CENTRAL ASIA

Democracy, Instability and Strategic Game in Kyrgyzstan

CENTRAL ASIA

Democracy, Instability and Strategic Game in Kyrgyzstan

P. STOBDAN

idsa
INSTITUTE FOR DEFENCE STUDIES & ANALYSES
NEW DELHI

PENTAGON PRESS

Central Asia: Democracy, Instability and Strategic Game in Kyrgyzstan
By P. Stobdan

First Published in 2014

ISBN 978-81-8274-752-4

Disclaimer: The views expressed in this book are those of the author and do not necessarily reflect those of the Institute for Defence Studies and Analyses, or the Government of India.

Published by
PENTAGON PRESS
206, Peacock Lane, Shahpur Jat,
New Delhi-110049
Phones: 011-64706243, 26491568
Telefax: 011-26490600
email: rajan@pentagonpress.in
website: www.pentagonpress.in

Branch:
Prime Arcade
Office #11
1154 Saifee Street
Opp. M.G.Road, Camp
Pune-411001
Email: pentagonpresspune@gmail.com

In association with
Institute for Defence Studies and Analyses
No. 1, Development Enclave,
New Delhi-110010
Phone: +91-11-26717983
Website: www.idsa.in

Printed at Avantika Printers Private Limited.

Contents

Annexures

Preface

The Central Asian states have completed 20 years of their independence in 2011. The five states have been undergoing an arduous and complex nation-building process, which is far from complete. They have suffered limitations due to centralised political and economic system inherited from the Soviet era; as such transformation has never been easy. While some states have achieved political success, others have done fairly well on the economic front. Except in Kyrgyzstan's case, the leaders of Kazakhstan, Tajikistan, Turkmenistan and Uzbekistan have strongly resisted political change and instead they have adopted internal political mechanisms with varying style to stay in power. The politics in these states still remains unpredictable. None of the aging Presidents of Kazakhstan, Tajikistan, and Uzbekistan appear to have clear succession plans despite some surreptitious intrigues among members of the ruling elite.

The region is unlikely to remain calm in the coming years as signs of unrest over worsening economic conditions, rising ethnic tensions, growing Islamic extremism and demand for a regime change would become more visible. The systemic breakdown of the Soviet built infrastructure is already causing socio-economic chaos in the region. This is especially true for Kyrgyzstan and Tajikistan. In essence, the basic politico-economic characteristics of these countries remain no different from those in West Asia. But unlike in the Arab cases, both Russia and China are likely to firmly insulate the Central Asian regimes from failing through the intervention of the Collective Security Treaty Organization (CSTO) and the Shanghai Cooperation Organization (SCO) structures.

Kyrgyzstan is the only country that from its inception as an independent state had uniquely followed a liberal polity and privatised economy. It was even called the *island of democracy* in the post-Soviet space. The country was ruled for 14 years by Askar Akayev, who was a liberal physicist, until he developed an authoritarian tendency and became corrupt, resulting into overthrowing of his regime in 2005 through an uprising, which came to be known as Tulip Revolution. Since then, Kyrgyzstan went through a very difficult political transition. The major test has been the transition from a Soviet Republic to a parliamentary democracy, though it had to witness another major uprising in 2010.

A shaky democratic experiment in coalition government is in place in Kyrgyzstan; but the institution of democracy and the rule of law remain underdeveloped. The country still remains locked in a difficult and intricate internal intra-clan discord that makes the Kyrgyz political process complicated. The country faces some tough challenges i.e., inter-ethnic rifts, inherent economic difficulties, rising threat of Islamic extremism, drug-trafficking, and the convoluted strategic games played by major powers. Kyrgyzstan is the only country in the world that hosts military bases of both Russia and the United States. Besides, China has found new means to retain its influence in Kyrgyzstan. But all in all, these difficult issues continue to keep Kyrgyzstan prone to instability

This manuscript is an attempt to provide an overview of the political and strategic process at work in Kyrgyzstan. It is an attempt to trace the events in Kyrgyzstan that erupted in 2005 and the subsequent developments that followed until 2012. The book does not in any sense purport to be an academic endeavour on Central Asian studies but merely a narrative, as well as, an analytical account and a result of my own self-education and understanding gathered through extensive interactions with wide sections of people in Kyrgyzstan and Kazakhstan, especially with the think tanks, academia, government officials and the diplomatic community. The subject is capsulated to provide a reading brief on the region by taking the case of Kyrgyzstan. An attempt has been made to highlight some of the impinging issues that shape the dynamics of Kyrgyz polity. The book contains aspects of India's interests in Kyrgyzstan as well, which should form a part of India's newly launched 'Connect Central Asia' policy.

While writing the manuscript, I have largely relied on the official sources and vernacular media reporting of *Akipress, 24.kg news agency, KyrTAg, Vecherniy Bishkek, Vesti.kg, Kyrgyz Television, Kyrgyz Radio-1, Nezavisimaya Gazeta, Interfax* and others. Some of the points identified as well as analysed are a result of my participation in various conferences, seminars and discussions held in the region. Some of the impressions gathered are based on personal visits to various places in Kyrgyzstan. The views expressed in the book are my own.

P. Stobdan

Introduction

The Kyrgyz are one of the most ancient peoples; their nomadic past tracing back to the legendary trilogy Epic Manas. The present Kyrgyz identity and nationhood revolves around this legendary hero. The statue of Manas is being resurrected in the centre of Bishkek. The country enacted a law in June 2011, which was meant to regulate the preservation and propagation of the trilogy of Epics: Manas, Semetei and Seitek. However, the Kyrgyz society is essentially divided into several major and minor clans and the matrix of their relationship is difficult for outsiders to fathom. In the modern times, especially under the Soviet rule, the multiple Kyrgyz tribes were co-opted into the Communist structure of governance. Their political cohesion and socio-economic wellbeing were well embedded within the socialist pattern of life. However, after decades of living under a communist but superpower's rule, for Kyrgyzstan to emerge and survive as an independent state has been an arduous challenge. During the last two decades the country went through a very difficult political transition. The major test has been the transition from a Soviet Republic to a parliamentary democracy, though it had witnessed two major uprisings, something not known in the former Soviet republics.

But uniquely, Kyrgyzstan from its inception as an independent state decided to follow a liberal polity and privatised economy. It was even called the *island of democracy* in the post-Soviet space. The country was ruled for 14 years by Askar Akayev, who was a liberal physicist, until he developed authoritarian tendencies and became corrupt, resulting in overthrowing of his regime in 2005 through an uprising, which came to be known as Tulip Revolution. Askar Akayev fled the country and took shelter in Russia.

Akayev had taken some important steps for political and market reforms. He introduced liberal investment and monetary legislation, launched privatisation and pushed Kyrgyzstan's membership into the WTO. But Akayev became a victim of his own doings. By embarking on a series of reform processes, he had prematurely given the most play to opposition and free media. As a result, the country became most unstable in the region. The trouble started when people challenged his wisdom of surrendering the country's territory to China in a clandestine manner. The ensuing violence set off a chain of events. Since then, political tensions in the country remained high. The rising tide of ethnic tension and Islamic radicalism, especially in the south became another reason. But, the situation got worsened after the 9/11, when the US military entered Kyrgyzstan to fight war against terror in Afghanistan. Akayev's family gained control over the flow of American money that permeated rampant corruption practice. Finally, growing popular dissatisfaction led to his fall. The condition was in fact similar to what has been witnessed in the recent case in the Arab countries that led to the 'Arab Spring' spreading across West Asia region.

Following Akayev's departure, a new leadership team led by Kurmanbek Bakiyev took up power. But President Bakiyev too gradually concentrated power in the hands of his family. The problems of corruption and economic crisis became more rampant. Thus, the 2005 Tulip Revolution too did not bring any change in Kyrgyzstan. In April 2010, Kyrgyzstan saw another revolution in which Bakiyev was thrown out on the same ground on which his predecessor AskarAkayev was ousted in 2005. The bloody uprising took place on April 7, 2010 when demonstrators stormed the government building. Over 85 persons were killed and 1500 persons were injured. Bakiyev fled to the southern city of Jalalabad and tried to rally support among southerners, but he too later fled the country and took asylum in Minsk under the protection of Belarus state. The second uprising came against the backdrop of the same syndrome of a failing regime that had not sufficiently enjoyed legitimacy at home and abroad. Bakiyev's period was particularly marred by frequent political instability and struggle with Parliament over constitutional balance of power. The opposition pressure heightened when his family virtually took control of affairs of the entire country. Among others, the US Transit Centre became the most corrupting factor that led to regime fall.

Following the April 2010 uprising and regime change, Kyrgyzstan saw a deadly ethnic violence. The interim government that came to power after ousting President Kurmanbek Bakiyev held a constitutional referendum, and parliamentary elections. Since then Kyrgyzstan has been coping to function as a parliamentary state, even though it seemed to be a painful process. The new governments that came to rule were seeking to avoid excessive state control over public life and to make the political process more transparent. By changing the constitution, the power and role of future Presidents was watered down. By voluntarily stepping down from the President's post, Roza Otunbayeva paved the way for the first peaceful transfer of power in Central Asia. The presidential elections in Kyrgyzstan on October 30, 2011 marked the completion of that process. The elections took place in an environment of freedom and impartiality.

The second revolution was though a major step towards democratic transition, but the deadly ethnic clashes between ethnic Kyrgyz and Uzbeks that erupted in June 2010 in the southern cities of Osh and Jalalabad had sent shock waves; reminding the world how fragile and volatile Central Asia could be. The conflict came as an extension of the uprising in April that year. Hundreds died in the rioting involving mobs of ethnic Kyrgyz and Uzbek. Three years have passed since the tragedy and several commissions of inquiry have gone into finding out the truth. An international inquiry commission has pointed towards complicity of the interim-government officials in the ethnic riot. However, the government has denied and repeatedly blamed Bakiyev's loyalists and Islamic extremists for fomenting the riots. The findings of numerous and muddled internal inquiry reports have seriously questioned the credibility of the Kyrgyz Government. The main culprits have not been brought to justice so far, and to some extent this has already undermined the rule of law, posing further risk to the stability of the country. From all accounts it appeared that ethnic crises were engineered and were part of the internal power struggle and influence. The ethnic divide between the Uzbeks and Kyrgyz remains the most explosive issue for the country and even a risk for its unity. Growing nationalism, partly even patronised by the state, is going to pose a serious challenge to Kyrgyz experiment and its urge for building a state on the prism of liberal democracy.

The politics and the issue of democracy in Kyrgyzstan though have always remained a dynamic process but the outcomes of these developments have been controversial if not doubtful. The country has seen fairly good amount of political reforms in the last few years, a shift away from authoritarian model that prevailed since independence in 1991. The country has vibrant political culture including the culture of protests by civil societies and political groups. The country also has a free media. However, both the Kyrgyz uprisings still remain one of the controversial and contested topics. Many questions are being raised whether they are internally grown processes or a part of the wave of democratisation that was seen in the former Soviet republics (Georgia and Ukraine) in the form of 'coloured revolutions'. On the face of it, the uprisings did appear indigenous with a broad domestic support base. But the consequences and analysis that followed the Tulip revolution gave the people a strong reason to believe that it was not a planned revolution. There was no clear political ideology or agenda by the opposition parties. It was rather an act of unrest carried out by a few hundred hooligans storming the main government building. Moreover, the new leaders who emerged on the scene were the same people who had fallen out with Akayev. They had simply regained power in a democratic guise. Many observers believed therefore that Kyrgyzstan had not experienced a genuine popular revolution; it resembled more a palace coup or a putsch. The people who took over the reins of power were directionless. They lacked unity and were essentially scrambling for power. Many were even battling over the control of the State's enterprises. Some analysts have concluded that they were less a revolution and more a process of state collapse. Therefore, serious issues were raised both at the conceptual and political level about the revolutionary process itself, although the Kyrgyz aspirations for a genuine democracy have a long history, especially in the context of Central Asia. However, the Kyrgyz example threw up several questions on how a young and fragile state had to cope with the political transition. In essence, Kyrgyzstan severely lacked a political class or an independent middle class aspiring for a genuine change. Until that happens, it will remain all about grabbing power including economic power that the state sways. The symptoms and desire for change do exist among the people in the country, but the time had not yet come for a broader change that will address the issues in true democratic sense. Kyrgyzstan was still far away from that to happen.

The early experiment with liberal democracy has been the primary reason for Kyrgyzstan to become a fragile state in the region. The democratic system, which is yet to be understood fully by the people, has induced rampant corruption in the system as well as in the society. The so called two revolutions have only added to its failing process. Moreover, being a young state Kyrgyzstan seemed unable to deal with complexities of religion, state and societies. The state had been taking steps from one extreme to the other. For example, while dealing with the religious groups, the regimes have shown a tendency to either flirt with the Islamic groups or comedown heavily on their activities depending on the political exigency. This is like in any democracy where the political groups rally support from any sources to gain political power. The increasing nexus between the enforcement agencies and organised criminal groups could be added as another factor contributing to the Kyrgyz chaos.

So far, many regional experts have not been optimistic about the Kyrgyz democratic success. Notwithstanding the transition towards a parliamentary system of governance, no substantial change has been observed by the ordinary people. The institutions of democracy still remain very weak. In fact, a coalition government fell due to serious corruption charges. Persistent infighting among power elite-clans, regional rivalry, rampant corruption, ethnic problem and economic crisis has in fact raised doubts about the success of democratic transformation. Of course, the experiment with parliamentary democracy is at its nascent stage, there are few challenges ahead:

Firstly, the formations of coalition governments since 2010 have been driven primarily by individual and group interests and not by any common ideology. Despite two uprising since 2005, nature of ruling class in Kyrgyzstan remained largely unchanged. Building a value based democratic structure in a society deeply rooted in tribalism therefore remains a major challenge. Three successive coalition governments formed since 2010 have proved unstable due to infightings. Atambayev had vowed to bring about a speedy change, but such efforts have been hindered by clan and regional rivalries. The fragile coalition system has led to rise in corruption and nepotism that continue to hinder any meaningful change. Many Kyrgyz political leaders still believe that a vital change can come only if a centralised power structure (presidential system) is restored. Even Atambayev who preferred to give up the Prime Minister post to become the President had clearly indicated that inclination. But to justify the overthrow of previous regimes, Atambayev himself supported the idea of a parliamentary system more suited to the nomadic spirit of Kyrgyz people. Although, the parliamentary system seems almost irreversible, there is always a strong desire for a centralised system which has to do with both Soviet legacy and perhaps also with the Kyrgyz politics of tribalism, which is traditionally anchored solely by one chieftain.

Secondly, in comparison to others, the country is sharply divided along regional and ethnic lines, and the country's politics have traditionally hinged on this thin line of regional balance between the north and the south. While the north remained more Russified and Westernised, the south remained more traditional and characterised by a large Uzbek minority—both Kyrgyz and Uzbeks with a roughly equal share of the population here. Since the independence, the regional imbalance could never be bridged, which continues to challenge the country's unity.

Thirdly, in addition to the ethnic rivalries, Kyrgyzstan has a nascent Islamic extremist movement in its southern regions. The fear was that the perpetual internal instability will allow Islamic groups to thrive. The influence of the Islamic Movement of Uzbekistan (IMU) and Hizb-ut-Tahrir (HuT) has grown over the years. Some Western powers tended to view the growing Islamist influence as part of the democratic process. So far, there has been no indication of the Islamic extremist forces actually playing a substantial political role in Kyrgyzstan. The political Islam, such as the power of HuT was unlikely to become a reality at least in the near term. Many experts also believed that even if Kyrgyzstan as a State collapses, the Islamists will not become a unifying force. This was even true for the southern Kyrgyzstan where despite the rampant ethnic and political crisis that have emerged so far in the wake of revolutions, the role of Islamic extremist groups were rarely noticed. However, there have been reports of terrorist activities in various parts of the country including in Bishkek suburb and southern Kyrgyzstan. Nevertheless, the growth of religion especially Islam has been quite rapid in Kyrgyzstan. The number of mosques and religious organisations has grown over the years. In 2012, over 3,000 registered religious organisations were operating in Kyrgyzstan. Islam was not only replacing public and the state institutions, of late, the state itself was initiating several steps to patronise Islam by introducing laws in the Parliament. Many regional experts have predicted that creation of the Islamic Caliphate is going to be a reality in the longer term.

Fourthly, it is a weaker state in the region in terms of economy. The country remains one of the poorest in the world; per capita GDP is below $1,000. Poverty and unemployment remains high. The economy depends heavily on remittances from migrant workers. More than 1.5 million Kyrgyz nationals are working in Russia and Kazakhstan and they contribute around $1.2 billion remittance which is about 20 per cent of the country's GDP. The country is dependent on donors support from various countries. The country's total debt had reached $3.107 billion in 2011 including external debt of $2.825 billion, which is over 58 per cent of the country's GDP. The country was not able to attract Foreign Direct Investment (FDI), as the investors were shying away due to political uncertainty.

The new government's attempts at controlling the Canadian Gold Company Centerra, which contributes 12 per cent to country's GDP, has dampened investors' confidence. Barring China, no other country has shown much interest in investing in Kyrgyzstan. The new leadership has been mulling over joining the Russian-led Customs Union. If Kyrgyzstan joins the Customs Union, it would further lead to inflation and unemployment as most of the Kyrgyz business depends on re-export of Chinese goods to other CIS countries.

Unlike others in Central Asia, the country has no rich hydrocarbon resources. The only asset it has is the abundant hydropower potentials. However, exploiting the rich water resources has never been an easy task for the Kyrgyz. In fact, Kyrgyzstan's political relations with outside are driven by water related issues, the management of which is getting problematic day by day as the mechanisms dealing with it during Soviet period has started to weaken. Its challenges are linked to neighbouring states with far more experience in political independence. Russia has finally agreed to construct the mega hydro project Kambar-Ata-I and other projects in return of security concession by Kyrgyzstan. The deal has emerged as a major achievement for the Atambayev government and its ability to maneuver the politics that compelled Moscow to agree to undertake the old promised projects. However, this may still be not easy. There would be many Russian conditions and also depends on Uzbekistan able to outdo the progress on the project. President Karimov of Uzbekistan recently said there will be war if the Kambar-Ata projects go through. A section of people have therefore suggested that for a conflict-stricken and economically weak country, the practice of parliamentary system is not suitable. The success of democracy would therefore mainly depend on how Kyrgyzstan will become an economically self-reliant and a viable state. Kyrgyzstan has no worthwhile resources to export and earn revenue.

Fifthly, Kyrgyzstan has become geopolitically a significant country in Central Asia. The country has drawn the attention of Russia, US, China and other neighbouring states and in fact has become vulnerable to manipulation by these powers; China has been aggressively trying to step up economic expansion and the presence of the US and Russian air bases continue to pose a challenge to the new parliamentary government. In fact, the Kyrgyz case has been an example of how a small state is unable to play the game with big powers. A tendency remains among the Kyrgyz ruling elite to factor Kyrgyzstan into the big power politics. After granting the US the right to use the Manas air field, the Kyrgyz regimes welcomed the opening of a Russian base in the country. The Kyrgyz hoped to play the two big powers off each other that in turn would boost their authority. But each regime got caught in this double-game. The foreign policy dilemma therefore continues to pose a challenge, especially when the external factors directly impinged on Kyrgyz internal dynamics. The US Transit Centre has long been a source of instability. Consequently, anti-American sentiments have increased over the years, which in turn also fuels Islamic extremism. But, despite occasional rhetoric, the political elite wish to maintain the country as a military hub for the US. Atambayev has repeatedly declared, before and after his election that Kyrgyzstan would not extend the lease of the Transit Centre after it expires in 2014. However, since 2012, the Kyrgyz have mellowed down a bit on the issue. Eventually, they are likely to agree to demand for the extension in return of an enhanced rent.

The Kyrgyz uprisings however did not affect the Russian-Kyrgyz relations. Importantly, unlike in the Georgian and Ukrainian case, the Kyrgyz revolutions were not built around anti-Russian sentiment. The new dispensations, therefore, are inclined to follow an approach that will result into closer political and security integration with Russia. But at the same time, anti-Russian feelings among the nationalist Kyrgyz were already setting in, even though the Kyrgyz leaders know that without Russia's blessings they cannot survive even a day in their offices. The new Kyrgyz regime has tried to bargain on the Russian military facilities in Kyrgyzstan including on the rent of Kant airbase. Significantly, the Russian-led CSTO's Secretary-General had announced in 2011 that its forces were ready to intervene in Kyrgyzstan if needed. This was a change in its position when the CSTO refused to intervene in 2010 that drew strong Kyrgyz criticism for not helping the country in its difficult times. The process of Kyrgyzstan joining the Russian-led Customs Union has intensified after Putin visited Bishkek in 2012. So far, Moscow has been able to keep the Kyrgyz leadership on a short leash, which in turn limits the Kyrgyz overplaying the democracy rhetoric.

While Kyrgyzstan is likely to remain aligned to Russian sphere of influence, the democratic governments have been giving significant importance to China in the economic space. China's responses to Kyrgyz uprisings have been muted and cautious. Beijing considered Kyrgyzstan to be a trouble spot and was wary of Kyrgyz instability impacting the situation in Xinjiang. China was also concerned about impact of Kyrgyzstan's new foreign and security policies on Beijing's regional strategic interests. But, China is the only country which has been making huge forays in Kyrgyzstan and poured in huge investments in several strategic sectors despite all the problems it confronts in Kyrgyz unstable environment.

The Kyrgyz democratic experiment looked very odd in a region traditionally ruled by presidents with near-absolute powers, but of course, a centralised presidential system also proved to be a failure in the Kyrgyz case. The neighbouring states have been taken off guard by the Kyrgyz democratic moves. The Uzbeks and Kazakh media were dismissive of the Kyrgyz development. The Kremlin too was not expecting problem free elections. The Russians remained apprehensive about the Kyrgyz experiment with open and representative parliamentary system that may impact the region. Kyrgyzstan's case only demonstrated that the post-Soviet authoritarian leaders were not immune to popular uprisings. To some extent the Kyrgyz example provided that hope. However, the Kyrgyz upheavals did not become a harbinger of change in the region, partly because the situation and style of rule in other states differed significantly. The other regimes have managed to shield themselves from the coloured revolutions and the Arab Spring. But the situation in Central Asia quite resembles the Arab world and it is essentially about authoritarian control of power and lack of multi-party system. While some regimes like in Turkmenistan and Uzbekistan still remain repressive, others like Tajikistan and Kyrgyzstan suffer from different political and economic problems that may fuel further instability. Even Kazakhstan has started witnessing social unrest and the spread of extremism challenging the authoritarian rule.

Lastly, beyond the challenge of balancing the strategic equation, Kyrgyzstan faces some other serious issues, including tense relations with its neighbours Uzbekistan, and Tajikistan over a host of issues including disputes over border, enclaves, and water resources. The ethnic issues with Uzbekistan, religious extremism and potential separatism in the south, and the threat of drug trafficking emanating from Afghanistan-Tajikistan borders pose serious security challenges to the country. Given the mountainous geography and complex ethnic composition of the country, finding enduring solutions is not likely to be easy.

The 2005 and 2010 Kyrgyz events provided some worst-case scenarios. However, the situations have been contained partly because Russia and China would never allow things to go out of control that would affect the whole region. Most external powers had opted not to risk destabilising the regimes, as the internal democratic forces were fractious and fragile. The optimists remain hopeful about its success. The experiment is expected to bring a decisive outcome for either uniting the country or reigniting fresh inter-ethnic violence and thereby opening the door to Islamist extremism.

So far, the new political formation has taken some positive and promising steps for normalcy. The economy has shown some recovery from the 1.4 per cent slump in 2010 to above 8.5 per cent growth in GDP in 2011. The government has announced plans to implement 40 nation-wide projects worth $8.9 billion during 2012-14 that are aimed to boost strategic sectors and create the basis for the long-term development of the country. Construction of China-Kyrgyzstan-Uzbekistan railway is one of the biggest projects in the transport sector. Other planned projects include development of new deposits of coal, tin and gold, construction of Kambar-Ata-1 hydropower plant and other hydropower plants of upper Naryn cascade, construction of Kemin-Almaty high voltage line, Data-Khujand line under CASA-1000 Project, hi-tech parks etc. The Parliament brought amendments to the existing laws on mining and mineral exploration to promote transparency and prevent corruption. The government has been largely successful in arresting further ethnic violence and stabilising the general law and order situation in the country. The new regime has tried to probe the causes of the June 2010 ethnic riots. The reports though largely blamed local Uzbek leaders and relatives of the former President for instigating the violence, but the authorities also took some of the blames. Roza Otunbayeva apologised to the nation for failing to prevent the violence.

A sense of optimism prevails when people talk about Kyrgyzstan having already made progress on the political front as compared to other Central Asian states which are yet to confront with the political reality once the authoritarian control fades away sooner or later. The West particularly viewed the Kyrgyz democratic example as a big achievement in contrast to other Central Asian states where elections are purely formal exercises to lend legitimacy to the ruling elites that remain unchallenged since the Soviet times. The overall Western assessment was that the Kyrgyz elections would set a democratic precedent for the region.

Following the successful parliamentary elections, Kyrgyzstan received closer international attention especially from the multinational institutions, including from NATO, OSCE, EU, CSTO, SCO, and other international financial institutions. India too had an opportunity to assist Kyrgyzstan's strive for building democracy which would have been in its strategic interest to counter extremist forces around its "extended neighbourhood". India did acknowledged Roza Otunbayeva's courageous step to establish and strengthen a vibrant democratic, secular and pluralist culture in Kyrgyzstan. After she relinquished her Presidency, Roza visited India. She met Indian leadership and spoke in various forums on the Kyrgyz experiment with parliamentary democracy. Otunbayeva remains in the whole of Central Asia as the strongest proponent of Indian democracy.

Kyrgyzstan perceives India as a large and successful model of democracy and secularism with expanding political and economic influence not only on Asian affairs, but also on the global stage. Following Kyrgyzstan's adoption to parliamentary form of democracy, it seeks to further deepen the vibrant relationship with democratic India. The Kyrgyz President Atambayev has a natural affection and love for India. He praised the role of India as a champion of democracy, for upholding cultural values in a diverse society and expressed great satisfaction with the bilateral relations. India's engagement with Kyrgyzstan is presently at a nominal yet steady rate. It may have, in the short term, several limitations for enhancing economic relations with Kyrgyzstan. However, Kyrgyzstan is gaining enormous strategic significance for regional security and great power interests and in this regard India's interests and engagement with Kyrgyzstan should gain merit. In order to clarify India's interests and find a new platform that could lay the groundwork for evolving an enduring policy, the Government of India had envisaged its new Connect Central Asia policy in 2012. The new policy outlines India's multifaceted and pro-active political, economic and people-to-people engagement with Central Asian countries, individually and collectively. The policy is anchored in broadening India's firm and long term strategic interest which will also serve to be commensurate with India's rising profile on the global stage. The greater emphasis will be given on extending India's soft power, for example by setting up of a Central Asian University in Bishkek that could evolve as a Centre of excellence to impart world class education in areas like IT, management, philosophy and languages. The new policy also envisaged replicating India's success of the Pan Africa e-network by creating a similar project of tele-education and tele-medicine connectivity, linking all the five Central Asian states. The new policy was launched at India's first Track 1.5 diplomacy in the framework of India-Central Asia Dialogue held in Bishkek on June 12-13, 2012.

CHAPTER 1

The Kyrgyz Revolution

Kyrgyzstan was once seen as the most stable and liberal of the ex-Soviet Central Asian republics and even hailed as the *island of democracy*. However, it descended into turmoil in 2005 when a popular revolt, dubbed as *Tulip Revolution*, had ousted the first post-Soviet President Askar Akayev, who was a liberal physicist, from power.

Askar Akayev ruled the country for 14 years since Kyrgyzstan's independence on August 31, 1991. He was the only apparatchik leader in Central Asia if not in the whole of former-Soviet republics to have embraced economic reforms (privatised economy) and political openness (free media and legal opposition).

Akayev remained an effective and popular leader in the initial phase of independence. However, after his re-election in 1995, he made a constitutional amendment extending the presidential powers. Akayev again got re-elected in 2000 that became controversial and judged by observers to be flawed. These trends took Akayev towards a more authoritarian direction and he began to resist power sharing with opposition. In the process, political reforms that he had initiated got stalled, the media was harassed and opposition leaders were jailed.[1] Due to relative lack of economic resource, the market reforms introduced in the country could not be sustained. The situation was further accentuated by growing poverty, rampant corruption and nepotism that had seeped into the system, mainly dominated by his family, his extended clan and supporters. The clan-based politics and the north-south regional divide got sharpened.

Akayev believed in the concept of democratic reforms to be achieved through a step-by-step 'organic growth'[2] approach and rejected outside imposed changes just as Communism was imposed on the Kyrgyz society in the past. From the early years of his presidency, Askar Akayev took some important steps to turn Kyrgyzstan into liberal democracy with a market economy by introducing a new constitution and a parliament. He also attempted to introduce liberal investment and monetary legislation, launched privatisation as well as pushed Kyrgyzstan's membership into the WTO.

Having sown the seeds of democracy and liberal political system, Akayev became a victim of his own doings. His regime became most unstable in the region mainly because he had given the most play to opposition and free media. In most Central Asian cases the regimes survived because the forces opposed to them were and still not strong enough to topple them.

Internally, the Kyrgyz politics have traditionally hinged on a thin line of regional balance between the north and the south.[3] The north remained more Russified and Westernised, the south remained more traditional and also characterised by a large Uzbek minority. In the aftermath of independence, the balance of power in the country got shifted to the north. Akayev's prolonged stay in power gradually led to marginalisation of the south and as a result, the semblance of national unity got weakened.

The first visible sign of Southern discontentment was manifested when in 2002 the demonstrators in the South in Aksy challenged Akayev's wisdom of surrendering territory to China in a clandestine way. The police shot six persons in the incident but it set off a chain of events in which the entire government had to resign and opposition leaders were jailed. Since then, tensions had remained high between the regime and its adversaries. Akayev lost his popularity in the South and gradually this got expanded to the North.[4] One of the key reasons that forced Akayev to stifle political opposition was the rising tide of Islamic radicalism, especially in the south.[5] Moreover, the situation got worsened after 9/11, when the US military entered Kyrgyzstan to fight the war against terror in Afghanistan. Akayev's family gained control over the flow of American money that permeated rampant corruption practice by his family. His fall became imminent.

The Tulip Revolution

The Kyrgyz March 24, 2005 uprising was mainly triggered by allegation of vote-rigging, but among other critical factors that brought Akayev down included popular dissatisfaction and pent-up frustration—culmination of a perception that his rule had foundered in pervasive corruption, persistent poverty, and unresponsive governance. The condition was in fact similar to what has been witnessed in the recent case in the Arab countries that led to the Arab Spring spreading across West Asia region.

But the uprisings in Kyrgyzstan still remain one of the controversial and contested topics. Many questions were then raised whether the upsurge was a natural process grown internally or was it a part of the wave of democratisation that had been seen in the former Soviet republics in the form of 'coloured revolution' as was the case in Georgia's 'Rose revolution' in 2004 and Ukraine's 'Orange revolution' in 2005.

On the face of it, the revolt did appear indigenous, with it having a broad domestic support base, but most observers believed that the event was simply orchestrated by Western NGOs to oust the pro-Russian Akayev regime. The timing of the event had of course coincided with the wave of democratisation elsewhere and to some extent those coloured revolutions may have definitely stimulated the Kyrgyz events. The rhetoric in the run-up to elections showed the intension of opposition parties adopting the Georgian and Ukrainian style of protest. Protestors wore yellow scarves and ribbons signifying the launch of the Tulip Revolution. Several youth organisations, including Kel-Kel and Birge had emerged in Kyrgyzstan ahead of the revolt.[6] Leaders of opposition party later used the youth to mobilise support for elections. In the subsequent political events, Youth Centres were set up and groups of youth were made to sit on the Gorky Square in the capital.[7] Much before the election, the opposition parties had forewarned that there would be revolution should the election be rigged.

The problem started when the supporters of the *Ata-Jurt Movement* protested over the refusal of Central Election Commission (CEC) to register former Foreign Minister Roza Otunbayeva as a candidate for the parliamentary election scheduled for February 12-13, 2005. Roza Otunbayeva under the Akayev's regime had served as Ambassador to London and later served as the UN's Deputy Envoy to Georgia. Slowly, other opposition parties also rallied behind *Ata-Jurt* and pledged to a unified struggle. Until then over 40 political parties never posed a credible challenge as they never showed inclination for unity. Akayev was well aware of this and perhaps in a way this made him complacent about his ability to manipulate and suppress opposition. In any case, one can say that Akayev failed in his democracy experiment because by 2005 the factions within his party proliferated along personalities, regional and clan affiliations.

The Key Factors

The March upheaval was though triggered by allegations of vote-rigging in the 2005 February parliamentary elections. The protests initially began in the Southern city of Jalalabad and later spread to the north. The CEC and President stood by the outcome resulting in flaring of the situation. But it was the hard aspects of economic weakness that was troubling the country for a long time. Kyrgyzstan lacked abundant energy resources of its neighbours. Half of its population lives under the poverty line. According to the National Statistics Committee (NSC), the Kyrgyz average monthly wage was \$54.9 as of January 2005. Kyrgyzstan's external debt had reached \$1.6 billion—five times the country's annual income. The Soviet built factories got shut down resulting in massive unemployment. Most of the skilled ethnic Russian labourers and professionals had migrated out. Almost a million Kyrgyz worked as labourers in Russia and Kazakhstan. In November 2004, the World Bank reported corruption as the single biggest brake on economic and social advancement in Kyrgyzstan. The state run factories were shut down or privatised, mostly falling into the hands of government officials and their clans. The Akayevs controlled one-third of the economy, including all financial flows, all levers of influence and big business, medium and small business.[8]

There was also the nasty struggle between regional clans competing for influence both in the south and the north. Akayev's cardinal mistake was that towards the end he had started over patronising the northerners thus upsetting the hitherto and unspoken power-sharing agreement between northern and southern clans. This resulted in the eruption of dissatisfaction in Osh, Jalal-Abad and Batken. But essentially, the conflict of interest revolved mainly between the so called democrats and despots. The opposition mostly included those who fell out of Akayev's favour on the grounds of differences over latter's social programme and territorial concessions to China. Akayev's nepotism and preparation for a dynastic succession, by bringing his son, daughter and extended family into the political process, came at the expense of even his northern allies. Slowly, even the bureaucracy lost the sense of loyalty to Akayev. This turned into Akayev's Achilles' heel and at the end even the top security officials of the interior minister refused to heed President's orders. This, in fact, also indicated that Akayev was unable to built strong institutions. During the revolution, the state machineries failed to control street protests. A handful of elites were willing to defend the president—even his closed confidants switched their loyalties to opposition, and at the end, the regime collapsed in a few hours.

The Kyrgyz case was also an example of how the culture of democracy and openness was introduced prematurely without the country having had any history of horizontal political power sharing experience. As a result, the country witnessed the birth of multiple political parties playing a vocal role. The relative media freedom and a large NGO presence added to anti-Akayev rhetoric. The media defied the censorship imposed during the crisis and harshly criticised his policy follies.

The role of Islam in the Kyrgyz revolution was suspected by most regional observers and there were many reasons for doing so. Islam in Kyrgyzstan will be dealt separately elsewhere. At this stage, the role and influence of political Islam like the Hizb-ut-Tahrir (HuT), and radicals such as the Islamic Movement of Uzbekistan (IMU) in stoking the upheaval were not visible despite their strong presence in the Southern part of the country. The HuT had called for election boycott and has rejected the opposition movement not being enough Islamic in content.

The media reports during that period indicated the key role played by political figures, who had been known for their connections with criminals. The strength of criminal network in Kyrgyzstan had been linked to drug trade from Afghanistan moving onwards to Russia. The politician-drug trade nexus had been growing over the years with some of these mafia dons reaching to position of influence. Many of these drug-barons, mostly from the South, gained immunity by being elected to the parliament. Their popularity grew by sponsoring community welfare and philanthropic activities in the pockets where the government had failed. It was known that drug barons maintained private militia under the guise of martial arts sport clubs. It was widely felt that the *Alysh* (traditional wrestling) groups had indulged in storming the state offices during the crisis. The media accounts also suggested about groups of hard-core activists and not the pro-democracy supporters who had confronted the police during the uprising. Similarly, suspected agents' provocateurs assaulted both police and protesters. The opposition did admit they were unprepared for Akayev's fall and were caught unaware by the unfolding events on March 24. The weakness of the leadership also played a negative role, allowing rioters and thugs to act as they pleased. Observers and political watchers contended that the Kyrgyz case was a premature revolution.

Kyrgyzstan was also a case of how a young nation at nascent stage faced the security dilemma that in essence compounded the internal political dynamics. The country's vulnerable security situation particularly rendered the opposition sufficient grounds to contest the regime. Kyrgyzstan is landlocked and surrounded by stronger Kazakhstan, China, Tajikistan and Uzbekistan. It had unresolved border disputes with Uzbekistan. The sporadic outbreaks of conflicts along borders with Tajikistan also created tensions with Dushanbe. But importantly, Akayev's fall exposed the play of a double and even multiple game by his regime, involving the US, Russia and China.

The country's well pronounced 'multidirectional foreign policy'[9]—playing major powers off each other (supporting the US war on terrorism, Russia's *Collective Security Treaty Organization* (CSTO) and China's *Shanghai Cooperation Organisation* (SCO)—could not be sustained. By 2004, the balance had begun to tilt strongly in favour of Moscow and Beijing with Bishkek hosting a CSTO-led large-scale military exercise and upgrading a Russian air base in Kant city. The subsequent American unequivocal call for holding free and fair election compelled Akayev to call Russia the country's most reliable friend. Akayev announced that the US air base exists only to support the antiterrorist operations in Afghanistan and will be closed down once stability in Afghanistan is restored; whereas the Russian base was meant to provide security throughout the region. At the point of time, Akayev had also endorsed Moscow's doctrine of pre-emptive military strikes against terrorist bases in Afghanistan. As Bishkek and Washington sparred over the elections, Kyrgyz Foreign Minister Askar Aitmatov announced on February 15, 2004 that Bishkek had rejected a request from Washington to deploy *Airborne Warning and Control System* (AWACS) aircraft at its base Kyrgyzstan. The US Ambassador quickly responded that Washington had never made such a request.

At the political level, Russia endorsed Akayev's position vis-à-vis political opposition and promised large-scale investment in hydroelectric projects. Bishkek also stepped up relations with China in 2004 by signing agreements for cooperation in large-scale joint economic ventures, communications, border trade, and energy and mineral exploitation. In 2004, China's trade with Kyrgyzstan increased by 83.6 per cent.

The Kyrgyz-US relations had begun to strain after the US envoy Stephen Young offered financial aid for fair elections. His comment 'if a peaceful transfer of power takes place in Kyrgyzstan, it could inspire the citizens of the neighbouring states' had irked Akayev. The US strongly warned Akayev against fiddling with the constitution before his term expired in October. Akayev clearly saw the US design for a Tulip Revolution and voiced concern about 'foreign-funded' revolutions.[10] Akayev's rigged-election apparently provided the US consultants an opportunity to infuse popular discontent into a potent movement. A group of former US Army officials of Turkish origin with the Soros were reported to have played a key role in this regard. A Russian intelligence input is said to have indicated activists from Kazakhstan, Chechnya and Uzbekistan taking part in the movement and that the finances came through the Soros Foundation. In fact, the US Ambassador Stephen Young said after the events that Washington had been providing aid to Bishkek for many years and now wanted to see the real results of its assistance.

For Russia, it was best to avoid the blunder in Kyrgyzstan after experiencing humiliation in Ukraine. Moscow managed to maneuver a position of neither being an enthusiastic supporter or a protector of Akayev. Russia's role has been one of mediation, displaying more neutrality, which was viewed by many as a sign of Russia's weakness. Moscow backed Akayev during his presidency and later gave him refuge following the Tulip Revolution. However, unlike in Ukraine and Georgia, there was no case for an anti-Russia platform in Kyrgyzstan. Russia blamed the Kyrgyz turmoil on the OSCE and Western NGOs.

Not a Genuine Revolution

Following the March 24 uprising and after Askar Akayev fled the country, a new leadership team led by Kurmanbek Bakiyev, a long-time Akayev's associate but later turned political opponent, formed a provisional government on March 25, 2005. Bakiyev was named interim President and Feliks Kulov becoming the interior minister.

However, what followed after the revolution was complete chaos and paralysis of the country, lawlessness, looting, violence and destruction. In the main capital city Bishkek, the citizens had to take matters into their own hands. The people from outside the city were making forays looking for opportunities to loot and create chaos. In fact, interim Foreign Minister Roza Otunbayeva accused the former officials still loyal to Akayev of provoking "the marauding of shops and trade centres."[11]

The post-revolution developments in Kyrgyzstan raised serious debate at both conceptual and political level of the revolutionary process itself, although the

Kyrgyz aspirations for a genuine democracy have a long history, especially in the context of Central Asia. However, the Kyrgyz example threw up several questions on how a young and fragile state had to cope with the political transition. Sequentially, Kyrgyzstan became the third country after Georgia and Ukraine where the opposition strived for regime change. On the surface, the Kyrgyz revolt did appear like other coloured revolutions. It was marked by violence, limited though. Like in the case of Tbilisi and Kiev, the Kyrgyz revolt too was also firstly caused by falsification of the elections results and other underlying grievances such as corruption and standard of living. Secondly, the Kyrgyz opposition too appeared to have received the Western support. Thirdly, Russia's position as usual had to side with incumbent authority.

But the consequences and analysis that followed the Tulip Revolution gave the people a strong reason to believe that it was not a planned revolution unlike what was witnessed in the Georgian and Ukrainian cases. The real purpose, therefore, may have been something else.

Firstly, the March 24 event did not resemble any sign of a genuine popular pro-democracy movement like the mass civic demonstrations witnessed in Kyiv. No political ideology or agenda was pushed by the opposition parties prior to the public protest to storm the government building. It was rather an act of strife carried out by a few hundred thugs or hoodlums armed with sticks fighting the militia and storming the main government building.[12] It is widely acknowledged by people now that these people were brought from outside the city and were paid for doing the job. An Indian doctor who worked at the VIP hospital in the centre of Bishkek said that the organisers distributed Vodka (alcohol) filled in tankers along the streets closed to the White House building where the President's office was located.[13] A Western correspondent Jean-Christophe Peuch of (RFE/RL) who was an eyewitness to the events in Bishkek noted that there was yet another mystery group, perhaps agents provocateurs, who on that day appeared suddenly and began assaulting the protesters.[14] Whether this group was defending the government or another group trying to stir up the demonstrators was not known to him. There are many mysteries surrounding the event which has not been answered so far. The people in Bishkek narrate all kinds of intriguing stories, at times difficult to believe.

Secondly, the manner in which the regime collapsed so quickly still remains a mystery. No one was clear whether the government had badly underestimated the protesting power or the regime had simply perished away. Observers said there was no one left to defend it. More surprisingly, President fled the country within an hour and a half.

Thirdly, a popular perception prevailing then was that the protest was aimed at settling the regional rivalry mixed with religious, social or sub-nationalistic tendencies. The opposition parties neither had a clear political programme nor were they prepared to confront the ruling regime. The opposition leaders including

Kurmanbek Bakiyev himself had admitted that the protesters gathered on March 24, had no idea that the regime will collapse so easily.

Fourthly, the new leaders emerged on the scene were the same people who had fallen out with Akayev. They had simply regained the power in a democratic guise. That is why many did not believe it to be a genuine revolution; it resembled more a palace coup or a putsch.[15] An International Crisis Group (ICG) report had called the Kyrgyz events "less a revolution than a process of state collapse".[16]

Fifthly, the country still lacked the grass-root networks or a political culture to facilitate democracy building. The people who took over the reins of power were directionless. There was lack of unity and the main leaders were scrambling for power. Persistent squabbles and infightings had raised the inevitable doubts about a coalition based future regime. The fragmented opposition parties were unable to put up a united agenda for governance. Instead they were pulling in different directions. Rivalry between Kurmanbek Bakyev from the south and Feliks Kulov from the north was further harming the prospects for reconciliation. What emerged in the aftermath was the personality driven process. There were conflicting claims by candidates for governor's posts that indicated weakening of the central authority. Centrifugal forces were threatening the country's unity. In fact, the situation seemed worsening after the regime change. But the new government led by coalition of pro-democracy was even trying to win over former Akayev's supporters in various provinces to restore order.

Sixthly, the situation was accentuated further when the ousted Akayev did not formally resign.[17] Akayev termed the March 24 events as a "coup," adding that "rumours about my resignation from the presidential post are deceitful and malevolent."[18] With this, the constitutional legality of the Kyrgyz revolution therefore did not stand on good ground. The new regime was unable to undo the previous constitutional arrangements. Even the flawed February 2005 parliamentary elections could not be reversed, because this could have questioned the legal dimension of the revolution itself that brought the new regime to power unconstitutionally. Therefore, it questioned the concept of revolution itself. The regime hoped to hold a referendum on Parliament's dissolution and a constitutional review but that process remained controversial and inclusive which eventually became a cause for the second revolution in 2010.

Seventhly, the struggle that was played out in the guise of revolution turned out be a battle over the control of the Akayev clan's enterprises. As a Russian Professor, Sergei Luzyanin noted that "This is a typically 'Oriental' process. What lies at the core is not the creation of a civil society or the arrival of a new political elite espousing new value and new domestic and foreign policies, but rather a struggle among clans. It is a battle among clans that have regularly alternated power over hundreds of years, in ruling the state or their regions."[19] This being the case, the civil society fronts and democracy advocates were bound to flop in the political process and the ultimate result was that the people were getting thoroughly disappointed.

The July Election

The presidential campaign for the country's presidential poll in July 2005 was a contest between the two strongmen of the revolution, Kurmanbek Bakiyev and Feliks Kulov representing north and south respectively. Kulov later withdrew from the race and agreed to become Bakiyev's Prime Minister once elected. The denial of a chance to Bakiyev of the south, hub of poverty and religious conservatism, would have further fuelled tension in the country. Kulov later admitted to Andrei Kokoshin, Chairman of the State Duma Commission for Commonwealth of Independent States (CIS) and Compatriots Affairs during his visit to Moscow on May 18, 2005 that the Andijan crisis in Uzbekistan had compelled him to withdraw his candidacy from the July Presidential elections and align with acting President Kurmanbek Bakiyev. Bakiyev was a Soviet-trained economist and considered as a technocrat.[20] Kurmanbek Bakiyev won a landslide victory by 88.9 per cent of the vote. Bakiyev got mass support from the southern cities of Osh and Jalalabad. As per the pre-election understanding, Kulov became the Prime Minister. For Bakiyev, the result was an endorsement for the March revolution. Interestingly, another presidential candidate, the Kyrgyz ombudsman Tursunbai Bakir uulu got 3.3 per cent of votes and came second in the race. He is known for his advocacy for creating an Islamic state of Kyrgyzstan.[21]

In a news conference, Bakiyev hailed the results as a decisive defeat "for counter-revolutionary" forces.[22] The campaign and also the election took place rather peacefully. The election results characterised as broadly fair by the international monitors. Bakiyev promised for happier days ahead. He promised ratification of constitutional changes and fostering more democratisation. With the change, the power had shifted from predominantly Russian speaking north to the southern Kyrgyz clans and ethnic Uzbeks. But this did not necessarily mean a political stability for Kyrgyzstan. In fact, a prominent Russian journalist Dmitry Kiselev opined that revolutions in Kyrgyzstan give way to each other but they don't make the life of Kyrgyzstanis better.

As expected, the Tulip Revolution and the July election did not bring any substantial change in Kyrgyzstan. In fact, President Kurmanbek Bakiyev had turned the country in effect into a one-party state, and in which problems of corruption and economic crisis became rampant. In the subsequent course of events, questions were frequently raised whether Kyrgyzstan was to become a viable state. The reforms were lacking, especially the judiciary, which remained under governmental control.

Bakiyev held a referendum on a new constitution to give more power to parliament. But in the subsequent election held in December 2007 he installed a parliament fully dominated by his newly formed Ak Zhol party. The Ata Meken opposition party won 9.2 per cent of the total vote but failed to achieve the required 0.5 per cent in each of Kyrgyzstan's regions. International observers described the elections as flawed. In order to gain more power and legitimacy, Bakiyev gradually concentrated power in the hands of his family and tried to copy the style of Putin governance during his first term. Interestingly, Bakiyev's protégées had advocated that Kyrgyzstan's liberal democratic model since 1991 had failed and that it had brought political paralysis. They argued for a shift and favoured Russia's model of strong presidency a la Putin with limited democracy and a weak opposition. The regime went on a radical privatisation drive, selling off much of the country's energy infrastructure.

As the country struggled to find political stability, the leadership faced a tough job in meeting people's high expectations. The country had faced crisis after crisis ranging from murder of high ranking politicians, financial crunch, economic crisis, collapse of health system to deteriorating social conditions including poor condition in its prison system with political overtones.[23] Rising food prices and frequent power cuts in Bishkek were causing deep popular disillusionment with the government and had created sufficient condition for people to question the need for a revolution.

The situation was worsened by criminalisation of politics. The disorder and anarchy created ideal conditions for people to illegally seize property.[24] In fact, all of these unleashed popular discontent among people and slowly the euphoria for revolutionary change had begun to wane. Many even charged that the revolution and its aftermath weakened Kyrgyzstan's delicate geo-strategic position and exposed it to unwelcome attention from powerful regional players like Russia and China.'[25]

The only positive change noticed was a freer atmosphere, an ideal situation for the media as compared to tight control over media in the neighbouring Kazakhstan and Uzbekistan. Of course, there were other sections of the society which felt that things have changed for the better.[26] The optimists viewed that the events will help infuse decentralisation which will ultimately anchor democracy in the country.

In 2006, the first anniversary of the Tulip Revolution was celebrated with a military parade, along with festivities throughout the country. In a speech, Bakiyev promised to improve the situation in the country. He said 'Anxiety and unease came to many families on that day (March 24, 2005). Honest businessmen suffered losses. ... We must ensure that we do not have such hard times again.'[27]

On the Akayev's exile, Bakiyev said "My impression is that ... Askar Akayevich [Akayev] and [his wife] Mayram Duyshenovna [Akayeva] don't realise what happened and why. If they have not realised this, it is not advisable for them to return. They must understand with their hearts and minds why this [the revolution] happened, and ask the Kyrgyz people to forgive them. Only then should they think about returning home."[28]

Even after one year, the factions continued to engage in disturbing power struggle. In 2006, Bakiyev faced a serious political crisis. A series of mass demonstrations questioned the limits of his power. In April 2007, the opposition demanded Bakiyev's resignation. He later signed constitutional amendments to reduce his own power, but the protest continued. Bakiyev though promised not to return to authoritarianism and promised a dynamic development for the country, his opponents remained skeptical about his pronouncements on the first anniversary.

The economic impact of the Tulip Revolution was the gravest for Kyrgyzstan. The business entrepreneurs were dejected and frustrated with the continuing corruption. The economic crisis was worsened by tax collection problems and weak administration. This allowed the criminal groups to fill in the vacuum with their economic and political power. In the Kyrgyz case, any political turmoil meant disruption in agriculture, delay in sowing especially in the south, which would mean crisis in the next autumn. In fact, this was a perennial problem for the country—a seasonal pattern in crisis. The problem also aroused over land seizures by people coming into urban areas. The squatters and enduring problems with land tenure added to the tension. The officials and leaders on the other hand continued to seize properties, mines and resources. Foreign investors were afraid of investing in Kyrgyzstan where the law frequently changed and the authorities in connivance with local populace evicted investors on some ground or the other. Justice under the law simply did not exit. This continued to remain one of the major complains of the Russians, Chinese and Turks, which have invested heavily in Kyrgyzstan in the last two decades. Of late this phenomenon is being phrased as "resource nationalism."[29] This phenomenon was more acute in the mining sector.

The immediate danger as a fall out of the revolution was the potential spread of organised violence. The mafia infiltrating in a weak central government was the instant criticism in the discourse in the post-revolution period. There were cases of murder of several parliamentary deputies linked to criminal groups, though organised crime was nothing new to Kyrgyzstan. Essentially, the power struggle remains among families and clans and the organised crime has been always part of the overall political dynamics in the country.

There was the emergence of many self-defence groups, described as 'southerners',[30] who participated in the anti-government protest in Bishkek and thereby exacerbating the existing North-South regional tension. Conversely, inter-ethnic strife in and around Osh region had posed the danger of sparking renewed hostility between Uzbeks and Kyrgyz as it had happened 1990s.

The hope for a democratic transformation was also mutated into anxiety over the spread of Islamic radicalism. The Afghan experience had sufficiently underscored fundamentalism having thrived in the uncertain political environments. It was envisaged then that if Kyrgyzstan cannot establish a strong central government, it could become a safe haven for international terrorist operations. The Russian officials had repeatedly cautioned a possible rise of Islamic radicals and indicated the Afghan Taliban, amnestied by Karzai fomenting troubles in Central Asia. Many had dismissed this as Moscow's attempt at diverting attention of its failure in Ukraine and elsewhere. Whereas, the region's media analyses indicated that the democratic process may weaken appeal for HuT, and may have already caused split in its ranks between those advocating a peaceful method and those who favouring a more forceful means.

The Kyrgyz media claimed the majority nomadic Kyrgyz to be secular following conventional and moderate Islamic practices and the revolution has only made it easier for them to gather at mosques to discuss political and economic problems, something restricted during Akayev's rule and continue to be impossible in neighbouring Uzbekistan. It was assumed that the appeal for HuT was bound to fade. Most Western analysts too endorsed the view that the widespread conditions to breed extremist ideologies, unlike in neighbouring Uzbekistan, were absent in Kyrgyzstan. However, Kyrgyzstan's 15 per cent population of Uzbek origin always remained a potential source for fermenting trouble in the south.

Reports at the time indicated that members of an Uzbekistan-based outfit Mazhab-e-Tahrir (Harkat) who were arrested in April in Osh confessed of their Pakistani nationality. They had been residing in Uzbekistan for the last 15 years as students, but later started working in mosques and developed links with the Mazhab-e-Tahrir. They were tasked by some US based Muslims to foment disturbance in the south Kyrgyzstan on a monthly payment of US $ 500 per person. The interim government in Bishkek had summoned Pakistani Ambassador in Bishkek Mohammad Alam Brohi in mid-May to assist in locating a group of suspected extremists allegedly received training in Pakistan. According to Kyrgyz officials, a group of six people in Bishkek was also preparing to attack US interests. Kyrgyz authorities also arrested on February 15, 2005, a HuT cadre and recovered a number of leaflets, CDs and books propagating HuT ideology. The individual was said to be in touch with an extremist group in the Karasau town of Kazakhstan.

As stated earlier, instability was also fueled by drug operation by various mafia groups which were well entrenched in the Bakiyev's regime. There were reports of increasing production of narcotics in Kyrgyzstan's own Chuu Valley apart from the flow of drugs from Afghanistan.

Kyrgyzstan, therefore, risked another round of violence. The symptom of a larger problem to surface sooner or later was clearly visible as one of the briefings of the International Crisis Group *'Kyrgyzstan: A Deceptive Calm'* August 14, 2008 noted 'If anger turns to violence, it risks being brutal, destructive and xenophobic—

and the remnants of the discredited opposition may not be able to channel demonstrations into a more controllable form.'[31]

In essence, Kyrgyzstan severely lacked a political class or an independent middle class aspiring for a genuine change. Until that happens, it is all about grabbing the power including economic power that the state sways. The systems and ingredients for all these existed or still exist in the country, but the time is not yet come for a broader change that will address the issues in true democratic sense. Kyrgyzstan is still far away from that to happen.

This was not to deny that there were no serious issues with the Bakiyev regime. The ultimate outcome of March 2005 uprising was no better. In any case, Kyrgyzstan provided hardly a model for the rest. But the Kyrgyz failure should neither be used as a justification for continued authoritarian rule elsewhere in the region.

The External Dimension

The US welcomed Kyrgyzstan's revolution and justified it as the American pursuit of the Bush Doctrine, which served as a major source of inspiration for Kyrgyz popular movement. Ironically, the US had embraced Akayev as an ally, who facilitated the Western forces to use the Kyrgyz Manas airport as a transit centre after the 9/11. It was this very US support that had turned the Akayev's regime to become more authoritarian.

The Kyrgyz case was also an example of how a small state was unable to play the game with big powers. After granting the US the right to use the Manas air field, Akayev welcomed the opening of a Russian base in Kant, also outside Bishkek. By doing this Akayev hoped to play the two big powers off each other that in turn would boost his authority. But he got caught in this double-game. The US has been annoyed with Akayev since then and perhaps it did not feel sorry when he was ousted.

The Kyrgyz experiment also had a strategic dimension for the US. The event may have encouraged the US to consider Uzbekistan's Karimov and Turkmenistan's Niyazov as regional security liabilities. The US officials believed that hard-line domestic policies of the two leaders were helping to swell the ranks of the HuT. Despite the change in regime, the US assessed that a possible escalation of terrorist activities in Kyrgyzstan could hamper its interests. To a large extent the Kyrgyz upheaval and also the Andijan episode in Uzbekistan had their origin in the belief of dislodging the American presence in the region.

Ironically, the new regime in Bishkek that replaced Akayev appeared reluctant to alter the country's foreign or domestic policies.[32] This was in sharp contrast to the changes seen in Kyiv and Tbilisi. In his first press conference Bakiyev talked about the possibility of closing a US military base in Kyrgyzstan. Bakiyev said that the situation in Afghanistan was stabilising, and the American military presence might not be needed for much longer. Surely, it did appear that Bakiyev was under pressure from Russia and China. In early July 2005, the SCO member states asked the US to set a deadline for the withdrawal of its forces based in the region. Earlier on July 7, Uzbekistan had issued a statement asking the American forces to vacate the Karshi-Khanabad air base. Both Uzbekistan and Kyrgyzstan had signed separate bilateral agreement to host the US bases after the 9/11. In the changed context, even Bakiyev seemed wanting to renegotiate the lease terms.

Later, Bakiyev's government had announced the continuation of key security policies, maintaining the need to entertain the US military base at Manas for cooperation in the war against terrorism, but also continue to participate in the Russian-led Collective Security Treaty Organization (CSTO) and SCO. This clearly explained the contradiction and pertinently raised the question whether events were about revolution or was it just a power struggle. It was also explained by the fact that notwithstanding the much claimed American indirect support for the revolution, the new regime in Kyrgyzstan showed inclination towards joining the Moscow-Beijing axis. The US was failing to induce the Kyrgyz for a security arrangement and in fact it barely struggled to retain a foothold by alluring the corrupt Kyrgyz leadership and through offering both military and economic aid. The talks between US Defence Secretary Donald Rumsfeld and the new Kyrgyz leadership saw no significant change as Bakiyev assured Rumsfeld that bilateral cooperation in the political, military, and economic spheres will continue. He only reiterated the earlier position taken by Akayev that Kyrgyzstan will not serve as a base for surveillance AWACS aircraft or additional foreign military troops.[33] If AWACS was to be based in Ganci, it could gather broad and detailed information regarding Russia, China, and other Central Asian states. This could have challenged Russia's direct security interest and Bakiyev would never have had the guts to accept the US request. Some observers said Akayev's decision was meant to placate Russia and win Moscow's support ahead of parliamentary elections in late February.

On March 28, 2005 Kurmanbek Bakiyev announced that his government had the support of the leaders of Russia, Kazakhstan, and Uzbekistan. Bakiyev while making the announcement in the upper chamber of the parliament said; 'I must report to you that the president of the Russian Federation, Vladimir Vladimirovich Putin; the president of Kazakhstan, Nursultan Abishevich Nazarbaev; and the president of Uzbekistan, Islam Abdugaliyevich Karimov, all support the interim government that I am heading today. I've talked to all three presidents and all three said in one voice: 'we're ready to help you.'[34]

Russian President Vladimir Putin initially expressed disappointment over the Kyrgyz events and said 'It is regrettable that once again, political problems in a post-Soviet country are being resolved in an illegitimate way and are accompanied by chaos and casualties."[35] However, he said, "We know these people [the opposition] very well as they helped develop relations between Kyrgyzstan and the Russian Federation when they held government positions for several years in the past. They have done a lot to establish today's level of bilateral relations."[36]

Of course, the countries which witnessed revolution and were opposed to Russian dominance had welcomed the Kyrgyz developments and offered their support to help Kyrgyzstan resolve the internal conflict. Georgian President Mikheil Saakashvili said that Georgia's sympathies are with the Kyrgyz opposition, Tbilisi is not in the business of exporting trouble. 'We are not exporters of revolutions ...our revolutions were similar [to Kyrgyz events]. That was not because someone fabricated them somewhere, but simply because people react to injustice in the same way in all countries.'[37]

As expected, the change did not affect the Russian-Kyrgyz relations. Russia, of course, managed to retain an edge over others due to geography, history and economy. Importantly, unlike in the Georgian and Ukrainian case, the Kyrgyz revolution was not built around anti-Russian sentiment. The new dispensations, therefore, were unwilling to display any anti-Russian rhetoric. It became easier for Moscow to deal the new leaders in the evolving scenario. Indeed, both Felix Kulov and Kurmanbek Bakiyev talked in favour of re-enforcing Russian military presence, particularly establishing a new base in Osh region, apart from the one in Kant.[38] In fact, the Kyrgyz acting President reported to have opined that the new base could be established, under the aegis of either the CSTO or SCO.[39] This had clearly indicated how important Russia was viewed of the new regime for playing a stabilising role in the country. For Russia, a constructive approach towards Kyrgyzstan was also important in the wake of the earlier crisis in Andijan in neighbouring Uzbekistan. The Russian Foreign Ministry on May 26, 2005 however denied having received any specific request about the new base. The, CSTO Secretary General Nikolai Bordyuzha refuted the report.

China's response to Kyrgyz uprising was remarkably muted and cautious. The Chinese Foreign Ministry called for an early stabilisation, and the SCO's Secretary General Deguang had emphasised the need for adhering to constitutional norms and restoration of a national accord. Deguang's statement summed up Beijing's concerns. In fact, many observers felt that China was least likely to benefit from the events in Kyrgyzstan.

Fearing trouble in Xinjiang, China immediately closed its border trading post at Irkeshtam.[40] (The opening or closing of trading post has been an old tool of Chinese diplomacy!) In the Kyrgyz cities, Chinese property and citizens became the target. At least two Chinese supermarkets were destroyed and looted by frenzy mobs. A group of Chinese entrepreneurs met the Kyrgyz Finance Minister and sought compensation worth Som 1,500,000,000 for losses suffered by the Chinese businessmen due to looting of shops during March 24-25 riots. The Kyrgyz Minister ruled out any compensation due to shortage of funds. The Chinese, however, sought concessions in custom tariff and visa regulations.

Beijing was naturally concerned about a possible change in Kyrgyzstan's position: (a) *vis-à-vis* the Uighur diaspora, estimated to be over 50,000 in the country, (b) a power vacuum in Kyrgyzstan triggering possible threats to neighbouring Xinjiang, (c) the impact of Kyrgyzstan's new foreign and security policies on Beijing's regional strategic interests.

The Uighurs are on both sides of the frontier. Akayev's government had been cooperative with Beijing on the Uighur activities. Over 50,000 strong Uighur diaspora lived in Kyrgyzstan besides thousands of shuttle traders who travelled back and forth between Xinjiang and Kyrgyzstan. In the past, Beijing had successfully impressed upon the Akayev Government to curb the Uighur activities. Many Uighur activists were detained and extradited to China. The Chinese were certainly concerned that in the light of democratic change in Kyrgyzstan, the Uighurs would make fresh attempts to regroup under the new dispensation in Kyrgyzstan. Beijing also knew that the Western powers were waiting for an opportunity to play up the Uighur case on the ground of democracy and human rights.

China feared a long-term instability in Kyrgyzstan creating a power vacuum, which may enable radical Islamic groups and drugs syndicates to entrench on its doorsteps. There was genuine reason for the Chinese fear as it suspected that the Kyrgyz revolution was part of the American larger and long term game plan detrimental to China's interests in Central Asia. The Chinese writings suggested growing US influence in the region after the Kyrgyz uprising. It was well known by that time that the new Kyrgyz leaders were propped up by Washington for democratic change.

But then like in the Russian and the American case, all top three new leaders, the acting President Kurmanbek Bakiyev, interim Foreign Minister Roza Otunbayeva and acting Prime Minister Felix Kulov also have had a long history of engagement with China during their careers. In fact, following the revolution, there was no visible indication of any policy change towards China. Otunbayeva had announced that Kyrgyz-China ties would remain intact and that mutual borders would be respected. Nonetheless, Beijing had been aware of the anti-China rhetoric that runs deep in Kyrgyz politics, particularly after Akayev had ceded territory to China in 2002 that eventually became one of the reasons for Kyrgyz revolution. In fact, the new President, Kurmanbek Bakiyev himself, when he was then Prime Minister, had resigned over this issue. Beijing was naturally wary about possibility of the new regime raising the bogey of territorial concession. China was also concerned about the new US activism, especially the new US-Kyrgyz partnership which could potentially impact China's strategic gains, particularly its profile within the SCO. The Chinese official *Xinhua* news agency in a series of articles had highlighted the US meddling in Central Asia through military and economic infiltration. The articles had argued that the US influence in region would grow after the transfer of power in Kyrgyzstan.

The reactions of the neighbouring states were either cautious or indifferent, because the uprising had posed serious implications for the other Central Asian republics. They too in varying degree carried widespread poverty and corruption, along with unresponsive government. The reports of Kazakh Chechen and Uzbek nationals in the demonstrations coupled with the fact that NGOs like the Soros Foundation were channelising funds to the opposition groups in the region was a cause of worry for others. Uzbekistan had forcibly closed the Soros office in Tashkent and Kazakhstan had declined to renew its registration. Kazakhstan and Uzbekistan sealed their borders with Kyrgyzstan and put restrictions on media outlets.

Nazarbayev had blamed Akayev's neglect of socio-economic factors and lax security measures. Nazarbayev said, "It is absolutely clear that social and economic problems that accumulated for years in [Kyrgyzstan] have led to mass poverty and unemployment...that sparked unrest in many parts of the country. The weakness of the authorities also played its negative role in allowing rioters and thugs to act as they pleased."[41]

Notwithstanding all the fears, the Bishkek upheaval did not become a harbinger of regional change in the region, partly because the situation and style of rule in other States differed significantly. The Kazak situation resembled that of Kyrgyzstan. Like Akayev, Nursultan Nazarbayev too had concentrated power in his extended family. But unlike in Kyrgyzstan, Nazarbayev had allowed limited media freedom that curtailed people to be aware of the corruption in the system even though the opposition in Kazakhstan remained stronger, better organised and more united. But, at the same time, Nazarbayev's regime also remained more organised, tougher, and more motivated than that of Akayev's. Nazarbayev was facing presidential election in 2006 end and the stake for him was high. But, instability in Kazakhstan was not anticipated in the immediate term, as the people society there was more prosperous, less religious oriented, and absence of a large middle class made demand for change less urgent. At the same time, the emerging new business class was increasingly becoming interested in political power as a means of protecting its interests.

The Uzbek official reaction came through a statement that called for the crisis in Kyrgyzstan to be resolved "within the legal framework and laws outlined in the constitution. The events are not spontaneous processes but are the result of the long accumulated...resentment of the population, which is unhappy with its appalling socio-economic conditions, hopelessness, and corruption."[42] The statement said Uzbekistan is ready to cooperate with a Kyrgyz leadership, government and parliament that have the "support and trust of the population."[43] Karimov held talks on phone with Kurmanbek Bakiyev and stressed on the need to use all available opportunities to solve existing problems within a legal framework and constitutional requirements. Uzbekistan was concerned about the situation in southern Kyrgyzstan, a part of the Fergana Valley, which always proved to be the epicentre of explosion of popular discontent in the past. It was a hotbed of opposition to Karimov's administration. The Uzbek authorities sought to clampdown on political activities. It had quickly controlled media, forbidding the press to carry information about developments in Bishkek. But, the Uzbek leader had quickly learnt from Akayev's mistakes. When similar surge took place in Andijan in June 2005, Islam Karimov took swift and brutal response against demonstrators. Tajikistan had maintained silence but it too closed borders with Kyrgyzstan fearing spread of instability. Turkmenistan remained tight lipped on the Kyrgyz events. However, there was a sense of euphoria among opposition parties and activists across the region. The opposition leaders in Kazakhstan congratulated the Kyrgyz people for overthrowing an authoritarian and undemocratic regime.

Among others, the Iranians too viewed Kyrgyz upheaval being engineered by the US. The political turnover dealt a blow to Iranian and also to Pakistan's foreign policy. Both had cultivated closer ties with Akayev. Pakistan's President Musharraf had paid a visit to Bishkek few weeks before Akayev was ousted. For India, it was important for these countries to shore up their independence so that negative forces do not fill in the vacuum and destabilise the region. India's security concerns are inextricably linked with turbulence in the region. It is clear that the changes in Central Asia are awakening resentment far beyond the section of population sympathetic to Islamic revolution. The strength of HuT was growing at that time, which could not have been possible without the domestic support and participation. However, it needed to be underlined that whether Islamists or nationalists, so far such groups have not shown any antipathy towards India. On the contrary, appeal for India among the majority people in Central Asia run far deeper than the region's ruling class. India was and is not in a position to infuriate any section of population in the region; instead a meaningful contact was needed to be built with all stake holders.

The Challenges Ahead

Kyrgyzstan's revolution and its aftermath development did not bring a degree of stability. Akayev's departure from the scene did leave a political vacuum. The semblance of unity that was visibly seen among the political elite in the run up to revolution was rapidly decaying. They were unable to check the political and social upheaval that continued to sweep across the country. Instead the country was veering off in an unpredictable direction. Persistent infighting among power elite-clans, regional rivalry, rampant corruption, ethnic problem and economic crisis raised doubts about the new regime's ability to infuse democratic transformation. Interestingly, Kyrgyzstan's peculiarity over its tribal nature of politics was described by Roza Otunbayeva herself, when she said that nepotism and clannism in appointments could lead to the collapse of the state system. At a ceremony of award to Kyrgyz civil servants she said "Regrettably, nepotism and clannism take place in our life. Despite contests to employ staff, ministries and agencies often have those who still want to appoint their relatives and their own people to posts. Parliamentarism has relatively protected the higher echelons of power from tribalism. You know that the ruling coalition appoints ministers. So they are politically appointed people. Deputy Ministers are also in part politically appointed. Administrative servants down the vertical line can count only on the protection of the law. People should work regardless of big bosses' political tendencies and preferences. This is important for us. Ministers come and go while civil servants should work permanently. Otherwise, this kind of appointment system could lead to the collapse of the entire state machinery."[44] This was a clear reflection of how a young democracy was confronting with problems that were unique to Central Asian tribal environment.

At that point of time, the entire governing structures in the provisional regions and towns across Kyrgyzstan had become engulfed in disorder. Some of these controversies remain unresolved due to constitutional ambivalence, further challenging legitimacy of Kyrgyzstan's new political order. In certain cases, especially in the southern Kyrgyz regions, a state of dual-power existed for a long time.[45] There were other issues, such as the north-south divide and the Uzbek ethnic problem, which were assuming alarming trends. They were likely to remain unaddressed and could become fresh sources of dispute and polarisation among Kyrgyz people.

A dilemma for the new regime arose when it came to foreign policy as well. Having played the bug strategic game by the earlier regime, it was going to be an uphill task for the new dispensation to sort out the external equations or balancing of strategic interests that directly impinged on Kyrgyz internal dynamics. The US military base had already become a source of instability. By that time anti-Russian feelings among the nationalist Kyrgyz had already set in, but it was also clear to all the Kyrgyz leaders that without Russia's blessings they cannot survive even a day in their offices. Besides, the challenges for Kyrgyzstan included finding a national consensus on the controversial territorial settlement with China, addressing the issues of enclaves and ethnic issues with Uzbekistan, religious extremism and potential separatism in the south, and the threat of drug trafficking emanating from Afghanistan-Tajikistan borders.

The above trends did provide an analysis that Kyrgyzstan had not experienced a genuine popular revolution as it had not gone through a genuine political process guided by a popular leader with mass participation. In essence, Kyrgyzstan severely lacked a political class or an independent middle class aspiring for a genuine change. Until that happens, it was all about grabbing the power including economic power that the state sways. The symptoms and desire for change do exist among the people in the country, but the time had not yet come for a broader change that will address the issues in true democratic sense. Kyrgyzstan was still far away from that to happen.

Reverse Tulip Revolution

After five year since Kyrgyzstan saw the first Tulip Revolution, the country faced yet another mass uprising in April 2010 when President Kurmanbek Bakiyev was thrown out on the same ground on which his predecessor Askar Akayev was ousted in 2005. The bloody uprising took place on April 7, 2010 when demonstrators stormed the government building. Over 85 persons were killed and 1500 persons were injured. Bakiyev fled to the southern city of Jalalabad but he did not resign and tried to rally support among southerners.[46] Later, Bakiyev agreed to resign provided his security was guaranteed. After five days of resistance he left Kyrgyzstan for Kazakhstan and later Bakiyev and his family took asylum in Minsk under the protection of Belarus state.[47] On April 20, President Alexender Lukashenko told his parliament that "Bakiyev and his family, four people in all, have been in Minsk since Monday, as guests.... Today they are here under the protection of our state, and personally of the president."[48] Bakiyev was later granted with Belarusian citizenship in February 2012.

The new interim government charged him in absentia with organising mass killings and put him on trial.[49] But, after arrival in Minsk, Bakiyev held a press conference on April 21, and stated "I, Kurmanbek Bakiyev, am the legally elected president of Kyrgyzstan and recognised by the international community. I do not recognise my resignation. Nine months ago the people of Kyrgyzstan elected me their president and there is no power that can stop me. Only death can stop me," and called Otunbayeva's administration an "illegitimate gang".[50]

Following Bakiyev's ouster, an interim government was set up under the leadership of former Foreign Minister Roza Otunbayeva. But, after months of turmoil on the streets, a country wide referendum, held on June 27, 2010 overwhelming (over 80 per cent of voters), supported Otunbayeva's proposal for reducing the power of the presidency and transform the country into a parliamentary democracy.[51] Subsequently, Otunbayeva was formally sworn in as caretaker president[52] till December 31, 2011 and she became the region's first post-Communist female leader.

The second Kyrgyz uprising came against the backdrop of the same syndrome of failing regime that had not sufficiently enjoyed legitimacy at home and abroad. As elaborated in the previous chapter, Bakiyev's period time in office was marred by frequent political instability, particularly struggle with parliament over the constitutional balance of power.[53] His opponents accused him of becoming more authoritarian and corrupt than the previous president. The opposition pressure backed by public discontent heightened when his family virtually took control of affairs of the entire country.

Bakiyev elevated his family members to prominent positions in the government.[54] His brother Janysh Bakiyev held the post of the presidential guard. His brother Marat Bakiyev was Kyrgyzstan's Ambassador to Germany. Another brother Adyl Bakiyev became an adviser to Kyrgyzstan's Ambassador to China. His son Maksim Bakiyev was the most powerful among all who controlled all the businesses including fuel contract of the US transit centre at Manas. Maksim was later charged among other things with embezzlement and abuse of power by the interim government for transferring about $35 million of a $300 million loan from Russia into his private bank accounts.[55] In June 2010 Maksim was arrested in the UK and continues to avoid extradition.

Bakiyev's rule was marked by a series of scandals over corruption and shady dealings by his son Maksim Bakiyev, who was even leading official delegations abroad. He had dealings with known underground mafia groups; drug deals, narco-barons etc.[56] He had even contacts with India's number one terrorist Dawood Ibrahim, who enjoyed Maksim's hospitality when the latter visited Kyrgyzstan in 2009. The particular importance was that Bakiyev's rule brought Kyrgyzstan closer to China. Within a short span the country was turned into shadow economy controlled by business lobbies from China. The number of Chinese businesses, labourers and students in Kyrgyzstan had risen during Bakiyev's period. Several projects were envisaged including the idea of connecting Kyrgyzstan with China through a high-speed rail network.[57]

After Bakiyev got re-elected in the 2009 Presidential election, he promised to carry out reforms. However, his critics remained skeptical and accused him for following the footsteps of Vladimir Putin and Nursultan Nazarbayev.[58] The country's chronic internal economic crisis, including power shortages during winter months, added to his unpopularity. Bakiyev's son was even accused of selling power to neighbouring Kazakhstan and thereby depriving Kyrgyz public of electricity. The power shortage was at peak during the winter 2008–09. The government later raised energy tariffs by many folds that further fuelled anger against his regime.[59]

To his bad luck, Bakiyev finally got caught in the high geopolitics of major powers. He announced in October 2008 to close the US Airbase and subsequently visited Moscow in February 2009 to strike a deal with President Dmitri Medvedev. Bakiyev promised the Russians that he will evict the Americans from Manas if Russia in return promised a $2 billion investment in Kyrgyzstan's energy sector. Moscow did agree to Bakiyev's conditions, but soon after he returned home, Bakiyev backstabbed Moscow by renegotiating with the US to keep the base. In the bargain, the USA agreed to more than triple its annual rent for the base.[60] Later, Kyrgyzstan, in a bit to balance the situation, tentatively agreed to allow Russia to open a second military base on its territory. But this did not cut much ice. Beyond the rhetoric, Moscow did not perhaps think it necessary to push for the US eviction, for it carried little significance for Russia. Kremlin continued to back Bakiyev's regime and waited for the right moment to teach him a lesson. By March 2010, a month before the April uprising, the Kremlin had launched an anti-Bakiyev campaign through the mass media.[61] Moscow also showed its displeasure by imposing duties on fuel exports to Kyrgyzstan. Stopping of fuel exports is a card that Russia had played in the past as well. The spike in fuel prices on April 1, 2010 was Moscow's last straw that ultimately caused public discontent, culminating in violent protests on April 7, 2010. Observers felt that this was an orchestrated reverse-tulip revolution.[62]

However, the gravity of Kyrgyz situation was not easy to ignore. This time the implications of mishandling the Kyrgyz crisis could have been severe for the whole region and the prospect of a wider civil war breaking up on ethnic lines in Fergana Valley was real and that could have engulfed other states as well. The deposed Kyrgyz leader had greater degree of support in the south, especially in Osh and Jalalabad regions, where ethnic Uzbeks constituted over 40 per cent of the population. Every possibility existed for orchestrating violence against the Uzbek minorities, which in turn would have widened the conflict into other parts of the Fergana Valley. Therefore, a careful handling of the Kyrgyz situation was required by the regional and international actors. Within days, the Kazakh Foreign Ministry issued a statement saying that President Bakiyev's departure from Kyrgyzstan was a result of negotiations between the Presidents of Kazakhstan, the US and Russia. It was clear that the OSCE and a number of other international players also played mediatory role.[63] The Kazakh statement said that this was done to prevent civil war and to let the interim government address the most pressing socio-economic issues in the country.

New Challenges

Bakiyev came to power on the back of the Tulip Revolution but he failed to meet the peoples rising aspirations. Instead he too got bogged down into corruption and nepotism. The democratic reforms were stalled and for those who fought for change during the Tulip Revolution there was disappointment. Nor could the first Kyrgyz revolution steered changes in other countries. Therefore, all eyes were now on the new Kyrgyz leaders who apparently were the same officials worked for the previous two regimes. The difference this time was that new leaders had learnt from the earlier mistakes of the pre-mature revolution and tried to make the change a genuine political process. The economy was in shambles. Reforms were required in the government institutions, but power struggle among the political elite persisted. The situation witnessed this time in capital Bishkek was the same as it was in 2005. For days, chaos prevailed, shops were looted and lands, private property and businesses were unlawfully seized by thugs and the powerful. One of the early and toughest challenges faced by the interim government was the deadly ethnic violence which erupted in June 2010 in the city of Osh and nearby Jalalabad. Hundreds died in the rioting involving mobs of ethnic Kyrgyz and Uzbek. The new interim-President Roza Otunbayeva pledged to re-write the constitution and hold elections within the next six months.

The Kyrgyzstan's case only demonstrated that the post-Soviet authoritarian leaders were not immune to popular uprisings. To some extent the Kyrgyz example provided that hope. But is also a fact that other regimes in the region have so far survived despite the Kyrgyz coloured revolution and also shielded themselves from the Arab Spring that unfolded in West Asia. The situation in Central Asia quite resembles the Arab world and it is essentially about authoritarian control of power and lack of multi-party system. While some regimes like in Turkmenistan and Uzbekistan still remain repressive, others like Tajikistan and Kyrgyzstan suffer from different political and economic problems that may fuel further instability. Even Kazakhstan had started witnessing social unrest and the spread of extremism challenging the authoritarian rule.

NOTES

1. Daan van der Schriek Akayev, "Faced Divided Opposition", *The St. Petersburg Times,*1055 http://sptimes.ru/index.php?action_id=2&story_id=3064 (Accessed March 25, 2005).
2. Michael A. Weinstein, "Kyrgyzstan at the Crossroads", *The Power and Interest News Report (PINR)*, http://www.pinr.com January 18, 2005.
3. Valentinas Mite, "Kyrgyzstan: North-South Divide Is a Factor in Politics", *Radio Free Europe,* http://www.rferl.org/content/article/1058107.html (Accessed March 24, 2005).
4. "Revolutionary Momentum Builds in Southern Kyrgyzstan", http://www.eurasianet.org/departments/insight/articles/eav032105.shtml (Accessed March 20, 2005).
5. Alisher Khamidov, "MP's Arrest Focuses Attention on Executive-Legislative Struggle in Kyrgyzstan", http://www.eurasianet.org/departments/civilsociety/articles/eav010902.shtml (Accessed January 8, 2002).
6. The *KelKel* (New Epoch), a youth organisation formed on the lines of what appeared in Serbia, Georgia and Ukraine. It was formed in January 2005 and drew its inspiration from Georgia's *Kmara* (Enough) movement to catalyze Kyrgyz youth for political change. The KelKe helped new authorities to restore order after the revolution but claimed no formal links with the opposition.
7. Gulnoza Saidazimova, "Kyrgyzstan: Youth Playing Key Role In Pro-Bakiyev Political Movement", *RFE/RL*, July 7, 2005.
8. BTI 2012 Kyrgyzstan Country Report, *Report. Gütersloh: Bertelsmann Stiftung, 2012* http://www.bti-project.de/fileadmin/Inhalte/reports/2012/pdf/BTI%202012%20Kyrgyzstan.pdf
9. "Kyrgyz minister sets out foreign policy priorities", *BBC Asia Africa Intelligence Wire*, October 19, 2004.
10. Akayev voiced concern about "foreign-funded" revolutions during a televised speech on December 25, 2004.
11. "KYRGYZSTAN: Protests ahead of elections", http://www.irinnews.org/print.asp?ReportID=45768 (Accessed February 24, 2005) or read Justin Burke, "Kyrgyzstan's Revolution: Be Careful What You Wish For", *Eurasianet,* March 24, 2005.
12. Mark Baker, 'Kyrgyzstan: Questions Remain About March 24 'Revolution' (Part I)' *RFE/RL* Prague, April 8, 2005.
13. Personal conversation with Dr Prem Kumar in Bishkek.
14. *RFE/RL,* April 8, 2005.
15. This was the analysis of most Russian academics. Read Jeremy Bransten, "Kyrgyzstan: Was 'Revolution' A Worthy Successor To Rose And Orange? (Part III)", *RFE/RL*, April 8, 2005.
16. Quoted by Central Asia-Caucasus Analyst", http://new.cacianalyst.org/publications/analytical-articles.html?start=488 (Accessed October 5, 2005).

17. *Kabar news agency*, March 24, 2005.
18. "Toppled Kyrgyzstan President Akayev denies he resigned", *Itar-Tass,* March 25, 2005.
19. Read Jeremy Bransten, "Kyrgyzstan: Was 'Revolution' A Worthy Successor To Rose And Orange? (Part III)", *RFE/RL*, April 8, 2005.
20. N.C. Aizenman, "Season of Unease after Kyrgyz Spring Revolt", *Washington Post,* May 31, 2005.
21. "Kyrgyzstan: Bakiyev Wins Election By Landslide", Bishkek, *RFE/RL*, July 11, 2005.
22. Gulnoza Saidazimova, "Election Commission: Kyrgyz Vote Valid", *RFE/RL*, October 7, 2005.
23. The prison crisis emerged in October 2005, when a member of parliament, Tynychbek Akmatbayev, was murdered while visiting a prison camp. The event led breaking out of riots several prisons simultaneously that sparked a political crisis. Read "Kyrgyzstan: The Prison Nightmare", http://www.crisisgroup.org August 16, 2006.
24. The most advertised of such incidents was the capture of a coalmine in Kara-Keche, in the Naryn region of central Kyrgyzstan, by workers of the enterprise. Read, Zoya Pylenko, Attempts at re-privatization follows Kyrgyz revolution", http://old.cacianalyst.org/?q=node/3198 (Accessed July 13, 2005).
25. Tom Wood, "Kyrgyzstan: Too early to pass judgment on revolution", *EurasiaNet* Commentary, January 20, 2006. Also read for greater analysis of the situation Swanee Hunt, "Kyrgyzstan at crossroads: Asian nation could be a democracy or a disaster", *Eurasianet,* November 28, 2005.
26. Gulnoza Saidazimova, "Kyrgyzstan: Did Revolution Sow the Seeds of Democracy? (Part II), Prague, *RFE.RL,* April 8 2005.
27. "Kyrgyzstan Honors Revolution, President Pledges Most Important Stage About to Get Underway", *EurasiaNet Commentary*, March 24, 2006.
28. Ibid.
29. A commonly used term to describe Kyrgyz problems by foreign investors.
30. A term locally used by Bishkek citizens.
31. ICG, Asia Briefing N°79, http://www.crisisgroup.org/en/regions/asia/central-asia/kyrgyzstan/B079-kyrgyzstan-a-deceptive-calm.aspx (Accessed August 14, 2008).
32. Gulnoza Saidazimova, "Kyrgyzstan: What Will Be New Government's Domestic, Foreign Policies?" *RFE/RL* Bishkek, July 12, 2005.
33. *RFE/RL,* Prague, April 14, 2005.
34. "Bakiyev: Russia, Neighbors Support Government", *RFE/RL*, Bishkek, March 28, 2005.
35. Valentinas Mite, "Central Asia: Regional Officials Cautious as Oppositions Rejoice at Events in Kyrgyzstan", http://www.rferl.org/content/article/1058131.html (Accessed March 25, 2005).
36. Ibid.
37. Ibid.
38. According to an agreement (September 2003) with Kyrgyzstan, an air base is presently being set up in Kant, 30 km east of Bishkek. Around 500 Russian military personnel, several Russian helicopters and aircraft, including Su-27, Su-25 aircraft and Mi-8 helicopters are currently located at the base.
39. *Kommersant,* Moscow, May 25, 2005.
40. "China: Border Crossing With Kyrgyzstan Closed" *China News Service*, March 25, 2005, *Reuters,* March 28, 2005.
41. Valentinas Mite, "Central Asia: Regional Officials Cautious As Oppositions Rejoice At Events In Kyrgyzstan", *RFE/RL Prague*, March 25, 2005.
42. *Uzbek National News Agency*, March 25, 2005.
43. Uzbek National News Agency, March 25, 2005 also read Valentinas Mite "Central Asian officials cautiously react to Kyrgyz uprising", *RFE/RL Prague*, 26 March 2005; also read

Daniel Kimmage, "Central Asia Report", *RFE/RL,* March 26, 2005.

44. "Kyrgyz leader says tribalism may lead to state collapse", *Kyrgyz Telegraph Agency (KyrTAg),* May 31, 2011.
45. *Kabar,* April 8, 2005.
46. *Kabar,* April 7, 2010.
47. "Kyrgyz ex-leader Kurmanbek Bakiyev flies to Kazakhstan", *BBC,* April 15, 2010.
48. "Ousted Kyrgyz president 'in Belarus'", http://www.bullfax.com/?q=node-ousted-kyrgyz-president-turns-belarus (Accessed April 20, 2010).
49. http://kg.akipress.org/news:194361
50. "Bakiyev defiant over Kyrgyz role ", *BBC News,* http://news.bbc.co.uk/go/pr/fr/-/2/hi/asia-pacific/8634292.stm (Accessed April 21, 2010).
51. http://en.beta.rian.ru/exsoviet/20100701/159656579.html (Accessed July 2010).
52. *RIA Novosti,* July 3, 2010.
53. *BBC,* October 10, 2012.
54. Bruce Pannier, "With First Son's New Role, Kyrgyz Government Remains A Family Affair", *Radio Free Europe,* November 5, 2009.
55. *RIA Novosti,* April 16, 2010.
56. "Maksim Bakiyev: A Groomed Puppet Who Never Came to Be King", http://www.boilingfrogspost.com/2010/07/18/another-%E2%80%98viable%E2%80%99-candidate-bites-the-dust-%E2%80%A6/ (Accessed July 18, 2010).
57. *24.kg,* March 23, 2010.
58. *The Eurasian Daily Monitor,* September 10, 2009.
59. Liat Asman, "Kyrgyzstan: Utility Price Hike Squeezes Citizens", http://www.eurasianet.org/departments/insightb/articles/eav020810.shtml (Accessed February 7, 2010).
60. Joshu Kucera,"Bakiyev Can Be Bought": U.S. Embassy Tied Rent for Kyrgyz Air Base to President's Reelection", http://www.eurasianet.org/node/64797 (Accessed January 5 2012).
61. *The Eurasian Daily Monitor* reported on April 1 2010.
62. "Tulip time is over", *The Washington Times,* April 21, 2010.
63. *BBC,* April 13, 2010.

CHAPTER 2

Ethnic Divide: The Osh Riots

The second Kyrgyz Revolution in 2010 was a major victory for those who remained dissatisfied with the democratic change that accompanied the Tulip Revolution of 2005. However, the deadly ethnic clashes between ethnic Kyrgyz and Uzbeks that followed the uprising in the country's southern cities of Osh and Jalalabadhad sent shock waves; reminding the world how fragile and volatile Central Asia could be. The conflict came as an extension of the uprising in April that year. The new Interim Government believed that it was orchestrated by the former President Kurmanbek Bakiyev who had fled the country on April 7.

The violence had erupted on May 19 in Jalalabad and quickly spread to Osh on June 10. The groups of Uzbek and Kyrgyz youth came from the neighbouring villages to join the clashes that continued for several days. When the situation went uncontrolled, the Interim Government declared a state of emergency on June 12. The Kyrgyz security forces fired at the mobs in which hundreds were killed brutally and thousands fled the cities in the ensuing violence.[1] The exact number is still unknown; different inquiry commissions gave different figures. The UN and others claimed that 400,000 people were displaced and over 111,000 people fled across the border to Uzbekistan.[2] The ethnic Uzbeks however claimed that at least 700 ethnic Uzbeks were killed in Jalalabad alone.[3] The media reported brutal cases of rape; burning of children alive, stabbing, etc.[4] In fact, several independent sources claimed the complicity of local military units involved in the ethnic clashes. Unable to contain the conflict, Kyrgyzstan called for Russia's intervention but was rejected by Moscow citing its inability to get involved in the Kyrgyz internal conflict. The CSTO too refused to dispatch peace keepers to contain the conflict.[5] Uzbekistan that borders with Osh region fortunately opened its borders to Uzbek refugees and also took sufficient measures to prevent any backlash across the border. Thus, a major inter-state conflict was forestalled.[6] In fact, the role of Karimov for preventing the escalation of ethnic conflict was widely acknowledged by Kyrgyz leadership later. Even the European Union (EU) had fully acknowledged the role of Uzbekistan in averting a major conflict.[7]

The Kyrgyz (nomadic) and Uzbek (sedentary) [8] dichotomy has been existing for very long time. Even the Soviets had a hard time in defining a cohesive strategy, for their differences were rooted deeply in history.[9] Following the Soviet collapse, the two ethnic communities in Osh fought fiercely over land dispute in June 1990. The Kyrgyz had then demanded that collective farms of the Soviet era be handed over to them. The bloody violence killed hundreds and the Soviet troops had to be deployed and borders between the Uzbek and Kyrgyz republics be closed.

The Kyrgyz, who have been living in the rural areas, had long envied the Uzbeks, who have largely controlled the economy and were more prosperous than the nomadic Kyrgyz. The Kyrgyz envy became more intense after the independence. There have been accusations that during Bakiyev's rule the officials had encouraged the Kyrgyz youth to occupy Uzbek land.

The reasons for the June 2010 riots had been widely contested by both sides. The Kyrgyz have blamed the Uzbekleaders for initiating the violence. The Uzbeks have been long accused for their irredentist moves, such as their demand for official status for Uzbek language, reservation of seats for Uzbeks in the Kyrgyz parliament among others. The majority Kyrgyz therefore viewed it as a separatist move; an attempt to split Kyrgyzstan along ethnic lines. The situation in any case had become volatile across the Fergana Valley; each state that shared the Valley perceived threat from each other. The Kyrgyz media regularly aired Uzbekistan's desire to annex Osh region. The border between Kyrgyzstan and Uzbekistan had been tense; Tashkent even fenced the borders.

But the needle of suspicion was mainly pointed at the former President, Kurmanbek Bakiyev and his son Maxim Bakiyev who were accused for spending $10 million for instigating the riots with the help of the Islamic extremists.[10]

The terrorist outfits such as the Islamic Movement of Uzbekistan (IMU) and Islamic Jihad Union (IJU) were separately blamed for creating instability to pursue their radical agenda. The officials cited that initially agent provocateurs with sniper-shooter infiltrated from Badakhshan across the border with Tajikistan. However, this could not be confirmed by the Kyrgyz security agencies due to lack of credible evidence.[11] Besides, no other country, including Uzbekistan, Russia, Kazakhstan and US had supported the view of the IMU and UIJ having instigated the violence. No comments came from the Afghan officials, NATO and others about terrorist movement around Badakhshan during that time. Bakyt Beshimov, a well-known political expert on Central Asia and Kyrgyz politician, who served as Kyrgyz Ambassador to India and currently a visiting scholar at Massachusetts Institute of Technology's (MIT's) Centre for International Studies and Harvard University's Davis Centre for Russian and Eurasian Studies, believed that if Bakiyev had links with international terrorist outfits, he should have been on the watch list of counter-terrorist agencies.[12] The Kyrgyz Government's accusation that Bakiyev instigated the riots in connivance with terrorist, therefore, did not hold much water. Even the Interpol had refused to cooperate with Bishkek. Belarus refused to cooperate with Kyrgyz authorities on Bakiyev's extradition.

However, Uzbekistan did mention about the role of a third force but it didn't perhaps mean the role of IMU.[13] To that extent, even the UN High Commissioner for Human Rights, Navi Pillay too viewed that there was compelling evidence of the events being preplanned. The UN High Commission representative for Human Rights, Rupert Colville made a following statement: "We have compelling evidence that these events were not spontaneous ethnic clashes. In some ways they were organised and well planned."[14] However, several inquiry reports had ruled out the role of outside powers and instead pinned on local reasons that got flared up due to absence of law and order.

Strategic Dimension: Role of Russia?

The strategic dimension was also not left out. The role of foreign powers especially the Russian and Kazakh hands in destabilising Kyrgyzstan was widely discussed. In fact, Kyrgyz and also Uzbek media widely covered the direct involvement of some Russian leaders in fomenting trouble in south Kyrgyzstan.[15] Uzbekistan's perception was that Russia had been engaged in steering the trouble in the Fergana Valley in order to consolidate its hold in Central Asia, and especially to punish Tashkent for defying Russia's dictum.[16] Many observers believed that Uzbek authorities had been predicting the event as far back as 2009. Uzbekistan had been particularly opposed to the idea of opening of a Russian military base in Osh that has been under discussion since the Bakiyev's time. The Western funded media outlets noted the Russian and Kazakh media were consistently attacking Kyrgyzstan.[17] A Turkish analyst Turgut Demirtepe in the article *"Last Tango in Bishkek"* published by *Hurriyet Daily News* (Turkey) in August 2009 believed that the IMU was tasked by the Russian Intelligence Service to instigate ethnic conflict in Osh.[18] Some direct statements came from senior Uzbek State officials during the conflict. For example, on June 15, 2010, Deputy Foreign Minister of Uzbekistan, Abdulaziz Kamilov, had voiced concern about the role of outside actors. He said" The impression is that these events are organised by outsiders. I do not doubt that a third party is behind bloodshed in Kyrgyzstan,as proven by the facts of large number of weapons and groups of mercenaries,skilled sniper-shooters on the ground."[19] During his visit to Ashgabat in October 2010, Islam Karimov blamed a third party for stroking the fire. He said, "Everything that happened in southern Kyrgyzstan, all these problems were created by those, who pursue far-reaching strategic goals. Uzbeks and Kyrgyz have become hostages of what was initiated by the third forces....Neither Uzbeks, nor are Kyrgyz guilty. People are born to be happy and to live well themselves and to provide better life for children. This is said in Muslim and Christian and other religions. If we talk through this prism, neither Uzbeks, nor Kyrgyz are interested in this confrontation. These people used to live together for centuries and will live together further. All that has happened in Kyrgyzstan, we experience as our pain, real national pain for those people who died in senseless massacre imposed on Uzbeks and Kyrgyz from outside."[20]

This perception was further substantiated when Uzbekistan called for an independent international investigation into June violence at the Third Committee of the UN General Assembly in 2010. The Uzbek representative Murad Askarov underlined that Kyrgyz and Uzbek community, jointly living for centuries, became hostages of well-thought campaign by the third forces. He believed that the events were a serious threat to Central Asian stability. The campaign, he believed, was "aimed not only at creating chaos and uncontrollable situation in the country, but also at envisaged far-reaching aims to attract Uzbekistan into cruel slaughter and turn inter-ethnic conflict into inter-state confrontation of two neighbouring states."[21]

During this author's conversation with several well-informed Kyrgyz sources, including officials working in the Prime Minister's office believed that only Russia had the motivation to stoke the fire in Osh. This was similar to the views expressed by a number of politicians and organizations in Uzbekistan who directly accused Russian Federal Security Service (FSB) of provoking a conflict in Osh. Moreover, the Interim President Otunbayeva in an interview with *Ekho Moskvy Radio is* supposed to have made an interesting comment that said "Bakiyevs had clearly drawn a plan; unfortunately, it was executed with help from Moscow."[22] This aspect is widely elaborated in the internal commissions' reports.

Interestingly, not just the Uzbeks but Kyrgyz and Tajik experts too believed that only Russia could have gained the strategic benefits out of the situation. It became quite clear when Russia tried to obstruct the proposal of the OSCE Police Advisory Group (SPAG) deployment in Osh. Earlier in May 2010, the Russian Foreign Ministry warned the EU and NATO not to intervene in the internal affairs of CIS countries. Moscow appeared to have arm twisted the Kyrgyz authorities on the issue. There was a sudden spurt of various groups in Kyrgyzstan protesting against the OSCE peacekeeping mission. The issue evoked much debate and criticism in the country with the Parliament Speaker seeking explanation from the Kyrgyz Foreign Minister over who authorised OSCE Police Advisory Group deployment in south Kyrgyzstan. According to the Speaker, the President, the government and the Parliament were unaware of the issue. Ministry of Foreign Affairs (MFA) explained by saying that the friendly countries (OSCE) was asked by the Interim Government on June 20, 2010 to deploy its Police Advisory Group to control the situation in Osh. Meanwhile when the OSCE considered the issue in August 2010, the reaction of the people was against it, hence the President closed this issue. It was explained later that the Kyrgyz Deputy Interior Minister Nikolay Soldasheko had addressed the OSCE Permanent Council on November 4, 2010 in Vienna and the Police Advisory Group began its work in Kyrgyzstan in January 2011.[23] Kyrgyz Foreign Minister Kazakbaev later told the Parliament that there was no OSCE Police Advisory Group in Kyrgyzstan now, though experts from various countries were in the country working under OSCE police reform project, but they are not OSCE police officers.[24] The Speaker Ahmatbek Keldibekov however decided to set up a parliamentary commission to establish how the OSCE police officers arrived in Kyrgyzstan and opened their office there. It only appeared that the government came under pressure from the SCO states, particularly Russia and China, to ascertain the OSCE police presence in Kyrgyzstan.

The Uzbek suspicion also grew when Russia ordered an investigation into the June violence under the auspices of CSTO but the report, it appeared, was never released. Uzbekistan also warily reacted to Russia's appointment of Vladimir Rushailo as its special envoy in Kyrgyzstan. The Kyrgyz have never blamed the Russian Secret Service's role in the Osh events, but the country's leadership has been critical of the role played by the CSTO's Secretary General Nikolai Bordyuzha in Kyrgyzstan. A plethora of commentaries and strategic analyses on the supposed role of Russia in the conflict are available in the public domain. At one point Atambayev made an oblique comment saying many states expected military conflict between Uzbekistan and Kyrgyzstan.[25] He was perhaps referring to Russia and Kazakhstan; both having strong intelligence presence in the Fergana Valley.

The Aftermath

In the aftermath of the events, the Interim Government led by Roza Otunbayeva had come under sharp attack for its failure to prevent the riots. Since then several national and international inquiry commissions had been set up to find out the root cause and the perpetuators of the June tragedy. In all there are more than eight inquiry commissions' reports. They include Ombudsman Abdygany Erkebaev's report, Amnesty International report, Union of Lawyers report, Human Rights Organiations's report, National Commission report, Parliamentary Commission report and Kyrgyzstan Inquiry Commission (KIC) (International) report. Some of them were conducted seriously, but most internal investigations were chaotic and inconsistent. They were meant to cover up the failure of the state though the International report too acknowledged the weakness of new regime -providing sufficient scope for various vested interests to exploit the situation. Most analysts who had access to other reports suggested that the chronology of events cited by them were 80 percent similar.

Among other things, the report accused the Kyrgyz militia for carrying out arbitrary arrests and illegal detentions of ethnic Uzbeks, ostensibly to seize weapons, in various villages and homes. The issue had widely featured in all the investigations conducted by rights groups and media. Those who had access to information coming out of Osh region observed frequent cases of torture, ill-treatment, prolonged detentions and extortion. Some Russian sources estimated 77 per cent detainees were ethnic Uzbeks.On the other hand, a series of articles and videos were in circulation throughout 2010 and 2011 that mainly blamed the Uzbeks as separatists. The nationalistic passion among the Kyrgyz has never gone down since then throughout the country.

The findings of the most internal investigation reports, including the one released by the National Commission of Inquiry and the Parliamentary Commission, have mainly held the Uzbeks leaders, linked to the former president Bakiyev, responsible for instigating the violence. The internal Kyrgyz inquiry reports though reprimanded the Interim Government for failing to avert the unrest, none had mentioned about Russia's role even though outside the government this has been widely discussed. However, the most important report brought out by the International Independent Commission of Inquiry, known as KIC, contradicted the official government version and other internal inquiry commissions' findings of the June ethnic violence. But the KIC report too ruled out the role of outside power in igniting the Osh conflict.

The Kyrgyzstan Inquiry Commission (KIC)

After much controversy, the Interim Government had authorised an International Independent Commission of Inquiry to be conducted to go into the Osh events. The inquiry came to be known as the KIC, which released its report on May 3, 2011.[26] The KIC was headed by the OSCE Parliamentary Assembly's special representative for Central Asia Kimmo Kiljunen and other members composed of legal experts and academics from Australia, Russia, and Turkey. The Kyrgyz Government mandated the Commission to ostensibly demonstrate transparency and willingness to address the problems. It was also backed by international human rights organisations to have its legitimacy under international law, while the criminal investigation was left to the responsibility of the Kyrgyz authorities. The Commission's enquiry had cost $1.4 million that was financed by the Crisis Management Initiative (CMI), a Finnish independent non-profit organisation, the EU and the US.

The report provided a detailed chronology of the events including the social, economic, political, and historical factors contributing to the violence. It had determined responsibilities and also made important recommendations with a focus on accountability measures. The commission based its report upon extensive analysis and interviews of 750 witnesses, 700 documents, nearly 5,000 photographs, and 1,000 video extracts. The report noted the following critical observations:

> The Kiljunen's report observed that the Interim Government that took over from Bakiyev in April 2010 had failed to guarantee security during the violence in Osh. The report noted there was a period of fluidity and weak authority in the aftermath of Bakiyev's overthrow.
>
> The report noted the Kyrgyz jubilant liberation movement had created the conditions for nationalistic overdrive which soured further after ethnic Uzbeks also demanded more rights. According to the report 470 people were killed,

1,900 injured and about 411,000 were driven from their homes.

The violence, according to the report had risen to the level of a "crime against humanity"[27] as defined by international conventions, if the evidence the commission saw were proved in court. It was though not called as war crimes or genocide.

Notably, the report said, in many instances crowds of attackers seized firearms and ammunition from the military and police....members of the crowd then committed murder, rape, other forms of sexual violence, physical violence against ethnic Uzbeks.

Kiljunen's report sharply criticised the complicity of the Kyrgyz security forces directly or indirectly, especially its uniformed soldiers participated in the violence; some military officers handed out weapons to Kyrgyz mobs that attacked Uzbeks. It noted the failure of the police commanders to maintain discipline or investigate the loss of armoured vehicles and weapons. The report implicated civilian and military officials including those still serving in government. The report singled out one general in particular, Ismail Isakov then Commandant of the south, for failing to use his soldiers to protect civilians. It also implicated a security force commander in the city of Jalalabad, Kubatbek Baibolov, who was Prosecutor General of Kyrgyzstan until March 2011.

Kiljunen's report noted the ethnic Uzbeks having suffered ill-treatment, arbitrary arrests and detentions in the Uzbek neighbourhoods or *mahallas* by the police. It added that trials and prosecutions following the events disproportionately targeted ethnic Uzbeks—and that this may be ongoing. According to the report ethnic Kyrgyz had also suffered, though in lesser numbers. The report supported a narrative of the violence conveyed by witnesses in the ethnic Uzbek *mahallas* in Osh.

The report ruled out any involvement of the third forces, therefore suggesting that Bakiyev was not involved in inciting the bloodshed. There was no proof of involvement of international terrorists but the criminal groups may have played a certain role in the events.

Kyrgyz Bellicose Response

The Kiljunen's KIC report became extremely controversial with Kyrgyz authority and its political class instantly rejected its conclusion as unacceptable and one-sided. The KIC report completely contradicted the official Kyrgyz version and other internal inquiry commissions' findings. The official statement came through the MFA that said "an overwhelming tendency that only one ethnic group has committed crimes, ignoring the victims and deaths of this very group, and portraying the other group solely as defenceless victims".[28] The government strongly countered the report and said that there was insufficient evidence of crimes against humanity and that it was the previous regime of President Bakiyev that had to be blamed, and that both ethnic Kyrgyz and Uzbeks suffered equally. The official

Kyrgyz accused the authors for giving too much credence to accounts by Uzbeks and also found that the research was incomplete.

A Kyrgyz MFA press release said, "Tragic events have a very deep historical, social, economic, and political background...they were provoked in the conditions of a very complicated situation in the country by the supporters of the former regime, which aimed to regain the power it lost on April 7, 2010."[29] The MFA said "it is important to take into account lack of political, financial, law enforcement and military resources available for the Interim Government to counter large scale provocations of inter-ethnic clashes during the conflict. Even in such severe conditions, the people and the authorities of Kyrgyzstan managed to stop violence and to localise the conflict within several days without assistance from outside."[30] It also noted the influence and involvement of organised crime groups, drug dealers among them, in the incitement and escalation of the conflict. However, the government said it was doing all it could to minimise the consequences of the unrest and to prevent such events from recurring. It said it will establish a special state commission to implement the international commission's recommendations and those of other groups that conducted investigations.

The Prime Minister Almazbek Atambayev asserted that not all things in the report of KIC were true. He said "Some international commissions want to accuse the Kyrgyz people and to blame the Interim Government for the events. Some say the genocide took place, crime against humanity. This is a lie; the disorders were organised by Bakiyev's supporters and separatists."[31] The Kyrgyz Defence Ministry also rejected the report and said that it was conducted in one-sided manner and without consideration of all relevant stakeholders. Defense Ministry said that the report describes only the negative sides of military and law enforcement agencies. All actions were taken in line with the laws of the Kyrgyz Republic and international laws. The ministry asserted that the publication of the report won't lead to reconciliation; on the contrary, the report could cause discontent of people and armed forces, whose positive contribution was not mentioned in the report.[32]

The report had sparked off a fresh political controversy. The Kyrgyz Parliament hurriedly conducted a session on May 26, 2011 to hear the findings of the Parliamentary Commission (PC) of inquiry into events of April-June 2010 and also to discuss the report of the International Commission of Inquiry (KIC) that was released on May 3, 2011.

The Parliament too instantly rejected the findings of the KIC report and overwhelmingly passed a resolution to declare Kimmo Kiljunen a persona non grata in Kyrgyzstan.[33] The parliamentarians ordered the authority to ban Kiljunen's entry for providing inaccurate and biased information about the tragic events to the international community and who has a scandalous and doubtful reputation in his home country.

The Parliament agreed with the comments of the government concerning the Kiljunen's report and said that it is an incitement to racial hatred and endangers the national security of Kyrgyzstan. It described the report as "biased, one-sided, does not contribute to peace, stability and serve to prevent further conflict."[34]

The Parliament tasked the government to adopt all necessary measures to communicate accurate and unbiased information about circumstances and conditions leading to the tragic events in April-June 2010 through diplomatic missions abroad. The General Prosecutor's Office, the interior ministry were tasked to bring to justice those guilty of production of inaccurate information able to incite inter-ethnic hatred and its dissemination.

All in all, the Kyrgyz Parliament's reaction to Kiljunen report was extremely harsh that invited sharp criticism from the international community. Kiljunen himself in a statement expressed his unhappiness about the *Jogorku Kenesh* resolution to ban his entry into Kyrgyzstan. He said "I can only say that the truth seems to add to the agony...we've produced an honest account of the events and analysed them objectively. Some circles of power seem not willing to face the facts."[35] Kiljunen stressed that "Kyrgyz government, unlike the parliament, agreed with the report's recommendations and conclusions though it has also criticised some of the report's interpretations."[36] He was astonished by the way all MPs, including his friends in the Kyrgyz parliament voted in favour of the resolution.[37]

What perhaps irked the Kyrgyz leaders was the KIC charge of "crimes against humanity if proven beyond reasonable doubt in a court of law that the Kyrgyz mobs attacked on Uzbek neighbourhoods."[38] This had caused notable discomfort in the country and was viewed by many officials as a slur against ethnic Kyrgyz which will only fuel more discontent. Of course, many of those who are guilty for the events may be sitting in the Parliament.

The United Nation supported the conclusions of the KIC report and called it an important step in the right direction but urged Kyrgyz Government to carry out further investigations addressing the issues of accountability. The UN particularly congratulated President Roza Otunbayeva for initiating the independent inquiry and giving it unrestricted access. The UN expressed readiness to assist Kyrgyzstan for the establishment of a special commission to implement the recommendations of the KIC report. The US Government too termed the Kiljunen's report most accurate and urged Kyrgyz authorities to take further steps to ensure accountability, promote reconciliation and prevent recurrence of violence. Similarly, the UK welcomed the decision of the Kyrgyz Government to allow the KIC to conduct its work unhindered, and its willingness to accept responsibility for some of the issues identified in the report.[39]

Significantly, the Russian Foreign Ministry also endorsed the conclusions of the report saying that they were balanced and aimed at preventing the repetition of similar events.

Meanwhile, the Human Rights Watch (HRW) and the Amnesty International (AI) in their statements urged Kyrgyz authorities to pay careful attention to the commission's findings and carry out investigations on how such systematic ethnic attacks took place with the complicity of Kyrgyz officials. The International Federation for Human Rights (FIDH) and its member organizations in Kyrgyzstan, Citizens Against Corruption (CAC), Legal Clinic Adilet and Kylym Shamy welcomed the findings and said that "it should bring to light the failure of the Kyrgyz authorities to fulfill their basic responsibility to stop the violence and protect their own citizens."[40]

However, the international community was surprised by the Kyrgyz dramatic response to the Kiljunen's report.[41] It was the newly arrived US Ambassador Pamela Spratlen who used "surprise"[42] expression in her reaction. She said the US would continue to support efforts to bring those responsible for the violence to justice. Subsequently, the Council of Human Rights Defenders of Kyrgyzstan too called the Parliament's move a shameful decision and said it should have taken longer to consider its response to the report by Kiljunen's commission.

In a telephone conversation on May 30, between State Secretary and Deputy Minister of Foreign Affairs of the Russian Federation Grigory Karasin and European Union Special Representative (EUSR) for Central Asia Pierre Morel, both expressed concern over harsh resolution of the Kyrgyz Parliament. Grigorin Karasin, however, urged that the resolution should not be dramatised. Karasin noted that "despite some criticisms of the document, its conclusions were taken into account by the Kyrgyz Government, which has decided to heed the recommendations. The main thing is that these steps should contribute to strengthening inter-ethnic harmony, preserving peace and stability in the Republic."[43]

The strong rhetoric over the KIC report also evoked angry response from the UN High Commissioner for Human Rights Navi Pillay. In her report filed for the 17th session of the UNHRC, she warned that "nationalist rhetoric ... used by some politicians" could affect the credibility of the coming presidential election. She urged the government to ensure the election's credibility and the protection of minorities residing in Kyrgyzstan.[44]

However, the Chairman of the Parliamentary Committee on Defence and Security, Ismail Isakov, took the US statement as intimidating. He said it was a hint addressed to the Kyrgyz authorities to fear us or else we will raise this issue at any time. Besides, Ismail Isakov charged the KIC head for taking bribes from Uzbek separatists. He said that Kimmo Kiljunen had ties to one of the authors of Yugoslavia dismemberment, in particular. Ismail Isakov said "They want to separate artificially two nations."[45]

A right wing member of the Ar-Namys party Tursunbay Bakir took a different stance questioning why the Kyrgyz authorities did not invite Muslim countries as members of the KIC. He said "They invited atheists who are absolutely not aware of Muslim relationships...when there is conflict between the Muslim countries, how can the representatives of other faith to resolve and understand it? Kimmo Kiljunen handed down a wrongful conclusion discrediting Kyrgyzstan."[46]

Of course, the Kiljunen's report caused considerable frictions among the political groups within Kyrgyzstan. The report came as an embarrassment to President Roza Otunbayeva who had authorised the Commission to be set up in the place. However, in the Parliament, she expressed her willingness to take full responsibility for authorising the international investigation. She explained the need for an inquiry and said "The press repeatedly mentioned the word 'genocide'. Representatives of other countries, including the Ambassadors, wanted an investigation. When I was in Osh in July 2010, local residents also requested that an international commission assess the events. When we received an offer from Kimmo Kiljunen we sent a message to Ban Ki-moon on September 29, 2010 expressing our readiness to allow an international commission to hold an investigation. But it was not only my decision; still I am ready to take the full responsibility."[47]

Otunbayeva also took the discussion and debate over the KIC report in a different spirit suggesting that opinions of political groups and the conclusion of such debates should serve as a strong foundation for building a parliamentary democracy in the republic. She believed that without assistance of the KIC, Kyrgyzstan would have to clear itself from genocide and armed conflict accusations for years. She said "The conclusion of KIC that there was no genocide and armed conflict is very important. The main thing now is to find the answer to the question what should be done to prevent recurrence of the tragedy in future."[48]

Speaking in the Kyrgyz Parliament on June 2, 2011, the President said she wanted to do her utmost to unite all ethnic groups[49] and the politicians not to use nationalistic ideas in their election campaigns for Presidential election. The President was clearly against "searching for culprits, but promised that KIC recommendations would be reflected in Kyrgyzstan's state policy.[50]

President Otunbayeva however did not agree that the work of the NGOs could be termed as the "third forces" in June tragedy. In an interview to *Radio Kabarlar*, Otunbayeva said that NGOs can't be interpreted as third forces and without assistance of NGOs it would be difficult to promote democratic processes in the country."[51]

When a Member of Parliament Myktybek Abdyldayev had questioned about the authorities' attitude towards the KIC report, Roza Otunbayeva blamed former President Bakiyev for committing crime against humanity by giving orders to shoot at innocent people. This evoked negative response from the leader of the Ata-Jurt faction, Kamchybek Tashiyev, asking her not to make unfounded accusations against anyone.[52]

There were certainly a guilt factor among every politicians and officials of the Interim Government including the President who were perhaps shocked by the Kiljunen's report. The guilt was visible from every statement made by them which were either defensive or they were diversionary in tactics. President Otunbayeva called upon Parliament to move away from disputes about June events and instead stressed on the need to achieve consensus, peace and friendship in the society.[53] The President was in favour of developing a national conceptual framework for peace preservation and inter-ethnic accord, but was opposed to reflecting the unconfirmed media information by the Parliamentary Commission. The President asked people not to suspect her nationalism. But her critics said that she had been making such statements when she was in opposition.[54] Certainly, Otunbayeva appeared loath to urgently find out the truth especially taking on the security services and political leaders that could cause a considerable political backlash, especially when the emotions among Kyrgyz were running high.

Probably in a move to divert the attention from the KIC report, a series of demonstration demanding the closer of the US Transit Centre were witnessed a week before the anniversary. The so called the "7th April Youth Movement" on June 1, 2011 demanded immediate closer of the US Transit Centre. Its leader Mirlan Bekitayev warned that if the government failed to evict it by October and November, they will settle this problem on their own way to close it in two hours and 45 minutes.[55] The Youth Movement argued that the US facility was causing huge ecological damage in the Chuy Region and wanted $1 billion compensation for the ecological damage. Similarly, the members of the National Congress of Parties (NCP) also voiced their position to the continuation of the US military facility at Manas and proposed a referendum on this issue during the Kyrgyz Presidential election. It said that the US presence in Kyrgyzstan was causing unease among the Muslim countries.[56]

Other attempts were also made either to deflect the KIC report or perhaps to divert the people's attention from the Osh event, the anniversary of which was falling on June 10. Suddenly, The Kyrgyz Youth Associations that included *Kyrgyzstan Zhashtar Keneshi* was fronted to express apprehension over the media report of NATO opening its office in Bishkek.[57] The leader of the outfit Almazbek Dzhasybayev wanted to know what transpired between NATO's the Special Envoy James Appathurai and Roza Otunbayeva in their closed doors meeting.[58]

Both political activists and media linked Kiljunen's report with the US Transit Centre and the US Ambassador's statement on opening the NATO Office in Bishkek. There was no doubt the protesting groups were fronted by interest forces, perhaps on the behest of Russia. The NGOs criticised the government and said, "If this office opens, confrontation between Kyrgyzstan and Russia will arise. This will lead to decrease in fuel supplies and soaring prices for transportation costs and food products, affect situation of migrant workers, relations with pro-Russian Kazakhstan, Tajikistan and Uzbekistan that may close the borders."[59] It further said "Our state is member of UN, CSTO, and SCO. This is enough to maintain security in the region. Our country is in a difficult economic situation. We do not need additional economic problems over unnecessary political games on the international arena."[60] According to the youth organisation leader Jazybaev, such actions were aimed at strengthening the military presence of the US and hinted that the implications of report of such commission in Yugoslavia followed a similar pattern. "It's unclear where the commission of Kimmo Kiljunen is rooted," activists questioned.[61]

Roza Otunbayeva later clarified in the Parliament that NATO Office rotates the host country every three years in Central Asia—a reason why it was shifting its office from Kazakhstan to Kyrgyzstan. She said "They allege some personal interests are pursued. This is not true as many countries receive NATO assistance. Russia receives assistance from NATO and hosts a big office of NATO. Kazakhstan sends its specialists to NATO for training. We turn this issue into politics immediately. If we do not receive aid, it is up to you not to ratify this agreement."[62]

But not everyone agreed with the Parliament's resolution on Kiljunen's entry ban. MP Shirin Aitmatova firstly charged that someone had voted for her on declaring Kimmo Kiljunen as persona non grata. She said "if you want to prohibit the entry of those, who tell bad things then you should start with Andronik Migronyan, a Russian political expert, who had said that it is necessary to divide the north and south of Kyrgyzstan."[63] But Speaker Keldibekov noted in return that Kimmo Kiljunen said not only "bad things", but also "lies".[64]

The KIC report and its fallout had forced Kyrgyzstan in May 2011 to dispatch a delegation to the US to participate in round tables held in the National Democratic Institute (NDI), Carnegie Endowment for International Peace and the Open Society Foundation (OSF). The Kyrgyz delegation presented its own version of the events and offered explanations to the KIC findings. The delegation held series of briefings at the US State Department, the US Congress and National Security Council (NSC) about the measures taken in the country on ethnic development, reform of law enforcement agencies and judicial system.[65]

The Parliamentary Commission (PC)

The Parliamentary Commission (PC) was set up in January 2011 and was headed by Tokon Mamytov. The PC included 25 members, five representatives from each parliamentary faction. On May 26, 2011, a session was called to hear the PC report. The Prime Minister, members of the government, head of the State Directorate for Reconstruction of Osh and Jalalabad, former Interim Government members, Prosecutor General, governors of southern regions and other officials were invited for the hearings. The Kyrgyz parliamentarians decided to invite Roza Otunbayeva, who had mandated the Commission for investigation, to plenary session to respond to the Kiljunen report. The Kyrgyz law makers also wanted foreign diplomats representing OSCE countries for the discussion. The idea was to set the record straight and convey the displeasure of the Parliament over the report. The Kyrgyz MPs also wanted Kimmo Kiljunen to report to deputies to explain the basis on which the report was prepared.[66]

The PC report broadly concluded that the tragedy was incited by the supporters of Kurmanbek Bakiyev and Uzbek separatists. However, there were many uncomfortable questions raised by the report that were directed against the members of the interim government, many of whom were still holding key posts. Besides, the members of Commission had no consensus on the final outcome of inquiry report. The parliamentarians decided to postpone the hearing on the first day of the hearing suggesting that they needed more time. Others insisted on preparation of one report instead of three. The members watched the documentary "*The Hour of Jackal*" presented by Member of Parliament Joldosheva, criticised the KIC report and dispersed.

The Commission constituted 25 MPs as its members. However, only 21 of them had signed the commission's general report, which was later released on June 1, 2011 by the parliament's press service. Three of its members Ismail Isakov, Jyldyz Joldosheva and Shirin Aytmatova did not sign it as their version and findings were not reflected in the final report. The Chairman of the commission also admitted that the report was written in haste.[67] In fact, it turned out to be three reports.[68] The first report was conventionally called Mamytov's report, the second was Isakov's report, and the third report was presented by Joldoshev. Mamytov's report was supported by 12 parliamentarians. Isakov's report was endorsed by three-four MPs and Joldosheva's documentary film was supported by none.

The head of the Parliamentary Commission PC, Tokon Mamytov in his version of the report identified a number of factors including the absence of a single state national policy, Bakiyev's control over power through clan structure, double standards in foreign policy, the growth in drug trafficking, and corruption in state bodies among others that had caused the June tragedy. The "Uzbek card" played by Kyrgyz ethnic Uzbek leader, Kadyrjan Batyrov was also a major factor. The report said attack by ethnic Uzbeks was preplanned, a reason why the law-enforcement bodies could not defend properly.

The report also blamed the Interim Government and its law enforcement agencies for their failure to prevent the ethnic conflict. Newly appointed officials including the police demonstrated poor professionalism as they had to work in difficult emergency situations; they were demoralised and allowed the seizure of arms.[69] Nevertheless, the report held the population responsible for escalating the conflict. The report detailed a chronology of chain of events that started immediately after the ouster of ex-President Kurmanbek Bakiyev in April 2010 culminating in the June conflict.

The report noted that the clashes in Osh and Jalalabad started after Bakiyev reached there on April 3, 2010 immediately after he was ousted from power; indicating that it was his last bit to fight back by dragging the political crisis into an inter-ethnic tinderbox. Mamytov said that subsequent events in May in Maevka village, Alamudun district, and in Dostuk village, Ala-Buka district, Bakiyev's supporters' intrusion into public administrations in Batken, Jalalabad and Osh oblasts, armed attack on the University of Peoples' Friendship etc were all linked to one chain. He said that the main goal of inflaming the ethnic riots was to reinstitute Bakiyev's regime. The report detailed how in May 2010 the mass media published phone conversation between Zhanysh and Maxim Bakiyev who discussed about hiring 500 militants to seize some public and government buildings and organise mass riots and conflicts. The findings also revealed that the State National Security Committee (GKNB) had information about Maxim Bakiyev's meeting with IMU in Dubai in April 2010 and subsequent development of Bakiyev's family members meetings with IMU, Taliban and former United Tajik Opposition (UTO) in Afghanistan. The report believed these terrorists outfits had agreed to support Bakiyevs.[70] In fact, a group of militants had infiltrated southern Kyrgyzstan through Badakhshan in June that year. The report however said that this information was not confirmed by GKNB. But, it said "subsequent events were developed in accordance to the scenario of Maxim and Zhanysh Bakiyevs that is proved by total absence of the relevant immediate work from GKNB."[71]

The report gave a vivid account of how the subsequent development took place especially the way pro-Bakiyev forces provoked the Uzbek population and the way the Interim Government was unable to prevent the inter-conflict intensifying.

On the April 2010 event in Bishkek, the report listed names of offenders responsible for the shooting of 1,500 citizens (87 of them were killed) in front of Government House in Bishkek on April 7, 2010. They included: The former Kyrgyz President, Kurmanbek Bakiyev; the former Speaker of Dzhogorku Kenesh A. Tagayev, Parliamentary official, Z. Kurmanov, the leader of the Ak-Zhol party, U. Ormonov), former Prime Minister D. Usenov, the Prosecutor-General's Office head N. Tursunkulov, Defence Minister B. Kalyyev, Interior Minister M. Kongantiyev, Chairman of the State National Security Committee, M. Sutalinov, and the Mayor of Bishkek, N. Tyuleyev. They were directly blamed for the events. The report blamed Kurmanbek Bakiyev and his closed associates for trying to seize administrative buildings in April and May 2010 to discredit the Kyrgyz interim government. It said that "When these steps did not yield the desired results, they began to raise ethnic and regional issues by deliberately stirring up ethnic intolerance."[72]

The report held Uzbek community leaders Kadyrzhan Batyrov, Inomzhan Abdurasulov, Karamat Abdullaeva, Jallalidin Salakhuddinov and other leaders of the Uzbek national cultural centre directly responsible for the June riots. They took advantage of the situation. Batyrov particularly wanted to strengthen his political and economic position and had taken support of the criminal groups.

On June 2010 events in Osh, the report said enormous financial resources were spent to run the media outlets. It cited the involvement of foreign mercenaries in carrying out the events. The Commission noted 426 people killed in the events that included deputies of local councils, police officials and military personnel. The report said "The facts of brutal killing of state officials—members of local councils: A. Shakirov, E. Murzabekov, E. Arapbayev; servicemen: Maj K. Abdyldayev, Sgt A. Surantayev; police officers, namely the chief of the Kara-Suu district police department, A. Sultanov, inspectors of Osh city traffic police department, B. Baykishiyev and B. Aydarov; and others are evidence of the involvement of dispatched foreign mercenary groups."[73] It was an act committed against representatives of state bodies at the instigation of foreign mercenary groups.[74] (This was clearly indicated at the Uzbek groups.) It said, mercenary groups had outnumbered the law enforcement and armed forces and the result was many ethnic Kyrgyz died. This prompted Kyrgyz response and in the ensuing development, organised trained forces arrived on the scene with weapons for retaliation. They were mainly motivated by the supporters of former Kyrgyz President Kurmanbek Bakiyev with financial resources. The report said "Many citizens who arrived in Osh to help their relatives of both Kyrgyz and Uzbek nationalities were involved in specific plans of supporters of Bakiyev and Uzbek community leaders. Ordinary people are not at fault."[75] The Commission also took a note of meetings and contacts of Kadyrzhan Batyrov with officials and leaders of the interim government that included Roza Otunbayeva, Almazbek Atambayev, Omurbek Tekebayev, and Emilbek Kaptagayev among others.

It added that growing confrontation between supporters of Bakiyev and the Interim Government led to the ethnic clashes between the Kyrgyz and Uzbeks. Besides, the Interim Government had failed to contain the events in Osh and Jalalabad oblasts. The situation therefore allowed Kadyrzhan Batyrov to take advantage of that. However, Mamytov's report did not provide any concrete facts and evidence of involvement of the third forces. It had admitted that the interior ministry and the National Security Sevice (NSS) did not provide any materials to prove that.

Tokon Mamytov called the KIC report as one-sided, because irrespective of which ethnic group (Uzbek or Kyrgyz), died or convicted, they are all citizens of Kyrgyzstan. The report called for the Interim Government to bear responsibility for significant human losses and destruction and suggested political and legal actions against those responsible regardless of their ethnic background. The commission also recommended President Roza Otunbayeva to dismiss heads of law enforcement, security and military agencies, including national security agency chief and defence minister.

Another version of the PC was that of its member Ismail Isakov who blamed former President Bakiyev and his regime for the tragedy. According to him the original report did not mention the responsibilities of the Constitutional Court, Supreme Court, government bodies, prosecutor general, NSS and others who acted in favour of one family. He particularly blamed the Uzbek separatists led by Kadyrzhan Batyrov and criminal groups for causing the events.

The third version of the PC report was that of its member Jyldyz Joldosheva, anationalist leader belonging to of Ata-Zhurt party. She had presented her own documentary film titled "*Koogalan*" on the tragedy. Her version was supported by member Ismail Isakov.[76]

Joldosheva in her documentary went into the deeper political conspiracy of how the Kyrgyz politicians had been playing games with Uzbek community leaders for simply gaining their support in the elections. She said "The political elite divided into the north and south, they were dividing power, some leaders were bargaining with leaders of separatists."[77] Jyldyz Joldosheva wasn't satisfied with the Parliament's decree and argued that nobody had been punished so far including those who were responsible for the events of June 1990. She took reference to Saidulla Akbarov who had made a separatist call in 1990, and in 2010 his children had called for separatism. Instead, both former Presidents Akayev and Bakiyev conferred Saidulla Akbarov with awards. For instance, she said, a street and a school in Jalalabad were named after Saidulla Akbarov, Akayev awarded Kadyrzhan Batyrov with Dank order, Bakiyev patronised and spoke to them in Uzbek.[78] She said Kurmanbek Bakiyev danced on Uzbek music on Independence Day with Kadyrzhan Batyrov and his group.

She had largely blamed Bakiyev not only for ruining the economy but also the state. In her documentary *Koogalan* Jyldyz Joldosheva gave description of corrupt practices during Askar Akayev and Kurmanbek Bakiyev regimes. It also showed how, after April 2010 revolution the brother of the interim President Bolot Otunbayeva and brother of Omurbek Tekebaev occupied key political offices.

The film showed the developments during June tragedy with some details of Uzbek preparedness. It included the demands made by Uzbek leader Kadyrzhan Batyrov for conferring autonomy for Uzbeks, recognition of Uzbek as official language, representation of Uzbeks in the government and army. According to her setting of Bakiyev's family house and the Kyrgyz flag on fire by Kadyrzhan Batyrov and Asylbek Tekebayev was the biggest mistake. The MP believed that it was the provisional government members and several politicians and not Uzbeks and Kyrgyz, who are to be blamed for the events. The film showed how the Governor of Jalalabad oblast Bektur Asanov welcomed Batyrov's statements.[79] For Joldosheva the main reason was the lack of consensus in the Interim Government after it took over from Bakiyev.

Joldosheva's accusation of Kadyrzhan Batyrov's connivance with Otunbayeva, Atambayev and Tekebayev had steered massive controversy. Ata Meken's leader Omurbek Tekebayev strongly refuted the charge as simply lies. Tekebayev argued that the facts were checked by several commissions, including the National Commission of Inquiry (NCI, led by Abdygany Erkebayev and Parliamentary Commission (PC led by Tokon Mamytov). Tekebayev said the investigations confirmed that the voices in the recorded conversation were not of Atambayev, Tekebayev and Batyrov. Similarly, the Prime Minister Atambayev refuted the charge and asked everyone to stop spreading rumours about his secret meeting with Kadyrzhan Batyrov.[80]

Joldosheva also suggested that the long cherished idea of creating a caliphate in Fergana valley was one of the causes of June tragedy.[81] She said this idea was hovering in the air for a long time. "Uzbeks leaders, extremist forces sponsored by the West are interested in that...everybody understands well that Kyrgyzstan will not exist as a sovereign state, if the country's south is lost."[82]

Jyldyz Joldosheva's film *Koogalan* showed no evidence of genocide, but she believed that it would be very difficult if the case was considered at an international court. She informed that the Uzbek leaders have appealed to The Hague Tribunal and if that is entertained by the Tribunal "only my report and a documentary *Koogalan* will save the country's authorities, especially members of the interim government.[83] According to Jyldyz Joldosheva, the original report of Tokon Mamytov did contain some strong conclusions, but they were removed later, suggesting that the interim government was shielding the guilty. Another powerful nationalist leader Azimbek Beknazarov too believed that "Kyrgyzstan is though not a member of an international court, and therefore does not fall under its jurisdiction. But as I understand, the head of the International Commission Kiljunen will submit a report to the OSCE; they in turn will pass it to the EU."[84]

While the hearing on the PC report was still going on, news erupted over how Kadyrzhan Batyrov transferred $100,000 to human rights defender Azimzhan Askarov's account for organising the ethnic disorders. Meanwhile, in the Parliamentary Session the Governor of Jalalabad region admitted that everybody including himself who supported Kurmanbek Bakiyev during elections was responsible for the tragedy.[85] The former Kyrgyz Interior Minister Bolot Sher too apologised to the country for his inability to prevent the deadly clashes. Sher had announced in the Parliament on June 2, 2011 about his intension to resign from the military rank of Lieutenant General and also quit from his party Ata-Meken.[86] Roza Otunbayeva took a nuanced position and said no one ethnos could be blamed for the crisis. Her view was people of different nationalities have been experiencing difficulties together with ethnic Kyrgyz people.[87]

Meanwhile, according to media report Jalalabad provincial prosecutor's office on April 29, 2011 had initiated criminal investigation against Uzbek community leaders in southern Kyrgyzstan; namely Kadyrzhan Batyrov, Inom Abdurasulov,

Abdrakhman Abdullayev, Makhamatrasul Abakzhanov, Khalilzhan Khudayberdiyev and Khavlon Mirzakhodzhaev. They were being charged under several criminal codes, i.e. organising mass unrest, indulging in separatist activities, threatening unity and territorial integrity of the country, inciting ethnic, racial, religious or interregional hatred and complicity to murder.

Earlier, one of the commissions headed by former Ombudsman Tursunbek Akun too had charged the same ethnic Uzbek leaders for financing and inciting the riots. Akun's report charged them for seeking to transform Osh and Jalalabad regions into autonomous regions of Uzbekistan. He charged them for having links with Uzbeks inside Uzbekistan who were opposed to Karimov.[88] Batyrov had been charged on different criminal cases in various parts of the country, something which he had denied. Batyrov had since fled Kyrgyzstan perhaps living in Ukraine. The other Uzbek leaders who were charged with separatism are also living outside Kyrgyzstan.

The three reports presented by the PC members were common in their assessments of the role played by Bakiyev's family and representatives of Uzbek diaspora, but the fact that the PC gave three reports indicated lack of consensus and differences of opinion as to what led to the tragedy to occur. Essentially the sanctity of the Commission's report was lost. However, unlike the KIC report the PC revealed more facts about sources of funding and preparation towards the conflict by the Uzbeks i.e. controlling the entry roads in Osh in the night of June 10 and 11, 2010. The PC also revealed the role of unidentified forces that incited the riots, though it did not give specific evidence of those forces. The KIC on the other hand ruled the role of third force in the conflict.

The two reports of PC mentioned the role of Colonel Mahmoud Hudoiberdiev, allegedly an Uzbek special services agent who was attempting to intrude into Kyrgyzstan on the night of June 13. This information was ascertained by the State National Security Committee (NSC) and was also confirmed by some Russian media. Kyrgyz leaders blamed Kiljunen for having deliberately concealed this fact. However, many observers doubted how by doing so Tashkent would have risked the Uzbeks living in Osh.

First Anniversary

On June 10, 2011, amid widespread rumours and threats of fresh outbreak of violence, Kyrgyzstan observed the first anniversary of the June 2010 inter-ethnic clashes in Osh. Prime Minister had signed the decree to proclaim June 10, as the Memorial Day for victims.[89] All state flags on government buildings, diplomatic missions of Kyrgyzstan abroad were flown at half staff on that day. The local state administrations and executive agencies organised the event. The Muslims boards and leaders of other religious confessions were asked to disseminate ideals of peace and accord among believers for the benefit of unity of the people and integrity of the country. The local media were encouraged to facilitate reconciliation through impartial coverage of the national tragedy.

A week before the anniversary the Ministry of Internal Affairs warned about various rumours of a possible repetition of the ethnic conflict. A film and a book entitled "*An hour of a jackal*" based on June 2010 events had already heightened the anxiety among the officials. The fear was that the separatist and extremist forces were waiting for an excuse to ignite the trouble again. The authorities also feared that many young people, who went abroad for training, had returned to the south to take revenge. The wide spread rumours about the Uzbek youth receiving training in Pakistan and Afghanistan were frequently heard in Bishkek. The fear also prevailed that Bakiyev's supporters might use extremist elements to foment trouble. In fact, the Kyrgyz Prime Minister warned about possible revenge by Kurmbanek Bakiyev's supporters. Almazbek Atambayev even accused some Kyrgyz parliamentarians of having links with Bakiyev and criminal gangs led by Bakiyev's son Maksim. He said "When I look at some politicians in the parliament, I can see leaders of criminal gangs Kamchy Kolbaev and Aziz Batukaev behind them," he said. "I can also see Kurmanbek and Maksim Bakiyev's ears protruding from behind (some lawmakers.) Dear compatriots, please, stay together! If the Kyrgyz will be divided, then we all will be eaten by 'wolves.'"[90]

The government had taken sufficient precautionary measures. The law enforcement agencies—the Defence Ministry, Ministry of Internal Affairs, NSC, Emergency Service, the Financial Police, Border troops and local administration had carried out exercises prior to the anniversary along the sensitive check posts at Furkat, Nariman, Airport and its adjoining areas.

On June 10, around 500 representatives of local communities were corralled in Osh city square to commemorate the victims of the riots. Important national and provincial leaders and the media were invited to attend the function. The entire diplomatic corps and members of international agencies were flown to Osh for the ceremony. President Roza Otunbayeva unveiled a monument named "*Mothers' Tears*" depicting two women representing Kyrgyz and Uzbek weeping and embracing. Roza Otunbayeva called for peaceful co-existence and urged people to refrain from mutual accusations and rumours over who instigated the violence. In her speech Otunbayeva said that ordinary people who helped one another to escape violence were not to blame for what happened. "My heart bleeds when I recall the June tragedy... standing at the foothill of the Holy Sulayman Mountain, I would like to stress again the need to join forces to preserve and to promote our statehood, peace and harmony on our land. We are all a single people and must respect, support one another, build together a new and true democratic society."[91]

The mood at the function was sour as minutes after the official ceremony dozens of ethnic Kyrgyz crowded the main square in Osh city to express bitterness over the events—some of them suggesting that the monument should not have included an Uzbek figure. No Uzbeks were visible at the site.

The city appeared peaceful but undercurrent of tension and fear were visible. One could feel the nervousness and the level of trust between Kyrgyz and Uzbeks remains elusive. The rights groups had warned earlier that the government has not tackled the divisions and the failure to deliver justice could spark more violence. The UNHCR cited individuals complaining of distrust and a high degree of suspicion between communities. Many said affected groups are not yet fully ready for reconciliation.[92] The author, during several trips to Osh, had found people carrying knives and weapons when they went out. Along the streets, burnt down houses and completely charred tea houses were visible. Authorities had sent reinforcement ahead of the anniversary to tighten the security. Police units were patrolling the streets, wearing bulletproof vests and wielding Kalashnikov submachine guns. Schools and Universities remained closed. The officials as well as the observers feared that extremists especially the IMU elements might seek to destabilise the country during the anniversary.

In Bishkek, the government commemorated the June anniversary separately attended by Prime Minister Almazbek Atambayev, First vice Prime Minister Omurbek Babanov, Chief of President's Administration Emilbek Kaptagaev, Vice Prime Minister Shamil Atahanov, Bishkek Mayor Isa Omurkulov and Ombudsman Tursunbek Akun attended the ceremony. Atambayev called "Kyrgyz citizens, especially the politicians and public figures, to realise that we are one multi-ethnic nation...we will be able to build a prosperous state only having united efforts of all citizens of Kyrgyzstan."[93] Atambayev expressed gratitude to the international organisations for assisting Kyrgyzstan in the reconstruction efforts. Importantly, one year after the tragedy the Kyrgyz leadership did acknowledge the balanced and wise position played by President of Uzbekistan Islam Karimov. This was also repeatedly acknowledged by the Roza Otunbayeva during my meetings with the former President.

Conclusion

Three years have passed since the tragedy and several commissions of inquiry have gone into finding out the truth. However, the present government has been so far denying any complicity in the violence and repeatedly blamed Bakiyev's loyalists and Islamic extremists for fomenting the riots. The main culprits have not been brought to justice so far, and to some extent this has already undermined the rule of law posing further risk to the stability of the country.

Since June 2010, Kyrgyzstan has witnessed several political developments, including elections for a newly adopted parliamentary system of government and elections for the first democratically elected President. However, the ethnic issue and the June 2010 tragedy continue to haunt both the Kyrgyz leadership and the population; causing lingering prejudice and endless politicking.[94] Among the Kyrgyz the sense of recrimination remained high, for they accused Uzbeks of initiating the violence. Most Kyrgyz take bellicose rhetoric how Uzbek minority attempted to secede from Kyrgyzstan and thus triggering the unrest. Kyrgyz fear primarily stemmed from Uzbek Diaspora nurturing irredentism. The Uzbeks on the other hand continue to assertKyrgyz nationalism as a driving force. The Uzbeks claim that they are not only excluded from political and economic life but also face ill-treatment by Kyrgyz law enforcement agencies—an allegation supported by KIC report.[95]

It appears; judging from all the reports that the interim government could not handle the political situation efficiently after Bakiyev was ousted. Clearly, the old ethnic tensions between Kyrgyz and Uzbeks were the easiest thing to be exploited. The organised crime and drug money that had seeped into Central Asia after the Soviet collapse had played an important role in southern Kyrgyzstan. The city of Osh is now a major hub for Afghan heroin on its way to Europe. The number of drug users is said to be growing every year. For several years now, the criminal gangs who thrived on the heroin trade enjoyed protection from government officials. The country was still awashed with small firearms. Hundreds of weapons had disappeared from the cities mostly seized by protestors during the Tulip Revolution in April 2010.As established by inquiry report security forces had lost control over more firearms in the south. Besides, proliferation of small arms across the border from Afghanistan and Tajikistan along the drug route was a major problem for Kyrgyzstan, which has no effective mechanism to control the flow of drugs and small arms; a reason why Uzbekistan and Kazakhstan close their borders with Kyrgyzstan every time there is a trouble there. The proliferation of arms represents a grave risk to national security. The security experts fear weapons would keep featuring in domestic political struggles.

The future of Osh does remain a subject of much discussion among aid agencies and others. The inquiry reports, though useful in drawing the international attention to the issue, had put this fragile country in a sticky situation with potentially far-reaching political ramifications. The Kyrgyz authorities view serious shortcomings and gaps in the report. If the recommendations of the reports are to be implemented, the tenuous authority of the present government would be at serious risk. It could also further fuel discontent and inflame nationalism in Kyrgyzstan. Kyrgyzstan is not a member of the Rome Statute of the International Criminal Court, and as such the government knows that it is not obliged to accept the KIC report in letter and spirit. Kyrgyzstan had adopted a fragile parliamentary system of government since the end of 2010 but the ethnic issues are unlikely to be solved by the parliamentary form of democracy, which itself appear somewhat shaky.

Beyond the ethnic tension, Kyrgyzstan still faces some other serious issues, including tense relations with its neighbour Uzbekistan and a possible spill over of violence from Tajikistan. Uzbekistan too saw the possibility of tension escalating during 2011. It had closed its border with Kyrgyzstan in 2010 and was still erecting additional barriers on the Uzbek side.[96] It is also possible that trouble next time could come from the Uzbek side of the Fergana Valley and in turn impact southern Kyrgyzstan.

The above mentioned issues, especially the domestic discords, will continue to make Kyrgyzstan geopolitically a significant country in Central Asia. The country draws the attention of Russia, US, China and other neighbouring states. There also remains a tendency among the Kyrgyz ruling elite to factor Kyrgyzstan into the big power politics. Despite occasional rhetoric, the political elite wish to maintain the country as a military hub for the US. The new Kyrgyz regime even tried to bargain on the Russian military base in Kant. The Chinese are pouring in money in several sectors to woe the Kyrgyz. All these factors, along with Kyrgyzstan's mountainous geography and complex ethnic composition make the country subject to much instability. Significantly, the Russian-led CSTO's Secretary-General had announced in 2011 that its forces were ready to intervene in Kyrgyzstan if needed.[97] This was a change in its position when the CSTO refused to intervene in 2010 that drew strong Kyrgyz criticism for not helping the country in its difficult times.

In March 2012, the International Crisis Group (ICG) published a report which stated that ethnic tensions between Uzbeks and Kyrgyz continue to grow.[98] The possibility that such clashes will be repeated was widely spoken about in the informed circles and among the members diplomatic community who often visit Osh for spot assessments. A common view is that the Uzbeks are waiting for an opportunity to avenge at some point and they cannot be prevented even by the most strong-mindedethnic nationalist like Melis Myrzakmatov who is the Mayor of Osh city.

On the other hand, according to the Crisis Group report, the anger among Kyrgyz is not a fringe phenomenon but is quite widespread even among educated middle-class Kyrgyz who cherish no conciliatory attitude.[99] The ethnic Kyrgyz dismissed the KIC findings which suggested that weapons were distributed to crowds by military personnel to attack the Uzbek communities.

Undoubtedly, the Kyrgyz nationalist assertion has grown since the Osh ethnic crisis. New leaders in the south have emerged with strong Kyrgyz nationalistic agenda. Melis Myrzakmatov, a Bakiyev appointee and current Mayor of Osh holds strong grounds in the city. The KIC report had censured Melisbek Myrzakmatov, but he published a provocative book of his own that blamed the Uzbek separatists and their sponsor.[100] Despite repeated attempts by the interim President Roza Otunbayeva through official decrees Melis could not be dislodged from the post.[101] This situation remained unchanged even after Almazbek Atambayev took over the Prime Minister's and later President's post. In many sense the authority in Bishkek has no control over the southern provinces.

The numerous and muddled internal inquiry reports and statements made by state figures on the Osh ethnic crisis have seriously questioned the credibility of the Kyrgyz Government in the eyes of its own population and for those outside. From all accounts it is very clear that the ethnic crises are being deliberately engineered by states and politicians for power struggle and influence. The Kyrgyz case is typical of that nature. Of course, the fault is not that of Kyrgyzstan's alone. Uzbekistan has its own share to contribute the mess. The Uzbek leadership, led by Islam Karimov has been playing the ethnic card for own interest. In the past, Tashkent had been indifferent to the issues pertaining to ethnic Uzbeks living in Kyrgyzstan for the fear of ethno-nationalism posing threat to Karimov's authority. But, when it suited them, the Uzbek political leaders exploited the ethnic factor to advance their political and commercial interests.

If the ethnic issue is not addressed for a prolonged period either through the government measures or by judicial intervention, the rift between the Uzbeks and Kyrgyz is likely to get widened, which would become very explosive in future; putting the country at the risk of collapse. So far, there is also little sign of measures being taken to integrate ethnic Uzbeks in the Kyrgyz national affairs. But, the way Kyrgyz nationalism is allowed to grow, partly even patronised by the state, inter-ethnic discord and language issues will always pose a serious challenge to Kyrgyz experiment and its urge for building a state on the prism of liberal democracy. It does appear that building a value based democratic structure in a society rooted in deep tribalism will always remain a challenge. Despite two upsrisings since 2005, the nature of ruling class in Kyrgyzstan remains largely unchanged. Many regional experts are convinced that Kyrgyzstan is clearly on the path of chaos. But a sense of optimism also prevails when people talk about Kyrgyzstan already having made progress on the political front as compared to other Central Asian states which are yet to confront with the political reality once the authoritarian control fades away.

NOTES

1. A National Commission of Inquiry in January 2011 gave 426 people died in the violence, including 276 Uzbeks and 105 ethnic Kyrgyz. The same figure was quoted by other inquiry commissions.
2. "Kyrgyzstan: Widening Ethnic Divisions in the South", *ICG Report No. 222*, 2March 29, 2012. http://www.crisisgroup.org/en/regions/asia/central-asia/kyrgyzstan/222-kyrgyzstan-widening-ethnic-divisions-in-the-south.aspx.
3. *Interfax*, June 14, 2010.
4. Galeev, Artur; Pavel Gronskiy, "Tragedy in Kyrgyzstan: Number of Deaths Reaching Thousands (In Russian)", *Komsomolskaya Pravda*, June 12, 2010, Retrieved October 15, 2012.
5. "Kremlin will not intervene with military in Kyrgyzstan", RT, June 12, 2010 http://rt.com/top_news/kremlin-humanitarian-help-kyrgyzstan.html.
6. The credit was later given by the Kyrgyz leaders to the Uzbek President Islam Karimov for taking a wise decision to close the border.
7. "EU: We highly value efforts of Uzbekistan on prevention of escalation of situation in Kyrgyzstan and region", *AKIpress*, November 12, 2010.
8. Sean R. Roberts, "What's ethnicity got to do with it? Healing the wounds of Uzbek- Kyrgyz

violence in the Fergana Valley", *PONARS Policy Memo No. 106*, The George Washington University, http://www.gwu.edu/~ieresgwu/assets/docs/pepm_106.pdf.

9. Towards the end of the Soviet period an Uzbek-rights group *Adalat* demanded autonomy for Uzbeks living in Osh. The main point of dispute was over land. To protect their interests, the Kyrgyz then formed an association, called *Osh-aimagy* (Osh-land). Two ethnic groups clashed for several days killing 320 Kyrgyz and Uzbeks in Osh. Read, A Timeline of Events: 1800-1990 http://www.onwar.com/aced/chrono/c1900s/yr90/fkyrgyzstan1990.htmimeline of Events 1800-1999 A *Timeline of Events* 1800-1999.
10. "Kyrgyzstan to seek extradition of ex-president's son over riots", *RIA Novosti*, June 15, 2010.
11. "Deupty Head of Kyrgyz Security Forces Denies his Words about Tajik Gunmen", *News.rambler ru.* Retrieved April 8, 2012.
12. Bakyt Beshimov in his interview to Turkish Weekly of *USAK Publication*, http://beshimovbakyt.blogspot.in/2011/01/jtw-interview-bakyt-beshimov-kyrgyzstan.html.
13. "President Karimov: Conflict in southern Kyrgyzstan was initiated by third party", *AKIpress*, October 20, 2010.
14. Cited by Bakyt Beshimov in his interview to Turkish Weekly of *USAK Publication*, http://beshimovbakyt.blogspot.in/2011/01/jtw-interview-bakyt-beshimov-kyrgyzstan.html.
15. *RFE/RL.* May 14, 2010.
16. "Kyrgyzstan: Eyes Turn to Moscow as Instability Grows", *Stratfor*, June 13, 2010.
17. *Eurasia Review*, 20 May 2010http://www.eurasiareview.com/20052010-bishkek-fears-russia-wants-a-protectorate-over-kyrgyzstan/. Retrieved June 9, 2012.
18. Cited by Bakyt Beshimov in his interview to Turkish Weekly of*USAK Publication*, http://beshimovbakyt.blogspot.in/2011/01/jtw-interview-bakyt-beshimov-kyrgyzstan.html.
19. Bakyt Beshimov: "Kyrgyzstan-How Political Success Justified Violence? and Who Incited the Kyrgyz-Uzbek Conflict?" http://beshimovbakyt.blogspot.in/2011/01/jtw-interview-bakyt-beshimov-kyrgyzstan.html.
20. "President Karimov: Conflict in southern Kyrgyzstan was initiated by third party", *AKIpress*, October 20, 2010.
21. "Uzbekistan calls for international investigation into June violence in southern Kyrgyzstan", *AKIpress*, October 22, 2010.
22. Cited by Bakyt Beshimov in his interview to Turkish Weekly of *USAK Publication*, http://beshimovbakyt.blogspot.in/2011/01/jtw-interview-bakyt-beshimov-kyrgyzstan.html.
23. *AKIpress*, June 2, 2011.
24. *AKIpress*, June 2, 2011.
25. "Atambaev: Many states expected military conflict between Kyrgyzstan and Uzbekistan", *AKIpress*, December 17, 2010.
26. Report of the Independent International Commission of Inquiry into the Events in Southern Kyrgyzstan in June 2010, *The Kyrgyzstan Inquiry Commission* (KIC), May 3, 2011, See the original text in annexure 1.
27. KIC report, original text annexure 1.
28. Comments by the Government of Kyrgyzstan in response to the report of the Kyrgyzstan Inquiry Commission into the events in southern Kyrgyzstan in June 2010. See annexure 2 http://www.fergananews.com/archive/2011/kg_comments_english_final.pdf Also visit the website of the MFA of Kyrgyz Republic, www.mfa.kg.
29. Ibid.
30. Ibid.
31. *AKIpress*, May 26, 2011.
32. *AKIpress*, May 26, 2011.
33. Except one 96 deputies present in Parliament voted in favour of the resolution. The resolution said "In line with the resolution, the Finnish national, Kimmo Kiljunen, does not have the

right to enter Kyrgyzstan and stay on its territory owing to the biased report of the commission he led. The government has been tasked to implement the resolution. In line with this, diplomatic offices in other countries should be informed of the decision to declare Kimmo Kiljunen persona non grata. The government should distribute true information in the international community about the causes of the June events," Parliament Speaker Akhmatbek Keldibekov said. Text of report was published news agency Kyrgyz Telegraph Agency *(KyrTAg), May 26, 2011.*

34. *The Associated Press,* May 26, 2011.
35. Ibid.
36. Ibid.
37. "International ethnic probe head upset by Kyrgyz decision", *Kyrgyz Telegraph Agency (KyrTAg)* May 26, 2011.
38. See the full KIC report annexure 1.
39. Minister of State, Foreign and Commonwealth Office; Conservative, Lord Howell of Guildford made the comment in the Parliament on May 18, 2011.
40. *24.kg* May 31, 2011.
41. The international media commented that after Sri Lanka, Kyrgyzstan is another country that rejected international independent commission of inquiry in the ethnic violence took place in June 2010.
42. U.S. Envoy 'Surprised' At Kyrgyz Reaction To Head Of Violence Probe, *RFE/RL* May 31, 2011.
43. "Russia - Deputy Minister of Foreign Affairs/State Secretary Grigory Karasin Speaks to EU Special Representative for Central Asia Pierre Morel by Telephone." Press release by the Ministry of Foreign Affairs of the Russian Federation, Visit the official site http://www.mid.ru/brp_4.nsf/0/A6767E3C66A8C693C32578A0005C58A7
44. "UN worried by Kyrgyz nationalist rhetoric" *CentralAsiaOnline.com,* June 4, 2011.
45. URL: http://eng.24.kg/politic/2011/05/25/18316.html.
46. *24.kg news agency,* 3 June 2011, Also visit URL: http://eng.24.kg/politic/2011/06/03/18493.html.
47. Excerpt from report by privately-owned online news agency Kyrgyz Telegraph Agency (*KyrTAg*) June 2, 2011.
48. *AKIpress,* June 14, 2011.
49. *Interfax news agency,* Moscow, in Russian, June 2, 2011.
50. Ibid.
51. *AKIpress* June 16, 2011.
52. *24.kg website,* Bishkek, June 2, 2011.
53. *AKIpress* June 2, 2011.
54. *AKIpress* June 2, 2011.
55. *KyrTAg,* Bishkek, June 1, 2011 .
56. *AKIpress* news agency website, Bishkek, June 1, 2011.
57. NATO secretary-general's special representative for the Caucasus and Central Asia, James Appaturai, visited Bishkek in early May 2011 and met Kyrgyz President Roza Otunbayeva to discuss boosting Kyrgyzstan's border security and border troops' technical potential by opening NATO's training centre in the country's south. They also agreed to open NATO's special office in Bishkek. *KyrTAg, Bishkek,* May 31, 2011.
58. URL: http://eng.24.kg/politic/2011/05/31/18411.html.
59. *AKIpress,* May 31, 2011.
60. Ibid.
61. Ibid.
62. "President Otunbayeva explains why NATO Office will be opened in Kyrgyzstan", *AKIpress,*

June 2, 2011.

63. *AKIpress*, May 27, 2011.
64. Ibid.
65. *AKIpress*, May 24, 2011.
66. URL: http://eng.24.kg/politic/2011/06/03/18507.html.
67. *KyrTAg, Bishkek,* June 2, 2011.
68. "Six reports on investigation of June events in southern Kyrgyzstan", *AKIpress*, May 26, 2011
69. *KyrTAg, Bishkek,* in Russian June 2, 2011.
70. Daniyar Karimov, Darya Podolskaya, "Chronicles of June tragedy: Version of deputies", Part I, *24.kg news agency*, May 19, 2011.
71. Ibid.
72. *KyrTAg,* June 6, 2011.
73. As reported in *AKIpress* June 1, 2011.
74. Ibid.
75. *KyrTAg,* June 1, 2011.
76. URL: http://eng.24.kg/politic/2011/06/02/18469.html.
77. *AKIpress,* June 2, 2011.
78. *AKIpress*, June 26, 2011.
79. URL: http://eng.24.kg/politic/2011/05/25/18313.html.
80. *AKIpress*, June 2, 2011.
81. Aizada Kutueva, "Zhyldyzkan Dzholdosheva: Idea to create the caliphate in Fergana valley is cause of June tragedy", *24.kg news agency,* June 13, 2011.
82. URL: http://eng.24.kg/politic/2011/06/13/18672.htm.
83. "Kyrgyz MP says ethnic Uzbek leaders wanted to build a caliphate in south", *Interfax news agency*, Moscow, June 13, 2011.
84. *AKIpress* June 13, 2011.
85. *KyrTAg, Bishkek,* June 2, 2011.
86. *RFE/RL's Kyrgyz Service reports* June 2, 2011.
87. URL: http://eng.24.kg/politic/2011/06/02/18475.html
88. *Fergana News Agency,* April 24, 2011.
89. *AKIpress* June 2, 2011.
90. Farangis Najibullah, "Supporters of Ousted President 'Seek Revenge,' Kyrgyz Prime Minister Warns", *RFE/RL*, April 7, 2011
91. The speech released by President's press service and as reported by *AKIpress*, June 1, 2011. The event was attended by this author.
92. Author's interaction with cross section of people in Osh in 2011.
93. *AKIpress* June 10, 2011.
94. Similar observations had been made by independent media reporters in 2011. Read Ted Trautman, "Kyrgyzstan's Ethnic Wounds Still Close to the Surface", *World Politics Review,* June 13, 2011.
95. The KIC report noted extensive torture and unfair trials of mostly Uzbeks. The Amnesty International had accounted Uzbeks having suffered 75 per cent of the casualties and 90 per cent of property losses. According to the official figures, 230 of the 271 people taken into custody were ethnic Uzbek.
96. The author witnessed it during a trip to Kyrgyz-Uzbek border in August 2011.
97. "CSTO: We'll Intervene in Kyrgyzstan If Necessary" http://www.eurasianet.org/node/63660 June 10, 2011. Also visit Russian site http://regnum.ru/news/1413956.html.
98. "Kyrgyzstan: Widening Ethnic Divisions in the South", *ICG Report No. 222,* March 29, 2012, http://www.crisisgroup.org/en/regions/asia/central-asia/kyrgyzstan/222-kyrgyzstan-

widening-ethnic-divisions-in-the-south.aspx.

99. Ibid.

100. Myrzakmatov's book entitled *(In Search of the Truth. The Osh Tragedy: Documents, Facts, Appeals, and Declarations)* described the Uzbeks as a separatist group. The book gives details about he and other patriotic Kyrgyz thwarted the Uzbek plot. Also visit http://www.operationspaix.net/DATA/DOCUMENT/6976~v~Kyrgyzstan__Widening_Ethnic_Divisions_in_the_South. pdf.

101. "Mayor of Osh Rejects Otunbayeva's Government", http://kyrgyzstan.carnegieendowment.org/2010/08/mayor-of-osh-rejects-otunbayevas-government/ Also visit http://www.kommersant.ru/doc/1489447.

CHAPTER 3

Parliamentary Democracy

The April 2010 uprising took place against increasing demand to overthrow the Kurmanbek Bakiyev's authoritarian regime. The interim government led by Roza Otunbayeva justified the revolt to undo excessive state control over public life under one man and to make the country's political process more democratic and transparent. By changing the constitution, Roza Otunbayeva and her co-revolutionaries pledged to build a system that would make it difficult for future leaders to concentrate too much power in their own hands. Introduction of a parliamentary democracy was the first step. The need for the parliamentary system had been much debated in the country. It was argued by most leaders that a representative form of government will be better suited for an ethnically diverse country like Kyrgyzstan.

The interim government managed to hold the parliamentary election on October 10, 2010 despite lot of political skepticism, especially when the internal political situation remained volatile following June's inter-ethnic (Kyrgyz versus Uzbeks) clashes in which more than 400 people were killed and thousands left homeless. The interim government had to struggle hard to control southern parts of the country.

Kyrgyz Parliament (*Zhogorku Kenesh*)

Under the new Kyrgyz constitution, the seats in the Parliament *(Zhogorku Kenesh)* were increased to 120 and they were to be filled through popular voting by party lists and not individual candidates. The ballots had names of the top five candidates from each party. The new rule envisaged that the seats are to be distributed proportionately to parties winning at least five per cent of the vote at national level and 0.5 per cent of the votes at regional level and two key cities. This was intended to prevent a party from winning representation if it lacks broad nationwide support. However, no single party was to be allotted more than 65 seats regardless of its election result.

In 2010, Kyrgyzstan had 2.8 million registered voters out of country's total population of 5.3 million. Under the new constitution, the Parliament will have a term of five years. The majority party will nominate a candidate for the Speaker and the Prime Minister. The President, who elected separately, could propose the Parliament twice to form the government. In case the Parliament fails to form a government twice, the President may dissolve the Parliament and seek new elections. The Prime Minister will be stronger than the President and have the right to appoint and dismiss Cabinet Ministers and Governors. However, the opposition will head parliamentary committees on the budget and law and order. The new constitution also stipulated that the President will have truncated powers and will play the role only as an arbiter between the constituent and executive powers. However, the President will have the right to appoint the Defence Minister and National Security Chief. The interim President Roza Otunbayeva was to be country's acting President until December 31, 2011. Future Presidential term will be limited to a single six-year term.

Parliamentary Election

The 2010 Parliamentary Election was held peacefully on October 10, 2010 even though there were reports of serious violations of the Code on Elections, including the facts of bribery of voters and rigging of votes at some polling stations.[1] No major incident of violence was reported. There were 29 major parties that had filled over 3,300 candidates for 120 parliamentary seats.[2] According to Central Election Commission (CEC), 1,614,427out of the total 2,852,751 registered voters or about 56.59 per cent turnout for voting by the end of voting. Osh city, where low voting was expected, had recorded 66.28 per cent turnout.[3] The US Embassy in Bishkek was prompt in issuing a statement congratulating the Kyrgyz Republic for carrying out parliamentary elections. The statement underlined that "the voters of the Kyrgyz Republic demonstrated their courage, choosing to take ownership of their future and shape their government by exercising their democratic right to vote."[4]

The period in the run up to the election was peaceful. No major incident of violence was reported. Considering that such an election was held for the first time, the campaigning by the 29 registered parties was conducted freely, transparently and democratically. The election process appeared competitive and highly visible. The parties held rallies and used posters, flags and advertisements through electronic and print media to attract voters. Parties' lists met gender requirements and the ethnic minorities were represented proportionately in their lists. According to observers, Central Asia has never seen such a competitive election race.[5] It was described as unprecedented for a nation that had until now remained under authoritarian regimes.

The CEC of Kyrgyzstan had registered over 848 foreign observers from 31 international organisations including CIS, SCO and OSCE. The OSCE and its Office for Democratic Institutions and Human Rights (OSCE/ODIHR), the OSCE Parliamentary Assembly (OSCE PA), and the European Parliament (EP) had taken active part in monitoring the Kyrgyz election. It had stationed 22 long-term observers and 300 short-term observers. The OSCE also wanted to deploy a Police Advisory Group (PAG)—a 52-member team to southern Kyrgyzstan after the election to help safeguard the fragile peace in the area, but several analysts suggested that this move was not received positively by the local Kyrgyz majority, perhaps on the behest of Russia and China.[6]

The OSCE/ODIHR that monitored the election campaign across the country characterised it as active and equal competition. This was the first sign of Kyrgyz experiment getting strong international legitimacy.[7] Similarly, the head of the EU delegation, Katarína Neved'alová observed that "The people of Kyrgyzstan have expressed their determination to turn a page in their history and to proceed towards a stable and effective democracy. The international community will take full account of this and expects the political parties to respect the results and form a stable government which can deliver a better future for Kyrgyzstan."[8]

The chorus of congratulatory messages followed the OSCE statement. Among others, the US President Barack Obama stated that the vote showed "positive attributes of a genuine democracy and the vote renews our conviction to help the courageous people of Kyrgyzstan consolidate their democracy, jump-start their economy, and maintain peace and security."[9] Similarly, the US Senate Foreign Relations Committee Chairman John Kerry (D-MA) in his statement called the Kyrgyz election as historic poll that could create Central Asia's first parliamentary democracy. The OSCE Chairperson-in-Office, Secretary of State and Foreign Minister of Kazakhstan, Kanat Saudabaev praised the peaceful conduct of the parliamentary elections attributing it to the wisdom and the courage the people of Kyrgyzstan. The Japanese Ministry of Foreign Affairs endorsed the OSCE's positive evaluation and added that the election has brought the country closer to meeting its international commitments on democratic elections. German Federal Foreign Minister Guido Westerwelle in his statement said that the elections were held peacefully and calmly is positive and deserves recognition. Importantly, Russia too welcomed the result of the Kyrgyz election. Sergey Lavrov hoped that the country's course of development based on international norms will continue. Another Russian statement made by the Foreign Ministry's representative Andrey Nesterenko said "Kyrgyzstan has another important stage in its political life ahead—formation of the coalition government based on the election results....Russia would like to hope that the new parliament and government of friendly Kyrgyzstan will work cohesively and effectively in handling tasks of stabilisation of situation, revitalisation of socio-economic infrastructure."[10] China was somewhat lukewarm in its response and had only hoped for stability after the elections. The Chinese Foreign Ministry spokesman Ma Zhaoxu stated that "China is a friend of Kyrgyzstan that pays attention to the situation in its neighbour. He added that the election proceeded smoothly."[11] India, Turkey, Uzbekistan, France, Kazakhstan and others had also congratulated the interim Kyrgyz government for conducting peaceful parliamentary elections.

It was a foregone conclusion that no single party will gain a majority 65 seats in the parliament and consequently it would be a coalition government. The main political parties that were expected to win the required republican five percentage and regional 0.5 percentages included the followings:

Ata Meken (Fatherland)
Leader: Omurbek Tekebayev, a leading figure in the interim government and author of the recent constitutional reforms. The party called itself a socialist "party of creators".

Social-Democratic Party of Kyrgyzstan (SDPK)
Leader: Almazbek Atambayev, a leading opposition leader and former prime minister in 2007 under Kurmanbek Bakiyev. He frequently visited Moscow. He met Russian Prime Minister Vladimir Putin in early September 2010. The party promised to bring economic reforms.

Ak Shumkar (White Falcon)
Leader: Temir Sariyev, a former opposition leader and entrepreneur who worked in the interim government. The party aimed to concentrate on economic revival.

Ar Namys (Dignity)
Leader: Felix Kulov, a former interior minister and one-time Bakiyev ally who served as prime minister after Bakiyev came to power in 2005. The party advocated a strong Presidency and sought to reverse the constitutional changes and remained fiercely critical of the interim government.

Ata Jurt (Motherland)
Leader: Kamchibek Tashiyev, a former emergencies minister having strong support base in the south especially from the ethnic Kyrgyz group. He is a pro-Bakiyev and opposed to the interim government.

Respublika (Republic)
Leader: Omurbek Babanov, a former parliamentary deputy and businessman. The party advocates the interests of business groups.

Against the backdrop of political fragility, there was intense speculation whether the parties unable to cross the dual thresholds of five per cent nationally and 0.5 per cent regionally would accept the elections results. The critics suggested that the coalition will remain fragile and thirst for power could result into abandoning the Parliamentary system. The pro-Bakiyev *Ata Jurt* party that has been staunchly opposing the interim government was expected to foment trouble in the aftermath of the results. According to some analysts, the Kyrgyz who are not used to party based affiliation would make their choices based on personalities rather than the parties, though there were no great statements or personalities among the leaders contesting the elections. The contestants were essentially the same senior officials from within the interim government that assumed control after the April 7 revolt or those earlier worked under Kurmanbek Bakiyev and Askar Akayev. In another word, the political class in the country was so small that people had not much choice. In fact, the main figures like Tekebayev, Atambayev, Babanov and Otunbayeva and others had worked for previous Presidents Akayev and Bakiyev. They were all members of the Soviet nomenclature.

Among the frontrunners in the 2010 Parliamentary elections included the SDPK, led by Almazbek Atambayev, who was deputy to Otunbayeva in the interim government. Atambayev was described then as the shrewdest leader who travelled to Moscow and played the pro-Russia card. He met with Russian Prime Minister Vladimir Putin in September 2010. His main rival was Omurbek Tekebayev, leader of the *Ata Meken* party and the architect of the constitutional reforms. Omurbek Tekebayev was identified as the most democrat Kyrgyz politician and also labelled as a pro-US leader. He was expected to form alliance with any party that opposed Bakiyev in the past.

Another strong contender was Feliks Kulov, a former Prime Minister and former Security Chief under Bakiyev. He headed the *Ar Namys* (Dignity) party. Kulov had a good chance of winning with good margin. He had a reputation as a law-and-order man, who appealed to the ethnic Uzbek, ethnic Russians as well as to the urban Kyrgyz. He was said to be enjoying the Russian support. Kulov was against the idea of introducing parliamentary democracy and instead his posters promised the "iron shield of the law."[12] Kulov also met the Russian President Dmitry Medvedev in September that year at his residence near Moscow. In Bishkek, some billboards featured the emblem of Vladimir Putin's ruling United Russia party next to the emblem of Kulov's party.

The general fear was that the election results could trigger new violence. The scenarios for trouble were drawn in the election aftermath, when the losers could challenge the results on the streets. One of the speculations was that the former President Bakiyev' supporter would try to foment violence in order to stage a comeback to power. Several associates of the former President's *Ak-Jol* Party had contested the election albeit through new platforms. For example, the former Secretary of State Adahan Madumarov had formed the *Butun Kyrgyzstan* party; a businessman Omurbek Babanov was contesting through *Respublika party*; the former minister of emergency situations Kamchibek Tashiyev was contesting through *Ata-Jurt* party. All of them have had strong linkages with Bakiyev. They also had the financial advantage and could manipulate the post-election situation. There was also the possibility of few fringe political parties creating trouble, such as *Butun Kyrgyzstan* which was protesting against the alleged vote irregularities and tampering.

A sense of skepticism and uncertainty had prevailed especially around the problem of forming a government. A strong resentment against pro-Bakiyev persons (mainly *Ata-Jurt*) party coming back to power was prevalent in Bishkek. In fact,

Ata Jurt had emerged as the strongest party and was popular among ethnic Kyrgyz in the south. It was also accused of enjoying the backing of criminal groups. Inevitably, *Ata Jurt* was expected to foment trouble should it not be allowed to form the government. As the winter months were approaching, the challenges before the new government were becoming even harder, though sufficient attention was being paid to affected population in southern Kyrgyzstan.

Though the election was considered to be free and fair, it took more than three weeks after October 10 election for the Central Election Commission (CEC) to announce the results. The official reason given was the demands for recounting, especially by the *Butun Kyrgyzstan* and other losers who formed a congress. In fact, the way the CEC had to go through a painful process of recounting of votes itself was cited by officials as the true proof of the democratic nature of the parliamentary elections.[13] In the past, election results were out within three days and they were a foregone conclusion.

The CEC had made admission of mistakes in counting by the election officials. It was also believed that CEC followed a cautious approach to resolve the tightly and closely contested elections.[14] The move was also calculated to forestall possible trouble. The results became known immediately after the polls, but officially the result was announced on November 1, and along the expected lines the following parties passed the five-percent entry threshold to enter parliament:[15]

Ata Jurt (8.7 per cent)	28 seats
SDPK (7.83 per cent)	26 seats
Ar Namys (7.57 per cent)	25 seats
Respublika (6.93 per cent)	23 seats
Ata Meken (5.49 per cent)	18 seats

No political party had achieved anywhere close to a majority. This was being viewed as a welcome departure from the past practices of ratifying the incumbent in power. There were no clear winners though five parties representing various interests and ideological groups have emerged as potential candidates to form a new government.

The *Butun Kyrgyzstan* was expected to clear the five per cent hurdle through the recounting and join hands with *Ata-Jurt* and *Ar-Namys*, giving them the necessary majority to form the coalition. But, after numerous recounts, *Butun Kyrgyzstan* had failed to clear the threshold. Such a formulation would have cast immediate doubt on the future of Kyrgyz parliamentary democracy, initiated by interim leader Roza Otunbayeva and supported by SDPK headed Almazbek Atambayev and *Ata-Meken* headed by Tekebaev. *Ata-Jurt* and *Ar-Namys* had both expressed skepticism for the parliamentary system and had promised to push for a reversal to Presidential system should they form a ruling coalition.

Formation of New Government

Meanwhile talks about creating a national coalition government comprising of all five winning parties dominated the discourse in the interim three weeks.[16] A strong belief was that Moscow was making deliberate move to scuttle formation of a parliamentary system in Kyrgyzstan that would set a bad precedent for other republics. After visiting Moscow, SDPK leader Atambayev said in a press conference "Russia is our strategic partner and we need to develop cooperation on a parity basis. But we won't change the Constitution to please someone's interests. The Constitution was adopted not so long ago and should work on it. Moreover, as the practice shows, presidential form of government has not justified itself and people rejected it." Atambayev said "no one has a right to dictate Kyrgyzstan how to live."[17]

Meanwhile, *Ata-Jurt*'s leader Kamchibek Tashiyev had openly declared his party to be pro-Russian but said that the party was rather willing to sit in opposition with an aim to restore peace and stability in the country.[18] This indicated that Tashiev did not receive sufficient support from Moscow. With this, the remaining three parties—*SDPK, Ata-Meken*, and *Respublika*—were expected to form the ruling coalition with the strength of 67 seats in the 120-seat parliament. However, there was also no clarity even on this formulation. SDPK leader Alamazbek Atambayev had admitted that talks for alliance were being held with the leader of *Respublica* party Omurbek Babanov but the party was not decided for alignment with *Ata-Meken* with which it had insurmountable issues especially on foreign policy matters. *Ata-Meken*'s leader Tekebayev was seen as overtly pro-West.

As per the new rules, the Parliament should convene its first session not later than 15 days after announcement of the election results. The CEC was to issue mandates to the elected MPs within three days; however, the process was withheld as the results were challenged in the court by some parties. The delay was proving to be unsettling for Kyrgyzstan which remained politically fragile and possibly even prone to sliding into chaos further and ultimately put Kyrgyzstan's nascent parliamentary experiment at risk. The possibility of going in for a fresh election was also not ruled out. The political parties and leaders particularly seemed unable to let go their ideological contradictions, personal ambitions and hidden agendas.

The initial attempt to form a coalition was made in early December by SDPK along with *Respublika* and *Ata-Meken*. Almazbek Atambayev became the first Prime Minister of the parliamentary form of government under the new constitution. However, it immediately got dissolved as they failed to vote on a speaker. But, after months of upheaval and political stalemate, a new coalition government in Kyrgyzstan was formed on December 17, 2010. The coalition was led by *Respublika* Party, with Social Democratic Party (SDPK) and *Ata-Jurt* Party as members and controlled 77 seats in the 120-member legislature. The government was led by the Russia-leaning leader of the SDPK, Almazbek Atambayev with 18 ministries and three state committees. Atambayev had previously served as Prime Minister in the interim government.

Interestingly, this time, the *Respublika* party leader and wealthy oil businessman Omurbek Babanov had managed to bring on board the nationalist *Ata-Jurt* party. *Ata-Jurt's* head, Akhmatbek Keldibekov was elected as the speaker in a 101-to-14 vote. Two prominent parties—*Ar Namys* and *Ata Meken* have decided to sit in opposition. *Respublika* leader, Omurbek Babanov, himself got elected as first deputy Prime Minister. However, the President has retained the right to appoint Chairman of the State National Security Committee (NSC) and the defence minister. The incumbent interim Foreign Minister Ruslan Kazakbaev and defence minister Abibila Kudaiberdiyev continued to hold their charges.

The largest and pro-Bakiev party *Ata-Jurt* joining the government had cast serious doubts about its durability in view of several contradictions that have underpinned the Kyrgyz politics.[19] Keldibekov's swift election as the Speaker surprised many. The victims of those killed in the April 2010 uprising feared that he would seriously try to influence the ongoing investigations and trials of those guilty for April 7 events. *Ata Jurt* had also been strongly opposed to the idea of introducing parliamentary rule and was fiercely critical of the interim government during the election campaign, whereas, SDPK and *Respublika* supported interim President Otunbayeva's plan to build parliamentary democracy for the country.

The new Prime Minister Alamazbek Atambayev in his first statement said that his first foreign visit would be to Russia.[20] But he had also hinted that the US Military base in Bishkek would continue to operate over the next four years until the five years term is over. He promised to pursue a balanced multilateral foreign policy.

But the challenges for the new coalition government came on the domestic front. The economy was particularly in a bad state and needed a functioning government to tackle its impending problems i.e., chronic energy shortages during winter. The problem was compounded by teachers going on strike demanding higher wages and the worsening security situation in the south. Lack of a legitimate government had caused difficulty in obtaining international assistance from donor countries. At a donor's conference held in Bishkek on July 27, 2010, representatives of 14 countries and 15 international organisations pledged assistance worth $1.1 billion aid to Kyrgyzstan to help rebuild the country after the worst ethnic bloodshed in its modern history. The World Bank and other international bodies pledged to render a mix of grants and favourable loans to the interim government of Kyrgyzstan.

In 2010, the country's economy was expected to shrink by five percent. It had 5.5 per cent growth forecast before the ethnic turmoil. The economy depends on remittances from citizens working abroad, mostly in Russia, which comprise as much as 40 per cent of GDP. Mining was the other major source of income. The Kumtor gold mine, operated by Canada's Centerra Gold, alone accounted for more than seven per cent of GDP and supplied a quarter of industrial output and a third of all exports in 2010.

Role of Roza Otunbayeva

The interim President, Roza Otunbayeva, the proponent of a parliamentary system, suddenly gained a strong national and international legitimacy as a new emerging leader in Central Asia. She was considered to be the brain behind the introduction of parliamentary form of democracy with a strong Prime Minister who can knit together the country's diverse political and ethnic groups.[21] Otunbayeva had been advocating the idea of doing away with the presidential system which she thought had not served well for the country. In October 2011, during a Bishkek conference to discuss the parliament's role in developing the Central Asian state, she stated "the president may be a mediocre person with secondary education...a president in power could fill the government with friends and family members."[22] Otunbayeva acknowledged that the parliamentary system had not become fully institutionalised in Kyrgyzstan, but the parliament could play a leading role in the state...there was a puppet parliament for 20 years of the republic's independence, but was dissolved many times; the MPs were expelled from the parliament, brought to the court and somebody rose to the ministers' posts."[23] In her speech, Otunbayeva acknowledged that she was inspired by the Mongolian democratic experiment that started immediately after the Cold War ended. However, she agreed that for Kyrgyzstan to reach to the level of democracy achieved by India was a long road ahead. India, she thought was an ideal model in Asia for countries like Kyrgyzstan to emulate from. In fact, when the Indian Defence Minister visited Bishkek, she complained about the Indian envoy in Kyrgyzstan not doing enough to promote democracy in Kyrgyzstan.

Otunbayeva's idea was widely perceived to have had the subtle backing of the US, at least in its pronouncement and the manner in which President Roza Otunbayeva was received by the US President in New York in September 2010. She was the darling of the West and even described as the Mikheil Saakashvili of Central Asia. Otunbayeva had received wide international admiration for holding the successful, free, fair, and surprisingly non-violent parliamentary election.

The parliamentary elections and the smooth transition in the aftermath also raised Roza Otunbayeva's strong national and international legitimacy as a new emerging leader in Central Asia. Otunbayeva was credited for restoring a semblance of stability after the months of inter-ethnic clashes in South Kyrgyzstan. She had taken a courageous step to rebuild democratic institutions over the months by drafting and ratifying a new constitution through a referendum on June 27, 2010, and holding successful elections for a new parliament on October 10, 2010. As stated before, by and large, international observers from the UN, OSCE, CSTO, CIS, SCO, OIC and regional observers, including a Russian Parliamentary group, had assessed the election as having met the basic requirements of a free and democratic election.[24] In fact, it was arguably described as the fairest election held in post-Soviet Central Asia. Even the opposition *Ata-Jurt* party leader, Kamchibek Tashiev said that "I respect President Roza Otunbayeva not as politician, but as mother and woman...frankly speaking, we are far from thought that she will be able to bring the country out of crisis."[25]

Clearly, Roza Otunbayeva enjoyed a clean reputation. She did not represent any interest group. She was essentially an academic-diplomat and had the ability to bring a balance among competing parties. As former Ambassador and Foreign Minister, she influenced the country's foreign and national security policies. Significantly, when President Obama met Roza Otunbayeva in New York on September 24, 2010, he expressed admiration for Otunbayeva's courageous efforts to rebuild democratic institutions in Kyrgyzstan. A Press Note said "Under Otunbayeva's leadership the Kyrgyz government removed restrictions on independent media, drafted a new constitution, which was ratified by a referendum on June 27, 2010, and will hold elections for a new parliament next month."[26] Obama also praised Otunbayeva's actions to end the June 2010 tragic violence and urged her to take further steps to prevent renewed violence, including approving the deployment of a Police Advisory Group (PAG)—a 52-member team appointed by OSCE. Obama advised her to initiate a credible international commission of inquiry to investigate the June events. Of course, at that point of time, the main interest of the US in Kyrgyzstan was the continuation of its military transit centre at Manas that was opened in 2001 to support anti-terror operations in Afghanistan. In February 2009, the Kyrgyz parliament voted for the closure of the Manas base after securing pledges of $2 billion in aid and credit from Russia. Washington later agreed to pay more rent to Kyrgyzstan to keep the base open. Dealing with the new Kyrgyz parliamentary democracy was, therefore, an important policy consideration for Washington.

As indicated above, the US seemed most excited by the course of democracy unfolding in Kyrgyzstan. Following the election results, the US Government had announced a new $15.8 million programme for the support of economic security of Kyrgyzstan and another $3.2 million for social institutions to maintain food security.[27] US Ambassador in Kyrgyzstan Tatiana C. Gfoeller announced a grant of $54.266 to the Kyrgyz Parliament for the purchase of technical equipments.[28] In 2010, the US Government allocated over $300 thousand to the Kyrgyz Parliament.

The US Deputy Assistant Secretary for South and Central Asian Affairs Susan Elliott visited Bishkek soon after and held meetings with President Otunbayeva and leaders of five parties, which had won seats in the Parliament. The stationing of the Transit Centre at Manas was discussed with the parties. Many observers noticed Washington was ostensibly changing its tact on Kyrgyzstan as compared to past policy of turning a blind eye to authoritarian rule, underscored primarily to retain the Manas air base. It has become more vocal about promoting Kyrgyz efforts to build a parliamentary democracy and has spent $5 million to facilitate the election process.

Most analysts viewed that renewed political stability in Kyrgyzstan would offer fresh opportunity for the US in the context of difficulties that it was facing in the way of NATO's supply lines to Afghanistan through Pakistan. A greater attention was expected to come on its Northern Distribution Network (NDN). Therefore, the US was seen as pursuing a more positive cooperative agenda to prevent further violence and disorder in Kyrgyzstan.

When Roza Otunbayeva visited Washington for the second time in March 2011, she was again received by President Barack Obama who reaffirmed US full support to Kyrgyzstan in its striving for democracy and political transformations. The US President expressed gratitude to Roza Otunbayeva for contribution into fight against international terrorism by hosting the Transit Centre and said the US is ready to continue its multi-faceted support to the Kyrgyz Republic in its democratic development.[29] She also had a meeting with Senator John Kerry who thanked Roza Otunbayeva for Kyrgyzstan's contribution towards the fight against international terrorism and regulation of the situation in Afghanistan.[30] President met with Senator John McCain who deeply expressed confidence that democracy and justice will prevail under the leadership of Roza Otunbayeva.

It had become quite clear that the US had politically invested in Roza Otunbayeva to prop her as an anchor of change in the post-Soviet Central Asian space. The National Democratic Institute, headed by Madeleine Albright, hosted a round table and lunch in Otunbayeva's honour. President gave a detailed account to the US policy think tank about the changes that had occurred in her country leading to establishment of parliamentary democracy. She also underscored the important role played by the US especially for its support in allocating assistance and grants from the international financial institutions. She said "During the last several months the people of Kyrgyzstan had to endure lots of shocks, which left pain in the heart of each citizen. At the same time, changes happened in the country during the last 11 months, which laid a foundation for real development of the country on the path of social, political and economic development."[31]

But in a most noteworthy act, the US Secretary of State Hillary Clinton conferred Roza Otunbayeva with the International Women of Courage Award at the ceremony on March 8 in Washington D.C.[32] Otunbayeva was considered for the award for her role in navigating the path of Kyrgyzstan towards establishing the first parliamentary democracy in Central Asia. The State Department said she was chosen because of her "tremendous courage, leadership, and tenacity."[33] The first lady attended the ceremony. Roza Otunbayeva became the first head of state ever to earn the State Department honour.[34] Secretary Clinton said on the occasion "She is a president who knows how to lead, but she also knows how to let go, because she has set an extraordinary example of what it means to relinquish power. She decided early on she would help to set up a new government, have a new constitution, and when the time came after the elections were finished, she would turn over powers to the new prime minister and that government. In so doing, she has offered an invaluable lesson to fledgling democracies everywhere. Otunbayeva stands "as an example for many leaders around the world about what democracy and power should be used for, to help the people that you are supposed to serve…and that….in the face of a collapsing government, regional divisions, economic privation, she emerged as unifier, someone who kept Kyrgyzstan whole after tragedy and upheaval."[35]

Roza Otunbayeva in her speech said "I accept this award on behalf of all the women of Kyrgyzstan who struggle from day to day to make their voices heard. This award belongs to those who, despite their condition, rise above and demand respect for their human dignity."[36] However, the award for Otunbayeva evoked sharp response from an Uzbek woman Mutabar Tajibaeva who received the same award in 2009. Mutabar announced to return her award in protest against Otunbayeva's inclusion, accusing her of failing to prevent the killings of Uzbeks during the 2010 Osh violence.

Regional Impact

The countries in the region, according to media reports, were taken off guard by the Kyrgyz election. The Uzbeks and Kazakh media were dismissive of the Kyrgyz development. The Kremlin, according to analysts, was not expecting a problem-free election. The Russians remained apprehensive about the Kyrgyz experiment with open and representative parliamentary system that could produce domino effect across the region,[37] besides its internal contradictions, rivalry among factions and clans will lead to violence and instability leaving Kyrgyzstan vulnerable to Islamic forces.

President Dmitry Medvedev had said on September 10, 2010 that "Russia does not want a system like that of...I fear for Kyrgyzstan—parliamentary democracy is a catastrophe."[38]

China considered Kyrgyzstan to be a trouble spot and was wary of mounting instability on its borders. China was keen to increase its influence in Kyrgyzstan which has abundant minerals and also acts as a corridor through which it supplies goods to Russian and other CIS markets. During the turmoil period, China appeared wary of Western countries monitoring the situation in Kyrgyzstan. It was for the first time the SCO had sent observers for the Kyrgyz elections.

The successful parliamentary elections also helped Kyrgyzstan receive closer attention and active cooperation from the multiple multinational institutions, including from NATO, OSCE, EU, CSTO, SCO, and other the international financial institutions. This was required to fortify Kyrgyzstan's newfound stability. India too had an opportunity to assist Kyrgyzstan's strive for building democracy which would have been in its strategic interest to counter extremist forces around its "extended neighbourhood". On the Kyrgyz request, India did provide 25 multi-functional computers to Kyrgyzstan to equip precinct election commissions. The computers were handed over by the Ambassador to the Chairman of the CEC, Akylbek Sariev in a ceremony on the eve of the first parliamentary election. India did acknowledge Roza Otunbayeva's courageous step to establish and strengthen a vibrant democratic, secular and pluralist culture in Kyrgyzstan. After she relinquished her Presidency, Roza visited India. She met Indian leadership and spoke in various forums on the Kyrgyz experiment with parliamentary democracy. Otunbayeva remains in the whole of Central Asia as the strongest proponent of Indian democracy.

Conclusion

Three successive governments have already been changed since 2010. After Atambayeva stepped down as the Prime Minister in late 2011, a new coalition led by Babanov was formed after a difficult political negotiation. However, on August 24, 2012, the President signed an order dismissing (technically termed as resignation) Babanov from Prime Minister's post. Babanov faced serious corruption charges, including an alleged bribe of a race horse from Turkish businesses. Ar-Namys was the first to withdraw from the coalition followed by Ata-Meken that precipitated the downfall of the government. A show down came as Babanov's own party members were demanding his resignation. The charges of corruption were backed by a legal circumstance. The next coalition was by another set of political parties and a former official Jantoro Satybaldiyev becoming the new Prime Minister of the country in early September 2012. According to a nationwide social telephone survey conducted by Human Rights Coalition "For Democracy and Civil Society" nearly half country's population was dissatisfied with the Satybaldiyev's government.[39]

The Kyrgyz experiment with parliamentary democracy is at its nascent stage though it appears very shaky. (a) the experiment looked very odd in a region traditionally ruled by presidents with near-absolute powers, but it is clear that a centralised presidential system also proved to be a failure, (b) in comparison to others, the country is sharply divided along regional and ethnic lines, both Kyrgyz and Uzbeks with a roughly equal share of the population in the south, (c) the formation of coalition governments since 2010 have been driven primarily by individual and group interests and not by any common ideology,[40] (d) economically, it is a weaker state in the region, (e) the country is vulnerable to manipulation by outside powers; China is aggressively trying to step up economic expansion and the presence of the US and Russian air bases continued to pose a challenge to the new parliamentary government, (f) the country is located on a drug trafficking route out of Afghanistan and shares the Fergana Valley—a hub of Islamic extremism. The optimists remain hopeful about its success. The experiment is expected to bring a decisive outcome for either uniting the country or rekindle fresh inter-ethnic violence and leave the south vulnerable to ethnic extremists and militant Islamists. The situation in the south remained particularly volatile. Relations between Uzbeks and Kyrgyz remained tensed despite attempts by some of the parties trying to portray plurality in their campaigns. However, many observers hoped that the parliamentary elections can be a step towards stabilisation.

NOTES

1. *AKIpress,* October 10, 2010.
2. *Kabar,* October 9, 20110.
3. *AKIpress,* October 10, 2010.
4. "U.S. Embassy Congratulates the Kyrgyz Republic on Elections", *Kabar,* October 10, 2010
5. International media generally hailed the Kyrgyz elections as free and fair.
6. Observation made by former Kyrgyz Foreign Minister, Askar Aimatov to the author.
7. The international legitimacy for Kyrgyz election came following the strong observations made by the Coordinator of the OSCE/ODIHR Morten Hoeglund when he said "Political pluralism, a vibrant campaign, and confidence in the central commission for elections or referenda characterised these elections. He noted that the "Fundamental freedoms, including the freedoms of expression, assembly, and association were generally respected." Morten Hoeglund said "I was impressed by the political pluralism, the civic responsibility and the spirit of the people of this country. I have observed many elections in Central Asia over the years but this is the first election where I could not predict the outcome." Source: "Kyrgyzstan's vibrant and pluralistic parliamentary elections constitute further consolidation of democracy" http://www.osce.org/odihr/elections/72409.
8. "Kyrgyzstan's vibrant and pluralistic parliamentary elections constitute further consolidation of democracy" http://www.osce.org/odihr/elections/72409.
9. "Obama: Kyrgyz Elections Offer Democratic Hope for Central Asia" http://iipdigital.usembassy.gov/st/english/article/2010/10/20101012142253nehpets0.5807917.html#ixzz2PIQKoa8W (Accessed October 10, 2010).
10. *AKIpress,* October 14, 2010.
11. "China hopes for stability in Kyrgyzstan" *24.kg news agency*, October 14, 2010.
12. Banners of Ar Namys in the Bishkek Streets featuring the slogan.
13. "A painful work of CEC on revision of voting data and number of voters is proof of democratic nature of elections—Chief of President's Administration", Bishkek, *AKIpress*, October 28, 2010.
14. "CEC Chair: Precinct election commissions made mistakes in voter lists across the country resulting in bigger number of voters", Bishkek, *AKIpress*, "Central Election Commission to streamline summary table with real figures from checked polling stations today", Bishkek, *AKIpress*, October 28, 2010.
15. *AKIpress*, November 2, 2010.
16. "Parties ready to form government in shortest possible time, says President Otunbaeva in her video blog", Bishkek, *AKIpress,* October 27, 2010.
17. Darya Podolskaya, "Atambayev said no one has a right to dictate Kyrgyzstan how to live", *24.kg news agency*, November 4, 2010. URL: http://eng.24.kg/cis/2010/11/04/14660.html.
18. "Kamchibek Tashiev: We orient to Russia and openly say we are pro-Russian politicians", AKIpress, November 3, 2010.
19. Tolgonai Osmongazieva, "Beknazarov: Coalition is likely to disintegrate in late March or early April", Bishkek, *24.kg news agency*, March 22, 2011.
20. *Kabar,* January 2, 2011.

21. "Otunbayeva: Presidential system not suitable for Kyrgyzstan", *AKIpress,* October 19, 2011
22. *24.Kg,* October 19, 2011. The author also participated in the conference held in the State residence in Bishkek.
23. *24.Kg,* October 19, 2011, http://www.universalnewswires.com/centralasia/kyrgyzstan/security/viewstory.aspx?id=10479.
24. "Kyrgyzstan's vibrant and pluralistic parliamentary elections constitute further consolidation of democracy" http://www.osce.org/odihr/elections/72409.
25. *AKIpress,* November 5, 2010.
26. Read-out of President Obama's Meeting with Kyrgyzstani President, www.whitehouse.gov/.../read-out-president-obamas-meeting (Accessed September 24, 2010).
27. Robert O. Blake, Jr. "The Emerging Importance of the U.S.-Central Asia Partnership". Testimony before the House Foreign Affairs Committee, Subcommittee on Asia, the Pacific, and the Global Environment, November 18, 2010, http://bishkek.usembassy.gov/tr_17_18_10.html.
28. Julia Mazykina, 'US Government pays for Parliament equipment", URL: http://eng.24.kg/community/2011/01/21/15895.html.
29. "U.S. President Barack Obama reaffirms support to Kyrgyzstan in its strive for democracy", Bishkek, *AKIpress,* March 29, 2011.
30. Ibid.
31. "President Otunbaeva attends round table discussion of NDI Board of Directors", *AKIpress,* March 28, 2011, Quoted from the Presidents' press release.
32. The U.S. State Department annually marks International Women's Day by designating 10 women from around the world "International Women of Courage". In 2011, women from Afghanistan, Cameroon, Hungary, Jordan, Pakistan, Cuba, and Belarus were given awards for their remarkable contribution for the well being of others.
33. Heather Maher, "U.S. State Department Honors 'International Women Of Courage'" http://www.rferl.org/content/us_state_department_international_women_of_courage/2332256.html, March 9, 2011.
34. "President Otunbayeva receives International Women of Courage Award", Bishkek *AKIpress,* March 7, 2011.
35. Ibid.
36. Ibid.
37. http://www.rferl.org/content/Can_Russia_Embrace_A_New_Model_For_Central_Asia/2184581.html
38. Stuart Williams, "Medvedev warns of parliamentary democracy 'catastrophe", http://www.google.com/hostednews/afp/article/ALeqM5gDgfbX1FnK1R4VieEG3fN012W7GQ*AFP,* September 10, 2010.
39. "Nearly half of Kyrgyz population unhappy about new government – survey", *Russian news agency Interfax,* September 1, 2012.
40. "A nation-wide Congress of Political Parties that included Akyikat party, the Youth Movement, Zamandash Party, Meken Tuu party, led by Urmat Baryktabasov assumed that the newly elected Parliament won't exist long", *AKIpress,* 7 April 2010.

CHAPTER 4

First Democratic Presidential Election

After successfully introducing the parliamentary form of government in late 2010, the country witnessed the Presidential elections on October 30, 2011. It marked the first peaceful and voluntary handover of power from one leader to another in the history of post-Soviet Central Asia. As mentioned before, it was Roza Otunbayeva's idea to build a system that would make it difficult for future leaders to concentrate power in their own hands. Roza Otunbayeva had opted out of the race but vowed to hold secure and legitimate presidential polls. In an address to the nation she said that "for the first the incumbent President is not taking part in the elections and does not resort to various tricks to stay in office. On the contrary, the leader is a neutral figure, an unbiased guarantor of free and democratic elections."[1] This decision earned Roza Otunbayeva a lot of international applause though a section of Kyrgyz population was demanding that she should contest the election for her exemplary contribution to the country. In her statement, Roza expressed hope that the new President will end the country's transitional period and bring the country to the path of long-term stability and development.

The Election

The nomination of candidates for the presidential election got started on June 30, 2011 and ended on August 16, 2011. The CEC received 83 applications of which 16 were nominated by political parties and remaining 67 were self-nominees. According to the law, a candidate can be registered for final fray if he/she was able to collect not less than 30 thousand signatures and deposit $2250 by September 10, 2011. A candidate had to pass a live, televised Kyrgyz-language exam. Official campaigning begins September 25, 2011. The election was to be held by direct, secret and non-transferable voting. A candidate getting 50 per cent or more votes would be adjudged as the winner. In case of fragmentation, the top two contenders were to enter a second round of election whereupon the one securing the maximum votes amongst the two will be declared the winner. According to the new constitution the President is elected for six years and for a maximum of two consecutive terms.

In the final phase of campaign, the number of candidates got considerably reduced. Out of initially 83 nominations, only 16 were left in the final race. The most prominent candidates included those who were already in the present government or have held important positions in the earlier governments. Interim President Roza Otunbayeva was to step down following the election but her main ally and the present Prime Minister Almazbek Atambayev of the ruling Social Democratic Party (SDP) was among the main candidates.

It is to be noted here that under the new Constitution the Prime Minister was to be made more powerful instead of the President. But, something was not clear to the minds of outside observers. Why would Atambayev seek the position of President when the power of the post had been truncated under the new Constitution? To an extent, this had clearly exposed the very motive of the revolution that overthrew Bakiyev. It became obvious at this stage that the main agenda of the revolutionaries was not about building democratic polity but was simply a means to capture the power from Bakiyev. As we move ahead this aspect of Kyrgyz democracy will be analysed in some detail.

Like in the parliamentary elections, the voting was expected to be polarised between North and South candidates—a regional rift that got sharpened after the 2010 bloody ouster of Bakiyev's regime. Moreover, the election was held against the backdrop of the previous year's political turmoil and ethnic tension that had brought severe economic hardship to the country. Russia had particularly increased its economic leverage over Kyrgyzstan, including regulating oil supplies, and entry in to Customs Union. Russia also hinted of support to return to 'strongman' politics.[2] The campaign itself was low-key, with rallies attracting a few hundred people at the most. With no candidate enjoying support across the whole country, the risk of political instability within Kyrgyzstan remained high. Media was also reporting about arms-cache being found and trained terrorists being caught by security agencies. The threat of violence before or immediately after the elections remained a high possibility.

The election was driven by personality rather than issues. Atambayev was to step down from Prime Minister's post in September to make a presidential run. He had, of course, emerged as the front runner in the election as he drew support from the Russified north, though he did not have much support in the south.

The second strongest candidate was the ex-parliament speaker and a pro-Bakiyev member Adakhan Madumarov of Butun Kyrgyzstan (United Kyrgyzstan) party whose main support base was in southern Kyrgyzstan. The third top contender was Kachimbek Tashiyev of the ultranationalist Ata-Jurt (Fatherland) party who also hailed from the south and was blamed for raising nationalist cause, and for being anti-Uzbek. Both Madumarov and Tashiyev were strong contenders from the south and were expected to pull votes on regional lines. Both were former Bakiyev allies and were in favour of resurrecting presidential powers that were watered down after the April uprising last year. Most of the other candidates had withdrawn in favour of front line candidate Atambayev Almazbek of the SDP. Therefore, the main contest was among the following:

Candidate	Party affiliation	Regional stronghold
ATAMBAYEV Almazbek	Social Democratic Party of KR	North
TASHIYEV Kamchibek	Ata-Jurt (Fatherland KR)	Pro-Bakiyev, South
MADUMAROV Adakhan	Butun Kyrgyzstan (United Kyrgyzstan)	Formerly pro-Bakiyev; South

Atambayev Almazbek had been a member of Kyrgyz political elite for a long time. In 1980s, he was a young communist-party activist. After the Soviet collapse he became a successful entrepreneur after setting up a printing house that published Russian translation of Mario Puzo's *The Godfather* series and other famous works. A businessman turned politician, he became an MP, then Minister of Trade and Industry before briefly serving as PM under former President Bakiyev. Later, he resigned and joined the opposition and became an ally of Roza Otunbayeva and together they ultimately threw Bakiyev from office in April 2010. Later, he became PM and leader of SDPK in the interim government. Atambayev belongs to northern Kyrgyzstan and normally enjoys Moscow's support as he travelled repeatedly to Russia and tried to push Kyrgyzstan closer to Russia during his tenure as PM. Unlike his predecessor, Atambayev is not viewed as a colourful politician and not very well oriented towards foreign policy except that he is keen on having closer relations with Russia and Turkey. Of late, he has become closer to China as well. At several occasions and during meetings with the author, Atambayev praised India's economic achievements and desired India's economic support to Kyrgyzstan in its difficult times.

KamchibekTashiyev, four-year old ex-Emergency Services Minister had won the largest share of votes in parliamentary elections in 2010. He is from the *Ata-Jurt* party and draws his popularity on the nationalist sentiments. Tashiyev plays the Kyrgyz and Uzbek ethnic divide. Tashiyev gained prominence for his violent physical assaults on fellow party members in the parliament in 2010. He is viewed by people as someone lacking political sophistication. In 2012, he has been jailed for attempting to storm the government building in Bishkek.

Adakhan Madumarov, 46-year old former parliament speaker and top security official, his *Butun Kyrgyzstan* (United Kyrgyzstan) party narrowly failed to secure seats in 2010 parliamentary elections. He draws his support mainly in the south. Madumarov was three-time national billiards champion. During a televised presidential debate he spoke about the need to "cut off the tongues and legs" of journalists smearing his reputation. Madumarov has strong links to the ousted Bakiyev regime. He favours a rollback to a presidential system of governance.

The nation-wide presidential poll was held on Sunday 30 October 2011. More than three million ballots were printed for the polls.[3] A total of 725 international observers from 47 organisations were accredited. The foreign TV channels, particularly the Russian channels were banned during the campaign to prevent interference in the polls.[4] Despite some shortcomings, the polling was free and fair as there were no reports of serious violations but the opposition declared the voting unfair suggesting technical errors including tens of thousands of people having not been registered in the rolls.[5] Interestingly, one of the presidential candidates, Kubanychbek Isabekov could not find his and his spouse name in the voter list. The candidates sought dismissal of CEC members and there were reports of even voters filing law suits.[6] The opposition leaders were outraged by the election. All the presidential candidates, Kurmanbek Osmonov, Kubanychbek Isabekov, Adakhan Madumarov, Sooronbai Dyikanov, Marat Imankulov, Kubatbek Baibolov, and representative of Kamchibek Tashiyev blamed the authorities for numerous violations including the misuse of administrative machineries. In a joint press conference, Kubanychbek Isabekov claimed that such a gross violation and misuse of administrative resource had not taken place even under regimes of Akayev and Bakiyev. They charged that even the university's teachers were forced to ensure presence of students at the polling stations in order to vote for the certain candidate. This was also true for other public sector employees.[7] The media also reported from a polling station in the Kyrgyz National University in Bishkek of how several teachers were seen calling their students by telephone to come for voting. Adakhan Madumarov noted "all fears about election outrages have come true. Such lawlessness is happening like never before in Kyrgyzstan and such distrust may lead to social explosion."[8] Kubatbek Baibolov blamed the authorities for organising public transport for voters supporting Atambayev. Similarly, Marat Imankulov didn't think the elections were legitimate and the authorities were creating the situation for public discontent.

There were also complaints of law being unequal. When the acting Prime Minister Omurbek Babanov appeared at polling station No. 1215 he had forgotten to bring his passport. Yet, nobody thought it was wrong, including international observers who didn't object. Babanov was able to vote while people produced his identity card later. It was not quite the same when opposition presidential candidate Kamchybek Tashiyev reached at the polling station No. 4321 in Aral village of Naryn province, he was denied voting.[9] There were thousands of such cases where voters had to return back home without voting. In an incident, the Mayor of Osh Melisbek Myrzakmatov had refused marking of the list. Yet, the EC official let the Osh city governor to take part in the elections. A media commentator, Julia Mazykina noted that the election officials not only discredited the entire CEC but the presidential election itself. She aptly compared Kyrgyzstan to George Orwell's novel "*Animal Farm*".[10]

However, neutral political commentators felt that the polls were largely fair and could not be termed as illegitimate. A known political scientist Tabyldy Ackerov had commented "The current presidential elections in Kyrgyzstan are quite democratic and transparent, despite the technical problems with voting lists."[11] Significantly, Otunbayeva too stated that the misuse of administrative resources and the claims of violations were unfounded. The international observers had largely praised the run-up to the elections and also described the polls largely fair and impartial. However, it was an accepted fact, judging from the swing in favour of Atambayev, that he may have made full use of state resources.

There were rumours of vote-buying making the rounds around the elections. Almost a million Kyrgyz work as migrants in Russia and elsewhere. They were not able to vote as there were only a few polling stations available. However, the biggest challenge this time was to keep the ethnic balance and bring the Uzbek minority back into political life. Voting pattern of the sizeable Uzbek ethnic population in south Kyrgyzstan was therefore critical. The OSCE election observers had noted that ethnic Uzbeks were reluctant to engage with the campaign and avoided participating in any events. Many local observers linked the low turnout in the south to people's distrust for the candidates.[12] The Uzbek voters stayed away from the poll due to lack of adequate security.

As mentioned earlier, the threat of violence before or immediately after the elections remained a high possibility. The neighbouring Kazakhstan particularly appeared worried about the situation in Kyrgyzstan. There were unconfirmed reports about Kazakhstan having supplied weapons worth $3 million to Kyrgyz security authorities to contain any possible trouble that may engulf the region. They had also tightened security at all the check-posts with Kyrgyzstan.

Learning from the past experiences, the Indian Embassy had also issued an advisory to all Indian students and citizens residing in Kyrgyzstan and restricted movement during the election. A contingency plan to meet any emergency for the evacuation of students from Osh was also kept ready. Based on the past experience and as a precaution, the Mission advised that no official visits be planned during this period.

The polls were held sharply along regional lines and it was driven by personality rather than issues. Atambayev's victory had been widely anticipated. The initial expectations were that none of the three top contenders would garner more than 50 per cent of votes, though the possibility of Atambayev securing the 50 per cent of votes in the first round did exist, especially when Madumarov and Tashiyev could split the southern vote. However, if Atambayev was unable to garner 50 per cent of votes then the second round would have pit him against a lone southerner—Madumarov or Tashiyev—a development that could have easily exacerbated a north-south rift as the losing candidates will attempt to declare any results invalid and bring protestors into the streets. In fact, tensions leading to spate of violence were expected immediately after the announcement of the second round. Already, Tashiyev had threatened to bring "millions"[13] of supporters onto the streets, if he perceived that elections were unfair. Both Tashiyev and Madumarov had repeatedly accused Atambayev for abusing administrative resources attempts to vote-rigging ahead of the elections.[14] The specter of a new wave of protests did cause apprehensions among people who were yet to reconcile with instability and chaos due to the political and ethnic violence.

A second round of voting would have forced Atambayev to share power with a southern Prime Minister that would have, in a way, helped to potentially defuse regional rivalries. Newspapers had been reporting behind-the-scenes negotiations between candidates for the purpose of trading withdrawal and support of stronger candidates for promised future positions. If Tashiyev were to gain sufficient votes in the south he could have negotiated with Atambayev for the coveted position of Prime Minister. His Ata-Jurt Party holds the most seats. But, both Atambayev's main challengers rejected the idea of joining forces.

Atambayev had positioned himself as the strongest contender. As required by law, he was to step down as PM temporarily during the campaign, which he did. Atambayev drew his main support from industrial north. He gained popularity when he had raised salaries and pensions of teachers that earned him good political fortunes. He was well-funded candidate and enjoyed wide public exposure by serving as Prime Minister. Strong gossips prevailed about how he managed to receive funding from Russia, Turkey and even China.[15] Atambayev in posture stood for unity of the country as opposed to others who raised their political agenda along nationalistic rhetoric. Both Madumarov and Tashiyev were using the southern card. As the Prime Minister of the country, Atambayev projected himself to be a strong advocate of closer relations with Russia. He paid numerous visits to Moscow during his time as PM, particularly during times of crisis as well as his support of Kyrgyzstan's entry into the Customs Union. Atambayev's frequent visits to Moscow indicated that he had enjoyed Moscow's blessings. Meanwhile he was also seen as cultivating good ties with China. But unlike President Otunbayeva, he did not appear keen on foreign relations and especially with the West. His public announcement to close down the Transit Centre in 2014 was also seen in the above context.

The CEC Member Jenish Akmatov announced that as per the law, the final result was to be declared within 22 days of the polling. Later, the deputy chairman of the CEC Gulnara Dzhurabayeva said that if the number of votes exceeded the allocated ballots, the results of that polling station will be considered void. But, as expected, Atambayev was dominating in the north; the other two contenders had dominant presence in the south. With a turnout of 61 per cent and 16 candidates running, it appeared that the incumbent PM looked set for a landslide victory leading the field with over 63 per cent of the vote. His strongest opponents, leader of Butun Kyrgyzstan Adakhan Madumarov and leader of Ata-Jurt, Kamchybek Tashiyev gained 14.7 per cent and 14.3 per cent respectively. None of the other 13 candidates had polled over 1 per cent. The CEC announced over 60 per cent voting and the turnout was large in northern Kyrgyzstan including in the capital Bishkek, while in southern part the turnout was lower, suggesting that the ethnic Uzbek population stayed away from the voting. According to the law, the winner needed at least 50 per cent in one round.

Atambayev was declared the winner in the first round itself. Voices of dissent were roped in to share the political dividends. Otunbayeva left her office as per scheduled and paved the way for the new President to take over. On December 1, 2011, Atambayev Sharshenovich Almazbek was sworn in as the President of Kyrgyzstan, with the oath read out by CEC Chairman.

New History

In ways more than one, the inauguration of President Almazbek Atambayev assumed significance for the whole region. It was for the first time when outgoing and incoming Presidents shared the dais, signifying a civilised transfer of power. The event itself attracted large public and media attention with VIPs coming in from far and wide. However, despite the rhetoric, no high-profile Russian officials attended the inauguration. The head of Russian Presidential administration, Sergei Naryshkin, was initially among the listed guests but only the head of Russia's constitutional court, Valery Zorkin was seen during the ceremony. The presence of Georgian leader Mikhail Saakashvili in the inaugural function was said to have put off Moscow. It appeared Roza Otunbayeva had invited the Georgian leader with whom she has warm relations. The presence of the President of Turkey Abdullah Gül was expected as Atambayev had very close ties with Turkey. But Gül left early citing ill health. Kazakhstan and Tajikistan preferred to send only their PMs. Turkmenistan had sent vice Speaker of the Parliament. Surprisingly, Uzbekistan was represented by the Chairman of the Senate. Others included Premier of Azerbaijan, the Speaker of Belarus Parliament, and the Chief of Staff to the Mongolian President. China was represented by the vice Speaker of the National People's Congress, while the US had sent Assistant Secretary Robert Blake. The attendance of Indian Minister of State for External Affairs E. Ahamad was cancelled at the last minute citing inability to travel during cold climate.

Atambayev's Agenda

Atambayev promised to open a new page in the country's history and called for ethnic unity and stability without which he thought Kyrgyzstan has no future. In his landmark speech at a parliamentary session on December 28, 2011, President Almazbek Atambayev called upon his countrymen to dispel the popular notion that Kyrgyzstan will disappear from the face of the earth as a failed state because of the rift in his country. While promising to build the country and live up to people's trust, the President expounded his priority agendas in the following ways:

Judicial Reforms—to create fair and responsible courts/ and justice system, (Parliament to bring about a number of laws)

Fight against Corruption and Organised Crime—to set up an anticorruption service under the State National Security Committee,

Infrastructure and Energy Security—to improve the depleted infrastructure and ensuring energy security, the construction of Datka-Kemin power line with Chinese assistance, to extract domestic oil reserves with Russia's Gazprom in the next two to three years,

Improving Connectivity—to construct the China-Kyrgyzstan-Uzbekistan railway line in the next five-six years, to build a highway linking south with north—an issue he considered as important as national security,

Food security—to launch new national agricultural projects, construction of new irrigation system, micro-credit to farmers and livestock breeders,

Mining and Industry—to improve and modernise mining capacity, to create necessary conditions to make the country a paradise for investors and entrepreneurs by reducing red tape and cutting down inspecting bodies,

Ethnic Relations and Language Policy—to make the learning of Kyrgyz language mandatory at kindergarten level, to create conditions for developing cultures and languages of all ethnic groups of the united Kyrgyz people and to fully investigate ethnic riots of June 2010,

Russia: Main Strategic Partner

On foreign policy, President Almazbek Atambayev had announced that it should be conducted only in the interests of the people of Kyrgyzstan, but identified Russia as the main strategic partner. He also indicated the intention of joining the Customs Union, and added Kyrgyzstan should become a transit country with the construction of the railway link and a new road with China. On cooperation with Russia, he said "Of course, our strategic partner is Russia. We intend to become a full member of the Customs Union. I am confident that this move will revive our industry, strengthen our security, open borders with neighbouring countries, [and] improve the standard of living of our people. We have a common history and a common future with Russia and our neighbouring countries."[16] He believed that Custom Union will eventually serve as the foundation for the proposed Eurasian Union. But citing the need to construct the railway line, he had hinted at developing close relations with China as well.

Turkish President Abdullah Gul during his visit to Bishkek was quick to announce the writing off $49.2 million debt; and an agreement was signed to this effect. Sensing that developments in Kyrgyzstan was inevitable, China obtained concession from the new Kyrgyz dispensation on policy on Taiwan, Tibet etc and indicated of deep cooperation with the republic.

US Airbase: Dangerous Target for Iranian Missiles

The presence of US airbase (Transit Centre) at Manas assumed a fresh political agenda for the new President. When he was the country's Prime Minister, Atambayev repeatedly threatened to shut down the base once the rent contract expires in 2014. He promised to make it a civilian transit centre together with Russia and other countries. His predecessor Roza Otunbayeva was largely in favour of retaining the US base. But now, Atambayev had started citing security concerns as the motive for the decision. Atambayev believed that keeping a military air base at a civilian airport was dangerous in the light of a possible military conflict between the US and Iran. Atambayev said Iran wants to close the Straits of Hormuz, while the USA will not allow it to do so. In such a situation, Iran might hit US facilities in Bishkek. Just before he took over as the President, Kyrgyzstan along with members of the Collective Security Treaty Organisation (CSTO) signed a landmark agreement in Moscow recently that will prohibit deployment of foreign military bases without the consent of all its members.

At the swearing-in ceremony, the new President vowed to fight corruption and put an end to power struggle between various branches of power. Soon after he resumed office, President Atambayev signed a decree on setting up an anti-corruption agency under the National Security Committee of Kyrgyzstan on December 14, 2011.[17] Bekten Sadygaliyev was appointed as the head of the newly established anti-corruption service. The decree said that "Corruption and abuse of office by high-ranking officials has become one of the main reasons that led to the people's revolutions in March 2005 and April 2010.... The state management is losing its effectiveness.... The people, as well as, local and foreign investors' trust in the government remains low, and Kyrgyzstan's prestige is being damaged in the world community.... The scope and nature of corruption is reaching the level that poses a threat to not only the stability in society but also to national security."[18] This was an important initiative, but no one could understand why Atambayev opted to make the most corrupt politician and a business tycoon Omurbek Babanov as the Prime Minster of the country.

Atambayev also promised to build a high power transmission line and a controversial railway project connecting Uzbekistan and Kyrgyzstan to China and to finish construction of Soviet-era hydroelectric power stations. Atambayev also stressed the need to remove the designation of ethnicity from Kyrgyz passports, leaving only citizenship.

Challenges Ahead

Despite the seeming promise of Kyrgyzstan's election, the country continued to face host of uncertainties both on the domestic and external fronts. Atambayev came to office at a time when the country was still marked by deep political, ethnic, and regional divisions. An official probe into last 2010 deadly ethnic clashes in Osh blamed local Uzbek leaders and relatives of the former President for instigating the violence. International investigation report chastised the interim government and its officials for failing to avert the unrest.

The ethnic issues have their roots in economic problems and it would require major reforms to defuse the divide. The outgoing President Roza Otunbayeva, in her final speech in the Parliament on December 1, 2011, had apologised to the nation for her failure to prevent the ethnic bloodshed. She said "I am really touched by and proud of the heroism and wisdom of the nation of Kyrgyzstan, but want to apologise again for my failure to prevent bloodshed."[19]

The country also faced a stagnating economy, pervasive corruption, struggling with narcotics trafficking, rising fundamentalist forces and an uncertain foreign policy dilemma—whether to join Russian led Custom Union or to benefit from its existing liberal trade arrangements with China.

In the political front, President Atambayev has some basic hurdles to cross before he makes Kyrgyzstan a functional country. Primarily, the roles and responsibilities of President, Parliament and judiciary were not well defined. Following Atambayev officially taking up office as President, Kyrgyzstan's fragile ruling coalition collapsed—a development certain to spur frenetic political bargaining. The main ruling Party SDPK faction pulled out of the coalition citing disagreements with its partners on judicial, political and economic reforms. The new coalition was to include as many as four parties and Atambayev was to give the SDPK a mandate to form a new coalition. A new ruling coalition was formed with SDPK, ArNamys, Ata-Meken and Respublika factions. Ata-Jurt party remained in the opposition.

In a first move, Kyrgyz parliamentary Speaker Akhmatbek Keldibekov had to tender his resignation at an extraordinary parliamentary session on December 12, 2011 that was called to discuss results of the findings of a parliamentary commission. Keldibekov was accused of having links to the criminal world and the abuse of power. His resignation followed a no confidence motion against him in the Parliament which was passed with 103-15 votes. After much bargaining, the Parliament elected Asylbek Jeenbekov of SDPK party as the Speaker with 78-25 votes on December 21.

After weeks of political bargaining, Omurbek Babanov of Republika party was able to pull together a new coalition. The Parliament approved the members of the government proposed by Babanov with 113-2 votes. The President appointed Shamil Atahanov as Chairman of the State National Security Committee and Taalaibek Omuraliev as the defence minister. Jantoro Satybaldiev was appointed in place of Emilbek Kaptagaev as the Chief of the President's Administration.

Conclusion

The presidential election came as the culmination of an uprising for political reform and move for democratisation in April 2010. It was held against country's constitutional reforms in the previous year that boosted the role of the Parliament as the main decision-making body but watered down the powers of the President.

However, the institutions of democracy still remained very weak. The politics and the issue of democracy in Kyrgyzstan always remained a dynamic process but the outcomes of these developments have been controversial if not doubtful. The country has though seen fairly good amount of political reforms in the last few years, a shift away from authoritarian model that has prevailed in the country since independence in 1991. A vibrant political culture including the culture of protests by civil societies and political groups exist today in Kyrgyzstan. The country also has a free media. Those who advocated democratic system believed that the presidential election would consolidate parliamentary system. In that sense, presidential election was a peaceful transition of power and a victory for democracy. In fact, in a conference on *Parliament's role in the Development of Kyrgyzstan* held in October 2011, President Otunbayeva cited significant achievements made by the country in building democratic institutions and the rule of law. (This author attended the conference) She said that the path was chosen following the success of democracy in Mongolia but it was still a long way to reach the achievements made by India.

The West particularly viewed the Kyrgyz democratic example a no small achievement in contrast to other Central Asian states where elections are purely formal exercises to lend legitimacy to the ruling elites that remain unchallenged since the Soviet times. Even in the Kyrgyz case, the critics say that in elections in the last two decades, the pattern remained the same until two former Presidents (Kurmanbek Bakiyev and Askar Akayev) were chased out by mobs.

The overall Western assessment was that the Kyrgyz elections would set a democratic precedent for the region[20] a reason why the OSCE and others have been watching the Kyrgyz elections very keenly. The international observers have lauded the wide range of presidential candidates on offer and reforms in electoral legislation in Kyrgyzstan. Douglas Wake, deputy head of the OSCE had said "It is a notable fact that both for Kyrgyzstan and for this region, we have a really active campaign with a large number of candidates who are really offering a competitive choice to voters."[21] Earlier, the US Secretary of State applauded Kyrgyzstan's efforts to establish a democratic government. She said "There are many who say democracy cannot work in Central Asia...we think Kyrgyzstan is proving that it can."[22]

The West also tried to link Kyrgyz developments to terrorism, drugs and general instability that have implications for the entire region. It was often seen that adroit Kyrgyz leaders play the terrorism threat card to draw the Western attention. For months prior to elections, the authorities had been warning about imminent threat from Islamic militants across Afghanistan and Pakistan.

However, some Kyrgyz have been skeptical, if not disillusioned, with the parliamentary system as they see no real change in the country. The coalition governments formed after 2010 collapsed several times and this was hampering the desperately needed economic reforms. Corruption and nepotism continued to hinder any meaningful political and economic reforms. Atambayev had vowed to combat graft but such efforts were hindered by political infightings based on clan and regional loyalties. The country is still one of the poorest in the world. The country's per capita GDP is below $1,000. The economy depends heavily on remittances from migrant workers. More than 10 per cent of the working population emigrates to Russia or Kazakhstan for jobs. Therefore, shades of opinion have emerged with a section of people suggesting that Kyrgyzstan is economically too weak to continue with the parliamentary system and it is viewed neither suitable for a conflict-stricken country. In fact, the new system was proving to be quite expensive for the country, which has no worthwhile resources to export and earn revenue.

Many Kyrgyz still believe that a vital change can come only if a centralised power structure is restored. It is here that both Tashiyev and Madumarov earlier vowed to restore a strong presidency. But, many suspected that this may also be the intention of Atambayev who too had hinted ahead of the election that the Constitution may be amended yet again, perhaps in favour of return to a stronger Presidency. But to justify the overthrow of previous regimes, Atambayev himself supported the idea of a parliamentary system more suited to the nomadic spirit of Kyrgyz people. However, this is not an easy thing and the parliamentary system seemed almost irreversible. Yet, there is always a strong desire for a centralised system which has to do with both Soviet legacy and perhaps also with the Kyrgyz politics of tribalism, which is traditionally anchored solely by one chieftain.

The year 2011 marked the 20th anniversary of the Kyrgyz Republic's independence and during these two decades the country went through a very difficult political transition. The major test has been the transition from a Soviet Republic to a parliamentary democracy, though it had to witnessed two major uprisings, something not known in the former Soviet republics. Following the April 2010 uprising and regime change, Kyrgyzstan saw a deadly ethnic violence. The interim government that came to power after ousting President Kurmanbek Bakiyev held a constitutional referendum, and parliamentary elections. Since then Kyrgyzstan has been coping to function as a parliamentary state, even though it seemed to be a painful process. The new governments that came to rule are seeking to avoid excessive state control over public life and to make the political process more transparent. By changing the constitution, the power and role of future Presidents was watered down. By voluntarily stepping down from the President's post, Roza Otunbayeva paved the way for the first peaceful transfer of power in Central Asia. The presidential elections in Kyrgyzstan on October 30, 2011 marked the completion of that process. The elections took place in an environment of freedom and impartiality.

The new political formation has been able to bring about some positive and promising steps on the path to normalcy. One of the achievements has been the recovery of country's economy from the 1.4 per cent slump in 2010 to above 8.5 per cent growth in GDP in 2011. The growth was attributed to double-digit growth in the mining (especially gold mining), industrial production and utilities. But in the agriculture sector growth was little low. The average monthly salary of a worker grew by 26.9 per cent in 2011. All in all, the government had placed a better tax administration and expansion of tax base. A higher output and export of electricity and global increase in gold prices had added to increase in the revenue earning, which helped the government to contain the budget deficit despite over 30 per cent increase in salaries of the employees in health care sector, social sphere, culture, arts, science, physical education and sports.

The total public debt had reached $2.985 billion in 2011 including external debt of $2.755 billion, which is over 58 per cent of the country's GDP.[23] More than half the total foreign debt consists of commitments to the World Bank, Asian Development Bank (ADB) and IMF. About 44 per cent of the debts included loans from Russia ($490 million), Japan ($330 million) and China ($151 million). The domestic debt was less than six per cent of the total public debt.

The foreign trade turnover also seemed to have increased since the fall of Bakiyev's regime. Gold remains the major export item. Increase in import of energy products was expected by 15.3 per cent. Trade was projected to grow up to $6.4 billion by 2013.

The government announced to implement 40 nation-wide projects worth $8.9 billion during 2012-14 aimed to boost strategic sectors and to create the basis for the long-term development of the country. Construction of China-Kyrgyzstan-Uzbekistan railway is one of the big projects in the transport sector. Other planned projects include development of new deposits of coal, tin and gold, construction of Kambar-Ata-2 hydropower plant and hydropower plants of upper Naryn cascade, construction of Kemin-Almaty high voltage line, Data-Khujand line under CASA-1000 Project, hi-tech parks etc. The Parliament brought amendments to the existing laws on mining and mineral exploration to promote transparency and prevent corruption. The Government also approved a mid-term development program for 2012-14 which includes reduction in number of licenses required for entrepreneurs, reduction and optimisation of government employees, visa regime reforms, and implementation of other state programs. Kyrgyzstan ranked 80th in the 2010 Index of Economic Freedom published by The Heritage Foundation. This had put Kyrgyzstan in the group of countries with moderately free economy. The corruption level in Kyrgyzstan continued to remain on a high level—Kyrgyzstan was on the 164th place among 183 countries, according to the Corruption Perceptions Index 2011 released by the Transparency International.

Some of the important changes brought to effect by the new regime included, an amendment passed by the Parliament of Kyrgyzstan stipulating the President to appoint diplomats and sign international agreements with approval of the Prime Minister. The parliamentary committee for defense and security passed the draft law on Defence Council on February 14, 2011. The new bill defined the legal status of the Defence Council, its objectives, functions and powers of members of the Council. CEC was revamped in July 2011. The Parliament approved the amendments to the existing laws on diplomatic service on November 17, 2011 withdrawing the powers of the President for determining the Kyrgyz Foreign Policy. The amendments prohibit recruitment of close relatives in diplomatic service and restrict the terms of service of ambassadors and other diplomatic representatives of Kyrgyzstan to three years.

On the corruption front, largely due to pressure from leaders of coalition partners and opposition parties, the First vice Prime Minister Omurbek Babanov had to leave office temporarily to enable the PC to investigate the accusations related to Megacom issue against Babanov, though he resumed office after the probe exonerated him of any wrong doing. But when he became Prime Minister of the country, he again became controversial relating his involvement in corruption. Babanov was forced to resign in August 2012 from the post of Prime Minister.

The government had been largely successful in arresting further ethnic violence in southern Kyrgyzstan and stabilising the general law and order situations in the country despite hundreds of political protests by various groups over a variety of national issues. The new regime tried to probe the causes of the June 2010 Osh ethnic riots. The reports though largely blamed local Uzbek leaders and relatives of the former President for instigating the violence, but the authorities also took some of the blames. Roza Otunbayeva apologized to the nation for failing to prevent the violence. However, there have been reports of terrorist activities in various parts of the country including in Bishkek suburb and southern Kyrgyzstan.

The Kyrgyz security agencies revealed that about 400 ethnic Uzbeks from the country were being trained at terror camps in Afghanistan and Pakistan. Under aegis of the CIS Anti-Terror Centre large-scale exercises codenamed Yug-Antiterror-2011 (South-Antiterror-2011) were being conducted in the south. Counter terrorism drills were also held in the Talas and Sokuluk regions of Kyrgyzstan. The law enforcement agencies had also busted several drug trafficking cases in various operations in Osh and Batken provinces.

Kyrgyzstan was inclined to follow an approach that will result into closer political and security integration with Russia. While at the same, it was giving significant importance to China in the economic space. The process of joining the Customs Union with Russia, Kazakhstan, and Belarus had intensified after Putin visited Bishkek in 2012.

Atambayev has repeatedly declared, before and after his election that Kyrgyzstan would not extend the lease on the base after it expires in 2014 and proposed to make it a civilian transit centre together with Russia and other countries. However, since 2012, the Kyrgyz have mellowed down a bit on the issue. Eventually, they are likely to agree to demand for the extension in return for an enhanced rent. But, it will depend upon how other powers like China will provide incentives to the Kyrgyz in return for the closure of the US base.

NOTES

1. *RIA Novosti*, October 29, 2011.
2. There was no indication of which candidate Moscow supported. Almost all the main contenders were visiting Russia to seek blessings from Russian leadership. The rumour of Moscow supporting a strongman with authoritarian style was widespread.
3. *AKIpress*, October 30, 2012.
4. *Kabar*, October 30, 2010.
5. *Akipress,* October 30, 2011.
6. Darya Podolskaya, "Voters file 10 lawsuits against the Central Election Commission in Kyrgyzstan", URL: http://eng.24.kg/politic/2011/10/30/21266.html.
7. Aizada Kutuvea, "Presidential candidates state about outrages during elections in Kyrgyzstan", 24.kg *news agency*, October 30, 2011.
8. "Several candidates declare about use of administrative resources in Kyrgyzstan", *Akipress,* October 30, 2011.
9. URL: http://eng.24.kg/viewpoints/2011/10/30/21261.html.
10. Julia Mazykina, "Elections: who is more equal?", *24.kg news agency*, October 30, 2011.
11. "The current presidential elections in Kyrgyzstan are quite democratic and transparent, despite the technical problems with voting lists –Tabyldy Ackerov", *24.kg news agency*, October 30, 2011.
12. Aizada Kutueva, "Low voter turnout in the south of Kyrgyzstan is most probably connected with the citizens' distrust of the presidential candidates – Dastan Bekeshev", *24.kg news agency*, October 30, 2011.
13. David Trilling, "Kyrgyzstan: Presidential Vote Could Aggravate Regional Rift", October 28, 2011 http://www.eurasianet.org/node/64402.
14. *AKIpress*, October 10, 2011.
15. This was the general impression in the diplomatic circle.
16. The author represented Government of India at the swearing in ceremony of the new Kyrgyz President. Also read "Atambayev Sworn in as Kyrgyz President" RFE/RL - Radio Free Europe/ Radio Liberty: December 1, 2011, http://www.ecoi.net/local_link/206597/326350_de.html.
17. *Presidential Press Release*, December 14, 2011. Also read "Kyrgyz leader sets up anti-corruption agency at national security service", *BBC Monitoring International Reports*, December 14, 2011.
18. *KyrTAg*, Bishkek, in Russian December 14, 2011.
19. For details see *Khabar* and *AKIpress*, 1 December 2011. *Radio Free Europe/Radio Liberty (RFE/RL)* December 1, 2011 and also see http://www.universalnewswires.com/centralasia/general/viewstory.aspx?id=10843.
20. Peter Leonard, "Voters in Kyrgyzstan cast presidential ballots", *Associated Press,* October 29, 2011.
21. Ibid.
22. "U.S. Secretary of State Hillary Clinton applauded the country's efforts to establish a democratic government", *Associated Press,* December 12, 2010.
23. Daniyar Karimov, "Kyrgyzstan's foreign debt exceeds $2.6 B", *24.kg news agency*, May 25, 2011.

CHAPTER 5

Islamic Extremism

In addition to the ethnic rivalries, Kyrgyzstan has a nascent Islamic extremist movement in its southern regions. For a long period the specter of Islamic extremism in Central Asia, especially in the Fergana Valley had been part of the discourse on the region. Scores of books on the subject have been written on the issue since the early 1990s. The discourse has focused on the prospects of the radicalisation of Hizb-ut-Tahrir (HuT) in the region.[1] The HuT has been advocating the creation of an Islamic Caliphate in Central Asia. The West has expressed concern about this growing phenomenon, so has also Russia. There has been sufficient literature available on the growth of political Islam and also on extremism in the Fergana Valley. The past literatures have suggested that Fergana had turned into a key sanctuary for extremists fleeing from Pakistani tribal belt and Afghanistan.

The Valley, which astrides borders of several countries, has been critical to regional security.[2] But countries, Uzbekistan, Tajikistan and Kyrgyzstan, that share the Fergana Valley have not been able contain infiltrations due to growing internal discords and effective border management systems. The growth of HuT and Islamic Movement of Uzbekistan (IMU) has also been directly attributed to growing economic crisis, poverty, rising population and rising unemployment after the Soviet collapse. The HuT and IMU have been skillfully using the public discontent to strengthen their cadres. Most analysts have been underlining that the populations demoralised by the regimes have looked towards political Islam as an alternative for justice, wellbeing, and internationalism. A UN envoy to the region, Miroslav Jenca had said that extremists were rushing into Central Asia to exploit social and economic problems there.[3]

The analysts have long been arguing that growing authoritarianism of the Central Asian governments will ultimately result in the spurt of radical groups opposing the ruling regimes like what has been happening in the Arab world in the recent years.[4] Some new forecast studies on the rise of political Islam have come out recently from the indigenous sources.[5] In fact, the trend had emerged soon after the Soviet disintegration, especially in Southern Central Asia, where

Islam traditionally had strong presence. In Tajikistan, Islamic parties shared power since the civil war broke there in mid-1990s. The bombings in Tashkent in 1999 and the incursions of the Islamic Movement of Uzbekistan (IMU) into Batken region in southern Kyrgyzstan heightened the fears of extremist threat. Since 2005, there have been series of anti-government violent protests in Uzbekistan and also several such attempts in Kyrgyzstan and elsewhere. These protests were fuelled by HuT and IMU cadre especially by exploiting the anti-government sentiments of people living in Uzbekistan's eastern regions of Fergana, Namangan, Andijan and Kokand. It is also well know that these groups have close nexus with the drug syndicate. Lately, even Kazakhstan has witnessed terrorist acts committed by Islamic groups.

In the context of Kyrgyzstan, the fear was that the perpetual internal instability will allow Islamic groups to thrive. This is partly true. It is also because Kyrgyzstan has been practicing a relatively liberal polity, openness and free press. But, so far, the situation in Kyrgyzstan has not been that bad. Most people, even in southern Kyrgyzstan, remain secular and those who are devout Muslims typically follow a more moderate and ritualistic Islamic practice, rather than the extremist form of Islam followed in Afghanistan and Pakistan.

Kyrgyzstan does not have a proper database on religious organisations. But according to the Religious Studies Centre that quoted an official information of having eight terrorist organisations, which are banned in the country since 2005. They include; HuT, Turkistan Liberation Organisation (TLO), Islamic Party of East Pakistan, IMU, Al-Qaeda, Taliban, Kurdish Labour Party, and Jihad Group.[6] In 2012, the number of terrorist outfits banned in the country remained the same, but the blacklist of the Kyrgyz State Committee for National Security (GKNB) contained other organisations like the Unification Church, Islamic Jihad Union and Tabliqi Jamaat as well.[7] According to the GKNB Chairman Shamil Atakhanov the most dangerous outfit was the HuT and other groups that advocated *Jihadism* in Kyrgyzstan. The Tabliqi Jamaat, which was most widespread in the country, according to the officials, posed no extremist threat. According to some statistics, over 10,000 Kyrgyz were registered members of the banned extremist groups. The officials admitted that these banned terrorist groups continue to operate their activities under cover of different social funds. There were endless names of *Jihadi* outfits that kept cropping up in the media. However, it was always difficult to verify their existence in the absence of proper information.

What was different in the case of Kyrgyzstan was that the repeated political uprisings and the so called revolutions have rather made the Islamists to come out in open. Their activities were more visible because of lesser restriction and state control, which still does not exist in the neighbouring Uzbekistan and Kazakhstan. Many experts have also been articulating that with the easing of religious restrictions, such as in Kyrgyzstan, the appeal of group like HuT was bound to dwindle.

Within the region, many analysts have argued that the bogey of Islamic threat had been raised by various interests groups for different political reasons. For example, Russian media had been regularly putting up news and analysis about Islamic radicalism. The main message has been that political Islam would bring the country like Kyrgyzstan to the brink of a civil war and in the process the whole region will be affected. An Osh-based independent political analyst Ganijon Kholmatov was quoted by RFE/RL in 2005 as saying that Russian media articulations were politically motivated. According to Kholmatov, after playing a failed game in Ukraine and Georgia, Russia was repeating a propaganda game suggesting that Central Asia is going to be embraced by Islamic extremism.[8] Russian commentators also contended that Islam and drug mafias were being patronised by the Americans to destabilise the region.

It has been opinioned by many observers that HuT though suffers credibility problem within the Muslim world, draws unusually large interest in Central Asia, especially among the intellectuals and media.[9] The media has been largely blamed for keeping the HuT in the limelight among Central Asians. There has been also a lot of academic research on HuT in the academia and elsewhere in Central Asia. The stories on HuT are said to draw the interests of general public as well.

In Kyrgyzstan's case again, the problem seemed less to do with extremism but more to do with ethnicity, especially the ethnic Uzbeks living in Osh and Jalalabad regions bordering with Uzbekistan. Attribution here was that Islam was more embedded among the ethnic Uzbeks as compared to Kyrgyz people who traditionally followed a mix of Shamanism with Islamic tenet. That is why, every time a crisis emerged in Kyrgyzstan, apprehensions were raised about the large scale disorder by ethnic Uzbeks. But, so far, there have been no indication of Islamic extremist forces actually playing a substantial political role in Kyrgyzstan. As the author could assess, political Islam, such as the power of HuT was unlikely to become a reality at least in the near term. Many experts also believed that even if Kyrgyzstan as a State collapses, the Islamists will not become a unifying force. This was even true for the southern Kyrgyzstan where despite the rampant ethnic and political crisis that have emerged so far in the wake of revolutions, the role of Islamic extremist groups were rarely noticed. It was a different matter that the chaotic political and economic situation has allowed HuT to attract more supporters for the organisation.

More importantly, the problem in Kyrgyzstan was associated with the way the country had introduced a liberal political outlook as compared to others. The early experiment with liberal democracy has been the primary reason for Kyrgyzstan to become a fragile if not failed state in the region. The democratic system, which is yet to be understood fully by the people, has induced rampant corruption in the system as well as in the society. The so called two revolutions have only added to its failing process. As elaborated elsewhere, the revolutions were being described as coup sorts; the same old officials coming back to power in a different format with different slogan.

Moreover, being a young state Kyrgyzstan seemed unable to deal with complexities of religion, state and societies. The State had been taking steps from one extreme to the other. The trends so far have indicated that the regimes have a tendency to either flirt with religious groups or comedown heavily on their activities depending on the political exigency. This is like in any democracy where the political groups rally support from any sources to gain political power. While doing so, the leadership has been gaining political dividends but they have been losing strategically to the extremists. In 2005, Bakiyev came to power on the plank of nationalism and played the Islamic card. He was hobnobbing with the extremists and drug mafia when they suited him. But, when the criminal gangs and extremists went beyond control and threatened his power, he came down heavily on them. Hundreds of extremist elements were in jail when Bakiyev was thrown out in April 2010.

Yet again, the increasing nexus between the enforcement agencies and organised criminal groups could be added as another factor contributing to the State's failing process. A report by Chatham House noted the drug factor having exacerbated the Osh events. The International Narcotics Control Strategy Report (INCSR) published on the site of the U.S. Department of State in 2011 had illustrated that the drug and crime situation, if continues, will destabilise the new regime in Kyrgyzstan, which was facing depleted financial resources and political turmoil. The report has said that 30 per cent of Kyrgyzstan, which is a key transit country to transport Afghan opiates to Europe, Russia and China remain virtually uncontrolled.[10] In Kyrgyzstan alone cannabis is grown in almost one hundred thousand hectares of land. It said that in 2010 no measure was taken to curb narcotics trafficking. In 2009, the authorities seized nearly eight tons of drugs and precursors but the figure declined by 41 per cent in 2010. Apart from the rise in drug baron-politician nexus, the problem was also accentuated by underfunding and understaffing of the Kyrgyz security agencies. Kyrgyzstan has 9,000 officers for a population of 5.5 million.

Extremism and Politics

The discourse on Islamic extremism and terrorism in Kyrgyzstan has always been polarised. As mentioned above and also opinion expressed by many informed circles, the threat of extremism had always been deliberately ratcheted up by the authorities for political exigency. In fact, all regimes in the region are notoriously known for conveniently playing up and even fabricating the threat of terrorism.

In the aftermath of June 2010 riots in Osh, the Kyrgyz authorities at one stage blamed the Islamists and the Uzbek irredentist for initiating the violence. Of course, the main needle of suspicion was pointed at the former President, Kurmanbek Bakiyev and his son Maxim Bakiyev who were accused of spending

$10 million for instigating the riot with the help of the Islamic extremists.[11] Both IMU and HuT were separately blamed for creating instability to pursue their radical agenda. The officials cited initially agent provocateurs with sniper-shooter infiltrated from Badakhshan across the border with Tajikistan. However, this could not be confirmed by the Kyrgyz security agencies due to lack of credible evidence.[12] Besides, no other country, including Uzbekistan, Russia, Kazakhstan and US had supported the view of the IMU and United Islamic Jihad (UIJ) having instigated the violence. No comments came from the Afghan officials, NATO and others about terrorist movement around Badakhshan during that time. However, Uzbekistan did mention about the role of a third force but it didn't perhaps mean the role of IMU.[13] So far, several inquiry reports including the one conducted by an international investigation committee had ruled out the role of Islamic extremists and instead pinned on local reasons that got flared up due to absence of law and order. The national commission that had investigated the Osh events held the Uzbeks minority responsible for the ensuing tragedy. The Commission listed Bakiyev's associates, religious extremists, criminal groups, inept officials of the interim government and 'unknown forces' (intelligence services of third countries) which played major role in inflaming the violence. This aspect is being elaborated in a separate chapter.

As expected and also in a significant way, Kyrgyzstan had witnessed a spate of terrorist incidents soon after the new government assumed power in 2010. This had raised the specter of possible Islamic threat with wide implications. While the overall political stability seemingly had been restored, security officials cited a new *Jihadi* group Jaysh al-Mahdi (JaM) that has emerged on the scene to challenge the State with armed resistance. The crackdown was laid following the killing of three policemen on January 4, 2011, bomb blast on November 30, 2010, armed assault at an American citizen and attempt to blast a City Police Station on December 25.[14] A blast rocked outside the sports complex in Bishkek—the venue of a high-profile trial against 26 top officials of the former government accused of killing dozens of people during a popular uprising in April. According to reports, the improvised explosive device without shrapnel exploded in Bishkek. State National Security Service Chief had linked the Bishkek blast to the Osh event and detention of Islamic groups.

There were several terrorist attacks in southern Kyrgyzstan as well. In fact, the security situation got heightened after a clash broke out on November 29, 2010 in Osh between security forces and Islamic militants. Three insurgents were shot in an operation while another militant blew himself up. Officials said the militants were believed to be members of the Islamic Movement of Turkestan. They belonged to different ethnic origins: Kyrgyz, Uzbeks and one Russian. They were planning a series of terrorist attacks in the country. Two policemen were injured in a gun battle during the raid. The Kyrgyz State National Security Service Chief revealed submachine guns, grenades and other improvised explosive devices were found at shootout scene in Osh. The Security Service also revealed that a terrorist group comprising of about 40 men had planned more than 30 acts in Kyrgyzstan.[15] They had planned to hit eight places in Bishkek, 14 places in Osh city and 11 places in Osh oblast. Eight people were detained, three of which were detained in Bishkek. Three terrorists were killed in Osh including the imam of the Farkhat Nurmatov mosque.[16] The terrorist group comprised of ethnic Russians (Muslim converts), Uzbek and Kyrgyz nationals belonging to the Islamic Jihad Union (IJU) and IMU. A part of the group had fled to Russia. However, the authorities maintained some secrecy and never divulged the full details. But, many suspected that there was possible involvement of former officials in organising the incidents. It was mentioned that some of the extremists had undergone training in Tajikistan's Tavildarinskiy region. The security agencies had averted other incidents of terror attacks in Osh and Bishkek and it did appear that the Kyrgyz authorities had managed to quelled terror attacks. Obviously, no report came about the ethnic angle. But, events that occurred in sequence did suggest that extremist groups were gaining strong grounds in Southern Kyrgyzstan.[17]

Interestingly, Kyrgyz authorities this time revealed a new outfit Jaysh al-Mahdi (JaM) "the Army of the Righteous Ruler" that was found to have links with Chechen and Ingushetia extremists, inspired by the ideas of Alexander Tikhomirov, a Russian convert to Islam who was born in Buryatia—a home to majority Buddhists. Alexander Tikhomirov was also known as Sayyid Buryatsky who headed radical movement in North Caucasus. Tikhomirov was killed in Ingushetia in March 2010. The JaM consisted only of ethnic Kyrgyz and the weapons used by them were those lost by the authorities during April 2010 revolution. National Security Chief said "a war has been declared on all of us" and that "evil is wearing the mask of a believer."[18] The JaM, officials revealed, had planned to hit even foreign embassies in Bishkek. (In November end the diplomatic Missions received a Note Verbal with the warning of growing terrorist threat and necessity to take precautionary measures.)

On a serious note, President Otunbayeva had announced that extremists may lay claims for power in the absence of a proper defence mechanism. Kyrgyz PM Atambayev too echoed a similar point when he said excessive nationalism was causing a serious threat to the country even to the point of disintegration of the state. He was referring to ethnic Uzbeks and Tajiks being more loyal to the neighbouring countries. Obviously, the situation was not good in the southern parts of the country.[19]

The reported terrorist events had led the Government to embark on a heightened measure including the setting up an Anti-Terror Centre. The Security Council was abolished to create the Defence Council (DC). The first meeting of DC underscored that (a) criminal and terrorist activities grew significantly during 2010, (b) unresolved border demarcation hampered border security, (c) drug trafficking across Afghanistan contributed towards escalation of tension.[20] The

DC, inter alia, recommended that country's innumerable mosques be subjected to screenings and local imams be vetted to assess their competence.[21] The governor of Osh Region had proposed to bring mosques under the government and offered to pay salaries to clergymen from the state budget as one of the measures.[22] Some fifty Kyrgyz *imams*, mostly from the south, had either resigned or were removed by the new government.[23]

The explosion underscored tensions in Kyrgyzstan and possibly took place against the backdrop of the following:

1. Events took place after the new regime took over in 2010. Possibly, the theory of pro-Bakiyev forces taking avenge may have been the cause, though nothing has been proved to that effect.
2. The role of Uzbeks was suspected as they were angry against the interim-government for orchestrating the June 2010 ethic riots in Osh and the atrocities committed against the Uzbeks following the ethnic violence.
3. There may have been genuine terrorist threats emanating from various sources. After all, to appease the extremists, the interim-government after assuming power in April 2010 reversed the Bakiyev's harsh policies and issued blanket amnesty to those previously convicted under terrorism. To gain popularity, not only had it toned down rhetoric against Islamists but also used them for electoral gains. These terrorists who were freed from jail may have decided to challenge the state. Initially, the political groups were busy squabbling for power. But when the deal was done to form the government, the authorities decided to exercise the Bakiyev-style crackdown and even blame Islamists for country's security woes. Among others things, the screening of *imams* had commenced since March 2011.
4. The security crackdowns were viewed as necessary steps to exert control over the country which was yet to come to terms with several shocks faced after political and ethnic related crisis in 2010. New protest potential was growing amidst people losing confidence in their leaders.
5. The incidents occurred when the country was witnessing strong undercurrents of inter and intra-party rivalries. Many suspected that it was part of the sensitive political bargaining over the formation of a new government. The power struggle among major clans had at one stage forced President to hint at even dissolving the Parliament. It only indicated that all was not well with the newly formed parliamentary system.
6. The Kyrgyz ruling elite may have been possibly using terrorism as a selling point to get external aid.[24] The economy of the country was in bad shape. The June violence had severely hurt the economic growth prospects as foreign investors were shying away. Many investors were virtually driven away by the new regime for having links with the previous dispensation. Almost 50 per cent of the country's national income

depended on remittances from migrant workers in Russia. About a third of the population lived below the poverty level. Economic issues any way gain prominence during the spring sowing seasons. After the June 2010 events, the donor countries though had committed over a $1 billion aid, but they were not forthcoming. During Secretary Clinton's visit in early March 2011, Bishkek projected itself as a front-line state for war against terror. A section of Kyrgyz politicians were keen to retain the US Transit Centre at Manas and play it as an important Kyrgyz contribution in the fight against terrorism in Afghanistan. The assertion had coincided with a meeting between Kyrgyz PM and US Deputy Assistant Secretary Susan Elliott. The Kyrgyz-US security consultation was resumed and Bishkek was looking for every opportunity to extract maximum concession over Manas air base, especially over fuel tax issues. It needed to be underscored that these terrorist attacks took place weeks before US Secretary of State Clinton was to visit Bishkek.[25] Otunbayeva also made a point during the Clinton visit that by spring (2011) the theater of military actions in Afghanistan would be shifting to the north that would pose a greater challenge for Kyrgyzstan.

7. Most analysts, the author had interacted, made the assertion that the local *Jamats* in Kyrgyzstan were still moderate in outlook and the deteriorating security problem, if existed, was attributed to the simmering ethnic tensions as well as political rivalry within. Many viewed the new measures for curtailing religion as a thinly disguised attempt to silence or purge opponents—many of them Uzbek—on the pretext of fighting against terrorism.[26]
8. The terrorist attacks could have been linked to unfairness seen in the trial of accused connected to the April 2010 violence that killed 80 people.[27] Over 20 former government officials of the Bakiyev regime were among the accused. The human rights activists had alleged that confessions of detainees were obtained through torture.
9. A perspective also came to the fore that the authorities were simply showing its enthusiasm to fight against terrorism for the sake of seeking funds from SCO, CSTO and other international institutions. President Roza Otunbayeva had vociferously raised the security issue at the SCO, OSCE, CIS and CSTO meetings and urged the organisations to redouble their efforts to assist Kyrgyzstan in its fight against terrorism and extremism.[28] Otunbayeva had asserted for changes in the CSTO's legal framework and sought the deployment of Collective Rapid Response Forces (CRRF) in member states to deal with localised military conflicts.[29] In fact, in the CSTO Summit in December 2010, Russian Foreign Minister did state that Kyrgyzstan has become a test of the organisation's future.[30]
10. The events took place when Kyrgyzstan and Russia had contemplated

> the idea of opening an anti-terrorist centre at one of the southern regions of Kyrgyzstan to reinforce security system. Talks were also held for the possible opening of the second Russian military base in the south Kyrgyzstan. In May 2010, the US was planning to build an anti-terror training centre in the southern Kyrgyz province of Batken. Russia also sounded that Kyrgyzstan should quickly join the Eurasian Union[31] citing reasons that the country cannot bring order by itself.

Interestingly, when the Kyrgyz parliament debated the issue, there were many flip-flops. The end result of the debate was that the JaM operatives were termed as "criminals" instead of "terrorists".[32] The officials earlier claimed that JaM operatives had received training in Pakistan and Afghanistan, but following a parliamentary hearing on January 12, 2011, Security Chief had replaced Pakistan with Tajikistan. At several occasions, the Pakistani Ambassador was seen objecting to the Kyrgyz President about against Kyrgyz officials naming Pakistan.

For many Kyrgyz analysts, Islamic presence was already a reality in Kyrgyzstan. Curbing the activities of IMU and HuT were unlikely to be helpful. The belief among the extremist groups was that the existing regimes would eventually decay themselves without any external impact. However, any hard measures by the State would only risk of inciting them to take violent path thus turning Kyrgyzstan into another Dagestan. Some observers viewed that should the new parliamentary system fail to swiftly carry out radical reforms, there could be every possibility of another revolution in Kyrgyzstan and this time it is going be with an Islamic fervour.[33]

The US-Russia jostling for geostrategic space was also attributed for exacerbating the Kyrgyz situation. Several right wing groups have been strongly opposing the American and Russian military presence in Kyrgyzstan. If the situation persists, many feel that Kyrgyzstan would be on the way to becoming another Pakistan. As mentioned before, the terrorist attacks in Bishkek took place weeks before Clinton's visit.

However, it was also visibly clear that the Kyrgyz society was slowly getting Islamised, especially in the rural areas where the Islamists have been carrying intense activities to recruit children and women in their organisations. Islam was not only replacing public and state institutions but also education. The HuT's influence was creeping into every level of Kyrgyz society and power structures not only in Osh region, but also all over Kyrgyzstan. The HuT has been recruiting students of prestigious universities, including the Kyrgyz State Medical Academy (KSMA) and the Kyrgyz State Construction, Transport and Architecture University in Bishkek. Regular lessons were given on one-to-one basis through websites.[34]

The authorities have been revealing almost on monthly basis the emergence of new *Jihadi groups* all over the country.[35]

Kyrgyz authorities also indicated that Haqqani Network had penetrated Kyrgyzstan. This was revealed by Emil Zheenbekov, head of the Interior Ministry's

Directorate for Counter terrorism.[36] No specific data was provided by the authorities, but they explained that the Pakistan-Afghanistan based network used methods somewhat different from the rest. The network co-operated with members of the underworld, especially with drug mafia. There was no clear indication that Haqqani Network had actually penetrated Kyrgyzstan but media extensively reported the terrorist outfit opening branches in Central Asia with the help of criminal groups. In 2009-10, even Dawood Ibrahim is said to have visited Kyrgyzstan to set up business and interestingly he was hosted by former President's son Maksim Bakiyev.

Among the most active religious movements in Kyrgyzstan included Tabliqi Jamaat organisation that has widespread network in the country.[37] Tabliqi received funding from abroad. However, it has not been showing any radical manifestation. The officials also admitted that Tabliqi posed no terrorist threat to the country. In 2011 the activities of Tabliqi Jamaat was more open and widespread. It had 18,000 registered members. The aim of Tabliqi too is to establish an Islamic State in Kyrgyzstan.

According to the Kyrgyz Interior Ministry, the activities of some extremist and terror organisations had gone up. In July 2012, 1,473 supporters of extremist organisations were registered by the Kyrgyz Interior Ministry.[38] According to the Ministry; the activists also included youth who were leaving for Arab countries for religious training. The authorities suspected that they were getting trained in religious extremism. Even in the urban areas, extremist tendencies were growing. In fact, in June 2012, a video address in Russian titled *Declaration of jihad against President Almazbek Atambaev* was posted on websites.[39] The activist had accused the President of violation of Sharia norms, namely worship of national hero Manas and erection of the monument to Manas.

The State National Security Committee had put out a figure of 200 websites operated by the extremist groups in the country.[40] The Interior Ministry had revealed that between 2005 and 2010, over 1,000 active members of radical extremist organisations were identified and detained.[41] Over 700 faced criminal proceedings. They had put strength of 7,000 supporters of extremist and terrorist organisations.

The officials revealed 72 per cent of *imams* did not have religious education, 25 per cent have general secondary education and only five per cent have higher religious education. There was no standard set for degree and the *imams* practiced religion at will. Some *imams* received religious education in Uzbekistan, Tajikistan, Russia, Turkey, Egypt, Saudi Arabia, Kuwait, Lebanon, and Pakistan. According to official data, over 1,000 people are studying at 30 foreign theological and foreign educational institutions. Most of them went through unofficial channels. The Prime Minister even stated that Kyrgyz have a different culture and there was no need for Muslims to emulate the Pakistani dress code.

The Kyrgyz media had begun reporting on the spurt of extremists activities in southern Kyrgyzstan following the Osh incidents in June 2010. Security experts frequently commented about the elements of the IMU gathering strength in southern Kyrgyzstan and were establishing links with terrorist camps in Rasht Valley (Tajikistan).[42] The IMU was said to have undergone a transformation and had become more robust outfit with broader outreach and goals.[43] Its foot soldiers are trained in the FATA region of Pakistan, which included recruits from Uzbekistan, Tajikistan and Kyrgyzstan.[44]

Kyrgyz experts on Islamic affairs suggest that *Jihadi* culture is spreading at an unprecedented rate and is threatening the secular regimes. The degree of frustration and discontent among people is said to be high in Tajikistan and Kyrgyzstan where the states are failing in carrying out political, social and economic reforms. Professor Kadyr Malikov of Madrid University has forecasted that Wahhabism can erupt in the north of Kyrgyzstan mainly in Chui province and Bishkek.[45] Malikov thought the influence of extremists will gradually cover all aspects of public life from politics and culture to business.

Interestingly an indigenous report entitled *Central Asia-2020: opinions from within* released in Almaty on August 20, 2012 noted that an Islamic Caliphate might emerge in Central Asia either as a single whole or at least in some parts of the region.[46] The report was prepared by well-known strategic experts that included Rustam Burnashev, Director, Kazakh Institute of Political Decisions, Yerlan Karin, Political Scientist, Sanat Kush kumbayev of the Institute of Strategic Studies, Aleksandr Sobyanin, head of the strategic planning service of the Russian Association of Border Cooperation and other specialists from Central Asian countries.

The report said a wave of Islamic opposition with support from outside is likely to emerge to challenge the ruling regimes. The document asserted that Islamists might come to power through street protests and revolutions. The report suggested that the probability of that scenario was no more than at the level of five per cent currently, but in the mid-and-long term the probability of the creation of Islamic Caliphate will grow from five to 30 per cent. The report noted that political Islam in Central Asia was presently at a formative stage—gradually expanding the network, resource base, viable and political demands to emerge as an alternative to the current authoritarian regimes. The experts believed that the greater threat from the Islamists is posed to Kazakhstan and Kyrgyzstan.

At least, in the case of Central Asian, a forecast is being made through a careful study based on the merging trend in the region. This is unlike the collapse of the Soviet Union itself and also the recent case of the Arab Spring that took everyone by surprise. In the case of Kyrgyzstan, the process of Islamisation of its polity is likely to be faster due to democratic transition.

Islamisation of Kyrgyzstan

As being illustrated above the growth of religion especially Islam has been quite rapid in Kyrgyzstan. A number of factors have contributed to this phenomenon. According to Constitution, the Kyrgyz Republic is independent, democratic, law-governed, secular, and unitary state. Article 7 of the Constitution says none of the religions can be set as state religion. Article 4 forbids formation of political party on religious grounds.

Experts point out that over the years the number of mosques has exceeded the number of schools. It appeared that Kyrgyzstan does not have a proper database on religious organisations. According to official information, Kyrgyz were Muslims and all Russians were Orthodox. Official statistics given by the State Commission for Religious Affairs, the country had 1,886 registered Islamic organisations.[47] A total of 2,270 religious organizations had registration in 2011. These included 1,881 societies, centres, foundations, 82 religious education institutions, 329 fraternities and sisterhoods. Islamic organisations constitute 1,886 while Christian organisations 368. In 2011, according to the Chief Mufti Chubakazhy Zhalilov, the number of mosques was 2050 and over 3,000 imams are working. Kyrgyzstan has three Islamic universities, seven institutes and fifty two *madrasas.*[48] Over 3000 registered religious organisations were operating in Kyrgyzstan in 2012.[49] Kyrgyzstan's State Commission for Religious Affairs (SCRA) had registration of 138 organisations which were allowed to operate legally in the country. The Religion Law has existed since 2009.

The graphics below illustrates the number of religious organisations put out the on-line edition by *Tazabek* with assistance of the EU-UNDP New Legal Framework Project.[50]

The number of mosques and religious organisations has grown rapidly in the country. Almost all the villages throughout the country have more than four-five mosques on an average. The Kara-Suy district of Osh province alone had 136 mosques and 124 religious schools.[51] As the graphics indicates that the maximum number of Islamic organisations are concentrated in the south, especially in Osh and Jalalabad regions.

Over the years, Islam was aggressively challenging the Kyrgyz traditional pagan religion that revolved around shamanism; worshiping of *Tengir* (sky worship) as well ancestral worship of their national hero the Manas king.[52] In fact, there is still legal tussle between Islamists and Tengirist, the former accusing the letter of subverting the growth of Islam.

As mentioned before the influence of groups like the HuT and TabliqiJamaat was creeping into every level of Kyrgyz society and power structures all over Kyrgyzstan. The HuT has been actively recruiting youth, especially women from schools and universities. Regular lessons were given on one-to-one basis through websites.[53] Often the followers gathered at city parks, cafes and public squares. Of course, there are competitions among various strains of Islam; mostly sponsored

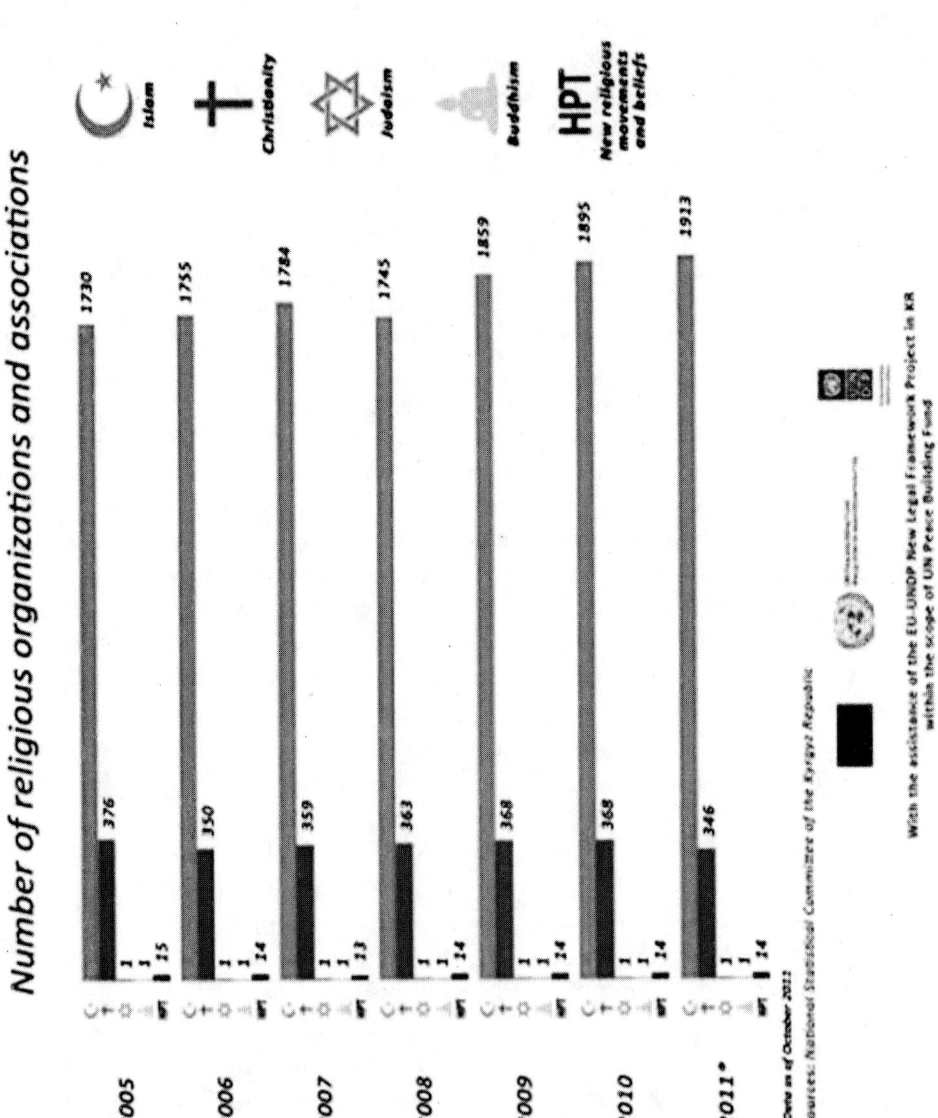
Number of religious organizations and associations
Islam
Christianity
Judaism
Buddhism
HPT
New religious movements and beliefs
2005
1730
376
1
1
15
2006
1755
350
1
1
14
2007
1784
359
1
1
13
2008
1745
363
1
1
14
2009
1859
368
1
1
14
2010
1895
368
1
1
14
2011*
1913
346
1
1
14
*Data as of October 2011
Sources: National Statistical Committee of the Kyrgyz Republic
With the assistance of the EU-UNDP New Legal Framework Project in KR
within the scope of UN Peace Building Fund

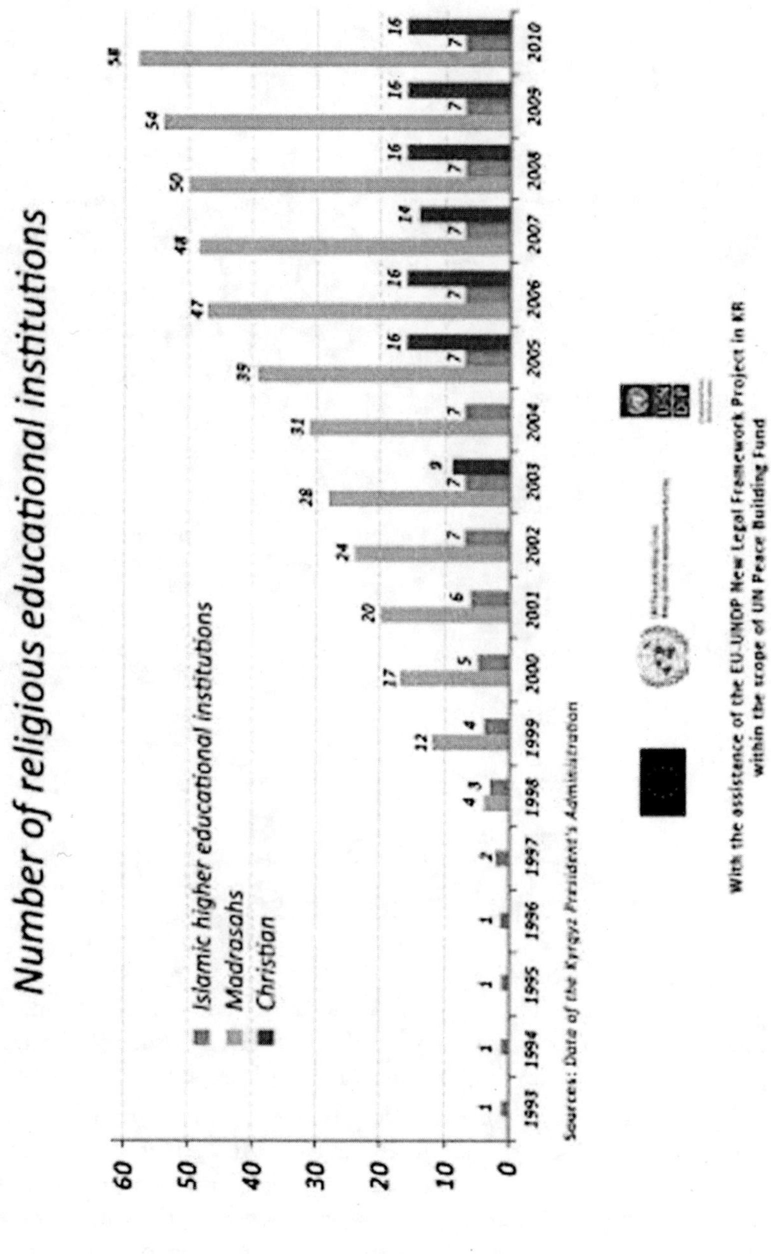
Number of religious educational institutions
Islamic higher educational institutions
Madrasahs
Christian
60
50
40
30
20
10
0
1993
1994
1995
1996
1997
1998
1999
2000
2001
2002
2003
2004
2005
2006
2007
2008
2009
2010
1
1
1
1
2
4
3
12
4
17
5
20
6
24
7
28
7
9
31
7
39
7
16
47
7
16
48
7
14
50
7
16
54
7
16
58
7
16
Sources: Data of the Kyrgyz President's Administration
With the assistance of the EU-UNDP New Legal Framework Project in KR
within the scope of UN Peace Building Fund

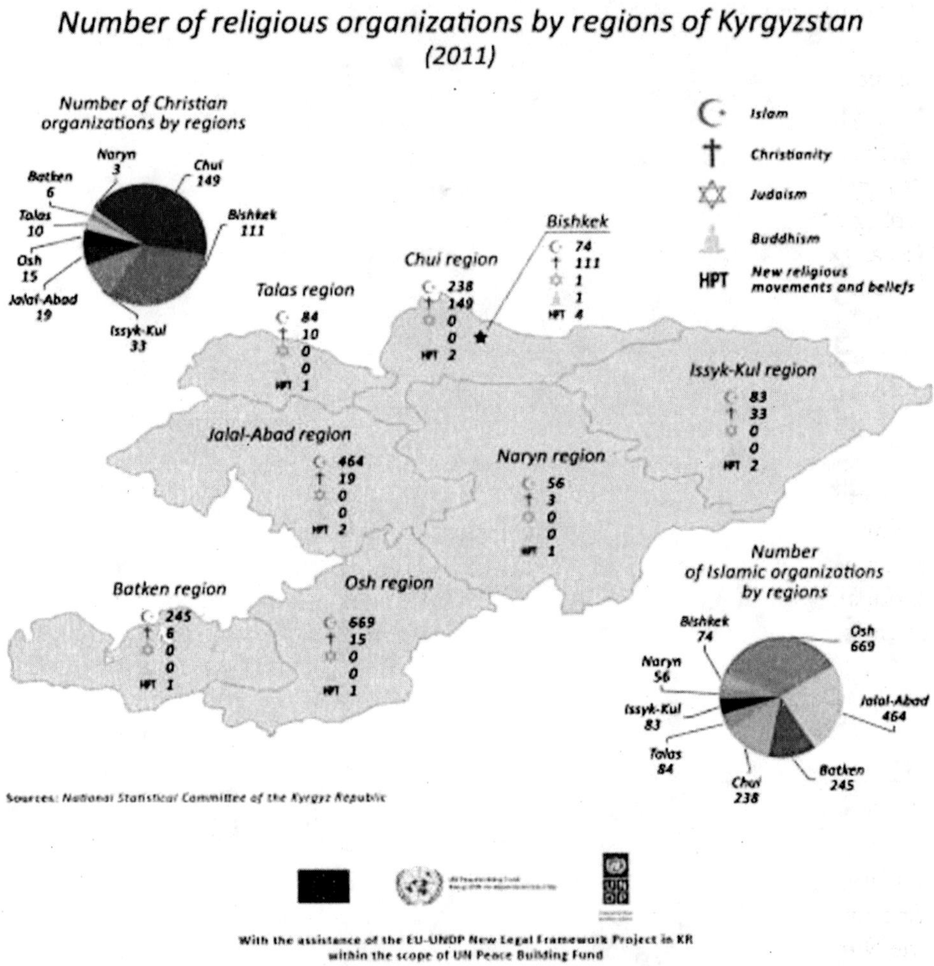

by foreign sources. Turkey, Saudi Arabia and other Arab countries were spending millions of dollars for building mosques in Kyrgyzstan. The Tabliqi Jamaat too has a widespread network in the country.[54] Tabliqi received funding from abroad. However, it has not been showing any radical manifestation.

Most of the Kyrgyz *imams* were receiving religious education in Uzbekistan, Tajikistan, Russia, Turkey, Egypt, Saudi Arabia, Kuwait, Lebanon, and Pakistan. Many have been visiting Tabliqi Jamaat Centre in Nizamuddin in Delhi in the guise of tourists. Bangladesh and Indonesia were other destinations where the young imams were getting trained. According to official data, over 1,000 people are studying at 30 foreign theological and foreign educational institutions. Most of them went through unofficial channels. The National Security Committee (NSC) revealed that children aged between 10 and 15 from Naryn region (Eastern

Kyrgyzstan) were taken by Tabliqi Jamaat to Bangladesh for religious training.[55] The Prime Minister even stated that Kyrgyz have a different culture and there was no need for Muslims to emulate the Pakistani dress code. There was speculation about early entry of Wahhabism even in the north of Kyrgyzstan.[56]

While the Tabliqis and Wahhabis/Salafis had been spreading the extremist version of Islamic practices, there were other groups such as the Turkish groups Nurgus that propagated moderate form of Islam. In fact, in Central Asia, the struggle for dominance within the non-Shia sects, particularly between the Arab (Salafi) and Turkish (Hanafi) missionaries have intensified. Whereas, the Shias have not shown much activism for proselytisation drive in the last two decades in the region. However, within Sunni variant, rivalry (ideological, sectarian, national, economic) persist aimed at influencing the spaces traditionally practicing Sufism, Tengirism, and Communism.

In the early 1990s, the Muslims in the former Soviet space (Azerbaijan, Turkmenistan, Uzbekistan, Kazakhstan, and Kyrgyzstan) have been lenient toward Turkish missionaries, even though some Muslims in the countries were traditionally followers of Shia sect. The Turkish groups were initially getting strong in these states, which tended to check the extremist Wahabbi variant. In general, Turkish groups always sought to reconcile Muslim and Modernity. Certainly, Turkish Islamic teachings had gone in parallel with Turkish nationalism.

The Nurjus are Turkish Muslims who follow the teachings of Said Osman Nurior Fetullah Gulen. Many young Turkish Muslims have been advocating Nurju in Central Asia since 1990s. They were mostly active in schools, colleges and business firms. The Nurju activities are funded by Nurjubusiness groups across Turkey.

Nurjus are said to be related to the Naqshbandya Sufi brotherhood, traditionally rooted in the region. Nurjus runs the Azis Mahmud Khudai Endowment that carries out a lot of charity works in the region. In Central Asia, the Nurjus or Nurjulars function in the name of Khezemet that has a large network with wide membership. The Khezemet aims to establish a stable, pro-Turkish environment in Central Asia. They conduct activities through clandestine operations. The membership is drawn from state institutions and business elite, who are able to lobby for promoting political and economic interests. Essentially, the Nurjulars works for countering Wahabbi and Tabliqi Jamaat activities sponsored by Saudis, Pakistanis and Egyptians in Central Asia. The group also works anti-Chinese interests while encouraging pan-Turkic ideas amongst the Uighurs in Central Asia.

Nurjus were and still are fairly successful in Kazakhstan but elsewhere such as in Uzbekistan, the Turkish group faced resentment from traditional Hanafi followers.[57] The Nurju schools are a bit elitist in orientation and as such enjoy less popularity among traditional Muslims. There was also resentment in Kyrgyzstan for Nurju for it practiced far stricter version of Islam than the Kyrgyz own version which was far more moderate in interpretation. The Nurjus are said to be a part of CIA operation in Central Asia.[58] Currently, the Tabliqis and Wahhabis and other Saudi and Pakistani sponsored groups pose greater challenge to the secular groups like the Nurjus.

According to Ekaterian Ozmitel, a head of Religious Studies Centre, several other cults were operating in Kyrgyzstan that included: Mormons, Krishnaite, Donald Hannong, Satanists, and Church of Moon etc. Ozmitel opined that relations between state and religion were getting tense due to lack of legal clarity.

Following the terrorist attacks in Bishkek and Osh in late 2010, the government had introduced many restrictions. The local *imams* were screened. Many Christian and non-traditional religious groups were outlawed.[59] Kyrgyz civil society though strongly protested against new restrictions imposed through the Parliament. The leaders of a number of public and NGOs reminded the deputies that "tax payers of the country can practice any religion or not to belong to any confession and deputies violate tax payers' rights and constitutional principle of religion derogation form the state, by creating special praying conditions for one of the religions in Parliament."[60]

In 2011, the Ahmadiyya Muslim Community was banned by the authority.[61] Ahmadiyyas had been banned from worshiping altogether and its registration was cancelled by Kyrgyzstan's State Commission for Religious Affairs (SCRA). The National Security Service (NSS) claimed that Ahmadiyya Muslims were a "dangerous movement and against traditional Islam."[62] Similarly, several other sects faced legal actions, as the officials said that these sects were challenging the traditional religion of Kyrgyzstan. In 2012, Kyrgyzstan's Prosecutor General's Office ordered the outlawing of the Unification Church, the controversial religious movement founded by Korean leader Sun Myung Moon. The prosecutors ruled the Moon sect was "a danger to the country's security."[63] The Kyrgyz NSS stated that the non-traditional sects posed a real threat to stability and public safety of the country.[64]

All in all, there was a prevailing sense that the authorities have opened the door to more fundamentalist strains of the religion.[65] The democracy has only facilitated the growth of various sectarian groups, depending on the funding they received from outside. Unlike, five years ago, today one can see the spectacle of tens of thousands men praying on the streets and corners of cities. Interestingly, several important political and official figures were frequently seen praying alongside the crowds.

Many also felt that over the years, Kyrgyzstan has become a testing ground for Islamic missionaries of all kinds. Analysts have suggested that the growing phenomenon was partly driven by internal economic reasons, but mostly it was promoted by external efforts to Islamise the Central Asian society. The Islamic countries, which had been active in Kyrgyzstan included Pakistan, Saudi Arabia, Kuwait and Qatar.

According to the opinions of liberal Russified population in Bishkek, Kyrgyzstan had adopted an open door policy on religion. They appeared concerned about growing radicalisation of the society.[66] However many Kyrgyz experts like Sultanov claimed that a full religious freedom was the best way to prevent the further spread of radical elements. A HuT activist Kadyr Malikov was quoted in the media by saying "The results of the Arab Spring have shown that secular governments are cracking under the pressure of political Islam. Muslims are an enormous human resource. The one who knows how to manage this force will rule the streets."[67]

In the recent years, the issue of *hijab* has become a huge controversy in Kyrgyzstan with lot of Muslims challenging the official restriction of wearing the veil by women and girls in the schools and work places.[68] In 2009, education official announced that school girls will no longer be allowed to wear *hijab.*[69] Media reported that many Muslim students were forced to remove their headscarf. Schools' officials cited guidelines to enforce the school dress code. But the rights activists challenged the government move by saying that headscarves do not pose a threat to national security.

An attempt to move from authoritarianism to theocracy was also surprisingly underway. New Kyrgyz MPs among others had started debating whether the Parliament should have a *namaz* (prayer) room and Fridays be declared day off from work. Clearly the issue was more political than religion. In fact, the Speaker of Kyrgyz Parliament, announced two-hour break for Friday *namaz* on December 24, 2011.[70] Tursunbai Bakir, a right-wing Member of Parliament mooted the idea of opening a prayer room in the Parliament. He was of the view that the move would not violate any laws. Bakir added that it "would be great to have each Friday as a national day off from work so that all Muslims could go to mosques for the traditional Islamic Friday Prayers."[71] However, the idea was opposed by many members of the parliament stating that Kyrgyzstan is a secular country and therefore there should be no prayer room in the parliament.[72]

Dinara Oshurakhunova, the head of For Democracy and Civil Society Coalition contended that idea of breaking for *namaz* into all official institutions contradicts the principle of the separation of religion from the state. She said, "The state must not violate human rights. But religious commitments are their choice. Nobody constrain deputies to go to any mosques, we have plenty of them now. Such initiatives cause tensions in the society. It is quite dangerous."[73] Similarly several MPs across the political parties made sharp criticism about the move to introduce religious practices in the parliament. Many MPs asked who is going to pay the deputies for these two hours of absence from work.[74] Nevetheless, right wing MPs insisted for the *namaz* break.[75]

Clearly, Kyrgyzstan was rapidly getting Islamised especially in the rural areas where the Islamists have been carrying intense activities to recruit children and women in their organisations. Islam was not only replacing public and the state institutions, but the State itself was initiating several steps to patronise Islam by introducing laws in the parliament.

NOTES

1. Nancy Lubin, Barnett R. Rubin, "Calming the Ferghana Valley: Development and Dialogue in the Heart of Central Asia", Published by *Council on Foreign Relations, Century Foundation* (Accessed March 2000)
2. Ben West, "The Tajikistan Attacks and Islamist Militancy in Central Asia", *Starfor*, September 23, 2010
3. Kirsten Schmidt, "Broad valley in Central Asia becomes militants' new sanctuary", *Dallas Morning News*http://www.dallasnews.com/news/20110109-broad-valley-in-central-asia-becomes-militants_new-sanctuary.ece (Accessed January 9, 2011)
4. Gulnoza Saidazimova, "Kyrgyzstan: Banned Hizbut-Tahrir Faces Dwindling Appeal, Internal Divisions", http://www.rferl.org/content/article/1058660.html (Accessed April 27, 2005)
5. "Kazakhstan: Pundits see Islamic caliphate in Central Asia in long run", *Interfax-Kazakhstan news agency, Almaty, in Russian,* August 20, 2012.
6. URL: http://eng.24.kg/community/2012/06/26/24909.html
7. "8 religious organisations on Kyrgyz blacklist, GKNB says", *RFE/RL*, May 5, 2012
8. Ibid.,
9. Impression gathered by author after attending several seminars in Central Asia on Islam for the last 20 years.
10. ZhannaKhusainova, "US Department of State: With Kyrgyzstan's depleted financial resources and political turmoil crime situation may affect the stability of the region", Bishkek, *24.kg news agency*, March 5, 2011
11. "Kyrgyzstan to seek extradition of ex-president's son over riots", *RIA Novosti*, June 15, 2010
12. "Deputy Head of Kyrgyz Security Forces Denies his Words about Tajik Gunmen", *News.ramblerru.* (Accessed April 8 2012)
13. "President Karimov: Conflict in southern Kyrgyzstan was initiated by third party", *AKIpress*, October 20, 2010
14. Farangis Najibullah, Daisy Sindelar, "Kyrgyzstan Blames Militants for Blast", *RFE/RL*, November 30, 2011.
15. Makhinur Niyazova, "Kolbay Musaev: Members of extremist groupings planned 33 terrorist attacks in Kyrgyzstan, *24.kg news agency*, November 30, 2010.
16. "Separatist group members reveal sensational evidence", *24.kg news agency*, November 30, 2010.
17. "Kyrgyz pundit says radical Islam threatening Central Asian "secular regimes", *Delo No, Bishkek, in Russian,* December 1, 2010.
18. *AKIpress,* December 30, 2010.
19. "Kyrgyz pundit says radical Islam threatening Central Asian "secular regimes", *Delo No, Bishkek, in Russian,* December 1, 2010
20. "Secretary of the Security Council: Kyrgyzstan tightens security measures to preserve public order", *24.kg news agency*, November 30, 2010
21. "Kyrgyzstan screening Muslim clergymen for possible terror links", *Kyrgyz radio on* December 9, 2010
22. "Kyrgyz governor wants to put mosques under government control", *Kyrgyz Radio 1* on December 9, 2010, Also see Julia Mazykina, "Kyrgyzstan to create a database of religious extremists", *24.kg news agency*, December 9, 2010
23. "Kyrgyzstan screening Muslim clergymen for possible terror links", *Kyrgyz radio* on December 9, 2010. "Kyrgyz governor wants to put mosques under government control", *Kyrgyz Radio*

1 on December 9, 2010. Also read BakytIbraimov and Stan Rogers, "50 Kyrgyz imams are fired or quit", *Radio Free Europe/Radio Liberty, RFE/RL*, January 22, 2011

24. Daniyar Karimov, "Official Bishkek urges OSCE to redouble attention to Kyrgyzstan and Tajikistan due to the situation in Afghanistan", *24.kg news agency,* December 1, 2010
25. Arthur Medetbekov, "incident in S. Kyrgyzstan may be an act of intimidation ahead of U.S. Secretary of State visit in Bishkek", *24.kg news agency*, November 30, 2010
26. Through discussion with local activist Sanjar.
27. Julia Mazykina, "Erlan Karin: Demoralization of law enforcement agencies and personnel reshuffle exacerbate situation in Kyrgyzstan", *24.kg news agency*, November 21, 2010
28. "President Otunbaeva to attend CIS Summit focused on economic, humanitarian and military cooperation", *AKIpress*, December 10, 2012.
29. "CSTO Presidents make changes in statutory documents over tragic events in southern Kyrgyzstan", *AKIpress,* December 10, 2010.
30. "Russian minister says CSTO crucial for security in former Soviet republics", *RIA Novosti news agency,* December 9, 2010.
31. "President Dmitry Medvedev does not exclude possibility of Kyrgyzstan's accession into Eurasian Union", *AKIpress*, December 10, 2010.
32. *24.kg news agency*, January 12, 2011.
33. The vernacular media had been covering the full spectrum of the possibility of the Third Revolution in the country.
34. *24.kg website*, Bishkek, July 12, 2012
35. Julia Mazykina, "Melisbek Myrzakmatov: Extremist organisations became active in the Central Asian region", *24.kg news agency*, May 3, 2011
36. Asker Sultanov, "Haqqani Network could surface in Kyrgyzstan-MVD watches for signs of Pakistani-Afghan group crossing border", *Central Asia Online*, June 13, 2012
37. "Kyrgyzstan government doing too little in fighting Islamist extremism – experts", *Interfax*, July 2, 2012.
38. "Religious extremism situation remains tense in Kyrgyzstan – official", *24.kg* website, July 31, 2012.
39. *AKIpress,* August 28, 2012.
40. Aizada Kutueva, "Kolbay Musayev: In Kyrgyzstan radical extremist organizations continue to strengthen their activity", *24.kg news agency*, September 12, 2011.
41. "Kyrgyzstan sees rise in religious extremism in first half of 2011", *AKIpress news agency*, September 12, 2011.
42. "Kyrgyz pundit says radical Islam threatening Central Asian secular regimes", *Delo No,* Bishkek, December 1, 2010
43. Alisher Karimov and RukhshonaI bragimova, "Terrorist camps possibly hidden in Kyrgyzstan",*CentralAsiaOnline.com*, November 20, 2010
44. "IMU's Evolution Branches Back To Central Asia", *Radio Free Europe*, http://www.rferl.org/content/imu_evolution_branches_back_central_asia/2240765.html
45. "Kadyr Malikov: Dissemination of Wahhabism ideas is expected in the north of Kyrgyzstan in the next five years", *24 kg news agency,* July 30, 2012
46. "Kazakhstan: Pundits see Islamic caliphate in Central Asia in long run", *Interfax-Kazakhstan news agency, Almaty, in Russian,* August 20, 2012
47. *AKIpress*, January 17, 2011.
48. Tolgonai Osmongaieva, "Kyrgyzstan numbers 2, 050 mosques", *24.kg news agency*, April 19, 2011
49. Makhinur Niyazova, "3000 religious organisation work in Kyrgyzstan", *24.kg news agency*, June 26, 2012.
50. Number of religious organisations and associations in Kyrgyzstan (info-graphics), Bishkek,

AKIpress, April 11, 2012
51. "Law enforcement bodies of Osh region are worried about increased number of mosques", *AKIpress*, June 15, 2012
52. The author has attended many ritualistic events organized by Kyrgyz Ordos in and around Bishkek.
53. *24.kg website*, Bishkek, July 12, 2012
54. "Kyrgyzstan govt doing too little in fighting Islamist extremism – experts", *Interfax*, July 2, 2012
55. "National Security Committee: Muftiyat staff and central mosque transported children from Naryn region to Bangladesh for religious training", *AKIpress*, June 12, 2012
56. "Kadyr Malikov: Dissemination of Wahhabism ideas is expected in the north of Kyrgyzstan in the next five years", *24 kg news agency,* July 30, 2012
57. "Islam in Kazakhstan and Kyrgyzstan: The Nurcu Movement and the Hizbut Tahrir", http://www.amerasianworld.com/ December 23, 2003.
58. Jeff Stein, "Islamic group is CIA front, ex-Turkish intel chief says", *Washington Post,* May 1, 2011. According to the story based on the memoir by former Turkish Intelligence Chief Osman Nuri Gundes, the Fethullah Gulen's worldwide Islamic movement based in Pennsylvania had provided cover for the CIA since the mid-1990s. The movement "*sheltered 130 CIA agents*" at its schools in Kyrgyzstan and Uzbekistan alone.
59. Mushfig Bayram, "Kyrgyzstan: Further Restrictions on Christian Activity a Result of Religion Law", *Forum 18 News Service,* December 21, 2011.
60. 'Kyrgyz civil society protests against conditions introduced by Parliament for religious customs performance", *24.kg news agency,* December 29, 2010.
61. URL: http://eng.24.kg/community/2011/09/12/20252.html.
62. Mushfig Bayram, "We have not been able to pray and worship together", *Forum 18 News Service*http://www.forum18.org (Accessed January 18, 2012).
63. "Kyrgyzstan to Ban Unification Church", *RIA Novosti*, February 6, 2012.
64. "Kyrgyzstan to outlaw Moon sect", *AKIpress*, February 6, 2012.
65. "Kyrgyz Islam: Embracing the future or breeding radicals?", *TV-Novosti*, February 4, 2012
66. "With rise of conservative Islam in Kyrgyzstan, country's liberals question how far religious freedom should go", *Russia Today*, February 29, 2012.
67. Ibid.
68. "Kyrgyz headscarf of discord", http://rt.com/news/headscarf-discord-kyrgyzstan-islam-193/ (Accessed February 25, 2012). "Kyrgyz Muslim activists protest over alleged headscarf ban in public schools", *Kyrgyz Television 1,* September 19, 2011.
69. "Unofficial' Hijab Ban Irks Kyrgyz Muslims", *OnIslam & News Agencies*, September 27, 2011.
70. Darya Podolskaya, "Parliament of Kyrgyzstan offers to introduce 3 hour break for Friday namaz in all official institutions of the country", Bishkek, *24.kg news agency*, December 28, 201110.
71. "Kyrgyz Ombudsman Opposes Prayer Room In Parliament", *RFE/RL's Kyrgyz Service,* January 15, 2011.
72. Julia Mazykina, "Dinara Oshurakhunova: Instead of thinking of where to go for Friday namaz MP have to think that food is rising in price in the country", Bishkek, *24.kg news agency*, December 28, 2010
73. Ibid.
74. Makhinur Niyazova, "Shall parliamentary deputies be paid for Friday namaz break? *24.kg news agency*, 28 December 2010
75. Aizada Kutueva, "Parliament of Kyrgyzstan insists on two hour break on Friday to perform namaz", *24.kg news agency*, 24 December 2010.

CHAPTER 6

National Security Concept

One of the highlights of Kyrgyzstan's transformation to parliamentary democracy has been the conduct of transparency relating to key national policies. Against this backdrop, Kyrgyzstan has brought out a new National Security Concept (NSC) that enshrined a remarkable insightful of the Kyrgyz strategic perspective on a range of national, regional and international trends. Kyrgyzstan's President Almazbek Atambayev signed the draft NSC into law on June 12, 2012.[1]

The document interestingly contains clear guidelines for Kyrgyzstan's defence, security and foreign policymakers. In effect, the new NSC also becomes a guide to international actors as they deal with Kyrgyzstan's security or in their efforts to assist the country in democracy building.[2] Besides, the preamble, the document is divided into five parts ranging from describing the global trends, defining the Kyrgyz interests, the contours of both external and internal security threats and the need for effective mechanism to mitigate those challenges.

The first section among others deals with the role of international multilateral security organisations and the role of Kyrgyzstan in them. It refers to the CIS, CSTO, the EurAsEC, UN, EU, NATO, SCO and OSCE. The NSC clearly singles out the CSTO and SCO as the most important multilateral security organizations relevant to Kyrgyzstan's national security. The role of CSTO is being described as the mechanism to deal with national and regional security issues within the CIS space. The SCO too has been cited as a cooperative mechanism to fight against terrorism and extremism in Central Asia.

The second part of the NSC defines Kyrgyzstan and its geopolitical position in the region. It identifies the real and potential threats posed by the ethno-regionalism, the lack of a national idea, and weakness in national identity among others. Section three deals with the nature of threats emanating from both internal and external sources.[3] The NSC describes the threats to national security as follows:

External Threats

1. Rising conflicts among major powers globally and in Central Asia, as well as between some countries of the region;

2. Expansion of international terrorism and religious extremism;
3. International drug trafficking in Central Asia;
4. Increasing water and energy security threats in Central Asia;
5. Unresolved border disputes amongst the countries in the region;
6. Unresolved demographic problems in the Fergana Valley;

Internal Threats

1. Growing separatist tendencies, inter-ethnic rivalries, ethno-regionalism and provincialism in social relations;
2. Declining public education, ethics and culture; greater influence of non-traditional religious sects in social life; demographic threats; unregulated external and domestic migration;
3. Ineffective government machineries;
4. Difficult economic climate and energy supply vulnerability;
5. Threat from the grey economy and corruption in all social spheres;
6. Increasing rate in crime, drug addiction, alcoholism and unemployment;
7. Lack of IT to protect from cyber threat and social media;
8. Ecological threat caused by degradation, exhaustion and unsustainable utilisation of natural resources, and an ineffective early warning and response system for natural disasters.

The Kyrgyz NSC illustrates the importance of the amendments made in the last CSTO charter in December 2011 that envisaged not allowing member states to station foreign military bases and sites without the consent of all member countries. Of course, this restricts the Kyrgyz room for maneuver for future options, but the document also underlines the security interests of the US and its Allies post-2014. China's intention to build Central Asia as a shield and buffer for Xinjiang is also understood by the Kyrgyz security planners. In essence, the NSC talks about balancing the divergent interests of major powers in Central Asia. The Kyrgyz NSC reflects the larger view of the global power politics from Central Asian perspective, especially on critical aspects of changes unfolding in the Arab world and also international standoff over the Iranian nuclear issue. The rivalry among powers also indicate that the competition for influence in Central Asia has grown both for containing security threats and securing raw energy resources from the region.

Of course, this is the first security document to be released in Central Asia after the NATO's announcement to withdraw from Afghanistan. The NSC elaborates little about the threat emanating from Afghanistan except suggesting that "the situation in Afghanistan and Pakistan, where terrorism, religious extremist forces, and special training camps for militants, such as Al Qaeda, Taliban, Islamic Movement of Uzbekistan, East Turkistan Islamic Movement, Jihad Group or the Islamic Jihad Union, and others are concentrated, possesses serious threat to security of the region and withdrawal of US and NATO troops from Afghanistan creates opportunities for penetration of those militants into Central Asian."[4]

As regards to the military, the NSC promised to release a new Military Doctrine that would be in line with the present-day conditions. The Military Doctrine was later released in early September 2012. The draft Military Doctrine contained aspects of military leadership and organisation, military security preparedness, military industrial-complex, the role played by the military and basic charters of the Kyrgyz armed forces.

The Kyrgyz security doctrine should also reflect the changes that had come about after the country has embraced parliamentary democracy. A transparency in dealing with key security issues in the public is indicative to this. The NSC paper and also the draft country's Military Doctrine were widely discussed through seminars participated by veterans and representatives of the Defence Council Secretariat, Defence Ministry, The Institute for National Security Strategic Studies (INSS), and Kyrgyz security agencies and general public.[5] Defence Council Secretary Busurmankul Tabaldiyev stated that it was the first time that the doctrine was discussed in an open forum.

Interestingly, the draft NSC also covers the non-traditional security aspects that posed challenges to the region.[6] The conflict over water resources in the region is particularly highlighted by the paper. Kyrgyzstan is the fountainhead for the lower riparian states like Uzbekistan and Kazakhstan. The conflict over water has been the source of inter-state tension for decades now. Recently, President Karimov stated that there would be war if Kyrgyzstan and Tajikistan manipulate with river waters.

President Almazbek Atambayev had justified the need for a security blueprint against the difficult security situation being faced by the country.[7] The draft plan defines the limits of Kyrgyzstan's core national interests and the need to protect them through co-operation with others. The key to the doctrine was to reiterate the need for strategic partnership with Russia and with other neighbours.

NOTES

1. "President approves Concept of National Security", Bishkek, *AKIpress,* June 12, 2012.
2. Makhinur Niyazova, "The National Security Concept of Kyrgyzstan does not involve a confrontation with other countries – Almazbek Atambayev", Bishkek, *24.kg news agency*, June 1, 2012.
3. Roger McDermott, "Kyrgyzstan's National Security Concept Legally Enshrines Strategic Balance", *Eurasia Daily Monitor* 9, August 6, 2012.
4. "After 2014 terrorist groups might penetrate to Tajikistan and Kyrgyzstan – National Security Concept", Bishkek, *AKIpress*, June 13, 2012.
5. "Kyrgyz discuss military doctrine", *Central Asia Online*, 25 September 2012.
6. "Central Asian conflict for water resources to aggravate in the future – National Security Concept", Bishkek, *AKIpress*, 13 June 2012.
7. Asker Sultanov, "Kyrgyz prepare draft national security plan", *Central Asia Online*, 2 June 2012.

CHAPTER 7

Politics of Hydropower

The success of democracy would mainly depend on how Kyrgyzstan will become an economically self reliant and a viable state. Unlike others in Central Asia, the country has no rich hydrocarbon resources. The only asset it has is the abundant hydropower potentials. However, exploiting the rich water resources has never been an easy task for the Kyrgyz. In fact, Kyrgyzstan' political relations with outside are driven by water related issues, the management of which is getting problematic day by as the mechanisms dealing with it during Soviet period had started to weaken. Its challenges are linked to neighbouring states with far more experience in political independence. Politics of water is said to be responsible for Karimov's rejection of Nursultan Nazarbayev's initiative for a Central Asia Union.

The tragedy is that Kyrgyzstan has plenty of hydropower potential. Central Asia's largest rivers (the Naryn, Chu, Talas, Saryjaz, Kara Darya, Chatkal, and others forming tributaries of the Syr Darya and Amu Darya basins) find their origin in Kyrgyzstan. Yet it faces the challenge of an energy quagmire, causing massive power fluctuations and cuts. This in turn entails major public outburst leading to frequent political instability. As it is that the politics over energy demand and supply inside Kyrgyzstan is ticking to explode as civil unrest grows caused by short supply of Uzbek gas.[1]

In the past, to achieve a cohesive integration among the five republics, the Soviet Union had ensured near-equitable construction of industrial units in the former Republics. This included the power transmission and supply lines that were there since 1920s. Likewise, the four Central Asian countries (Tajikistan, Kazakhstan, Uzbekistan and Kyrgyzstan) had powerful and reliable integrated regional power system inherited from the Union. The Central Asian grid was linked to State Commission for the Electrification of Russia (GOELRO), adopted in1920 that serves as a common power grid even today.

Overall, Kyrgyzstan has 20 major power plants producing 3,680 MW. 2,950 MW comes from 18 hydro power plants and approximately 725 MW comes from two heat and power plants. The power grid combines more than 10,000 km of power lines of 35kV or greater and over 58,000 km of 0.4-10kV lines. All 18 of existing Hydro Power Plants (HPPs) are heritage from the Soviet times. They are in poor condition and in need of repair because of lack of maintenance in previous years.

During the Soviet rule, much of Kyrgyzstan's energy requirement was imported from Uzbekistan, which in turn was dependent on Kyrgyz water resources; extra fuel was shipped to Kyrgyzstan in the winter to feed their power plants, and the water stayed behind in the dam was to be released in the summer. Even then, Uzbekistan was in a dominant position to supply gas not only to Kyrgyzstan but also to Tajikistan.

Tajikistan and Kyrgyzstan have the highest water resource potential—530 billion and 142 billion kWh a year. However, Kyrgyzstan's exploits are less than nine per cent of its total hydroelectric potential. The main source of water power in Kyrgyzstan is the Naryn River which rises in the Tien Shan Mountains and flows downstream to Uzbekistan and Kazakhstan where it renames itself as Syr Darya, before merging into the Aral Sea which is gradually drying up.

The water-gas-electricity sharing arrangement ended after new states of Central Asia came into being in 1991. In the southern Kyrgyzstan, the Toktogul reservoir was built on Naryn River and hydro power was harnessed. This Hydro Power Station has production capacity of 1,200 MW which caters to about 40 per cent of Kyrgyzstan's needs. Toktogul hydropower is transported by the Chaldovar power transmission line that passes through Uzbekistan and Kazakhstan and then comes back to Kyrgyzstan. Overexploitation, of the Toktogul reservoir has been a recurring issue; a major incident happened in 2008, which resulted in many crises.

Earlier, Toktogul Reservoir water was used for irrigation purpose with large summer releases for irrigation in Uzbekistan and Kazakhstan and low winter releases. When more energy was required, Kyrgyzstan resorted to increased releases from the Toktogul Reservoir during winter for power generation and lower summer releases. To address such problems, the states entered into annual agreements on water allocation-energy exchanges in an attempt to re-establish the pre-1991 operating regime and signed a Framework Agreement on the joint use of water and energy resources in the Syr Darya Basin in 1998. However, the implementation has not been easy.

Situation has accentuated as Kyrgyzstan needed to buy fossil fuel from downstream countries at market price, while the downstream states used water free of charge. This disturbed the intricate relationship for a barter exchange with major implications for geopolitical balance in the region.

Unlike others Kyrgyzstan does not possess hydrocarbon resource and as such hydro power generation and gold mining are linked to its aspiration to achieve economic independence, each contributing 10 per cent of GDP.

Table 1: Existing Power Plants in Kyrgyzstan

Name of the Power Plant	Categories	Installed Capacity (in MW)	River
Bishkek Heating Plant	Thermal	678	
Osh Heating Plant	Thermal	50	
Toktogul HPS	Hydro	1200	Naryn Lower
Kurpsai HPS	Hydro	800	Naryn Lower
Tashkumyr HPS	Hydro	450	Naryn Lower
Shamaldysai HPS	Hydro	240	Naryn Lower
Uchkurgan HPS	Hydro	180	Naryn Lower
Karbulak HPS	Hydro	149	Naryn Upper
Karabulun HPS	Hydro	163	Naryn Upper
At-Bashy HPS	Hydro	40	Naryn Lower

Source: Ministry of Industry, Energy and Fuel Resources, Kyrgyz Republic, 2010.

Table 2: Hydropower Plants Proposed or under Construction

Name Installed Capacity	River (in MW)	Probable construction timeline
Kambarata-1	1900	2010-2020
Kambarata-2	360	2007-2012
DJilanaryk-1	100	2007-2010
DJilanaryk-2	100	2007-2010
Akbulun	200	2010-2014
Saryjaz	1200	2010-2025

As a downstream state, Uzbekistan is opposed to large hydroelectric projects in Kyrgyzstan. Ties between the two countries have worsened on all fronts since Kyrgyzstan announced plans to build the hydropower plants. Uzbekistan has on several occasions in recent years stopped exporting electricity to Kyrgyzstan during the winter resulting in power blackouts in northern Kyrgyzstan. The possibility of an external investor in water resources in Kyrgyzstan is also fraught with the risk of spoiling relations with downstream countries.

Kyrgyzstan's water woes are exasperated by power distribution system. The energy situation in Kyrgyzstan is in a very bad condition. The problem is compounded when Kyrgyz and Tajik state energy companies defaulted on payments to Uzbekistan for gas supplies. Uzbekistan usually responds by restricting gas and power supplies to Kyrgyzstan who then considers using more of water to generate additional electricity. This perpetuates a vicious cycle.

Recently, Uzbekistan announced its intention to leave the Central Asian United Energy System (UCAES), while Kazakh, after threatening several times, promised not to leave the system, citing "good will gesture" towards the Kyrgyz. Violating a 1999 agreement between Kazakh, Kyrgyz, Tajik and Uzbek, of late, Uzbekistan is accused of stealing electricity from Kyrgyzstan's Kazakhstan grid—Kazakhstan Electricity Grid Operating Company (KEGOC)—upsetting both Kazakhstan and Kyrgyzstan. If Kazakhstan leaves the UCAES, Kyrgyzstan's electricity supplies will decrease by 70 per cent, and if Uzbekistan leaves the grid, Southern Kyrgyzstan's Osh oblast will face 50 per cent electricity rationing and Batken oblast will face 85 per cent rationing.[2] For the time, good news is that the issue has been resolved as a result of talks held in Astana with representatives of Kazakhstan Electricity Grid Operating Company KEGOC and Uzbekenergo.

Multilateral Mechanisms

Attempts by all five Central Asian leaders to come to a compromise solution by keeping Kyrgyzstan and Tajikistan supplied with Turkmen electricity through the winter months, and thus allow the reservoir volumes to reach normal capacity again have failed. One keeps hearing the idea of creating energy diplomacy specialists, who will address these complex issues. One of the solutions is the creation of an International Water and Energy Academy in Central Asia.

It seems that the UN law forbids the sale of water as a commodity but to trade services associated with water, such as release and storage.[3]

Kyrgyzstan has been refusing to accept Uzbekistan demand to recognise the trans-border status of the Syr Darya that becomes a reason for Uzbekistan's objection to the construction of hydro-power plants in Kyrgyzstan.

Geo-Political Issues

The border provinces of Kyrgyzstan (Osh, Batken and Jalalabad) have a sizeable Uzbek/Tajik population. As if the water-induced tensions are not enough, the inter-ethnic troubles often keep the sparks alive between these states. For instance in June 2010, Osh witnessed a violent retribution resulting in over a thousand deaths and about four lakh people fled to Uzbekistan. Mutual distrust, corruption, religious extremism and drugs/weapons are other compounding factors in the game.

The power station Kambar-Ata-1 (K1) with a capacity of 1,900 MW was planned by the Soviet Union in early 1980s. However, the construction started in 2009 with a promised $1.7 billion aid by Russia, with an additional $300 million given to Bakiev government as part of package to support the state budget—with an understanding to evict US from the Manas Airbase.[4] At that point of time, Russia also offered assistance worth $150 million and a write-off of $193 million debt of Kyrgyzstan in exchange of a 48 per cent stake in Dastan Torpedo plant. Bakiev reneged on his assurances causing Russia to suspend the aid.[5] In fact the issue had become a sore-point in Kyrgyz-Russia relations. The issue is beginning to be resolved since later 2012 with Russia agreeing to fund the Kambar-Ata projects.

The K1's most vocal opponent has been the Uzbek government. Here comes the role of Russia, which is easily able to exploit the inter-State contradictions. Moscow funded Bishkek when Uzbekistan President Karimov was giving difficult times for Russia. In fact, when Karimov sounded alarm about environmental risks from K1, Moscow ignored it.[6] However, when the Uzbek-Russia relations started to improve Moscow began to cite environmental concerns to delay the project. It wanted an international study to examine the possible risks posed by K1 and asked the World Bank to undertake such a study.[7]

As already explained, Uzbekistan has consistently opposed more Kyrgyz dams which restrict the natural water flow depriving Uzbeks of vital irrigation in summer. Uzbeks know that Kyrgyzstan would be able to store enough water and use it as greater leverage against the downstream state.[8]

The think-tanks in Kyrgyzstan observed that if the aim is to delay the process, say five or six years, all the parties will be happy. An opinion also prevailed that considering the complexities involved, it would be preferable not to hand over control of Kyrgyz energy resources to any one government, regardless of which country it is, Russia, the US, Kazakhstan or China.[9] Corruption in all state-agencies reigns at a high level.

The construction of Kambar-Ata-2 (K2) will be more expensive and Kyrgyzstan would require more resources to cover the costs of production.[10] Kambar-Ata plants are viewed more a political investment. By selling water services to Uzbekistan it could recover the costs. But this is not easy to come by and involves lots of geopolitical interests. Frustrated by delay from Russian side, Kyrgyz leadership has even talked about seeking Chinese investments.

In April 2012, the Chinese Ambassador Wang Kaiwen in Bishkek said Kyrgyzstan's rich water resources are not used properly and offered cooperation by way of dam construction.[11] He said Kyrgyzstan could export power to Xinjiang (western China, bordering Kyrgyzstan). First, there is an ease of distribution (locational advantages). Second, China especially desires access to clean green power in order to mitigate the climate-changing effects of coal. Therefore, Chinese company Tebian Electric Apparatus Stock Co. Ltd. (TBEA) signed a loan agreement for $208 million for construction of new Datka substation with the capacity of 500 KW in the Bazar-Korgon district of Jalalabad province which is be completed in 2013.[12] This will offset about $8 million presently spent for transportation of power from Uzbekistan.[13] Kyrgyz authorities have highlighted this project as crucially important for development of economy and secure energy independence.

Datka-Kemin power transmission line and Kemin substation, will allow Kyrgyzstan to create its own energy ring and to connect the Kambar-Ata hydropower plants to the power grid. Once the Datka-Kemin power transmission line is completed, Kyrgyzstan also wants to export electricity to Kazakhstan by extending the Kemin line to Almaty.

After construction of the Datka-Kemin line, Kyrgyzstan will launch the second hydroelectric unit of Kambar-Ata hydropower plant, which will take two years. Plans are afoot also to complete Kambar-Ata-1 project which will take eight years.

Kambar-Ata Projects

As explained above, the construction of Kambar-Ata-I (K1) was halted for various reasons over a prolonged period. However, the geo-political compulsions (chances that Kyrgyzstan might follow Uzbek in slipping out of CSTO or into the Chinese hands for the construction of projects) have enabled both Russia and Kyrgyzstan to achieve a thaw. President Atambayev Almazbek met with President Putin in St. Petersburg on July 30, 2012, where a preliminary agreement on the construction of K1 was reached. However, the final deal was signed when President Putin visited Bishkek in September 2012. Under the new term, Russia agreed to the construction of Kambar-Ata 1 hydroelectric power station and Verkhnenaryn chain of hydroelectric stations. Russia will fund the hydro projects on 100 per cent loan basis. Under the new agreements, Kyrgyzstan will obtain 50 per cent shares in two projects. Kyrgyzstan agreed to put its 25 per cent shares under fiduciary management arrangement with Russia in order to generate faster returns. However, the property will be owned fifty-fifty and dividends will be shared by the same scheme. The terms of the loan was to be decided later. The construction of the Kambar-Ata-1 was to cost around $2.5 billion and Russia will invest about $455-500 million into other hydro projects on the upper Naryn River. The feasibility study is expected to be completed in February 2013.

The details of the Russian commitment to build Kambar-Ata are covered in the section Kyrgyz-Russia Relations. The deal has emerged as a major achievement for the Atambayev government and its ability to maneuver the politics that compelled Moscow to agree to undertake the old promised projects. However, this may still be not easy. There would be many Russian conditions and it also depends on Uzbekistan able to outdo the progress on the K1. President Karimov of Uzbekistan recently said there will be war if the Kambar-Ata projects go through.[14]

Kambar-Ata-II (K2) is designed to have three units with turbines of 120 MW each which can work only in summer when there is huge water flow. The first unit produces 360 MW/year and was launched on August 30, 2010 with an outlay of USD 200 million. There are plans to build the second and the third unit with Chinese assistance. In any case, China was seriously envisaging building a cross-border grid project to share electricity between Xinjiang Uyghur Autonomous Region and neighbouring Tajikistan and Kyrgyzstan. Zhang Xin, Chairman of Tebian Electric Apparatus Stock Co., Ltd. (TBEA), said during the China-Eurasia Expo 2012 that "Tajikistan and Kyrgyzstan have abundant hydro-electricity resources in summer, but they experience power shortages during the dry winter season. With the grid, they could import electricity from Xinjiang in winter and export electricity in summer. Xinjiang largely relies on coal-firing stations for power."[15] Zhang believed that TBEA's projects in the two Central Asian countries will pave the way for launching the cross-border project in the future.[16]

The energy experts doubt the possible attraction of Chinese investment to Kambar-Ata-1 and the controversy is lot to do with the 'inefficient and spontaneous foreign policy' of Kyrgyzstan.[17] They also argue that the arrangements for joint Kambar-Ata project are becoming complex—leaving scope for ownership to slip away from Kyrgyzstan entirely.[18] Now with the agreement between Russia and Kyrgyzstan, that issue is no longer valid.

On K2 and other projects, if Kyrgyzstan goes ahead, they also risk Uzbekistan turning off gas supplies. However, if the Kambar-Ata projects are built, it will get market access beyond Central Asia into Western China, Pakistan and India. Other customers, still close but not contiguous, could be developed in partnership with other states. For instance, in partnership with Tajikistan, the Kambar-Ata projects could bring power to Pakistan and India. Northern Afghanistan could, in the medium or long term, become a customer for Kyrgyz and Tajik hydropower. In partnership with Uzbekistan, Southeast Turkmenistan could also access some of this hydropower capacity.

Yet many of these customers and some of the potential states for cooperation add to the elements of risk involved in this project. The most underserved market is of course, Afghanistan, which is also the market with the most risk. Developing utility export customers such as Uzbeks, Kazakhs, and Afghans would also require further investment in infrastructure, such as power lines across mountains and substations in seismically active areas or areas of political unrest.

One of the problems for a state that owns upstream water is that it also incurs obligations to downstream states, which have a right to water under international law, no matter what the improvements or diversions made by the upstream state. Therefore, water, surely more valuable than even hydrocarbons, makes the resolution very complex. There is a sense that Kyrgyzstan as an upstream state is too protective of what title it holds to water. The ambiguous ownership between domestic and international claimants should naturally be solved under the international law. But given the geopolitical complexities, Kyrgyzstan's efforts to exploit its hydro potentials are going to be mired into major controversies.

CASA 1000 (Central Asia-South Asia): Exploring Export Potentials

As stated elsewhere, Kyrgyz power export potentials are great but it faces several challenges for both building hydropower stations and repairing the Soviet-constructed transmission lines which are in bad shape. There was a sense of optimism as the Kyrgyz leadership relentlessly talked about a unique chance to have the second boom in development of energy sector.[19]

The CASA-1000 plan was formulated in 2004 when Afghanistan, Kyrgyz Republic, Pakistan and Tajikistan signed a memorandum on energy cooperation. As per the plan, Tajikistan and Kyrgyzstan would provide 1,300 MW of electricity, of which 300 MW would go to Afghanistan and the rest to Pakistan. Asian Development Bank (ADB) allotted funds for an elaborative project feasibility study. The overall cost of the project according to the feasibility study is $953 million.

On a technical level, the junction point of the 1,227 kilometres long power line is to be built on public-private partnership basis; shall originate from Datka substation in Kyrgyzstan and run to Tajikistan's Khodjent substation. A 457 km-section will pass through Kyrgyzstan costing $206 million to implement its part of the project. Kyrgyzstan had announced sanction for the Datka substation project to be financed by China. This is expected to be completed by 2013.

After remaining dormant for three years, the project was revitalised when the Inter-Governmental Council (IGC) comprising Energy Ministers of Kyrgyzstan, Tajikistan, Pakistan, and Afghanistan was held in Bishkek on September 19-20, 2011. Representatives of the US, Russia, China, Kazakhstan and Uzbekistan attended the meeting. The IGC signed a document under which a working group would discuss tariff issues, options for creating a legal entity, identification of jurisdiction and project operation schedule. Under the Bishkek MoU, each country was required to establish a national working group dedicated to implement CASA-1000 project. By this time, Bishkek secured China's approval for concessional loan for the Datka-Kemin power transmission construction.

Both ADB and the World Bank seem interested in funding the CASA-1000. But in the IGC meeting, Ikhtikor Alik, Adviser for energy issues of the World Bank's Department for Sustainable Development of Europe and Central Asia, said that they would not like the project to go through uncertainty in power transmission lines. The terms including pricing has to be worked out through talks by power exporters and importers.[20]

The fifth meeting of the CASA-1000 Working Groups (WGs) held in Almaty, on April 12-13, 2012 was attended by representatives of all four countries and the World Bank, Islamic Development Bank (IDB), USAID, IFC and IGC Secretariat. The WG has decided on hiring country advisors to coordinate with the World Bank.

Some progress was achieved at the meeting of the IGC for CASA-1000, held at Dubai on May 16-17, 2012 when Russia announced its interest and to provide $500 million for the project. Other decisions taken at the IGC were with respect to project structure, appointment of Executive Director for the Secretariat, roles and responsibilities of Country Working Groups, various financing options for the project and all other important issues to speed up implementation of the project. All the member countries reiterated their full commitment towards it.

The financial institutions also expressed their full commitment for financing it as well.

The Afghan Minister for Water and Power Ismail Khan had assured of complete security for the project and informed the meeting that a number of important projects have been started in Afghanistan and are being provided complete security. It was also learnt that the four states have been pursuing the development of electricity trade through the establishment of a Central Asia-South Asia Regional Electricity Market (CASAREM). The WB representative proposed to start the project construction by February 2014, while all procedural requirements including bidding, hiring of consultants would be completed.

For Kyrgyzstan, the construction of the Datka substation and the Datka-Kemin 500 kV power transmission line would substantially improve its infrastructure for export. There is a plan to construct the Kemin-Almaty power transmission line that will allow supplying power to Kazakhstan. Kyrgyzstan wishes to export power year-round but after analysis shows that it has energy excess available only in summer months.

Presently, Kyrgyzstan's only customer is Kazakhstan whose requirements are not large enough to consume the full scale energy, when produced.[21] Hence, Kyrgyzstan's viable alternative will be to export power to Russia, western China, and possibly to India. However, a mere capacity to produce alone is not sufficient to run a profitable show. The key issue here is availability of a reliable buyer. This can be understood after observing the statement by Kyrgyz Energy Minister who expressed hope to build a power transmission line to China, since Xinjiang was rapidly developing;[22] and Kyrgyz MPs also were of the view the government should start summit level talks on exporting electricity to China. A Kyrgyz Member of Parliament, Ravshan Zheenbekov noted that in the light of neighbouring province of China facing deficit of energy, Kyrgyzstan should start collaborative projects for energy export to China, and through it—to Pakistan and India."[23]

The Kyrgyz Energy Minister earlier admitted that Kyrgyzstan has no transmission line, resulting in apprehension among investors that Kyrgyzstan might step down from the project any time. In fact, Energy Minister Askarbek Shadiev, who led a Kyrgyzstan delegation to Dushanbe in December 2011, was candid in saying that there was nothing concrete yet as Kyrgyzstan needs to defend its interests fearing that "Tajikistan and Afghanistan should not earn money on us"[24]

But considering the water resources and the huge potential, and seeing the CASA progress, he announced the unique chance for Kyrgyzstan to have the second boom in development of energy sector. The Minister said "I think the day when energy sector will work is not far. The energy sector should bring huge money in future and we should implement lots of social projects with help of energy sector,"[25]

The analytical assessment is that there would be many uncertainties before CASA-1000 is fully realised. Some of these are highlighted below:

- Kyrgyzstan and Tajikistan remain competitors in hydropower production. Tajik capacity is said to be nearly twice more than Kyrgyz. Once Tajikistan puts Roghun into operation which is likely in six-seven years, it will outpace the capacity of the Kyrgyz.
- Both the Kyrgyz and Tajik plans to build mega hydro projects are mired into serious regional politics, which might also lead to inter-state conflict.
- Uzbekistan being a downstream country has serious objection against both Kyrgyz and Tajik plans to construct dams on the Naryn and Roghun rivers. Besides, Uzbekistan is keen to build a hydro plant on the Swat River in Pakistan to have a grip on the regional electricity market, giving tough competition for Tajikistan. This will possibly lessen Pakistan's dependence on CASA, thereby diluting the prospects.
- Once completed, the pricing of power is going to be a complicated process.
- There are no accurate safety guarantees—instability in Afghanistan and North-West Pakistan are potential areas of security breaches.
- Kyrgyzstan has no funds and availing loans comes with several hard obligations that are difficult to be avoided.
- Nikolai Kravtsov, an independent energy expert said that "If Kyrgyzstan undertakes to deliver two billion kWh, who will guarantee that tomorrow Kyrgyzstan will not suffer lack of water and energy deficit?[26] Kyrgyzstan's applying of energy export undertakings in conditions of its autumn-winter deficit in domestic market can deprive the majority of country's consumers of the energy. It can cause damage to business, aggravate tension in society. Kyrgyz people experienced power limitation without having such projects."
- Electricity market of Pakistan looks lucrative but there exists several competitors as Tajikistan and Uzbekistan can supply cheaper power to Pakistan.
- Tajikistan would not encourage Kyrgyzstan joining the CASA-1000 project on energy delivery to Afghanistan and Pakistan.[27]
- There is also no guarantee that Tajikistan will remain committed to exporting Kyrgyz electricity across its territory fearing potential revenue loss; creation of Distribution Company would be problematic.[28]
- Distribution network in Afghanistan is of greater implication as the majority grids are out of work; to have a distribution system is a long way.

Who will Control CASA 1000?

There is also the politics of who will control the CASA-1000, which is again linked to large geopolitics as it involves the future of Afghanistan. Even though, it may have been the American agenda, Russia appears to be seeking a major say in the project and hence Moscow pledged $500 million for CASA-1000 at the Dubai IGC. However, Tajikistan got an advisor provided by the US who supported RESET Project. Pakistan Working Group also reported that the USAID was funding for two Country Advisors (legal and commercial).

Kyrgyzstan wanted US endorsement of the project, and several Kyrgyzstan delegations visiting Washington had sought assistance of the World Bank and the IMF for the high voltage power transmission line. There was an indication that the World Bank would provide support to the Project, but ADB was still deciding whether to drop from it. The World Bank had proposed to divide the project into two phases. It proposed Kyrgyzstan and Tajikistan to join in the second phase as it will have lesser risks of losing financing.

Pakistan's desire to directly import electricity from Central Asia is also being propped by the US policy. The idea was to dissuade Pakistan from going ahead with the Iran-Pakistan gas pipeline. Besides, Afghanistan also began to generate indigenous electricity of about 220-kilovolt. The ADB has been funding a project to build 500-kilovolt capacity grid running from Turkmenistan to Kandahar. Of course there are projects like the Turkmenistan, Uzbekistan, Tajikistan, and Afghanistan to Pakistan (TUTAP) that would make Afghanistan more self reliant than importing power from Tajikistan and Kyrgyzstan.

The CASA-1000 project would not be economically viable without Tajikistan's own ambitious plan to build the massive Roghun hydropower plant. The Roghun is still mired in controversy due to lack of funding and strong objections from neighbouring Uzbekistan. The World Bank has commissioned a study on the Roghun project but its findings are not known. In addition to the Roghun, Tajik and Afghan officials also discussed construction of the Sanobod hydropower project, which would generate some 100 MW of electricity per year.

Clearly Tajikistan seems more serious about its Roghun dam and hydropower projects. The Tajik authorities have been garnering international support for the project. Dushanbe has been spending enormous funds and even tried to link these projects with efforts to stabilise Afghanistan. Tajikistan's Foreign Minister Hamrokhon Zarifi claimed that the CASA-1000 project would help to fundamentally reverse the existing situation in Afghanistan—reviving Afghan irrigation system and rebuilding its agriculture economy. However, many experts believed that the US efforts to link Afghanistan with CASA-1000 will drag the latter in a wider regional controversy.

The neighbouring Uzbekistan is locked into major dispute stalling Tajikistan's and Kyrgyzstan's plans of constructing major hydropower projects. The Uzbeks argue that the dams will lead to environmental disaster taking a toll on agriculture in downstream countries. The Uzbeks fear that Tajiks will gain powerful political negotiating leverages for example on territory dispute settlement. Tashkent also apprehends that building of world's tallest dam 336 metres on a permanently active seismic zone could threaten heavily populated territories of Uzbekistan, Afghanistan and Turkmenistan.

Against this backdrop, Islam Karimov had recently warned that attempts to build large power stations might spark a military conflict in the region.[29] Tashkent is being blamed for various armed conflict between Tajik troops and alleged Islamic militants for example in Rasht Valley in 2011.[30] Uzbekistan reacted strongly against Pakistan's decision to import electricity from Tajikistan and Kyrgyzstan at the diplomatic level, as also its objection to the CASA-1000 project, suggesting that it would lead to a "serious conflict".[31] Uzbekistan had been pressurising the Russian companies to abandon their participation in Roghun. In fact, Uzbek-Russia relations are closely regulated around Russia's position on the dam construction.

The issue of water resources in Central Asia could turn into a very complex problem. Interestingly, Pakistan was trying to prove its capability for facilitating a peaceful resolution to the water dispute in Central Asia.

So far, the World Bank has pledged $1 billion for the erection of electricity transmission lines as part of the CASA-1000 project. World Bank head in Bishkek Alexander Kremer had announced in 2011 that $200 million would be invested in Kyrgyzstan under CASA-1000 Project for five years at 20 per cent per annum, and $250 million to Tajikistan, while Afghanistan would need around $350 million in loans and Pakistan another $200 million.[32] The World Bank expects that the profit will cover the costs and Kyrgyzstan is expected to earn an annual income of $45-50 million.[33] All in all Kyrgyzstan hydropower prospects would hinge on multiple factors. But, in the medium term there does not seem to be a clear picture on how the Kyrgyz aspiration for exporting electricity in a big way will be realised.

NOTES

1. "Electricity TARRIFS in Kyrgyzstan are lowest in Central Asia, about1.5 cents per kilowatt-hour ($.015 US) and the government has no plan to reduce electricity tariffs", *24kg,* January 13, 2011.
2. *AKIpress,* January 19, 2012.
3. Erica Marat, "Hydroelectricity or Irrigation: a Central Asian Dilemma", *Eurasia Daily Monitor* 5(229), December 2, 2008.
4. This incident ultimately led to Coloured Revolution in 2005 resulting Bakiyev to flee the country. But efforts to obtain Russia's US$1.7 billion loan for Kambar-Ata-1 continued.
5. Russia reportedly suspends funding of Kyrgyz power plant's construction," *24kg,* February 18, 2010.
6. Anton Lymar, "Knyazev: Russia not to conflict with Uzbekistan for Kambarata construction", Bishkek, *24.kg,* 26 January 2010.
7. "International study to be made for Kyrgyz hydroelectric plants project", *Central Asia General Newswire, Interfax* via Lexis-Nexis Academic, February 27, 2010

8. Uzbekistan raised the issue at the General Assembly Second Committee on October 4 2011 in New York. The Uzbek envoy Murad Askarov called the proposed gigantic hydropower facilities in the upper streams as "counter-productive and dangerous" and said that it will negatively impact the socio-economic development of the entire Central Asian region. Read *AKIpress*, October 5, 2011.
9. A well know Kyrgyz strategic expert Valentin Bogatyrev felt it is a bad idea for Kyrgyzstan to place the Kambar-Ata project in Russian hands.
10. "The first generating unit of Kambar-Ata-2 was launched on 30 August 2010 with $200 million costs and started to run by October 2010 with full capacity. The news covered by *24.kg news agency*, September 22, 2010.
11. *AKIpress,* April 27, 2012.
12. "China's TBEA begins construction of Datka substation in southern Kyrgyzstan", *AKIpress,* July 28, 2011.
13. "The transit of electricity through Uzbekistan cost Kyrgyzstan $8 million every year", *24.kg,* July 28, 2011.
14. Uzbek President during his visit to Kazakhstan tried to garner Kazakh support to stop the construction of big hydro dams in Tajikistan and Kyrgyzstan that would affect the downstream countries like Kazakhstan and Uzbekistan.
15. "Chinese firm mulls cross-border power grid with Tajikistan, Kyrgyzstan", *Xinhua,* September 6, 2012.
16. TBEA has $500 million grid construction project in Tajikistan and another $580 million grid construction project in Kyrgyzstan.
17. URL: http://eng.24.kg/politic/2010/01/26/10227.html.
18. A well know Kyrgyz strategic expert Valentin Bogatyrev felt it is a bad idea for Kyrgyzstan to place the Kambar-Ata project in Russian hands.
19. Kyrgyz Energy Minister, Askarbek Shadiev said "I think the day when energy sector will work is not far. The energy sector should bring huge money in future and we should implement lots of social projects with help of energy sector," *interview with Business AKIpress* March 31, 2012.
20. *AKIpress,* September 19, 2011.
21. "Askarbek Shadiev: Kyrgyzstan has only one foreign buyer of electricity – Kazakhstan", *24.kg,* February 25, 2011.
22. *Akipress,* December 18, 2011.
23. *24.kg news agency*, December 18, 2011.
24. *AKIpress,* December 18, 2011.
25. Askarbek Shadiev's interview with Business, *AKIpress*, March 31, 2012.
26. "Energy Preparedness in Kyrgyzstan: Kyrgyzstan shall construct power transmission line to implement its part of CASA 1000", Bishkek, *24.kg news agency*, March 16, 2011.
27. Head of National Electric Networks OJSC Medetbek Aytkulov expressed such a view at a seminar "Energy security of the Kyrgyz Republic", *24.kg,* March 16, 2011.
28. "Tajikistan may become stumbling block for Kyrgyzstan in implementation of CASA-1000 – expert Kravtsov", Bishkek, *AKIpress,* June 29, 2011.
29. Uzbek President during his visit to Kazakhstan tried to garner Kazakh support to stop the construction of big hydro dams in Tajikistan and Kyrgyzstan that would affect the downstream countries like Kazakhstan and Uzbekistan.
30. "CASA-1000 and ailing Uzbekistan" *Najot,* Dushanbe March 25, 2011.
31. Khaleeq Kiani, "Uzbekistan opposes Pakistan's plan to import electricity from Tajikistan", *Dawn,* March 13, 2011.
32. *The Kyrgyzstan Newswire,* 19 December 2011.
33. *AKIpress,* December 19, 2011.

CHAPTER 8

External Relations

Since its independence, Kyrgyzstan has been in a state of inevitable dilemma of nation-building. The country had been trying to follow what it termed as a "multi-vector" foreign policy, but in reality it had to pursue a conventional approach to go along with Russian choice of policy direction. It had been proved more than once that for a poor and fragile state like Kyrgyzstan, the so called multi-vector foreign policy, which essentially entailed manipulation of ties with Russia, USA, China, and other key countries in the region became untenable. Realising its vulnerability to external pressure, it had explored all options aimed at greater flexibility in external conduct. Kyrgyzstan became a member of all important multilateral forums like UN, OSCE, SCO, OIC, CSTO, ECO, IMF, World Bank, ADB, EBRD, CAREC, and CASA-100 and others. It gave greater stress on involvement in regional and extra-regional organisations.

Since 2005, the country has witnessed two mass uprisings resulting in regime change. These were part of country's move towards democratic transition. But, this has also been a period of turmoil and struggle. In these circumstances, directing the course of foreign policy for country has not been an easy task.

In the post-9/11, largely owing to the consolidation of US presence in Central Asia, Kyrgyzstan's foreign policy conduct had become more complex. The opening of a US airbase at Manas 2001 altered the Kyrgyz course of events. The country has fallen into a strategic trap. The US entry particularly changed the fortunes of Kyrgyz ruling elite; a temptation the corrupt leadership could never resist. Kyrgyzstan's multi-vector policy since then became somewhat complicated.

Although, the leaders who came to power after the coloured revolution are the same pro-Russian lot, intense debate and confusion prevailed as to how and who has to formulate the country's foreign policy, for they appeared passing through a period of experiments with parliamentary democracy. The need for a sound foreign policy was debated both in the Parliament and outside in public domain.

Finally, on July 5, 2012, Kyrgyz President Almazbek Atambayev signed a bill adopted by parliament on June 28, 2012. The draft law *on the interaction of Kyrgyz state bodies in the area of foreign policy*[1] envisaged the country to pursue a single effective foreign policy aimed at developing equal relations with foreign countries, international organisations and other subjects of international law. The law drafted by MP Kanybek Imanaliyev was a bit vague about who should form the foreign policy.[2]

Kyrgyzstan has seen intense internal debate as to who should formulate the country's foreign policy.[3] Of course, the debate had emanated in the context of country's transition to parliamentary system of governance. The new parliamentarians have been pushing for a law that forbids President to shape the foreign policy. It was not clearly defined in the Constitution whether the president or the government shapes the foreign policy. Most democrats viewed that the government should shape the foreign policy and president should only approve it. While others believed that government must implement the foreign policy and the President must shape it.[4] In fact, the Parliament Speaker Asylbek Jeenbekov said at a parliamentary session on May 30, 2012 that "the entire nation expressed confidence in the President who will lead the country for six years. I do not have much faith in the stability of the parliamentary coalition and the government."[5] Those who believed that foreign policy should be President's prerogative argued that the new form of governance should be interpreted as a parliamentary-presidential one, rather than purely parliamentary. An MP argued that foreign policy requires a long stable course and the current parliament is prone to the principle of 'the swan, the pike and the crayfish' which is inappropriate.[6] These arguments in favour of President setting the foreign policy agenda only reflected the authoritarian tendency of the past practices, therefore, posed several question marks about the sincerity of Kyrgyz leadership pursuing a genuine parliamentary democracy.

However, Roza Otunbayeva advocated continuity of country's multi-vectored policy, which it was thought suited the country with an authoritarian background. She was naturally opposed to a single vector policy i.e. complete dependence on Russia. Otunbayeva commented once "why can't we cooperate with China? Our economy is based on the trade and cooperation with China. Why not with the European Union? For Russia, cooperation with the EU is of high priority. Why then small Kyrgyzstan must refuse it?"[7] On another spectrum, many leaders support the idea of sticking to Russia and neighbours in Central Asian region—Kazakhstan, Uzbekistan, Tajikistan.[8]

Whatever foreign policy approach the country may follow, the new regime that came after the 2010 revolution did receive quick international legitimacy.[9] The Kyrgyz Foreign Ministry, guided by President Otunbayeva, a veteran diplomat, quickly engaged in negotiation with the outside world on a variety of issues, so much so that Kyrgyzstan had given a stiff challenge to Pakistan for the contest of non-permanent seat at the UNSC in 2012. Kyrgyzstan was one of the competitors along with Pakistan and Fiji for the non-permanent UNSC member seat (from the Asian region) for the term of 2012-2013. During the general debate of the 64th session of UNGA, Kyrgyzstan stood for broader representation in the Security Council and improvement of its methods of work and suggested to increase the number of permanent members by including Asian, African, Latin American and Caribbean countries. Kyrgyzstan was taking an active part in peacemaking and security processes, economic cooperation and environmental sustainability at the global and regional levels. The Kyrgyz Foreign Ministry brought out a Non-Paper illustrating its role in the global peace.[10]

Relationship with Russia, which felt cheated by former Kyrgyz President Kurmanbek Bakiyev, has now been repaired after much hard work by the new leadership. Again many experts believed that Kyrgyz foreign policy was much to do with leaders pursuing personal interests. Almost a unanimous assessment of all experts is that Kyrgyz foreign policy is only driven by money. Some experts subscribed Kyrgyzstan's worsening relationship with Russia to President Almazbek Atambayev's huge personal business interests in Turkey. Ankara has agreed to write off Kyrgyz debt $51 million when Atambayev visited Turkey.[11]

Turkey has been developing substantial interest in Kyrgyzstan.[12] Turkey and Kyrgyzstan have signed more than 100 agreements and cooperation protocols in various fields such as education, culture, trade, economy, transportation, communication and military. The Eternal Friendship and Cooperation Agreement were signed in 1997 by the Presidents of the two countries. Kyrgyzstan is also a member of Cooperation Council of Turkic Speaking Countries and the Parliamentary Assembly of the Turkic Speaking Countries as well (TURKPA).

Turkey's more than US$ 300 million investment in Kyrgyzstan covers all important sectors such as education, construction, retail trade, agro-food sector, health-care, banking, hotel/restaurants etc. More than 250 Kyrgyz-Turkish joint ventures are active in Kyrgyzstan. In 2011, Turkish Prime Minister announced to invest around US$ 450 million in Kyrgyzstan.

The new government under Atambayev showed serious inclination for changing Kyrgyzstan's geopolitical orientation if it receives no substantial benefits from Moscow. In this, Turkey has increasingly emerged as an alternative patron for Bishkek and Ankara has demonstrated its ambition. Relationship with Turkey deepened after Atambayev's ascent to the Presidency. Kyrgyzstan had even thought about selling its only industry *Dastan*, a military enterprise which produces torpedo for India and weapon parts for the Russian Army and Navy, to Turkey.

Kyrgyzstan has provided land for the Turkish university in Bishkek. On April 26, 2011, Recep Tayyip Erdogan and Atambayev created a Supreme Council of Strategic Cooperation.[13] Atambayev proclaimed that Ankara was indeed Bishkek's strategic ally. Agreements were signed for increasing the number of Kyrgyz students in Turkish diplomatic and military academies. Turkey had also decided to build a military academy in Kyrgyzstan to help Bishkek develop its defence industry.

Kazakhstan

The other important countries with which Kyrgyzstan has got significant relations included neighbouring Kazakhstan. Traditionally, the relationship between the countries has been very strong. The Kyrgyz and Kazakh are very close in terms of language and culture. The richer Kazakh tried to assist Kyrgyzstan in its difficult times. However, non-payment of gas supply by Kazakhstan often created tension between the two. Kazakhs have also been wary of Kyrgyz democratic drive and every time there was revolution in Kyrgyzstan, the Kazakhs would close the border points. The new Kyrgyz leadership accused Kazakhstan for interfering in Kyrgyz internal affairs. There were rumours about the role of Kazakh secret services hand in the Osh ethnic conflict in 2010.

Kazakhstan provided substantial assistance to Kyrgyzstan; about $10 million in 2010 and $4 million was granted in 2011. Astana has given Kyrgyzstan with $30 million of humanitarian aid so far.[14] During Almazbek Atambayev's visit to Astana in May 2012 President Nursultan Nazarbayev called Kyrgyzstan as an ally and important strategic partner in Central Asia. He also talked of affinity and brotherhood of the two nations. Nazarbayev told the Kyrgyz to get into action of doing something to boost the economy.[15] Significantly, Nazarbayev supported the political processes that have taken place in Kyrgyzstan.

Kazakhstan is a large trading partner for Kyrgyzstan with trade turnover exceeded $750 million. The trade grew by 27 per cent in 2011. Kazakhstan has so far invested over $1 billion into the economy of Kyrgyzstan. More than 20 large and around 300 small and medium-sized enterprises were operating in Kyrgyzstan with the participation of Kazakhstan. For Kazakhstan, the issue of Kyrgyzstan joining the Custom Union is extremely important. For Kyrgyzstan, residential stay of Kyrgyz nationals in Kazakhstan assumed important public demand. The Kazakhs have agreed for the stay of Kyrgyz national in the country for 90 days with registration to be made within five days after arriving. This was done to boost the cross-border cooperation.

In 2012, both sides signed an agreement on military assistance in training of Kyrgyz military at education institutions of Kazakhstan's Defense Ministry. In economic sphere, Kazakhstan purchase more than 1 billion kWh of electricity power from Kyrgyzstan and supply thousand tons of coal, petroleum products and grains to Kyrgyzstan. Kazakhstan provided substantial humanitarian and technical assistances to Kyrgyzstan in 2010. The relationship has further bolstered with creation of "Kyrgyz-Kazakh investment fund" with equity capital of $100 million provided by the Government of Kazakhstan recently. President Nazarbayev visited Bishkek in August 2012.

In recent years, Kazakh President has agreed to sell gas to Kyrgyzstan at a far lower price than Uzbekistan has been supplying so far. Nazarbayev's decision to sell cheap gas to Kyrgyzstan prompted the Kyrgyz Parliamentarians to propose Kazakh President's name for a Noble Award nomination list (2011) for his contribution to *national building and global leadership in nuclear disarmament.* 91 Kyrgyz parliamentarians out of 113 present voted for the proposal. Kyrgyzstan has been gratifying other world leaders by naming mountains after them. A Kyrgyz peak was named after Vladimir Putin in 2011. A mountain peak in the Pamirs was also named after Boris Yeltsin.

Uzbekistan

Relations between Uzbekistan and Kyrgyzstan in general have been far from cooperative and friendly. Uzbekistan dominates southern Kyrgyzstan both economically and politically, based on the large Uzbek population in that region of Kyrgyzstan and on economic and geographic conditions. Much of Kyrgyzstan depends entirely on Uzbekistan for natural gas; on several occasions, Uzbek President Karimov has achieved political ends by shutting pipelines or by adjusting terms of delivery. Following the interethnic conflicts in Osh and Jalalabad oblasts in June 2010, in which several hundreds of Uzbeks were killed, Uzbekistan has closed its border transit points with Kyrgyzstan. The situation on the state border and in the Sokh enclave of Uzbekistan continues to deteriorate.

Recently, the Kyrgyz parliament has adopted a resolution seeking the return of the Severniy Sokh gas storage facility as well as the Severniy Sokh and Chongara-Galcha gas and oil fields in southern Batken Region to Kyrgyzstan.[16] The controversy erupted after the Soviet Union fell when Kyrgyzstan had allowed Uzbekistan to use its facilities which existed on Kyrgyz territory. The Kyrgyz Government then had no resources to use those facilities. Now the issue has become a bone of contention between the two states. Frequent incidents take place along the border with Uzbekistan. In 2010, 26 incidents on the Kyrgyz-Uzbek border were reported. The talks on Kyrgyz-Uzbek state border delimitation have been in progress since February 2000. Kyrgyz side say 55 meetings of working groups and 23 meetings of governmental delegations were held until 2010. The two sides have near agreement for 1,058.83 km but differences persist over the length of 320.3 km.[17]

Attempts at resolving a host of issues including the border between Kyrgyzstan and Uzbekistan have not succeeded so far.[18] But when Atambayev came to power, and he vowed to strengthen cooperation and remove all misunderstanding with Tashkent.[19]

Tajikistan

Kyrgyzstan's relations with its southern neighbour Tajikistan have been quite tense for years now. The borders between the two countries have been under dispute for 20 years. Thousands of families inhabit these disputed areas in southern Kyrgyzstan and Tajikistan. They often clash over property, land, water and roads. Rising nationalism on both sides have only accentuated the tensions in the recent years. The negotiations over border disputes between Kyrgyzstan and Tajikistan have been in progress since December 2002. Since then 19 rounds of talks have been held. The two share 970.8 km (467.5 km of the border are not demarcated yet), including 564.3 km in Batken oblast (251.1 km are demarcated and 313.2 km are not delineated).[20] Tensions between ethnic Kyrgyz and Tajiks remain high especially along the un-delimited border areas in Batken Oblast. The incidents of inter-ethnic strife are often reported.[21] Border towns constantly remained in conflict. The Kyrgyz in this area alleged that Tajiks are illegally buying up Kyrgyz land. Inter-ethnic incidents were intense in December 2011 in Andarak village of Lyalak District followed by Kyrgyz taking hostage of 19 Tajik traders in Batken in June 2012 for release of their relatives who were caught in Soughd province of Tajikistan for smuggling 90 kilograms of red mercury. The borders are porous and serve as easy gateway for smugglers, drug-traffickers and organised crimes.[22] In 2010, 24 incidents were reported on the Kyrgyz-Tajik border.[23] Residents and troops on both sides have destroyed property and detained each other. As a result border check points are often closed for traffic.[24] Incidents like these could overgrow into armed conflicts that may snowball into serious ethnic conflict spreading to entire Fergana Valley. Trans-boundary crime had posed serious threat to all the states in the past. The Kyrgyz authorities often accused terrorists and extremists infiltrating from across the Tajik borders. Refugees and antigovernment fighters in Tajikistan have also crossed into Kyrgyzstan several times, even taking hostages. Kyrgyzstan attempted to assist in brokering an agreement between contesting Tajikistani forces in October 1992 but without success.

Pakistan

Pakistan is projecting Gwadar port as the gateway to the sea for the land-locked Central Asian countries including Kyrgyzstan. For several years, Islamabad has been actively advocating the use of the road link through Almaty, via Kyrgyzstan - China (via the Karakoram highway) - Karachi. In May 2010, Kyrgyzstan and Pakistan signed a cooperation agreement for Pakistan assistance in Kyrgyz staff training on combating terrorism and in sharing of intelligence. During Prime Minister Sayed Yousuf Raza Gilani's visit to Kyrgyzstan in March 2011, both sides signed an agreement on Defence Cooperation and agreed to collaborate in fighting terrorism. Pakistan aims to import electricity from Kyrgyzstan and Tajikistan through a transmission line under CASA-100 project. Being the members of Organisation of Islamic Cooperation (OIC) and Economic Cooperation Organisation (ECO), Pakistan and Kyrgyzstan support each other on various global and regional issues as well as during the elections to key posts in international organisations. Recently, Kyrgyzstan contested against Pakistan for the non-permanent seat in the UNSC. However, it lost in the final voting.

One of the achievements in the economic co-operation between the two countries is the opening of the branch of the National Bank of Pakistan (NBP) at Bishkek. Pakistan is extending help for Kyrgyz nationals under the Technical

Assistance programme in the field of education, diplomacy, banking, English language and postal services, etc. A few Pakistan nationals have established their business concerns in the fields of hotel, pharmacy and tourism in Kyrgyz Republic. Most Pakistani expatriates in Kyrgyzstan are engaged in border trade with China. They also substantially control the 'second-hand car' business imported from Japan.

Prime Minister of Pakistan Sayed Yousuf Raza Gilani paid a rather self imposed visit to Kyrgyzstan ostensibly to enhance bilateral cooperation. But the actual motive was to impress on the Kyrgyz leadership to opt out of the race for UNSC seat for which both Pakistan was also contesting. It was suggested that Gilani had offered financial incentives to the Kyrgyz side but no specific amount was committed even after Prime Minister Atambayev raised the question.[25]

A Joint Declaration was issued that announced establishment of Joint Business Council (JBC), declaration of Islamabad and Kyrgyz capital Bishkek as sister cities, cooperation in intelligence-sharing, checking drug-trafficking in the region and exchange of parliamentary delegations. The Joint Declaration also affirmed comprehensive cooperation in trade, economic relations and investment.[26]

This time, Pakistan made renewed efforts to re-activate the Quadrilateral Traffic in Transit Agreement (QTTA) originally signed between Pakistan, China, Kyrgyzstan and Kazakhstan in 1998. To remove obstacles, the Kyrgyz side agreed to revive the pact and Pakistan hosting a meeting of experts from the four member countries.[27] It is pertinent to note that the QTTA did not achieve Pakistani desired results so far mainly due to (a) lack of awareness, (b) difficult terrain, (c) economically unviable, (d) frequent closure of Karakorum Highway (KKH), (e) Chinese unease over Uighur activities and extremist incursions. Pakistanis remained slow on it owing to natural disaster in Attabad/Hunza and adjoining areas. Of late, to revive interest, Pakistan wanted Kyrgyzstan to hold an expert meeting to get Tajikistan and Afghanistan joining the QTTA. Pakistan once again projected Gwadar port as the gateway to the sea for Kyrgyzstan and stressed that the two countries should fully exploit this potential.

Fresh attempts are being made to increase Pakistani commercial activities. Allocation of funds was made to Bishkek Branch of National Bank of Pakistan (NBP that provides soft lending to Pakistani businessmen. NBP is said to have issued nearly Rs.5 million rupees (2.5 million soms) for business crediting in Kyrgyzstan, which according to Minister of Economic Affairs of Pakistan Hina Rabbani Khar was the best way to promote trade.[28] Pakistan in the past provided Kyrgyzstan with $10 million loan, but later it had transformed it into grant.

Gilani pushed the idea of purchasing Kyrgyz electricity and the Kyrgyz Prime Minister fully agreed to facilitate Pakistan to buy electricity from Kyrgyzstan in the framework of Central Asia-South Asia Regional Electricity Market (CASAREM) which envisages export of electricity from Kyrgyzstan and Tajikistan to Afghanistan and Pakistan.[29] The export of hydropower is extremely critical for

Kyrgyzstan and it was looking for new markets. Kyrgyz lacks financial resources to implement its part of CASA 1000. The Kyrgyz, therefore, view Pakistani proposal in the context of the construction of a cascade of four hydroelectric power stations on upper streams of the Naryn River with the support of Russia's Unified Energy System and RusHydro Company. Kyrgyz PM was to discuss the issue with Russia during his Moscow visit starting March 17, 2011. However, Kyrgyzstan's plans to supply power to Afghanistan and Pakistan through Tajikistan were unlikely to materialise anytime soon due to host of political, technical and economic problems. Inter-state rivalry, especially Uzbekistan's objection against construction of big hydro projects complicated the CASA 1000. Uzbekistan had opposed Pakistan's plans to import 1000MW of electricity from Central Asia, saying the proposed projects are in violation of international laws.[30]

Pakistan, on its part, offered Kyrgyzstan the shortest land access to seaports Djaladaru and Karachi. The offer is considered by Kyrgyz side as useful and timely. Kyrgyzstan supported Pakistan's entry into the Central Asia Regional Economic Cooperation (CAREC) in November 2010. Pakistan has been separately seeking Transit Trade Agreement (TTA) with Afghanistan for transit rights to access Central Asia through Afghanistan.

Emphasis was laid on raising the level of cooperation in cultural and educational spheres besides pursuing national and regional security interests i.e. struggle against international and religious terrorism, separatism, and arms and drugs trafficking. Pakistan was pursuing regional stability, peace and prosperity and called upon the Kyrgyz Government for joint efforts.[31] On Afghanistan, impression was given that Pakistan was the part of solution and not the problem and stressed that any solution should be "Afghan-led".[32] Gilani said that any decisions should be negotiated with the leadership of Afghanistan and added that "We agreed to combat terrorism collaboratively. We have common enemies—drug trafficking and terrorism. We are ready to cooperate; this is why I came here to discuss the strategy of fight against terrorism."[33]

Discussion on sorting out the issue of both countries applying for non-permanent seat in the UNSC did not appear in the press. However, Pakistani side seems to have sought Kyrgyzstan's support for membership in the SCO. The visit by Gilani was generally lukewarm though the Kyrgyz PM called the Pakistani PM visit to Kyrgyzstan a historic event and a new chapter in the bilateral relations. It was the first visit by Pakistani PM to Kyrgyzstan after 15 years. Benazir Bhutto had visited Bishkek in 1995.

It was not clear though why Gilani chose to visit Bishkek when both Kyrgyzstan and Pakistan were passing through severe domestic problems. Timing of the visit was also not understandable particularly when the Kyrgyz coalition government remained fragile and survived on a day to day basis. The volume of Pakistan's trade with Kyrgyzstan was insignificant—about $3 million during 2010.

Nonetheless, Gilani's visit to Kyrgyzstan assumes importance after Islamabad secured a Free Trade Agreement (FTA) with China and a closer economic relationship with Tajikistan. Significantly, Pakistan's attempts to develop road links to both the countries from existing links to China must be taken note of. China, on its part, has been separately strengthening economic relations with both Kyrgyzstan and Tajikistan. The implementation of QTTA may not be easy, though Pakistan could be selling the idea for reasons other than trade ties with Central Asia.

Pakistan had been seeking an agreement on military training for Kyrgyz officers in Pakistan for a long time. The Kyrgyz side had been indifferent to the Pakistani offer even though it was told to the Kyrgyz that Pakistani military was being trained on the American pattern and were suited to deal with counter terror operation. This time too, the matter bothered many Kyrgyz as well. When the proposal was discussed at the meeting of Foreign Affairs and Inter-Parliamentary Cooperation Committee (PCC) of the Kyrgyz Parliament, two Kyrgyz parliamentarians had expressed reservations on the defence agreement with Pakistan. Their objection was particularly in the context of the deal might adversely impact on the country's relations with India.[34] The MP KanybekImanaliev asked the Kyrgyz Foreign Ministry to study all the aspects before considering it especially in the context of good relations with India. Similarly another MP Bakhtiyar Kadyrov noted "Kyrgyzstan does have not very close relations with....Many terrorist organisations operate in Pakistan. We should consider the issue more carefully to reveal pros and cons."[35] The Kyrgyz First Deputy Minister of Defence Asylbek Ormokeev defended the agreement by saying it will increase the efficiency of national military training in Pakistan as all expenses will be met by the host country. When MP BakhtiyarKadyrov questioned why Pakistan needs it for? The Deputy Defence Minister replied by doing so Pakistan wants to improve its image and further added that "It's no secret that the military institutions of Pakistan were built in cooperation with European countries, and this country has a good base for military education."[36]

The Kyrgyz Minister of Foreign Affairs Ruslan Kazakpaev too justified the agreement with Pakistan on military training by saying there would nothing wrong if our military will improve their skills in this country. The Foreign Affairs and Inter PCC of Zhogorku Kenesh later approved the agreement with the Government of Pakistan on cooperation in military education.[37]

It did suggest that Pakistan was trying to compete with India's engagement in Central Asia on security and defence cooperation issues. In the light of Kyrgyzstan assuming key strategic importance both from China and now from Pakistan angle, India needed to be seeking a more proactive engagement with Kyrgyzstan.

There were further developments following Gilani's visit, meeting of heads of special service and law enforcement agencies of Pakistan and Kyrgyzstan was held in Islamabad in May 2011. The aim was to discuss cooperation in combating international terrorism. An agreement was signed for training of personnel on combating terrorism and exchange of information necessary for security of both countries.[38]

Iran

Kyrgyzstan has maintained good relations with Iran, not for ideological reasons but purely for commercial interests. Iran has been quite active in Kyrgyzstan for political reasons and also due to the presence of US military presence at Manas. Iran views its relations with Central Asian countries in the context of major challenges it faces from international isolation. In fact, this is an important part of Iran strategy for the region. In 2012, Iran had showed strong indication of warming relations with Kyrgyzstan and wanted to invest $10 billion in Kyrgyzstan.[39] On July 12 the Iranian President met Kyrgyzstan's new Finance Minister, Akhylbek Japarov and called for greater ties between the two nations. Japarov discussed the resumption of direct flights between Bishkek and Tehran as well as other projects to boost their joint trade and developments.[40]

The two countries signed a memorandum on provision of $1 million Iranian aid for the development of Kyrgyzstan. The 10th Iran-Kyrgyzstan Joint Economic Commission proposed to cooperate in halal-industry, banking system, cement production, implementation of the joint projects in geology survey, energy, gas and tourism.[41] Minister Japarov and Minister for Mines and Trade, Ghazanfari also signed a protocol of the inter-governmental commission. Ghazanfari announced Iran's readiness to invest into economy of Kyrgyzstan more than $1 billion for short term and $10 billion for long term projects.[42] Iran and Kyrgyzstan also agreed to significantly increase their annual trade to $5 billion over the long term.[43] Trade turnover between Kyrgyzstan and Iran remained low. In 2011, trade turnover totalled $50 million mostly exports from Iran. According to the Iranian Ambassador in Kyrgyzstan, the reasons for such a low level of trade turnover were political instability and lack of transparency of certain laws and regulations in Kyrgyzstan.[44] Iran mainly exports clothing, nuts, paints and flooring to Kyrgyzstan and imports meat, grain and steel scraps. Ghazanfari said 180 industrial units were operating in Kyrgyzstan through joints ventures and mostly investments from Iran.

Earlier on October 18, 2011, the Iranian Majlis Speaker Ali Larijani paid an important visit to Kyrgyzstan and held wide ranging discussion with Kyrgyz leadership. Importantly, Ali Larijani during a meeting with Kyrgyz President Roza Otunbayeva expressed readiness of Iran to stand by Kyrgyzstan in its efforts to promote democracy. It did seem to suggest that Iran was looking at the political transition in Kyrgyzstan as a part of the popular uprisings unfolding across Middle East and North Africa region. Larijani said, "The Islamic Republic of Iran supports the freedom-seeking movements in Egypt, Tunisia, Libya, Bahrain, and Yemen because it believes that these protests are calling for the restoration of the rights of the people and democracy.... The people of the region have become fed up with dictators who are subservient to the hegemonistic powers."[45]

Larijani was particularly interested in replicating Iranian success of building power plants and dams in other countries in Kyrgyzstan.[46] Of late Iran was also planning to connect its power grid to Central Asian states. In July 2012, Iranian Energy Ministry's official suggested that the plan is to build two power transfer lines to Turkmenistan. Iran has a 400 kilovolt (kV) line with Turkmenistan for the exchange of electricity but it wanted to have an agreement to build two new 400-kV lines to exchange electricity with Kyrgyzstan, Uzbekistan and Tajikistan as well. This is perhaps one of the justifications given by Iran to pursue its civil nuclear programme. Larijani signed a MoU with Kyrgyzstan on inter-parliamentary exchanges.[47] Larijani also announced the allocation of $1 million for construction of the sport complex in Osh city. Interestingly, the Kyrgyz Speaker asked Ali Larijani to support the candidacy of Kyrgyzstan in non-permanent membership in the UNSC against Pakistan on which Iranian side readily agreed to support Kyrgyzstan's candidacy.[48]

Kyrgyzstan does have security agreements with Iran aimed primarily at taking action against drug trafficking, terrorism and organised crime. However, there were other issues involved between the two countries. In 2012, two Kyrgyz nationals were still under the detention of Iranian authorities on the charges of threatening Iran's national security.[49] One Kyrgyz national was detained in 2010 in an operation against an anti-Shiite group led by Abdulmalik Rigi in Baluchistan. A plane carrying Rigi from Dubai to Kyrgyzstan was grounded by Iranians on the way and Rigi was killed. A Kyrgyz national was also involved in the incident.

In early 2012, Iran had factored itself in the US-Kyrgyz relations particularly over the stationing of the US transit Centre at Manas and the possible use of the base for launching missile attack against Iran. Tehran was pressurising directly or indirectly through Russia on Kyrgyzstan to close down the US Military Transit Centre at Manas. In fact, it was Russia that had first flagged the issue. The Russian Foreign Ministry spokesman Alexander Lukashevich had said in February 2012 that the US might use its airbase at Manas to attack Iran, though he hoped such an apocalyptic scenario will not be realised."[50] Russia was perhaps trying to scare the Central Asia states by suggesting that any cooperation by them with the US could invite possible military retaliation by Iran. Many observers thought it was a smokescreen by Moscow to retain its hold in the region. But the Russian signal was taken seriously by the leaders in the Central Asian countries. The issue was even raised at the SCO meetings. The message was more directed at Kyrgyzstan which hosted the US military base at Manas. This led to eruption of debate in the country. The fear was related to the risk of retaliatory strike from Iran. President Atambayev feared Kyrgyzstan getting embroiled in the US-Iran conflict.[51] He had earlier talked about a possible conflict between the US and Iran and Tehran could deliver a missile strike at American facilities in Kyrgyzstan. He suggested that the US Transit Centre cannot be used against Iran and it is only being allowed to carry out operation in Afghanistan.[52]

The Iranian Ambassador to Kyrgyzstan welcomed President Atambayev's decision on vacating the US base. In fact, Ambassador Manouchehr Moradi had earlier said in a statement that the Kyrgyz top leadership will not allow US to use its territory for military actions against Iran.[53] Iranian Embassy's press-service in Bishkek quoted the Ambassador saying "The territory of the Manas transit transportation centre belongs to Kyrgyzstan...we are sure that the Kyrgyz government, as an independent state, will not allow any other state to use this land in a war against the third country. After 20 years of fruitful and close cooperation, our friendly nations will not let the events to develop in this direction."[54] He, however, believed that a war between the West and Iran was unlikely and that most probably there was a psychological pressure. The Kyrgyz Ambassador to Iran Medetkan Sherimkulov, at the hearing in Kyrgyz parliament on June 25, 2012, told that Iranian leadership from top to bottom were waiting for Kyrgyzstan to take an early decision on the US airbase.[55]

The specter of Iranian missile hitting Bishkek in case of the US-Iran military standoff was also raised by other Kyrgyz leadership and politicians. Of course, Atambayev had been repeatedly threatening to close the US Transit Centre once the current lease expires in 2014. He was doing this for domestic political reasons and also to appease Moscow. It seemed that Atambayev's constant threats to close the US base was also a part of a game to extract more rent from the US in the same way former President Kurmanbek Bakiyev did in 2010.

But, the US itself immediately dismissed the assertion made by Kyrgyzstan, Russia and Iran that the Transit Centre at Manas will be used against Iran. The US Ambassador in Kyrgyzstan Pamela Spratlen made it very clear that the Transit Centre at Manas is meant to "perform one single mission which amounts to supporting the stabilisation process in Afghanistan and preventing the appearance of havens of extremists there."[56]

In fact, it appeared somewhat naïve on the part of Kyrgyz President to link the US Transit Centre with Iran. Probably he was under pressure from both Iran and Russia on the issue. A serious President of a nation needed to know few basic political realities. Firstly, if the US has to attack Iran, it could launch air attack from any other nearby bases located in Turkey, Bahrain or from Afghanistan. Secondly, why would the US choose Kyrgyzstan, which would require crossing at least two other countries' airspaces on the way? The US knows that Kyrgyzstan falls under the Russian or CSTO air defence and any violation of the Russian space would invite trouble from Moscow.

However, judging from their activities, Iran's role in Central Asia, especially in Tajikistan and Kyrgyzstan was destined to rise in the near future. Iran has deliberately avoided playing its theological card and has not indulged in any activities, which give rise to suspicion among Central Asian secular regimes. Iranian attitude in Central Asia has been to project itself as regional players. It hopes to play a lead role in developing Central Asia's hydropower resources, by supporting the Tajik Sangtuda-2 plant. Moreover, Iran sells itself as a potential transit country for energy exports, and that it could provide Central Asian states with access to sea port.

Kyrgyzstan was also seeking closer relations with Azerbaijan primarily to set up an oil refinery by State Oil Company of Azerbaijani Republic (SOCAR) in the South of Kyrgyzstan. The idea was to get rid of dependence on Russia. The idea of an Azeri oil refinery in Kara-Balta later failed as Baku did not probably want to get into the Kyrgyz political and financial games.

Kyrgyzstan has tried to factor itself in the Afghan issue and has taken several steps to enhance its role in Afghanistan. Foreign Minister Ruslan Kazakbayev was seen active in all multilateral fronts taking about the need to resolve the Afghan conflict. The Kyrgyz Foreign Minister held talks with the UN Secretary-General Ban Ki-moon and expressed his country's readiness to take part in all international, regional and country initiatives, as well as programmes on the economic restoration of Afghanistan. In 2012, the Kyrgyz official also held a meeting with OSCE Secretary-General Lamberto Zannier to discuss cooperation with Afghanistan. Kyrgyz Foreign Minister had proposed a cooperation plan for Afghanistan in the aftermath of 2014. The US too had keenly been trying to engage Kyrgyzstan in the Afghan reconstruction programmes.

Clearly, on the foreign relations front, though the political public voice favoured a pro-Russia ideology, the tilt displayed by President Atambayev in his various meetings displayed an urge to reach out to non-traditional players like Turkey, Iran, Azerbaijan and the Middle-Eastern states. By 2011 Saudi Arab, Qatar and other Arab states were opening diplomatic missions in Bishkek. Atambayev was obviously trying to diversify the sources of material supply. This was coming at the cost of relations with Russia and US. With US, Atambayev was forceful on vacation of Manas air base, while continuing in the anti-terror activities. With Russia, the issues of old-debt, transfer of shares in hydro-electric and defence companies, Russian citizenship of Kyrgyz migrants etc. were the main irritants. Untimely, the issues with Russia were resolved but Atambayev played a hard game with Moscow. Kyrgyzstan intensely played the China card simultaneously in 2011-12, which compelled Moscow to make a conciliatory move despite all the annoyance Russia had with Kyrgyzstan over a number of sensitive issues. The real test would be whether Russia will be able to bring Kyrgyzstan into the fold of Custom Union eventually, which is very much linked to containing Chinese growing economic and political influence in Central Asia, especially in Kyrgyzstan. The Kyrgyz pressure on the US continues at high gear, but a deal will be struck before the draw down in 2014.

Being a landlocked state and surrounded by much powerful neighbours pose difficult challenges to Kyrgyzstan's foreign policy conduct. Over the years, even the competing rivalry for regional hegemony between Uzbekistan and Kazakhstan has impacted Kyrgyzstan. The choice of foreign policy direction has also been mired by internal power struggle among major Kyrgyz tribal clans. The country has traditionally aligned itself with Russia, but this has not been an easy experience. Relationship with Russia has seen many twists and turns. So far, Kyrgyzstan has not found a viable and durable foreign policy option, which also remains one of the strong reasons for its domestic instability.

NOTES

1. The President's press service, July 5, 2012.
2. "New law expands Kyrgyz leader's foreign policy powers", *AKIpress news agency,* July 5, 2012.
3. A comprehensive analysis of Kyrgyzstan's foreign policy entitled "*External policy: blunder, and one more blunder"* authored by Nina Nichiporova, Alexander Tuzov, Evgeny Denisenko, published by *Vecherniy Bishkek*, April 20, 2012.
4. "MP Ismail Isakov: President shouldn't shape foreign policy", Bishkek, *AKIpress*, February 15, 2012.
5. "Kyrgyz speaker says president should set foreign policy" Kyrgyz news& analytical agency *Vesti.kg,* September 30, 2012.
6. Ibid.
7. Daniyar Karimov, "Kyrgyzstan should keep multi-vectored policy –Roza Otunbayeva", *24.kg,* June 13, 2012.
8. "Kyrgyzstan shouldn't look for beyond the seas allies - party leader", *24.kg*, April 9, 2011.
9. Irina Pavlova, "Kyrgyzstan: Curves of foreign policy", Bishkek, *24.kg news agency*, April 9, 2012.
10. See Annexure 3.
11. "Turkey writes off $51 million debt to Kyrgyzstan and provides $10 million grant", *News Agency I...IUIypress,* January 20, 2011.
12. An expert on Central Asia Baete Eshment was quoted in "Kyrgyzstan: Curves of foreign policy", *24.kg news agency*, April 9, 2012.
13. Dmitry Shlapentokh, "Turkey and Kyrgyzstan deepen ties", *CACI Analyst*, March 21, 2012.
14. Kazinform, *http://engNews.gazeta.kz/art.asp?aid=362644* May 10, 2012.
15. "We regard Kyrgyzstan as an ally and important strategic partner in CA, Nursultan Nazarbayev", http://www.inform.kz/eng/article/2462500 (Accessed May 10, 2012)
16. "Kyrgyz MPs decide to return oil, gas facilities used by Uzbekistan", Kyrgyz Telegraph Agency (*KyrTAg)*, June 20, 2012.
17. "President Otunbaeva: Only equal land exchange can be discussed in enclave talks with Uzbekistan", *AKIpress*, February 8, 2011.
18. "Foreign Ministers of Kyrgyzstan, Uzbekistan discuss border limitation and demarcation", *AKIpress,* April 8, 2011.
19. "Kyrgyzstan wants to change relations with Uzbekistan dramatically – Atambaev", Bishkek, *AKIpress,* December 30, 2010.
20. "President Otunbaeva: Only equal land exchange can be discussed in enclave talks with Uzbekistan", Bishkek, *AKIpress*, February 8, 2011.
21. David Trilling, "Kyrgyzstan: New Ethno-Political Trouble in the Fergana", *EurasiaNet,* February 2, 2012.
22. K. Kumkova, " Kyrgyzstan & Tajikistan: Disputed Border Heightens Risk of Conflict", *EurasiaNet*, August 2, 2012.
23. "Tension growing between Kyrgyz, Tajik minority over murder case", *24.kg website,* April 27, 2012.

24. "Kyrgyzstan closes border crossing with Tajikistan", *KyrTAg, Bishkek,* May 15, 2012.
25. Information gathered from an official from the Kyrgyz Prime Minister's office.
26. "Defence Ministries of Kyrgyzstan, Pakistan sign cooperation agreement", *AKIpress,* March 15, 2011. "Prime Ministers of Kyrgyzstan, Pakistan sign joint declaration", *AKIpress,* March 16, 2011.
27. Shumaila Andleeb, "Pakistan, Kyrgyzstan agree on reviving four-nation trade pact", APP, March 15, 2011
28. Julia Mazykina, "Bank of Pakistan issued nearly 2.5 million soms in loans in Kyrgyzstan", Bishkek, *24.kg news agency,* March 16, 2011
29. "Kyrgyz, Pakistani prime ministers discuss energy cooperation", *Kyrgyz Telegraph Agency (KyrTAg)* March 16, 2011
30. "Uzbekistan opposes Pakistani plan to import Tajik electricity", *Dawn website,* March 14, 2011
31. "Prime Minister of Pakistan says it's necessary to counter such regional problems as terrorism and drug trafficking collaboratively", Bishkek, *AKIpress,* March 15, 2011
32. Shumaila Andleeb, "Pakistan, Kyrgyzstan agree on reviving four-nation trade pact", *APP,* March 15, 2011.
33. "Kyrgyzstan, Pakistan to jointly fight terrorism, drug trafficking", *Krgyznews agency 24.kg website,* March 5, 2011
34. Aizadakutueva, "Kyrgyz parliament profile committee approves agreement with Pakistan Government on cooperation in military education", Bishkek, *24.kg news agency,* February 21, 2011.
35. Ibid.
36. Ibid.
37. URL: http://eng.24.kg/politic/2011/02/21/16411.html
38. "Special services of Kyrgyzstan, Pakistan discuss cooperation in terrorism fighting", *AKIpress,* May 24, 2011.
39. Read more: http://www.businessinsider.com/iran-to-invest-10-billion-in-kyrgyzstan-2012-7#ixzz20UcwJ7Ge
40. *IRNA news agency,* July 12, 2012.
41. "Iran is ready to invest $1 billion into short term and $10 billion into long term projects in Kyrgyzstan", *AKIpress,* July 11, 2012.
42. Ibid.
43. *IRNA News Agency,* July 10, 2012.
44. *AKIpress,* May 3, 2012.
45. Ibid.
46. "Iran will help Kyrgyzstan go down the path of democracy: Larijani", *IRNA,* October 19, 2011.
47. "Parliament Speakers of Kyrgyzstan, Iran sign memorandum of inter-parliamentary cooperation", Bishkek, *AKIpress,* October 19, 2012.
48. "Iran to support Kyrgyzstan's bid for UN Security Council's non-permanent seat", *Kyrgyz Television* 1, Bishkek, October 19, 2011
49. Elvira Temir, "Two Kyrgyz held in Iran on security threat charges – official", *Vecherniy Bishkek,* May 22, 2012
50. "Russia says U.S. might use Kyrgyz airbase in Iran strike", *Interfax,* February 22, 2012
51. Joshua Kucera, "Russia: U.S. Could Attack Iran From Manas", *EurasiaNet,* February 22, 2012. Read more: http://www.dailystar.com.lb/News/Middle-East/2012/Feb-22/164220-russia-says-us-might-use-kyrgyz-airbase-in-iran-strike.ashx#ixzz1nBnuGSmK (*The Daily Star,* Lebanon News, http://www.dailystar.com.lb)
52. "Russia says U.S. might use Kyrgyz airbase in Iran strike", *Interfax,* February 22, 2012

53. "Iranian ambassador: Kyrgyzstan not to allow U.S. to use Manas against Iran", *24.kg,* February 15, 2012 Iranian embassy's press-service in Bishkek.
54. Ibid.
55. "Everyone" in Iran waiting for Kyrgyzstan to close US transit centre – envoy', *AKIpress,* June 5, 2012
56. *Akipress news agency,* March 9, 2012.

CHAPTER 9

Russian Interests in Kyrgyzstan

Kyrgyzstan, even though, followed an independent and relatively a more democratic political path, had remained as part of the CIS single strategic space and Russia continued to wield considerable influence in Kyrgyzstan, both through bilateral cooperation as well as under the aegis of the CSTO. Kyrgyzstan has been consistent in its efforts to project itself as a reliable strategic ally and friend of Russia in Central Asia. Russia has maintained an airbase at Kant near Bishkek and other military facilities in the country. A large number of Kyrgyz military personnel are being trained in Russian military institutions. The Kyrgyz Army is equipped with Russian equipment and remains dependent on Russia for supply, repair and maintenance of equipment. Out of an almost six million population, roughly one million Kyrgyz nationals are of Russian origin. Almost a million Kyrgyz nationals work in Russia and send remittances home which contributed to at least 20 per cent of Kyrgyz GDP each year.

The two countries have signed nearly 100 bilateral agreements for cooperation, including security and military areas (defence of Kyrgyz air space by Russian forces, supply of military hardware, cooperation between military industrial establishments of both the countries etc.), on economic and industrial cooperation, cooperation in the fields of science and technology, education and cultural cooperation etc. Trade turnover between the two countries was $ 1.8 billion in 2008. In 2010, it fell to $ 1.4 billion. Russia's exports accounted for $1.2 billion, and imports for about $300 million. Russia's share in the Kyrgyz turnover makes up 18 per cent.

However, the relationships between the two countries have remained inconsistent due to internal political instability and power struggle among Kyrgyz power elite. The Kyrgyz relationship with Russia particularly soured when former President Kurmanbek Bakiyev had started playing a double game with Moscow. Many say he had practically cheated Russia.[1] Bakiyev in 2009 had managed to get $150 million from Russia on the promise that he will close the US Manas Airbase. He also secured Russia's commitment to spend $300 million for Kambarata-2 hydro construction. The Kyrgyz side had agreed to part with 48 per cent of Dastan OJSC shares to Russia in exchange of the $180 million debt. Moscow immediately released $300 million through Bakiyev's elder son, Maksim Bakiyev's Central Agency of Kyrgyzstan's Development Investments and Innovations (KCADII). Bakiyev did not push for the Manas closure and instead signed with the US a fresh agreement with enhanced rent. Maksim along with $300 million disappeared. Therefore, for Russia to deal with Kyrgyz authorities was not an easy business.

However, after Bakiyev was ousted in the post-Tulip Revolution, some progress was made to regain the Russian trust by the interim government and by the first parliamentary elected government. But, basic mistrust over a number of issues, including the continuation of the US Military Transit Centre at Manas, non-payment of debt by Kyrgyzstan, Russia's non-payment of rent for leasing the Kant air base etc continued to persist between Russia and Kyrgyzstan. By 2011, Russia also started putting pressure on Bishkek to join the Customs Union. For Russia, it had to simply use some of its traditional key cards to protect its interests. Levy of custom duties on petroleum products was one such example which made the post Bakiyev regime to fall in line. For the new regime in Bishkek, fuel supply was essential to deal with country's perilous economic and political situation, particularly the chronic budget deficit which would have posed a threat to Kyrgyz national security. The government spending in 2011 was expected to exceed the country's total revenues by more than 18 billion Kyrgyz som. This difference amounted to almost eight per cent of GDP.

In early 2011, as the trouble phase in the country was coming to an end, the Kyrgyz new leadership was firmly trying to reinter into the Russian orbit. This was contrary to the initial belief that Moscow's clout might decline if a new parliamentary system was established in Kyrgyzstan. Many had thought that the second time revolution under Roza Otunbayeva will orient Kyrgyzstan towards the West. But the first parliamentary election results clearly brought back the same pro-Russian political parties to power though in a coalition format. Only, one party *Ata-Meken*, seen as somewhat pro-Western oriented, remained in opposition. This clearly indicated that Moscow had succeeded in influencing the process and the outcome of Kyrgyz April 2010 revolution as well as the subsequent parliamentary election. Most Kyrgyz leaders, barring those who sought pro-West tinge, seemed to have understood that they have no other option but to accept Russian tutelage; a reason why almost all political parties had earlier gone to the electorate with a pro-Russian policy lines and their leaders had visited Moscow for consultations before the elections. Moscow too did not appear keen to press Kyrgyzstan to return to Presidential system though this was a major subject of debate prior to the parliamentary election.

The first democratically elected Kyrgyz Prime Minister Almazbek Atambayev promptly visited Moscow in December 2010 to regain the loss of trust and to open a fresh chapter in the bilateral relationship.[2] Atambayev met Vladimir Putin and managed to secure inter alia two crucial goals: (a) $200 million loan to support Kyrgyz state budget and (b) lifting of extra export duties for oil products exported to Kyrgyzstan that was introduced in April 2010 after discovering that its fuel was used for Manas. Among other things, Kyrgyzstan in principle had agreed to facilitate construction of dozens of hydroelectric stations by Russian RusHydro Company. Russia's long pending proposal to push Gazprom in Kyrgyzstan for joint exploration with Kyrgyzgas was also being agreed upon. To bolster Kyrgyz agricultural sector, Russia was offered to open its procurement offices in each region of Kyrgyzstan. Most importantly, Atambayev announced Kyrgyzstan's intention to join the Russian led Custom Union and common economic space. A Kyrgyz observer was to join the Union's Supervisory Board for preparatory. This was basically meant to hurt neighbouring China. Until then, China had been able to dump its goods into Commonwealth of Independent States (CIS) market through open border with Kyrgyzstan. On the strategic front, Kyrgyz Defence Minister had announced that a draft agreement on setting up a Joint Russian Military Base (JRMS) in Kyrgyzstan in 2011 will be submitted to the Kyrgyz Parliament. (Four Russian military facilities were on the territory of Kyrgyzstan)

By 2010 end the Kyrgyz-Russia relationship had returned back to 2009 level, when the two had enjoyed full trust and strategic partnership until Moscow had started arm-twisting Bishkek on the issue of US Transit Centre at Manas. In the changed situation, Manas had not factored into the making of new Kyrgyz-Russia relationship. Meanwhile, Kyrgyz parliamentarians too were only keen to know from the government about the economic benefits from the Transit Centre.

Moreover, Gazprom's agreement to lift export tariffs indicated that the Kyrgyz government and the Russian firm had reached a deal on fuel supplies to the US Transit Centre. In this regard, plausibly a compromise formula may have been worked out with the US, prior to the formation of the government, that Russian and Kyrgyz companies will have 50 per cent stake in the fuel supply to the Transit Centre, which meant that all sides had agreed to cut out partially the middleman and original contractor, Mina Corp Inc, which had been supplying TS-1 jet fuel to Manas for six years.

The new Kyrgyz Government even announced to name one of the unnamed peaks in the Tian Shan range after Vladimir Putin.[3] Finally, Russia was set to gain large-scale contracts in Kyrgyzstan, especially in hydropower, mining and industry. However, as usual and by doing so, Russia risked hurting the sensitivities of neighbouring republics, especially complicating relationship with Uzbekistan. All in all, a new geopolitical balance was created by resolving the Kyrgyz crisis, of course on the Russian terms. In this entire game, the sense one got was that euphoria of democracy had simply died down. The uprising was only about change of power in different hands.

However, as times passed by, the relationship with Russia was affected by various internal political developments within Kyrgyzstan such as scandals over corruption, power struggle among numerous clans and the Kyrgyz desire to diversify relationship with other countries. By beginning of 2011, fierce political acrimony erupted within the Kyrgyz coalition partners. This led to Russia's growing discomfort over Kyrgyz government backsliding on a number of issues detrimental to Moscow's key strategic and economic interests. The immediate cause of tension was linked to the nationalisation of Kyrgyz largest mobile service provider MegaCom Company and associated scandals around it. The company was nationalised after the April 2010 uprising by interim government since it was allegedly owned by Bakiyev's son Maxim Bakiyev who controlled 51 per cent holding. Maxim Bakiyev had allegedly obtained from Moscow-based Eventis Telecom in 2006. The Russian share holders were also squeezed later for their alleged links with Maxim Bakiyev. The Ministry of State Property took control of 51 per cent that was held by Maxim and later it claimed that the state had 100 per cent shares. However, in early February 2011, two Russian directors of Megacom were charged with abuse of power for failing to declare $10 million in profits and fled Kyrgyzstan. Eventis had been attempting to retrieve its shares back since the fall of Bakiyev's regime. The MegaCom row shook the Kyrgyz fragile coalition government and risked serious implications for the country's economy, besides ruining relations with Russia. The Russian leadership and media strongly reacted to the Kyrgyz corruption scandals. It was viewed as attempts to cheat Russian investors. MegaCom scandal involved the role of then First vice Prime Minister Omurbek Babanov who was accused extorting $50 million from Russian investors. The case was being probed by a parliamentary committee.

The MegaCom issue resulted in opening the old wounds that had not been healed despite the change in regime. Moscow started raising the pent up issues mostly connected to noncompliance by the Kyrgyz of previously undertaken commitments for joint projects. It only appeared that despite Russian decision to wave off tax on fuel and large-scale assistance in the form of aid and grant running into $40 million and possibly another $30 million interest-free credit to bail out the country from economic crisis, the Kyrgyz had shown complete apathy and refused to resolve the issues for over the past 10 years. These included Kyrgyz failure to pass over 48 per cent stakes in a Soviet-era torpedo plant that had been negotiated since 2009. Bishkek had promised to hand over the stakes in exchange for $193 million in debt relief and over $2 billion in investments and credit. The Kyrgyz had received $150 million, but never handed over the shares to Russia. The transfer was expected after the April 2010 change in power, but the Kyrgyz leadership abruptly announced in February 2011, during the visit to Bishkek by Turkish Prime Minister Recep Tayyip Erdogan, that it would sell Dastan torpedo plant to Turkey instead. Moscow has been critical of this move and Russian media considerably played it up.

Russia's Kant Airbase (KB) has long been another key sore-point since 2009. KB was established at the Kyrgyz request after militants intruded into southern Kyrgyzstan in 1999. Russia wanted to unite three of its military facilities, including KB, now under CSTO, into a Joint command for which it wanted a rental agreement for KB for 49 years plus a clause for another two years extension. The Kyrgyz side expressed disagreement and instead sought enhanced rent for KB from currently about $4.5 million a year.

Almazbek Atambayev was therefore in a difficult situation. During his last visit to Moscow, he had assured Vladimir Putin that Kyrgyzstan would revive all the Russian projects earlier cancelled by former President Bakiyev. But, now did not seem able to control his First vice-Prime Minister Omurbek Babanov, who was rampantly indulging in corruption scandals i.e. oil delivery to Manas air base, cases with Dastan plant and MegaCom Company. Omurbek Babanov was accused in the parliament for introducing a special payment for jet fuel supplies to the US Transit Centre.[4] In fact, the issue of imposing tax on fuel supplies to the US Transit Centre in Bishkek had put Prime Minister Almazbek Atambayev on the spot. He had to strongly disapprove the move and felt that by playing such a game Kyrgyzstan will not only flout the Kyrgyz-US agreement on fuel supplies and but will lose what had been gained already.

But, at the same time, Russia's pressure on the new Kyrgyz Government over some of the old pending issues had given rise to increased nationalistic rhetoric among Kyrgyz against Russia. The media in Kyrgyzstan mounted a sharp attack on Russia and its policies towards the CIS adding a new twist to the existing political inconsistency. The worst and painful issue for Russia was the rise of Kyrgyz nationalism, which was increasingly aimed at the Russian-speaking citizens in Kyrgyzstan. There were series of media reports about atrocities against persons of Slavic origin that led to many of them leaving Kyrgyzstan.[5] In April a four-year-old boy of Russian ethnicity was founded wounded in Bishkek. Another two-year-old ethnic Russian girl was wounded in the city of Osh.[6] Russian speaking citizens became immediate target with increasing demand for introducing Kyrgyz as working language. Many Russians lost their jobs creating a strong panic. There were reports of mass migration of ethnic Russian leaving Kyrgyzstan. An editorial note observed "The country, once proud of bilingualism and ethnic tolerance, gradually becomes like militant political enclave, where "title" ethnic group runs the show on the rights of the owner."[7] The power struggle among political class and the Russian factor in their game play did spill over into the society. At one point of time, Kyrgyz language mass media created an anti-Russian hysteria which invited intense criticism from the Russian mass media. The deputies of Russian Duma during the visit by to Bishkek had directly charged Kyrgyz First Vice-PM Omurbek Babanov for his involvement in scandals relating to fuel supply to Manas Transit Centre, cases with Dastan plant and MegaCom Company. Even Russian Ambassador Valentin Vlasov had issued a strong warning to the Kyrgyz authorities to stop violating Russian citizen's rights. The Russian Mission was monitoring and keeping close watch on the situation around Alfa Telecom CJSC.[8] However, spurt of nationalism in 2010-11 was also considered as artificial phenomenon and many viewed that it was linked to internal and external players. Even Atambayev noted that certain forces in Kyrgyzstan are interested in inciting inter-ethnic conflicts.[9]

It did appear that the Kyrgyz leaders have underestimated or possibly were not able to connect their interests with Russia's larger strategic and economic interest in Central Asia. Moscow appeared unable to hide its discomfort with Kyrgyz leaders who initially came to power on pro-Russian platform but suddenly chose to play up the nationalistic rhetoric—seeking an end to Russia intrusion into Kyrgyz affairs. Russian media went hysterical about Kyrgyz leaders' inability to protect Russia's interests. Moscow did come to a stage when it realised that even the pro-Russian oriented leader like Atambayev is unable to protect Russian investments, but rather, on the contrary, becoming a threat to Russian security. Moscow, therefore, could not hide the disappointment; both the tough official statements and the views in the Russian mass media proved it. Local Kyrgyz media noted that such sharp criticism from Russia was never seen in the history of independent Kyrgyzstan.[10]

Russia ultimately used its strongest instrument of slapping fuel duties on Kyrgyzstan.[11] Moscow had earlier promised to lift the duties on fuel export—imposed since April 2010—by February 15, 2011, but was held back due to political reasons and on the pretext that Kyrgyz were re-exporting Russian supplied fuel to third countries.[12] The delaying tactics by Moscow and even the reports about cancelling lifting of duties had created panic among ruling circles in Bishkek, for it would lead to social explosion especially when demand of Kyrgyz farmers for gasoline shoots up during spring sowing season. Inevitably, Moscow's tough talks, if not arms-twisting, became a kind of moment of truth for the coalition survival. The pro-Russia inclined Atambayev had though assured Vladimir Putin in December 2010 that his government will restore joint projects that were cancelled by Bakiyev regime. But, for him keeping together assertive coalition partners also seemed a difficult task. It appeared that Atambayev had no choice but to kowtow to Kremlin and concede to every Russian demand. It was a real victory for Russia's battle for influence. Atambayev visited Moscow on March 17-18, 2011 and Moscow won a string of heavy concessions in Kyrgyzstan at least in commitment, which included:

- 48 per cent stake for Russia in Dastan Torpedo manufacturing company.
- A building in Bishkek to host Russia's Trade Office in exchange of Kyrgyzstan's debt redemption. (Kyrgyzstan owes $190 million plus $11 million interest to Russia).
- The length of Russian Kant base was to be decided through a discussion at the expert level and parliamentary committee. No enhanced rent to

be paid to Kyrgyzstan on the ground that the base serves the interest of Kyrgyz security.

- A new agreement to allow 75 per cent stake for Gazprom in the Kyrgyz gas company.[13] (This was done to avoid crisis during the sowing season. Moscow had been warning that it will not supply duty-free fuel if Bishkek is not able to fulfill its earlier commitments.)
- Kyrgyzstan to expedite regulation of its debt to Russia. Russia will assist Kyrgyzstan obtaining credit from the Eurasian Economic Community Anti-Crisis Fund.
- Moscow on its part agreed to resume duty-free gasoline for an unknown period subject to specific terms and conditions and ensuring transparency of fuel supply for domestic consumption of Kyrgyzstan. Kyrgyz will save $400 million a year.
- Kyrgyzstan to join the Customs Union and Common Economic Space. (The issue has been widely debated in the country fearing this will put an end to the grey market space enjoyed by Chinese traders.)
- Russia also nudged the prospects for entering Kyrgyz energy sector, particularly in the construction of Kambar-Ata-1 hydropower plant costing $1.7 billion and hydroelectric stations on the Naryn River with $800 million investment. These proposals were linked to Pakistani offer of purchasing electricity from Kyrgyzstan.
- Significantly, Kyrgyzstan promised to oust the controversial US fuel supplier Mina Corp, on the grounds that the company was linked to Maxim Bakiyev. However, this decision was to put Kyrgyzstan on a collision course with US for breach of its legal commitments to protect foreign investment from expropriation and refrain from interfering with US contractors supplying the Transit Centre. A US Congressional inquiry 2010 year had found no evidence of financial links to Bakiyev family. It will also contravene the compromise deal struck with the US DoD in December last year under which Mina Corp was allowed to supply 50 per cent and a Kyrgyz-Russian joint company would supply 20 to 50 per cent of the fuel to Manas Transit Centre. (Gazpromneft-Aero-Kyrgyzstan joint venture started supplying jet fuel to Manas international airport in April 2011. The Kyrgyz Government was upbeat about the development since this was the first time in the CIS that the same company will supply fuel to both civil and military aircrafts.)[14]
- On the issue of hosting the US Transit Centre, Kyrgyzstan seemed committed to continuing it until 2014, but the indications were that the Centre might be transformed ultimately into a civil international transit centre, which will also have Russian participation. There were also calls by politicians to impose a tax on fuel supplies to the US Transit

Centre. Atambayev had to warn the critics that this would not only flout the Kyrgyz-US agreement but the country will lose what has already been gained if games continued to be play around it.

With these, some of the contentious issues in Kyrgyz-Russian relations appeared to have been resolved. But the main issue has been the perpetual delay by Russia in implementing its promised projects in Kyrgyzstan. Some of the earlier Russian commitments for investment had been delayed for years and the Kyrgyz have been quite frustrated on this issue. As a result the Kyrgyz had started to look elsewhere, especially to China and Turkey, for investment and assistance. But for Russia, Kyrgyz internal power struggle, instability, corruption and frequent changes in laws have deterred serious investment in Kyrgyzstan.[15] It remains to be seen how Kyrgyz Government would protect the interests of Russian investors in Kyrgyzstan. While the Prime Minister negotiated with the Russians, the interim President Roza Otunbayeva had earlier discussed setting up an US anti-terrorist centre and Cantonment in Southern Kyrgyzstan and also declared increased co-operation with NATO. It only indicated that the Kyrgyz political situation was quite shaky.

Following Atambayev's visit to Moscow, a high profile economic forum "*Expansion of interregional cooperation of Kyrgyzstan and Russia as factor of sustainable economic development*" was held in Bishkek on March 23, 2011. A high-level Russian delegation included EurAsEC Deputy Secretary General Sergey Glaziev, Chief of President's Interregional and Cultural Ties with Foreign Countries Department Sergey Vinokurov, Deputy Foreign Minister Gregory Karasin, Deputy Regional Development Minister Maksim Travnikov, Omsk, Orenburg and Altay governors and other Russian officials traveled to Bishkek to attend the economic forum.[16] The forum discussed the prospects of future cooperation between the two countries. The head of the Russian delegation, Sergey Vinokurov noted that the economic and trade factors should compel both the countries to improve relations. He said that this will be possible only in circumstances of socio-political stability and added that "Russia was and will remain a reliable friend and partner of Kyrgyzstan at this crucial stage of development of the state of the country."[17] In the Forum, Prime Minister Almazbek Atambayev admitted that previous agreements remained unimplemented due to failure from the Kyrgyz side. He favoured joining the Russian-led Customs Union and Common Economic Space which would be in the interest of Kyrgyzstan's future. It was perhaps for the first time that such a conference with such a large and important Russian delegation was held in Kyrgyzstan.

Atambayev witnessed provocation even before he left for Moscow. But he strongly defended relations with Russia and called on politicians not to try Russia's patience. He complained about games often being played in Kyrgyzstan as there were many instances of Kyrgyz officials having deceived Russia into signing an agreement.[18] Atambayev said that the country's destiny had been linked to Russia in the past and will remain so in the future. "It would be difficult to imagine the future if Kyrgyzstan and Russia is not together. From now on, we should not cheat anyone and we should understand that Russia's assistance is as a friend's hand and a brother's shoulder."[19] For the time being Atambayev seemed to have succeeded in arresting Kyrgyzstan's serious drift from Russia that was underway for quite some time.

However, the positive atmosphere created after his first visit to Moscow did not last very long. By mid-2011, Kyrgyzstan got into presidential election mode and Prime Minister Atambayev was running for the presidential post. Therefore, during 2011, there was no seriousness on both sides to fulfill their commitments to resolve the pending issues. In fact, the Kyrgyz leadership was not yet clear how he will manage to fulfill Russian economic, strategic and the rights of Russian Diaspora in Kyrgyzstan. For him, playing up the nationalistic card was essential to garner support for his presidential contest. The mutual acrimony continued as Russia further delayed the projects in Kyrgyzstan.

In February 2012, after he was elected as the President, Atambayev again made some provocative statements that added fuel to the fire. He cited that the CSTO base in Kant was not useful and sought its closure, despite a valid agreement for another 45 odd years. What he perhaps meant was that the Russian military presence in Kyrgyzstan did not help to resolve the country's internal instability caused during the Osh ethnic riots. Kyrgyz new President had also sought the replacement of Nikolay Bordyuzha, Secretary General of the CSTO saying that he interferes in the internal affairs of the state. In fact, Atambayev also invited the wrath of Kazakh officials when he apportioned blame to the Kazakh intelligence services of fomenting trouble in Kyrgyzstan.

There were instant media outbursts over Russian authorities working out a consolidation of the Russian military facilities in Kyrgyzstan into one structure, and amendment of CSTO charter to intervene in a member state's affairs to maintain security. Kyrgyz media also attributed double standards to Russia's policy—demanding closure of Manas while offering airport in Ulyanovsk to NATO. The Russian Ministry of Foreign Affairs instantly dismissed the news and quoted UNSCR 1386 as basis for providing facilities to ISAF/NATO forces. Russia further clarified that simplified procedure of combine rail, road and air transit—for non-military cargo of ISAF is under consideration by the government. In any case, the transit will be carried under Russian customs control; neither the military nor the civilian personnel of NATO will be involved. Russian Foreign Ministry also clarified that they welcome Kyrgyz leadership's intention to transform the airbase into civilian international transport hub with no military component. Moscow thought it was an important strategic step to ensure Kyrgyzstan's security on its own and relying on the CSTO.

Almazbek Atambayev visited Moscow in March 2012, this time as President, and had a meeting with Dmitry Medvedev. The contentious issues particularly pertaining to Kyrgyz-Russian military relations were once again raised by Atambayev that irked the Russians.[20] Clearly, Moscow was unhappy with the policy of Kyrgyz President Almazbek Atambayev. The Russian officials seemed to have taken exception to Atambayev's demands. Russian media also carried out analytical pieces to attack Atambayev for his earlier utterances over shutting down of the Russian military base in Kant, bargaining on the Dastan torpedo plant shares, and over his earlier criticism of the CSTO head Nikolay Bordyuzha. *Itar-Tass* commented that "Atambayev might go wobbly on his vow to kick the US out of Manas in 2014."[21] The media quoted a Russian official stating that Kyrgyz President was not only creating new problems for bilateral relations, but also for the CSTO activities. The official said "If earlier the CSTO brought together six allied countries and one country with the special position that is Uzbekistan, after the presidential elections in Kyrgyzstan we received a President, who does not realise always what he is saying."[22] The Russians also expressed doubts on whether Atambayev will keep his promise to shut down the US military base Manas by 2014. The Russian viewed Atambayev repeating the same mistake committed earlier by former President Bakiyev. Several commentators noted that Russian salvo against Atambayev resembled the similar campaign by Moscow against former president Kurmanbek Bakiyev prior to his overthrow in 2010. The Kyrgyz had subsequently shut down a Russian media portal *Fergana.ru.*

In the bilateral summit meeting, he had also taken up with Medvedev the matter of dues recoverable on the Russian Kant airbase amounting to a paltry $15 million. Medvedev instantly ordered to pay $15 million in 10 days. But, the issue of the repayment of Kyrgyzstan's public debt ($493 million) to Russia was still not resolved. However, at the official level, Russia had showed understanding with Kyrgyzstan's difficult financial and economic situation, and agreed to seek a viable option to resolve the issue. Moscow decided to send delegations from the Russian Ministry of Energy and big power companies to Bishkek to focus on cooperation in hydropower sector, oil and gas industries.

Notwithstanding Atambayev's tough bargaining, Moscow at this stage did not take counter measures against Bishkek. However, Russia did introduce a tougher rule that would make the entry of Kyrgyz emigrants to work in Russia more difficult. The Russian Migration Service annulled a rule where Kyrgyz citizens had a simplified citizenship acquisition procedure. Though, during the election run up, Putin did indicate of such an acquisition process for the EurAsSec member-states, it was announced following the rhetoric by Kyrgyz President. (Tajikistan ran into similar problems with the detention of the two Russian pilots in 2011)

As to buy peace, Atambayev said Kyrgyzstan would like to be a member of the Eurasian Economic Union and reiterated that Russia is a strategic partner. Russia supported Kyrgyz efforts with it within the framework of the Custom Union and the Common Economic Space (CES). Atambayev also tried to play on the historical bonding between Kyrgyzstan and Russia. He unveiled in Moscow a monument of the Kyrgyz legendary hero Manas. The significance of it was that Manas had come from Russia's Altai Mountains. Here, Atambayev was trying to convey the point that Kyrgyz and Russians had common roots. He said in Moscow, "not only Manas came from Russia; Moscow was defended in 1941 by Frunze based Panfilov Division headed by General Panfilov, military commissar of the Kyrgyz Republic."[23] In his meeting with Medvedev he said "over all these years, our peoples tried to build a united country. There was Siberia—the Kyrgyz khanate—more than 1,000 years ago and then there was the Russian Empire, also a khanate in its way, and finally the Soviet Union. Now we are striving to build the common economic space in part simply because it is in our genes now, in the genes of the Kyrgyz, Russian, and all peoples here. Our common future lies in unity."[24] All these comments were meant to clear the air of misunderstandings.

There was no clear explanation as to why Kyrgyz had decided to take some hard stand on problems with Russia at this point of time, though the Kyrgyz leadership was quite hard pressed to resolve the country's economic situation, which could not be possible without the Russian support. Looking towards China for help would not have been liked by Russia. Atambayev also probably may have felt that as the new President, legitimately elected through democratic means, should take a strong stance vis-à-vis Russia. He was also mindful of high expectations from the people, and moreover he was preparing to stand for president's post by the end of the year. On the whole, the media had created sufficient public acrimony between the two people. The political class was also playing up its part in furthering the divide. A noted Kyrgyz politician and the father of the country's last Constitution OmurbekTekebayev noted that Russia needed to change its Central Asian policy because Kremlin's old approach to dealing with the former republics was failing. He said Russia has made promises in the last 10 years, but never fulfilled them; whereas, other countries are already carrying out specific projects in the region. He said, "If the Russian elite think that we are dependent on them and as a result, we have to integrate, then they are mistaken. Geopolitics and relations in the world are changing."[25]

A comment from a political expert Mars Sariyev was equally strong, which said "Moscow has still not worked out an effective systemic policy...consequently; Russia is slowly leaving Central Asia. Uzbekistan's recent exit from the CSTO is a proof of this. While it is still possible to make up for the loss, as Russia cannot be a small stand-alone European country. It will either be an empire or cease to exist."[26]

Interestingly, the matter did not end there. In May 2012, on the eve of Vladimir Putin's taking over as Russia's President, Almazbek Atambayev aired his observations on relations with Russia in a national television.[27] He had again emphasised that the US airbase will have to be converted into a civilian hub, post June 2014. Atambayev remarked that the situation in Afghanistan vis-à-vis

Kyrgyzstan will decide the future course of action, and hinted that the allies will be consulted on this matter. But, by this time, Atambayev was insisting on status-quo regarding the shares in Dastan and also on the issue of Kyrgyz debt. Interestingly, Kyrgyz President criticised Russia for not averting the Osh crisis in June 2010, and justified the demand to shut down the airbase at Kant. He wished Kyrgyzstan to develop a strong army to remain independent with no leaning on Russia, but was also hopeful of taking the relations with Russia to a higher level. Atambayev also cited Russia's largesse to African countries and felt the Russian authorities can be more 'proper' to Kyrgyzstan hinting at easier terms.

However, Atambayev did not mention amends to CSTO charter to provide better internal-member-security, duty free fuel, or migration of Kyrgyz labour, but criticised Russia for not averting the Osh crisis, and demanded closure of Kant base. He was signaling a tough posture on Russia and to make up for the possible loss of content, he was getting closer to China, and often started using the term 'strategic allies'. In a clear signal to Moscow, Kyrgyz President discarded the fear of China threat.[28]

Obviously, everything seemed not going well in its relations with Russia. On July 12, 2012, the Kyrgyz Defence Minister Taalaybek Omuraliyev, during his visit to Moscow, talked about Kyrgyzstan's intentions to raise the rent for Russian military facilities from 2014 citing inflation as the reason.[29] It was clarified however that this was only about the Russian facilities such the military communications centre in Kara-Balta, (northern Chuy Region), a radio seismic laboratory in Mayli-Say (in southwestern Dzhalal-Abad Region) and a base for underwater weapons tests in Karakol (northeastern Issyk-Kul Region). Kant base was excluded in this and the defence minister said that the base is being used in the interests of the Collective Security Treaty Organization (CSTO).

No one though quite understood why Kyrgyzstan suddenly raised the rent issue of Russian facilities. But, critics doubted inflation as the reason. An interesting comment on this came from a local political analyst Mars Sariyev who was quoted by media as saying "It would be logical if an economic body announced an initiative of this kind.... But when such statements are made by the Defence Ministry, they clearly take on political overtones. What is more, there is still a lot of time until 2014. It would seem that there was no need to make relations with Russia worse ahead of time. The situation can be explained by the fact that the move is a diplomatic gesture to the USA. As is known, Kyrgyzstan decided to close the Manas transit shipment centre in 2014 under Russian pressure. The US troops are set to withdraw from Afghanistan soon. After that, the USA will distribute its military hardware between the countries of the region. A sharp pro-Russian tilt would not help Kyrgyzstan to get part of the hardware. Thus, by raising the rent for the Russian bases, Kyrgyzstan demonstrates to the USA its impartial attitude."[30]

The defence minister's statement became quite controversial after Russian media hyped it up, which led the Kyrgyz President's international department to clarify the official position. The head of the department, SaparIsakov had clarified that the rent was not a priority. A statement circulated by the President's press service on July 12, 2012 said "The term of the agreement between Kyrgyzstan and Russia on the status and conditions of the Russian air base in Kyrgyzstan on September 22, 2003 is valid until 2020. In addition, the agreements between the Kyrgyzstan and the Russian Federation on the use of Russian military facilities in Kyrgyzstan and the status of the armed forces on July 5, 1993 are automatically extended in accordance with the terms of the Agreement until 2017."[31] At the same time, SaparIsakov noted that discussions on a Kyrgyz-Russian draft agreement on the terms of deployment and the status of the Russian military base on Kyrgyzstan are under progress and the amount of the rent would not be a priority. Separately, Kyrgyz Foreign Ministry said that this was not souring the relations between two countries. Kyrgyz Assistant Foreign Minister Aseyin Isayev rejected the idea that the rent issue was going to sour relations with Russia. He said that when the duration of the agreement expires, the terms of the agreement are reviewed.[32] However, the Russian Ambassador to Kyrgyzstan Valentin Vlasov differed with Kyrgyz's version. According to him the issue of uniting three Russian military facilities and Kant airbas has been under discussion since 2009.[33] Russia, as per international norms had proposed signing a rent agreement for the military facilities for 49 years plus extension and a provision to extend it for another 25 years, ruling out any possibility to cancel it. Obviously, Ambassador was suggesting that Kyrgyz side was backing out from the previous understanding which was not acceptable to Russia.[34] Obviously, tensions between the two countries continued, especially when media on both sides tried to flare up the matters.

But in August 2012, during the Kyrgyz Prime Minister Omurbek Babanov's visit to Moscow Dmitry Medvedev, bluntly told Babanov that Kyrgyz authorities should not expect Russia and other partners just forget and forgive debts.[35] There was no doubt that following Atambayev's assuming President's office, Kyrgyz negotiations with Moscow has been quite tough. But so were Russian responses. Even Russian Foreign Minister Sergei Lavrov, during his visit to Bishkek in March 2012, insisted hard on several tough requirements regarding Russian investments in Kyrgyz hydropower projects. In a changed tactic, Russia started seeking 75 per cent shares in several hydro projects including Kambarata – 1, 2 and hydroelectric stations cascade on Sary Zhaz River, and the cascade on the upper Naryn that was agreed upon in 2008. Originally, the agreement stipulated Russia's Inter RAO UES was to have 50 per cent stakes. But, Russia's fresh argument was that the 50-50 proportion did not reflect the real contribution of two sides. Media reports have suggested that Kyrgyz side was seeking seven per cent increase in Russia's duty-free fuel supplies in return of allowing 75 shares in the Kambar-Ata plants.[36]

The Russian Energy Minister Sergei Shmatko, during his visit to Bishkek in March 2012, reiterated Russia's seriousness in reaching to a key decision on implementation of energy projects in Kyrgyzstan.[37] However, the meeting was a deadlock as the Kyrgyz side rejected Russia's fresh condition and insisted to work on the previous agreements. Shmatko promised to provide a package of documents containing a list of comprehensive conditions for the conclusion of intergovernmental agreements with specific deadlines for implementation by April 10, 2012.

The Kyrgyz media reflected the views of the Kyrgyz officials' stubbornness or unwillingness to concede on crippling Russian terms. The media quoted sources in the Kyrgyz officials saying that the government will not act contrary to the national interests and even if the situation becomes hard (stoppage of fuel supply) they will be compensated through investments from Turkey and China.[38] In fact, the Chinese activism in Kyrgyz grew around that time. A well-known Kyrgyz scientist Professor Hyder Aliev who was dealing with Kyrgyz energy issues told the author that a Chinese delegation was in Bishkek to lobby for opening a think tank to study the prospects of Sary Zhaz hydro power project. Of course, there were talks about the danger of getting dependence on China as a result. But, President Almazbek Atambayev assured that the country was not afraid of being caught into Chinese trap.[39]

Interestingly in the Kyrgyz case, the problems appeared to have been arising from misgivings in the mind of Russian officials (military and civilian bureaucracy). The top Kyrgyz leadership always claimed that there was never any misunderstanding at the political level.[40] Instead, they felt, that mistrust and apathy towards the Kyrgyz existed mostly among Russian officials.

However, a sense of thaw in the relations prevailed when President dispatched a special delegation under the First vice Premier Igor Shuvalov to Bishkek in August 2012 to fix all pending issues (military, energy and financial) with Kyrgyzstan. A positive environment was created and the two countries were ultimately able to secure several key agreements on all issues. On the eve of President Vladimir Putin's visit to Bishkek on September 20, 2012, Kremlin spokesman announced its plan to sign a number of important Russian-Kyrgyz documents, including inter-governmental agreements on the status and terms of the Joint Russian Military Base (JRMB) in Kyrgyzstan; on the construction and operation of the hydroelectric power plants Kambarata-1 and Upper Naryn cascade; and on settling Kyrgyzstan's debt to Russia.[41]

Kambar-Ata

Russia agreed to the construction of Kambar-Ata 1 hydroelectric power station and Verkhnenaryn chain of hydroelectric stations. Russia will fund the hydro projects on 100 per cent loan basis. Under the new agreements Kyrgyzstan will obtain 50 per cent shares in two projects. Kyrgyzstan agreed to put its 25 per cent shares under fiduciary management arrangement with Russia in order to generate faster returns. However, the property will be owned 50-50 and dividends will be shared by the same scheme. The terms of the loan was to be decided later. The construction of the Kambar-Ata-1 was to cost around $2.5 billion and Russia will invest about $455-500 million into other hydro projects on the upper Naryn River. The feasibility study is expected to be completed in February 2013.

Kyrgyz President Almazbek Atambayev in his interview to Kyrgyz TV on September 26, 2012 said that if impracticable things or intriguing things were included in the previous agreements, the new agreements are precise. Even though Kyrgyzstan will not spend any money for the project, yet critics were dissatisfied with 50-50 stake basis. There were apprehensions that Russia will end up controlling the entire operation. Atambayev instead said that Kyrgyzstan will give an additional 20 or 25 per cent of stake to Russia until the money invested by Russia is recovered. He expressed firm decision to go ahead with the controversial hydropower stations on the River Naryn irrespective of opposition from his Uzbek counterpart, Islam Karimov, who had recently warned that attempts to build large power stations might spark a military conflict in the region.[42] For Russia, the difficulty was to keep the balance and it wanted all countries of the region to take part in the projects. Putin explained "We are in favour of involving both Kazakhstan and Uzbekistan in this work. The Kyrgyzstani side supports us."[43] Kyrgyz President Almazbek Atambayev too welcomed the neighbours to take part in the Kambar-Ata 1 hydropower project. Atambayev recalled that the Kambar-Ata 1 was drawn up in Tashkent at Giproproject [design institute] during Soviet times.[44] Once completed, discharged water from Toktogul reservoir will only solve problems of irrigation in Uzbekistan and Kazakhstan. Atambayev promised to discuss everything with the neighbours transparently but he said that the rules of cooperation should be set so that the project poses no threat.[45] He said "The main thing is that neighbours should live in harmony with each other. We do not need a war. We need peace. In the first place, we should provide our people with jobs and fill the coffers of our state with money with the help of all these projects."[46] At the same time, he stated that "we are not a country to fear someone if he scares us. Everybody should understand that we are an independent state."[47] However, construction of these mega hydropower projects on Naryn River may confront with multiple challenges, including financial and geopolitical obstacles.

Although, the Russian State Duma may have passed the resolution to go ahead with the building of the giant dams Kambar-Ata 1-2 and other hydropower projects on the upstream of the Naryn River. But there is already growing anxiety in Russia whether it will be able to fulfil the energy ambitions in Central Asia due to several reasons including the risk and cost factor, economic slowdown in Russia and the potential risk of spoiling relations with Uzbekistan. The critics have already questioned Moscow's wisdom of investing for a longer period in Kyrgyzstan, which is known for its 'rowdy' politics.[48]

The Russian sponsored project though appears quite impressive; the total annual output is projected to be over five billion kilowatt hours. While RusHydro is planning to build the four generators on the Upper Naryn Cascade, Russian state-run company, Inter RAO, will oversee the $2-billion Kambar-Ata-1. The total cost of all the projects will be over $3 billion. Inter RAO already reported to have incurred loss of $721 million in 2012. In March 2013, Inter RAO awarded Canada's SNC-Lavalin a $5-million tender to undertake a feasibility study of Kambar-Ata. However, there is no clarity whether the construction will begin soon.

Joint Russian Military Base (JRMB)

Under a fresh negotiation, the term of presence of Russian military facilities, including the torpedo testing site at Lake Issyk-Kul, has been set for 15 years i.e. 2017 and valid until 2032. The rent to be paid by Russia for these facilities will be $4,502,495 a year. It was calculated at the rate of $0.5 per 1 sq. m. of land and $0.1 per 1 sq. m. of water area. The rent is to be paid in US dollars from January 1, 2012. Russian unit will have the rights to sail its ships in the Issyk-Kul Lake. The JRMB will enjoy full immunity from civil and administrative jurisdiction of Kyrgyzstan. The personnel of the JRMB including their family members will enjoy diplomatic privileges and immunities.[49]

The original agreement was signed by Russian Prime Minister Dmitriy Medvedev and ex-Kyrgyz President Kurmanbek Bakiyev in Cholpon-Ata (Issyk-kul) on August 1, 2009, according to which the Russian airbase was to stay in Kyrgyzstan for 49 years with a further automatic extension for another 25 years. Atambayev's government had been insisting the stay for 15 years citing national interest.

The draft agreement on JRMB was approved by the Kyrgyz Parliamentary Committee on Defence and Security.[50] But some Members of the Parliament wanted the JRMB to pay for public services, electricity and water. Kyrgyz First Deputy Defence Minister had to explain that under the CSTO charter the lessor provides free electricity, water and public services to military formations so that they can fulfil their tasks.

The matter was drawn to conclusion when some of the Kyrgyz political leaders acknowledged the importance of stationing the JRMB, which in itself is not only important for the country's security, but also provides capability to counter international terror attacks. Importantly, under the fresh negotiations, Russia will jointly fight with Kyrgyzstan in case of military aggression or terrorist attack from outside to protect the sovereignty and security of the Kyrgyz Republic. The agreement also ensured provision of Russia to supply modern weapons to Kyrgyzstan's armed forces. It was for the first time that such a clause was included in the agreement. Essentially, Kyrgyzstan has been turned into a protectorate state.

The MP from Ar-Namys (Dignity) party and the Deputy Chairman of the Parliamentary Committee on Foreign affairs, Nurlan Torobekov quickly issued a statement justifying the need to resolve the issues with Russia. He said it was necessary taking into consideration the post-2014 US withdrawal from Afghanistan and the possible deterioration of security situation in the region. Importantly, he added that the decision was a political one and was linked to other bilateral issues, specifically, the writing off of the country's debt and the construction of hydropower stations.[51] Atambayev too strongly justified the agreement and said "God willing, our army or our armed forces will certainly stand on their own two feet in 15 or 20 years' time, but someone must help us if a war or other disaster breaks out by that time. We need this agreement."[52] In fact, a joint Kyrgyz-Russia military exercise was conducted around that time with the participation of pilots from the Russian Central Military District (CMD) at the Kant base over a simulated scenario of illegal armed groups equipped with modern weapons and communications and tracking equipment intruding in Central Asia.[53]

Atambayev drew JRMB's similarity with Japan's military agreement with the USA. In an interview he elaborated the need for having such a military agreement with Russia. He said "The Kyrgyz armed forces have not stood on their own two feet yet...We need to set up our own army within the next five to 10 or 15 years to be able to protect our country on our own, instead of counting on others. However, we need a friend who will fight jointly side by side with us by that time. Take the military base, for example, it is we who need it. One must realise this and stop playing games. If there were games in previous agreements we have done away with all of them now. We have included new clauses. We have changed 74 years lease period to 15 years."[54]

Kyrgyz Debts to Russia

Kyrgyzstan had two big debts to Russia—around $189 million of September 5, 2005 and $300 million external debt of February 3, 2009. In accordance with the new agreements and the signed protocols, the two countries agreed that the debt of 2005 would be written off in full in a lump sum. As for the second debt, the countries agreed that it will be serviced until 2016 and after that it will be written off in equal shares within 10 years. Interests would not be accrued and also not be paid. The agreements were to be signed before October 15, 2012 and countries will implement internal procedures before November 30, 2012. Prior to Putin's visit Kremlin said that the cancellation of Kyrgyzstan's debts to Russia worth nearly half a billion dollars is being considered after taking into account the development of full range of cooperation with Kyrgyzstan.[55] On September 21, 2012, Russian Finance Minister Anton Siluanov had said in State Duma that Russia's efforts to write off debts of developing countries (Kyrgyzstan and North Korea) increase its political weight as a donor. He was quoted as saying "In such cases we receive mostly political dividends since Russia along with other developed countries is helping the countries with developing economies and countries who do not possess serious resources to develop their economy."[56] He noted that as a rule, the debts which would hardly be recovered are written off but decision to write-off the Kyrgyz debt foresees the promotion of Russian interests in this country, including the energy and military spheres.

The agreement on settling the debt issues was agreed upon on February 3, 2009 in Moscow, but it never came into force. Kyrgyzstan was to repay the part of the debt to Russia before December 1, 2009 after handing over 48 per cent stake in the Transnational Corporation Dastan worth $19.4 million and the building of the Trade Delegation of Russia for free use for 49 years. The remaining part of the public debt was to be written off within seven working days upon handover of the assets to Russia. In an interview Atambayev justified the new negotiation on the debt issue which had been pending since former President Askar. He said a $300 million borrowed by President Bakiyev was also being forgotten and this was not correct. He promised to repay these debts within thirty years period.[57]

Transnational Corporation Dastan OJSC

Importantly, the handing over of 48 per cent of Torpedo Plant Dastan's shares to Russia no longer remained an issue. Instead, Kyrgyzstan has reserved the right to offer Dastan shares for sale through the auction to interested investors. Key experts were to study this issue. Kyrgyzstan also retained ownership of the building of the Trade Delegation of Russia. In early 2012, Russia demanded revision of the earlier agreed arrangement and sought 75 per cent stake instead of 48 per cent earlier agreed upon in the TNC Dastan. This was to be done in exchange for $180 million debt to be written-off by Russia. Russia demanded 75 per cent on the pretext that since 2009, the assets of Dastan depreciated due to wear and tear of the equipment. As mentioned earlier, the Kyrgyz were against such plan.

These agreements between Kyrgyzstan and Russia were a major breakthrough. Two sides were involved in mutual disputes and had created a major source of irritants leading to worsening of bilateral relations in 2009-10. Russia had constantly reminded Kyrgyzstan about the debt and the Kyrgyz officials would always dodge Moscow on some pretext or other. The Kyrgyz probably thought that they could get away by saying that the money was squandered by the former regime and the prevailing economic situation does permit them to pay back the debt. Even the public opinion was in favour of paying back the debt.

Of course, the Kyrgyz leadership had its own games to play with Russia. In April 2011 the Kyrgyz Government approved a plan to join the Customs Union with Russia, Belarus and Kazakhstan with which it had 45 per cent of foreign trade. The joining of the Customs Union has considerably delayed which also caused several mistrust among the Russians. More recently, relations further soured after the visit by President Atambayev to Moscow in 2012. His statements on the debt issue, Russian Airbase at Kant and criticism over the role of Russian special service in Osh in 2010 had angered the Russians. The matter worsened to such an extent that the Russian officials advised "not to search enemies among friends."[58] Moscow only had to play the fuel and migrant cards to tighten the Kyrgyz.

The breakthrough came during Russia's First Vice Premier Shuvalov's visit to Bishkek in August 2012. However, it was Putin who finally put seal on the agreements that were crucial to both countries. Russia finally pacified the Kyrgyz President Atambayev, who just few months back was up in arms against Moscow and did not want to hear about the presence of Russian military bases in Kyrgyzstan. This time he once again declared Russia as key strategic partner. The final outcome was that Kyrgyzstan bargained hard on Russian security interests to gain economic benefits for self; Russia squeezed the Kyrgyz on economic matters to secure a good security deal.

Under the new agreement, the Russian military will remain in Kyrgyzstan for at least another 20 years. In return, Russia will partially write-off Kyrgyzstan's debt measuring almost half a billion dollars. However, Putin reminded the Kyrgyz that it was Kyrgyzstan which asked for the Russian military base when armed terrorists entered the country in early 2000. Putin explained that the security threat from extremism, drug trafficking and terrorism has not changed and may in fact worsen as the situation in Afghanistan would hardly improve in the immediate future. Only Russian military presence in the region will help to ensure stability, he said.[59]

Atambayev once again categorically assured that Manas airbase will be turned into a civilian airport starting from 2014.Vladimir Putin promised to help to transform America's Manas base into a civilian facility. Putin responded by saying if Kyrgyzstan is interested in seeing the airport make a profit, Russia is prepared to fill it with economic content.[60] Putin also lured Kyrgyzstan to join the Eurasian space including its accession to the Customs Union and the Eurasian Economic Community (EAEC).[61]

Atambayev hoped that this will mark a new stage in their relations. He said that the signing of these agreements have been realised after waiting for decades, and many would still not believe this would actually happen considering there was so much mistrust against Kyrgyzstan. The two sides noticed that the actual hero who actually repaired the damaged relationship was Andrey Belyaninov, Co-chairman of the Intergovernmental Commission and Head of the Federal Customs Service. The Kyrgyz President conferred him with an award and said that Andrey "is a great friend of Kyrgyzstan and our little Kyrgyz in Moscow... We have had various problems, but he always campaigned for quite different relations."[62]

For Russia, settling the pending issues with Kyrgyzstan was a big strategic achievement. The Russian analysts termed it as forward policy in a geopolitical zone. The development was viewed in the context of securing energy interests, military interests and in the context of post 2014 Afghan situation. Some analysts even linked it to the American missile defence system in Kyrgyzstan.[63]

The creation of a JRMB in Kyrgyzstanis though was not a new thing because it contains the same old items. But the Russian side has put it in a different strategic context and situation. The Kant airbase has been a component of the CSTO in the past. Similarly, the Russian Federation Navy's Marevo communications hub in Kara-Balta, the radio-seismological laboratory at Mayly-Suu, and the torpedo testing site Ozero at Karakol on the Issyk-Kul Lake have already existed there. The only new thing is the period of their presence that has been extended for 15 years and will come into force in 2017.

Russian security experts, excited by the development, felt the necessity to have a full-blown military base in Kyrgyzstan in the light of increasing American forays into Central Asia. Aleksandr Sobyanin, leader of the Border Cooperation Association's Strategic Planning Service was quoted in *Nezavisimaya Gazeta* saying, "Russia has limited room for geopolitical maneuvering...forced to play according to American rules as clearly visible from President Putin allowing the opening of a US-NATO Air Force logistics centre in Ulyanovsk as part of the Northern Distribution Network (NDN) for carrying cargo to Afghanistan."[64] According to Sobyanin, the Americans are gambling with radical international Islamist groups to reformat the region. Importantly, Sobyanin noted "The American strategy entails the creation of military bases, logistics centres, relay airfields under the "Lily Pad" special programme, and training centres for security structures and the handover of some of the armament and military equipment of the US troops being withdrawn from Afghanistan...ensuring a massive presence makes it possible to tie individual Central Asian regimes to themselves and to give logistical support to allied Islamist combat groups."[65]

In fact, Russian and Kyrgyzstan had signed a MoU on the creation of a base in southern Kyrgyzstan in the town of Kyzyl-Kiya. Moscow had been interested in creating it in Osh but the Kyrgyz had insisted on Batken located closer to Afghanistan. The new agreement on a Joint Military Base does not mention the possibility of creating a permanent base. However, Russia emboldened by new achievements in Kyrgyzstan may push for it in the near future.

Not just the Afghan and the US factor, the need for a full-blown Russian military base in Kyrgyzstan is also being considered essential by Russian strategic community in the context of possible contradiction between Russia and China in the future. According to Yuriy Gromyko, Director of Management of Human Resources, "Whatever people might say about friendly relations with China, Beijing rigidly considers Kyrgyzstan in the zone of its interests and, given a suitable occasion, will take Moscow's place."[66]

If such a thing shapes up, Russia is likely to choose Osh as a key strategic point in Central Asian Theater to counter all possible threats; for instability in Osh affects the entire Fergana region. Osh is sufficiently located not only in proximity to southern Russia but is also the epicentre of Central Asia. However, such a military base in Osh will entail strong protest from Uzbekistan so long as President Karimov is in power. Certainly, Russia seems to be keen on strengthening its military position in Central Asia now that Moscow has been able to bring Kyrgyzstan back under its wing after some of the Kyrgyz democratic leaders such as Roza Otunbayeva and others hobnobbed with the Americans briefly and brought coloured revolution there.

Russian experts viewed that the Americans were building a missile interceptor system at the Manas Transit Centre in Kyrgyzstan with a capability to track down objects from distance. According to some reports, the radar system was constructed by Turkish company Serka.

The Russian had to be worried because prior to Putin's visit to Tajikistan and Kyrgyzstan, the US Assistant Secretary of State Robert Blake during his visit to Uzbekistan promised $ 2.8bn direct investments in the country. The US also agreed to make bulk purchases in Uzbekistan for its group in Afghanistan.[67]

Shortly after Putin's visit to Bishkek, Russian Defence Minister Anatoliy Serdyukov announced on September 21, 2012 that the Russian military base at Kant will be able to receive strategic bombers once the modernisation of airbase is completed in six months. Serdyukov also detailed some more information about the organisational structure of the airbase which will be brought under a single command and control.[68] The Kyrgyz Defence Ministry listed terrorism as the main external threat to national security in its new military doctrine released in September 2012. The First Deputy Defence Minister, Col Ilyazbek Subankulov said "The following figure among internal threats in Kyrgyzstan's new military doctrine: separatism, localism and religious extremism. The situation in the Middle East, Afghanistan, the incursion of armed groups into Kyrgyzstan and terrorism are part of the external threats."[69]

The agreement for a JRMB seemed to have caught the strategic imagination from both Kyrgyz and Russian side. The Kyrgyz enthusiasm appeared to have grown into its leaders seeking additional military packages from Moscow, including supply of arms and uniform for the Kyrgyz armed forces worth $1 billion. A strong rumour had spread in the public domain when information leaked in media in November 2012 that Russia was preparing to deliver military equipment worth $1.1 billion to Kyrgyzstan and $200 million to Tajikistan.

The information drew mixed reaction in Kyrgyzstan; optimists welcoming the news, while the skeptics feared that the country was going to lose the last remnants of independence and become an appendage to Russia.[70] Of course, there was no official confirmation about the news. However, many observers viewed that Kyrgyz are unlikely to turn down such an offer by Moscow. It remains to be seen how the new found relationship between Russia and Kyrgyzstan will last, but one thing is clear that Russia is now keen on taking the opportunity to turn Kyrgyzstan into a strong military bastion in Central Asia.

The post-2014 Security Scenario

As the drawdown dates of Alliance forces from Afghanistan are approaching nearer, Central Asian states are redesigning their security charts to profit from the reverse transit. Since May 2012, they have signed fresh agreements with NATO on ground transport routes to move out non-lethal equipment along the Northern Distribution Network (NDN). Although, signing of these agreements came against the backdrop of Russia's own approval of a transshipment centre for NATO in its Ulyanovsk city, the developments since then have snowballed into weakening of the Russian-led CSTO.

After Uzbekistan announced its withdrawal from the CSTO, Tajikistan and Kyrgyzstan too have started bargaining for more dividends from Russia's military presence in their territories. As already illustrated above, while Tajikistan has demanded $300 million yearly rent for the presence of Russia's 201st military base in its territory, Kyrgyzstan announced plans to increase the rent and place new conditions for the presence of three Russian military facilities including a Torpedo testing centre No 954 in Karakol, a military the 338th communications centre in Kara-Balta, and a radio seismic laboratory in Mailuu-Suu starting from 2014, when the existing term expires. Even the Kant airbase, which is operating under the CSTO auspices, the Kyrgyz President, during his visit to Moscow earlier this year, made a huge hue and cry about a $15.5 million debt outstanding against Russia. The amount was immediately released by the Russian Defence Ministry following a direct intervention by the Russian President.

The other three bases have been in existence under a 1993 agreement by which Russia agreed to train Kyrgyz military personnel and provide military equipment, though media reports have said these conditions have not been met since 2008, allegedly due to the deteriorating political situation in Kyrgyzstan.

In Tajikistan, the 201st Motorised Infantry Division was deployed in 2005 under a mutual assistance agreement. About 7,000 Russian servicemen are deployed in Dushanbe, Kurgan-Tyube, and Kulyab, serving as a key element of the common security system in Central Asia. The fate of the 201st army base had been turned into a riddle for quite some time as both Moscow and Dushanbe have exchanged conflicting signals for the continuation of the facility after 2014. But like the Kyrgyz, the Tajiks too asserted that the issue is not about money but about respect of their national interests. Tajikistan has been taking tougher stance linking the issue with host of problems such as from the ill-treatment of Tajik labourers working in Russia to seeking lower import duties on oil products coming from Russia. Russia finally managed to sign a deal with Tajikistan in October 2012 to extend the lease of the Russian Army's 201st Division's base to until at least 2042, with possible five-year extensions afterwards.

Besides the above, there was also a dispute over the lease of the Gabala radar station in Azerbaijan by Russia. The underlying motives seem driven both by geopolitical as well as due to economic interests. Since the 9/11, politics of military bases in Central Asia has been determined mainly by question of commercial yield, and in the face of rising economic recession and the lack of substantial sources of incomes in Tajikistan and Kyrgyzstan, it is likely to be a continuing feature.

Russia's State Duma, ratified in April 2013 both agreements with Tajikistan and Kyrgyzstan on extending the presence of Russian military bases.[71] The bases according to Russia media are meant as bulwark against the threat of Islamist extremism and drug-trafficking in Central Asia.

But, it is also clear that individual states are trying to readjust their policies to meet the post 2014 security scenario. For example, Uzbekistan's decision seems to be based on much deeper considerations of its domestic politics and the security challenges it foresees from Afghanistan. It has done such a rebalancing earlier as well.

But assessing the general situation, countries like Kyrgyzstan would seek to benefit from the three-way geopolitical struggle. The growing US interest for using Central Asia as a staging ground, and China's intention to build Central Asia as a shield and buffer for Xinjiang and Russia's interest to retain its strategic hold in the region. Thus far, Moscow has managed to get a security foothold in Kyrgyzstan until 2032 as part of a package deal signed in exchange of committing investment in hydropower projects as well agreeing to immediately write off Kyrgyz debt. Russia also hopes to bring Kyrgyzstan into the fold of the Moscow-led Customs Union. But all these issues are embedded into a very complicated regional geopolitics. One only hopes that the Kyrgyz will prove lucky this time and that Kyrgyzstan will become an exporter of energy someday.

NOTES

1. Evgeny Troitskiy, "*Political Turbulence in Kyrgyzstan and Russian Foreign Policy*", Tomsk State University, UIbrief no 10 November 14, 2011 http://www.ui.se/upl/files/66217.pdf
2. http://english.ruvr.ru/2010/12/17/37106366/
3. "Putin's Peak: Kyrgyzstan Names Mountain after Russian Leader", *Associated Press,* February 18, 2011http://dailycaller.com/2011/02/18/kyrgyzstan-names-mountain-after-putin/#ixzz1EOmLIiOj
4. "Kyrgyzstan wants to slap tax on US base", *Associated Press,* February 3, 2011
5. A senior scientist of Russian origin working at Dastan Plant told the author about 30,000 Russians on average leave Kyrgyzstan.
6. "Kyrgyz police chief, Russian envoy meet to discuss child murder case", *AKIpress news agency,* April 17, 2012.
7. Daniyar Karimov, "Politics.kg: Point of no return", *24.kg news agency,* March 15, 2011
8. "Russian Embassy demands—to stop violating Russian citizens' rights", URL: http://eng.24.kg/community/2011/03/16/16876.html
9. He said in an interview with the Public Service Broadcasting Corporation *OTRK.* March 8, 2011; "PM Atambaev: We shouldn't allow rampant nationalism" *AKIpress,* March 9, 2011.
10. Daniyar Karimov, "Politics.kg: Point of no return" *24.kg news agency,* March 15, 2011
11. Russia had been providing duty free petrol, almost 25 per cent less, to inject a rare boost of confidence into Kyrgyz economy.

12. There were reports of Kyrgyz big officials re-exporting Russian supplied fuel to Tajikistan and perhaps even to China. It was believed that First Vice-PM Omurbek Babanov was involved in fuel smuggling.
13. "Kyrgyzstan offers 75% of the "KyrgyzGaz" to Russia. Moscow is preparing to lend $30 mln to Bishkek", *Ferghana News*, March 21, 2011.
14. "Fuel Kyrgyz-Russian joint venture starts operations in Kyrgyzstan", *24.kg news agency*, April 1, 2011
15. Russian Ambassador in Bishkek frequently complained about over 150 Russian companies operating in Kyrgyzstan being frequently harassed by Kyrgyz officials
16. *AKIpress*, March 21, 2011.
17. DaniyarKarimov, "Sergei Vinokurov: Direct interaction of the Russian Federation and Kyrgyzstan—an important factor of integration between the two countries", *24.kg news agency*, March 23, 2011, http://eng.24.kg/business/2011/03/23/17025.html
18. In an interview to national television channel on March 20, 2011, Atambayev said nobody should make money on Kyrgyzstan's security. We shouldn't forget that the Russian air base was established at the request of Kyrgyzstan when militants from Afghanistan intruded into the country in 1999."
19. *Khabar*, April 20, 2011
20. Atambayev lacked diplomatic skills and had no idea about international politics. There was much discussion in the Bishkek based foreign diplomatic circle about his lack of political acumen.
21. Joshua Kucera, "Moscow Airs Grievances over Kyrgyzstan's Military Moves", *EurasiaNet*, March 22, 2012.
22. Ibid.
23. "Meeting with President of Kyrgyzstan Almazbek Atambayev", http://eng.kremlin.ru/news/3469 February 24, 2012.
24. Ibid.,
25. "Kyrgyz experts urge Russia to change its "failing" Central Asian policy", *Vesti.kg*, Bishkek, in Russian, July 5, 2012.
26. *Vesti.kg*, Bishkek, in Russian, July 5, 2012.
27. *Kyrgyz Television 1*, Bishkek, May 2, 2012.
28. Ibid.
29. *AKIpress*, July 12, 2012.
30. *Vesti.kg*, Bishkek, in Russian 0517gmt July 12.
31. President's press service, also see *AKIpress*, July 12, 2012.
32. "Review of accord on Russian military base not to "sour" ties-Kyrgyz official", *KyrTAg*, Bishkek, July 13, 2012.
33. Ambassador Valentin Vlasov, said in an interview with Bishkek's *Piramida TV channel* on March 22, 2012.
34. *Interfax news agency*, March 22, 2011.
35. Islam Duvanaev, "Debt bondage for Kyrgyzstan", *24.kg news agency*, August 2, 2012.
36. Kyrgyzstan imports 750,000 tons of duty-free fuel from Russia which amounted to some $240-280 million per annum. But the issue of stopping fuel supply is always hot political issue for landlocked Kyrgyzstan. In 2010, Moscow had to just restrict the supply and the Bakiyev's regime fell in 1.30 hours.
37. *AKIpress*, March 28, 2012
38. *AKIpress*, March 29, 2012
39. URL: http://eng.24.kg/cis/2012/03/27/23553.html
40. "Problems and games arise at the level of officials", *Kommersant*, April 6, 2012
41. *Interfax news agency*, September 19, 2012

42. Uzbek President during his visit to Kazakhstan tried to garner Kazakh support to stop the construction of big hydro dams in Tajikistan and Kyrgyzstan that would affect the downstream countries like Kazakhstan and Uzbekistan.
43. 'Russian paper details Putin's visit to Kyrgyzstan", *Rossiyskaya Gazet, September 21, 2012*
44. Atambayev said in an interview to *Kyrgyz TV* I, September 26, 2012
45. "President says Kyrgyzstan to go ahead with controversial power project", *AKIpress,* September 26, 2012.
46. Atambayev said in an interview to *Kyrgyz TV* I, September 26, 2012.
47. Atambayev said in an interview to *Kyrgyz TV* I, September 26, 2012.
48. Chris Rickleton, "Russian Concerns over Central Asia Threaten Kyrgyzstan Hydroelectric Plant", *Eurasianet,* April 30, 2013.
49. "Putin to extend Russian military base stay in Kyrgyzstan till 2032 – aide", *Interfax,* September 19, 2012.
50. "Kyrgyz parliamentary committee approves draft accord on Russian military base", *AKIpress,* September 10, 2012.
51. "Russian military base to help ensure security in Kyrgyzstan, Central Asia – MP", *Interfax news agency,* September 7, 2012.
52. Atambayev said in an interview to *Kyrgyz TV* I, September 26, 2012.
53. "Russian air base in Kyrgyzstan conducts military exercises", *AKIpress news agency,* September 11, 2012.
54. Interview to *Kyrgyz TV* I, September 26, 2012.
55. *Interfax news agency, Moscow,* September 19, 2012.
56. "Russia's move to write off debts brings political dividends - finance minister" *BBC, Interfax news agency,* September 21, 2012.
57. Interview to *Kyrgyz TV I,* September 26, 2012.
58. URL: http://eng.24.kg/business/2012/08/02/25164.html.
59. "Russia's military presence in Kyrgyzstan factor of stability in region – Putin", *Channel One TV, Moscow,* September 20, 2012.
60. *Rossiyskaya Gazeta,* September 21, 2012.
61. "Russia backs Kyrgyzstan's accession to Customs Union - presidents' statement", *Interfax,* September 20, 2012
62. *Rossiyskaya Gazeta website, Moscow, in Russian,* September 21, 2012
63. *Nezavisimaya Gazeta,* September 20, 2012.
64. Ibid.
65. Viktoriya Panfilova, "Russian daily views Putin's visit to Kyrgyzstan", *Nezavisimaya Gazeta,* September 20, 2012.
66. Quoted by *Nezavisimaya Gazeta* on September 20, 2012.
67. *Regnum news agency,* Moscow, in Russian, October 7, 2012.
68. "Russian strategic bombers could be landing in Kyrgyzstan within six months', *Interfax-AVN military news agency,* Moscow, September 21, 2012.
69. "Terrorism tops list of threats in new Kyrgyz military doctrine – official", *KyrTAg, Bishkek, in Russian,* September 25, 2012.*Also read* 'Kyrgyz border chief warns of rise in border security threats in 2014", *Kyrgyz Telegraph Agency* (*KyrTAg*), July 12, 2012
70. "Russian daily views Kyrgyz reactions to reports of possible military aid", *Nezavisimaya Gazeta,* November 8, 2012
71. "Russia ratifies Central Asia base deals", *RIA Novosti,* April 20, 2013.

CHAPTER 10

Kyrgyz-US Relations: Politics of Airbase

The importance of Kyrgyzstan to the United States increased only in the aftermath of the September 11, 2001 events. Until then the US was only helping Kyrgyzstan, like it did to other Central Asian states, to enhance its sovereignty, political and economic reforms, strengthen human rights, prevent weapons proliferation, and more particularly to strengthen capacity to combat transnational terrorism and drug trafficking.

Prior to 2001, the total US assistance to Kyrgyzstan from 1992 to 2008 was $953.5 million.[1] The USAID had launched wide-ranging programmes supporting institutional building, ostensibly aimed at supporting democracy, open society and a free market economy. Besides, the US has also been playing a key role in influencing international financial institutions like World Bank and IMF to extend sustained assistance to Kyrgyzstan.

Politics and Diplomacy over Manas Transit Centre

However, things changed drastically in December 2001when Kyrgyzstan offered to host the US forces at its Manas international airport located outside Bishkek. Since then, the US and NATO have been using the air field for aerial refueling, airlift and airdrop, medical evacuation, and for the transit of coalition personnel and cargo in and out of Afghanistan. In 2009, in an interesting geopolitical game, the Kyrgyz Government, under the former President Kurmanbek Bakiyev, had threatened to close down the US airbase after receiving a financial assistance package from Russia. But in an interesting twist Bakiyev reversed the decision in June 2009 after the United States had agreed to increase payments that rose from $17.5 million to $60 million annually. The airbase was renamed as the Manas Transit Centre. However, some reports indicated that the USAID was spending colossal amount of money in Kyrgyzstan's democratisation programme through a no-bid contract to Development Alternatives, Inc. (DAI).[2] Most of such no-bid contracts given by the US government to Kyrgyzstan were meant for fuel supplies to the Manas Transit Centre, but it was indicated that sums involved were thousands of times bigger than part of US spending on the war in

Afghanistan.[3] These contracts did become scandalous and were under congressional investigation.

After Bakiyev was thrown out in 2010 uprising, the US provided $90 million urgent humanitarian aid to Kyrgyzstan to deal with the deadly ethnic violence that erupted in Osh in June 2010. In return, the new interim Government headed by President Roza Otunbayeva, supported the continued presence of the US Transit Centre, although the new authorities sought few changes in the lease. Roza Otunbayeva had been known for her pro-US stance. She has been viewed by many as the key point person of Washington in Central Asia.

It was not without a reason that the US Secretary of State Hillary Rodham Clinton in a special gesture visited Bishkek in December 2010 soon after the first Kyrgyz parliamentary elections was held under Roza Otunbayeva's supervision. Secretary of State applauded Kyrgyzstan's efforts to establish a democratic government. She said "There are many who say parliamentary democracy cannot work in Central Asia....we think Kyrgyzstan is proving that it can."[4] Clinton praised Otunbayeva and promised commitment to work for the future Kyrgyzstan.

In fact, after a visit to Washington in March 2011, President Roza Otunbayeva announced the possible opening of two military training centres funded by the US and Russia in Kyrgyzstan.[5] The US centre was to be located in Batken and the Russian facility was to be opened in Osh.[6] Of course, both have not been implemented so far. Otunbayeva also mentioned about training centres in Koi-Tash and Tokmok where the US was providing military training for Kyrgyz conscripts. She had emphasized that this was not a balancing act but to receive support from both Russia and US to fight against terrorism.[7] In fact, this time, the Kyrgyz leadership was trying to capitalise on the Obama's "reset" policy that led to closer US and Russia cooperation.

The presence of the US airbase in Manas in 2001 did become the main reference point for Kyrgyz-US relations. It was not only a major strategic breakthrough for the US but also for Kyrgyzstan and its geopolitical status in the region, especially for its unsettling impact on its relations with Russia and China. Obviously, the Manas Transit Centre remains in a position to extend operational range vis-à-vis both China and Russia. The facility is located particularly in close proximity to China's sensitive Xinjiang province. Both Russia and China have been been wary of the US military facility and had put constant pressure on Kyrgyzstan to have it vacated. But the successive Kyrgyz leaders continued to play game around the US facility to extract maximum financial benefits from the US. In fact, the Manas base and the rent it generated became a key factor for internal political squabble resulting in the overthrow of two Presidents through mass uprisings.

New Challenge for the US

The parliamentary elections and the regime largely headed by nationalist and also pro-Russian Kyrgyz leaders that replaced the pro-Washington Roza Otunbayeva had badly upset the US plans in Kyrgyzstan.[8] The US was hoping to get an easy extension of lease for the Manas Transit Centre. Besides, Otunbayeva had promised to allow US sponsored counterterrorism and anti-narcotics training center in Kyrgyzstan. All these plans got washed out after Otunbayeva left the Kyrgyz political scene voluntarily after conducting the parliamentary elections. This was a setback for the US. The US Ambassador was called back to Washington after Otunbayeva left office.

The Kyrgyz new leader Almazbek Atambayev who took over power, first as the Prime Minister in 2010 and a year later as the President, had repeatedly threatened to close down the Manas Centre once the existing leasewith US expires in 2014. This time, President Almazbek Atambayev took a non-commercial overtone and said in a statement "we know that the United States of America is often involved in various military conflicts. This was the case with Iraq, now Afghanistan, and now there's a tense situation in Iran. And I don't want any of these countries to attack the military base one day. The civil airport should be a civil airport."[9] Of course, the statement was more in line with views of Russia and China.

Since this statement came from Atambayev, the US stepped up its efforts and sought diplomatic maneuvering to retain its military facility in Kyrgyzstan. A string of US delegation visited Bishkek following the statement. The US Deputy Secretary of State William Burns was negotiating with the Kyrgyz Foreign Minister Ruslan Kazakbaev in February 2012 on the sidelines of the Third Ministerial Conference of Paris Pact partners on combating the Afghan Illicit Opiate Trade held in Vienna.[10]

Almazbek Atambayev in February 2012 though agreed to resume Kyrgyz-American security consultations and proposed to discuss possibilities of strengthening security cooperation. But, he bluntly told the visiting US delegation led by US Deputy Assistant Secretary of State for South and Central Asia, Susan Elliott that after the summer of 2014 there should be no foreign military troops at Manas Airport.[11] Kyrgyz President maintained a position that "any future cooperation with the US will be built around his country's national interests, and democratic development will serve as a factor in strengthening bilateral relations."[12] Susan Elliott was accompanied by Deputy Assistant U.S. Secretary of Defence for Afghanistan, Pakistan and Central Asia, David Sedney, Director of the Office for Central Asia at the U.S. National Security Council (NSC) Lynne Tracy, and Major-General John Nicholson. Lynne Tracy conveyed to Atambayev a message of greetings from US President Barack Obama.[13] Through the visit, the US was trying not only to placate the Kyrgyz but was also offering them a role to play in the Afghan stabilisation process. The US delegation told the Kyrgyz leadership that finding a political solution to the Afghan conflict is essential to prevent the region once again becoming a safe haven for terrorists and a source of drug trafficking that would also destabilise Kyrgyzstan and the whole region.

Similarly, in the same month, a US congressmen delegation led by member of the House of Representatives of the Republican Party of California, David Dreier visited Bishkek to hand over invitations for cooperation between the Commission "Partnership for Democracy" of the U.S. House of Representatives and the Parliament of Kyrgyzstan.[14]

Earlier in January 2012, the US National Democratic Institute (NDI) invited a group of members of Kyrgyz Parliament under the Kyrgyz Parliamentarism Strengthening Program. The visit programme included meetings with US Congressmen, US Department of State, US Helsinki Commission, Washington-based Non-Governmental Organisations (NGOs), legislators of the state of Maryland and other officials.[15] In January 2012, a delegation of Kyrgyz Defence Ministry attended conference in Suffolk, relating to preparing a scenario of the Regional Cooperation 2012 anti-terror exercises.[16] The exercises were meant for strengthening security and stability in the Central Asian region through collaborative measures to deal with the contemporary challenges and threats i.e., enhancing regional and national capacities to curb Weapons of Mass Destruction (WMD), as well to strengthen information exchanges. The military from Afghanistan, Kazakhstan, US, Pakistan, Tajikistan and Uzbekistan were traditionally invited for the exercises.

However, Atambayev, who is known for his pro-Russia stance, remained adamant and, in fact became, more vociferous about the need to close down the Transit Centre. He insisted that airport be converted into a civilian cargo centre with the help any country willing to become a partner. He was primarily referring to Russia, USA and Turkey. In fact, the issue was raised by Atambayev during his meetings with Turkish officials. Of course, like other Central Asian leaders who talked about developing their airports into major transit hub, Atambayev too saw the need to boost Kyrgyzstan's status as a major logistic hub between Asia and Europe. Similarly, he has been consistently pushing for the construction of railway lines and strategic motorways from China to Kyrgyzstan. However, Atambayev's idea of turning Manas into a major transit hub came under question. Observers viewed that being a mountainous country; Kyrgyzstan was unlikely to ever be a major stop-off on trade routes between East Asia and Europe. However, some collaborative initiatives in this direction had begun, including a proposal to start a flight to Delhi by a joint Turkish-Kyrgyz Air company.

Interestingly, unlike his predecessor former President Bakiyev, who negotiated with the US through backdoor channel to extend the lease of Manas, Atambayev was playing a new game while mobilising mounting public pressure for the closure of the base. Since he assumed power, a series of protests outside the US Embassy in Bishkek were held demanding an end to the US presence, with placards "Obama, respond to us!" and "Yankee, leave our land!"[17] Even before the Presidential election, representatives of the nation-wide congress of political parties were expressing anxieties over the continued presence of the US Transit Centre at Manas. To drum up nationalism, some political groups even sought a referendum on the issue during the presidential elections.[18] Protesters cited the pretext of the planes dumping fuel during landings that have considerably damaged their crops in the Chu Valley where Manas is located. The US Embassy was quick to issue a statement saying there was no scientific evidence to prove the claim. Apart from environmental issues, the specter of Iranian missile hitting Bishkek in case of the US-Iran military standoff was also raised by Kyrgyz leadership and politicians. This has been elaborated elsewhere. Alikbek Jekshenkulov, former Foreign Minister and the head of the nation-wide congress of political parties thought that the US presence was creating tensions in Kyrgyzstan's relations with many Arab countries and other states. Another party "The Voice of People" instead voiced for closer cooperation with Kazakhstan and Russia, which share common history, language, cultural ties and experience of co-existence with Kyrgyzstan.[19]

At one point, Atambayev too, while constantly threatening to close the US base, was trying to bargain for additional rent from the US albeit in a different way. The Kyrgyz leadership appeared mindful about the US urgency against the growing Pakistani resistance for NATO supplies to Afghanistan.

Probably, Atambayev was also playing to the gallery, as his repeated statements were pleasing to both Russia and China. It became also clear, considering the business background of Atambayev, that his foreign policies were driven more by business rather than political consideration. For, he knew that China and Russia were more relevant economically and would be more helpful in the coming years in terms of trade and security partners. Interestingly, only 30 per cent Kyrgyz viewed the US in a positive light, which is the lowest within Central Asia.[20]

Military Base to Fuel Supply Contract

In a curious political wrangling, the Kyrgyz officials had been pressurising the US to suspend the award of fuel contract to an unknown private firm Mina Corp., and Red Star Enterprises Inc., that has been supplying TS-1 jet fuel for Manas for six years. The agreement signed in early 2011, allowed the Kyrgyz state-run Manas Refueling Complex to supply up to the 50 per cent of jet fuel to the Transit Centre. The deal was intended for the entire period of the Transit Centre's presence in Kyrgyzstan. The base needed 360,000 tons of jet fuel a year. Separately, the two firms were under the US Congressional investigations since April 2010 for their alleged purchase of 1.8 million tons jet fuel from Russia through six Kyrgyz firms without paying an import duty since 2005. The DoD had terminated collaboration with the companies shortly after Bakiyev's fall and the probe into the firm's activity had begun. In fact, the interim-President Otunbayeva had lobbied with President Obama in September 2011 for a new arrangement that would involve a Kyrgyz-Russian joint venture to take over fuel supply responsibilities. She had been seeking a cooperative approach between Russia and US on the Manas and believed that the resetting of the US-Russia relations would benefit everyone. The US initially welcomed the joint Kyrgyz-Russian venture proposal and even agreed to modify its tender specifications for the supply of up to 50 per cent of Manas' fuel needs.

However, a fresh controversy erupted when the Defence Logistics Agency (DLA) of the US Department of Defence (DoD) on November 3 2010 awarded a new $315 million contract to Mina Corp., and Red Star Enterprises Inc., for the supply of jet fuel to the Manas Centre. The fresh award came after a six-month investigation by the National Security and Foreign Affairs Subcommittee of the House of Representatives' Committee on Oversight and Government Reform that finally said it has found no credible evidence of underlying corruption in the contracts, or that Bakiev's family had profited from the fuel contracts with the US. The DoD maintained that the new contract was awarded after a competitive bidding process andin a transparent manner. It was considered as an important step forward. The companies too had denied wrongdoings and said they are the victims of misinformation spread by rivals.

But, the fresh contract infuriated the Kyrgyz interim government, which did not believe that the Congressional investigation had been thorough. A Foreign Ministry statement on November 5, 2010 said that Washington must suspend cooperation with Mina until the the prosecutors have not completed an investigation. It said that the April 2010 downfall of the Bakiyev government had revealed corrupt dealings around fuel supplies to Manas base. The new Kyrgyz dispensation had been accusing the two firms for their corrupt ties to the former President Bakiyev and his family. In fact, the popular outrage surrounding the issue did become reasons for toppling the two previous regimes.

Kyrgyz authorities wanted a new arrangement that would involve a Kyrgyz-Russian joint venture to take over fuel supply responsibilities. They hoped that if the fuel supplies are channelised transparently, the country could gain up to $60 million per year. The controversy was linked to the political jockeying for election and formation of the new coalition government. The US had finally fulfilled its commitment to agree to the Kyrgyz demand even though the US DoD's award of contract to Mina Corp. was made after a competitive bidding process. For the Kyrgyz, the issue was also a crucial element for putting together a coalition government that took care of all interests groups, especially on the foreign policy front and in which Russia was convinced of the need to continue with the US base for Kyrgyz economic exigencies. The Kyrgyz side intends to use the extra funds to be received for the jet fuel for health care and education expenses.

The Kyrgyz officials hoped that their plea for change in contractor would be considered by Washington given the prevailing internal political situation. They have been widely articulating that if the fuel supplies are channelised transparently the country could gain up to $60 million per year. But several times, the US had decided to ignore Kyrgyz demand, especially when its decision could possibly be misinterpreted or become unpopular that could eventually strain its relationship with Bishkek. The DoD claimed that it received no information on Mina Corp., that would prevent awarding a contract to the company. One probability was that Pentagon probably doubted whether a Kyrgyz-Gazprom joint venture would technically or financially be capable of playing the supplier's role.

What had irked the Kyrgyz was that the new deal was more lucrative for Mina Corp., than the previous contract. The decision had stirred tension in Kyrgyzstan because the controversy was fed in part by political jockeying in the parliamentary elections, which had even boosted the clout of politicians hostile to Mina and Red Star. The issue could also have snowballed into a round of controversy and may once again reopen the debate whether the US should be allowed to continue its Transit Centre at Manas. The notable Kyrgyz politicians who were known opponents of Mina Corp. included Atambayev and Bananov, who were any way assuming top jobs in the new government. Finally, Washington did agree to provide an additional succor to the Kyrgyz, when the US changed the jet fuel supplier by replacing previous deals with a more transparent system.[21]

This was not the only issue. When Babanov assumed office of the Prime Minister after Atambayev, he tried to squeeze more money out of the Transit Centre by slapping a tax on aviation fuel supplies.[22] The fresh Kyrgyz move obviously violated the lease agreement with the US. Yet, attempts were made to introduce a bill in the parliament for an enhanced tax on fuel supplies. The bill was however postponed or canceled in view of the controversy.[23] In fact, the issue of imposing tax on fuel supplies to the US Transit Centre in Bishkek had put Prime Minister AlmazbekAtambayev on the spot. He had to strongly disapprove the move and felt that by playing such a game Kyrgyzstan will not only flout the Kyrgyz-US agreement on fuel supplies but will lose what had been gained already. He said "The US embassy has already expressed objection...we must realise one thing, that we may get an extra $40-50 million...but the USA plays a very great role in all financial organisations, no matter whether it is the EAEC, the ADB, the EBRD, the IMF or the World Bank. We will lose what we have already if we begin playing a game or if we go after more. We are on the verge of losing two billion soms in a bid to earn 30 biilion soms."[24]

Fresh Diplomacy over Transit Centre

Despite all the rhetoric about evicting the US Transit Centre, the US was open to negotiation with the Kyrgyzstan, possibly even trying to keep the facility at Manas beyond 2014. The Transit Centre accommodated about 1,200 US troops and handles over 15,000 coalition servicemen and 500 tons of cargoes a month.[25]

Surprisingly, in March 2012, US Defence Secretary Leon Panetta visited Kyrgyzstan on the way to Afghanistan. He was still trying his diplomacy with the

Kyrgyz leaders by expressing gratitude for Manas Transit Centre support. Panetta thought Kyrgyzstan and its Central Asian neighbours were "key link in logistic system of import to Afghanistan which proved its importance during the last months".[26] Panetta's statement indicated that Kyrgyzstan did play an important role when Pakistan was uncooperative to the NATO. The Kyrgyz President did not meet the US Defence Secretary.[27] But meeting was held behind closed doors with the Defence Council Secretary of Kyrgyzstan Busurmankul Tabaldiev, who straight away told Panetta that after 2014 the Bishkek airport Manas will become a "commercial" object. Tabaldiev did acknowledge the new challenges emanating from Afghanistan that threatened the country's security. He was quoted as telling Secretary Panetta "Kyrgyzstan is interested in ensuring security and stability in the country and is ready to participate fully in the efforts of the international community to assist Afghanistan. The Kyrgyz Republic understands the USA necessity for Transit Centre's stay at Manas Airport as a strategic point of the "northern corridor" to support the international coalition efforts in Afghanistan. At the same time the Manas Transit Centre infrastructure will be used as a civil transit centre and it should not have military presence after 2014. This position is dictated solely by national interests of Kyrgyzstan."[28] Tabaldiev added that "After 2014 Kyrgyzstan is ready to provide assistance to the US Government for continued transportation of goods to Afghanistan in view of the opinion of the people, interests of the state and safety of the country."[29] Busurmankul Tabaldiev felt there was no sense in protraction of the issue and wanted a decision on this issue before the end of 2012 though he said the matter was not about bargaining, but was based on firm belief that the civilian airport should not have military facilities. A commercial project to create a transit hub was reemphasised. At the same time, Kyrgyzstan was also interested in the global effort for the Afghan stabilisation process and expressed readiness to export electricity and goods to Afghanistan. Tabaldiev had confirmed Kyrgyzstan's intention to build a high-voltage power transmission line in Afghanistan, Tajikistan and Pakistan.

The Kyrgyz officials also indicated about willingness to transport non-military goods to Afghanistan after 2014.[30] Busurmankul Tabaldiyev said "Areas for joint cooperation can also be found without military presence at an airport."[31] Of course, no particular detail appeared in the media but it was widely known later that Panetta, in response to the Kyrgyz threat, told them that he had not come to negotiate but to convey his thanks to the President for his continued support for the transit center at Manas. Secretary Panetta added, "I am also here to commend Kyrgyzstan for the very successful transition through the democratic process."[32]

What had finally emerged was that the Kyrgyz side was still keeping the issue of Transit Centre somewhat open-ended, subject to further commercial deals. In another words, use of the airport for shipment purpose to Afghanistan was not the key issue. Perhaps, for the Kyrgyz the issue was more about commercial terms, instead of the existing strategic cooperation. The sense gathered then was that the

Kyrgyz side had privately indicated to keep the options open for further negotiation. In fact, Secretary Leon Panetta later indicated that officials in Kyrgyzstan were open to extending use of an air base.[33] The media quoted a senior US official traveling with Panetta saying there may be some "wiggle room"[34] for additional negotiations for a longer term contract. Therefore, the US was not taking Atambayev's position on Manas as the final word on the matter. All and all, Pentagon was hopeful about extending the lease long enough to get troops and equipment out of Afghanistan. The Kyrgyz seemed to have suggested that the issue can be negotiated as long as the price is right. This was the first step in a long process.[35]

In fact, in May 2011, Special Representative for Afghanistan and Pakistan Ambassador Marc Grossman also visited Bishkek and told the Kyrgyz officials about the US policy goals in Afghanistan that involved three mutually reinforcing tracks- "a military offensive against al-Qaida terrorists and Taliban insurgents; a civilian campaign to bolster the governments, economies, and civil societies of Afghanistan and Pakistan to undercut the pull of the insurgency; and an intensified diplomatic push to bring the Afghan conflict to an end and chart a new and more secure future for the region."[36]

By summing up the developments, the US Ambassador Pamela Spratlen later said the US has heard the President's position on the withdrawal of the Transit Centre after 2014 clearly. She said, "I think that the two features of his position that are important to us at the moment are one that the current agreement will be fulfilled to its conclusion in 2014. And on a number of occasions the President has said we should talk about the future and those, the discussions about the future of the transit center have already begun (the expert team visited Kyrgyzstan in April)...so I think we will continue to talk about the needs and requirements of each side as we talk about the future."[37]

It needs to be underlined that Manas Transit Centre provided the best route for transiting troops and equipments back home from Afghanistan. If the Manas is lost, the US and NATO would be potentially vulnerable to losing a supply chain to Afghanistan. The strategic importance of Kyrgyzstan lay here. More than 580,000 troops' transited and almost 4,800 refueling sorties passed through the base in 2011. Nonetheless, the pressure for closing down the Transit Centre continued through protest rallies in Bishkek.[38] Protestors used the possibility of Iranian retaliation as a pretext.

In April 2012, Atambayev once again reminded the US Assistant Secretary of State on Central Asia Robert Blake that after two more years a civic commercial centre should be in Manas airport without any military component. Obviously, the US had stepped up its officials' visiting Bishkek for negotiation ostensibly this time to explore how Kyrgyzstan can be involved in Afghanistan issue by giving more incentives. The diplomatic pressure was likely to intensify further. Knowing the Kyrgyz past behaviour, the American interlocutors were quite hopeful for a breakthrough.

The US had further intensified its efforts to engage Central Asian states in the affairs involving security issues in Afghanistan. In fact, the media reported Secretary of State Hillary Clinton visited Kyrgyzstan probably in May 2011 on her way from Europe to Japan without the knowledge of Kyrgyz Government and the public. It was in June 2011, the Head of the US Transit Centre, Col. Dwight Sones had disclosed that an aircraft with Secretary Clinton on board was flying from Europe to Japan landed in Manas Airport over shortage of jet fuel. The aircraft stayed at the airport for 1.5 hour.[39] Sones said nobody met with Secretary Clinton during this time and nobody from the Kyrgyz Government saw her. Col. Sones said "I did not see her either. I met only with the crew. She was sleeping in the plane all this time."[40]

The American renewed activism started following its deteriorating relations with Pakistan and the closure of the NATO supply line to Afghanistan through Pakistan. Of course, this provided Russia as well as the Central Asian states with new leverages. Efforts to strengthen the NDN that carried large quantities of non-lethal supplies from Europe to NATO troops in Afghanistan through Russia, the Caucasus and Central Asia had increased considerably.[41] In fact, even before closure of all supply routes through Pakistan (after NATO forces killed 24 Pakistani soldiers on November 26, 2011), the NATO countries were not only seeking to expand the volume of cargo through the NDN but were negotiating fresh agreements with the Central Asian states for the reverse flow of transit from the NDN rather than through Pakistan. While the Pentagon officials were negotiating with the Kyrgyz, the US was also talking about upgrading defence cooperation with neighbouring Uzbekistan that was stopped in 2005 due to human rights concerns.[42]

The US Assistant Secretary of State Robert Blake visited Tashkent and held extensive talks with Uzbek President Islam Karimov in Tashkent in August 2012.[43] Blake visited Almaty, but skipped his scheduled visit to Kyrgyzstan. Blake was scheduled to stay four days in Tashkent. Uzbek television reported on August 15, 2012 that Blake and Karimov only discussed the "peaceful reconstruction of Afghanistan."[44] In fact, alternatively, the US also appeared looking for a base elsewhere, including the possibility of hiring the Aini airbase in Tajikistan.

Subsequently, the aid for Uzbekistan was bumped up to $1.5 million a year. In 2011, the US was paying $500 million a year to the governments of Central Asia for their services in running the NDN, which was more than the other international aid that goes into the region. Kyrgyzstan and Tajikistan were getting $1.5 million, Kazakhstan $1.8 million and Turkmenistan $685,000.

Many observers thought that Russian policymakers were taking comfort from the fact that NATO's Afghan mission was getting hostage to Moscow's good will.

In 2009, a Russian Lieutenant General Leonid Sazhin, analyst for the Russian Federal Security Service (FSB) had observed: "If the Khyber Pass and the road to Kandahar get blocked by the Taliban, then the US and NATO have no choice of other ...alternative routes through Central Asia. And as airplanes can't deliver much, ground transport corridors are necessary and here Americans need Russia."[45]

Since the 2009 Russia-US "reset" Moscow had permitted NATO's supplies to Afghanistan through Russian territory in exchange for financial compensation.[46] Of course, Russia had its own interest and wanted the NATO to achieve its success in Afghanistan against the Taliban and Al-Qaeda who were training the Russian Chechen rebels. Many political observers viewed that Kyrgyzstan was an important component of such cooperation. The "reset" was developing when Russia's own military and political presence in Kyrgyzstan was growing. As Stratfor noted "Kyrgyzstan is not the most important issue for Moscow and Washington, but it is a strategic part of their relations because it hosts the only U.S. military base in Central Asia, the Transit Centre at Manas."[47]

As mentioned elsewhere, Moscow had increased the supply of fuel to the Manas Transit Centre. Agreement was also signed for Russian crude and refined products to be supplied to the US in Kyrgyzstan for re-export to Afghanistan. According to Sratfor, the Russians were doing several conciliatory moves towards the US.[48] By and large the US-Russia reset was positively impacting Kyrgyzstan. The Deputy Assistant Secretary of State Daniel Russell was quoted in a seminar at American Enterprise Institute (AEI) as saying that the interaction with Russia in Kyrgyzstan is a "field" of successful cooperation.[49] He said "In Central Asia, our relations have obviously changed, I would have highlighted the situation in Kyrgyzstan. We no longer feel the pressure of Russia on the issue that we should close our transit centre at the Manas airport."[50] Whether Kyrgyzstan was kept in the loop or not was not clear.

Beyond the Transit Centre

Earlier in December 2011, the US Embassy in Bishkek issued a statement on occasion of 20 years of friendship and cooperation between Kyrgyzstan and the US that summed up some of the US policy goals and achievements in bilateral relations with Kyrgyzstan. It was clear from the statement that the US had given stress on the Kyrgyz choice for democratic reforms that seemed to have enabled the US to foster ideas about liberal values among the Kyrgyz. The statement said "In two decades, over three thousand citizens of the Kyrgyz Republic visited the US through our government-sponsored exchange programmes, in addition to countless others who have traveled to the U.S. for business or tourism. Kyrgyz high school students have lived with American host families and attended American schools. Students were exposed to American university life and some even obtained master's degrees or completed post-doctoral research in the US. Professionals toured the U.S. to compare best practices with their American counterparts."[51]

The statement also detailed the US activities especially in the field of education in Kyrgyzstan. It was widely known that thousands of Peace Corps Volunteers had lived in Kyrgyz homes and taught in schools or worked with local organisations in the 1990s.

On the political reforms, the US admired the Kyrgyz progress on democracy and the way competitive and open elections were conducted by the governments. It quoted the US Secretary of State Hillary Clinton's statement on Kyrgyzstan's achievements to "the strong character of the Kyrgyz people, the incredible resilience that you have shown since independence, but, most importantly, the path of democracy that you have chosen now…You are pioneers. Look around you in this region. You are trying to do something that no one else has done."[52]

The statement further said, that "US is a proud friend and partner of the Kyrgyz Republic….firmly in support of the people...have contributed over one billion dollars in assistance through the USAID and other U.S. Government institutions. We are fully committed to cooperating with the government and as the business environment improves, we hope to expand trade and investment ties."[53]

The statement further added that relations went beyond the people-to-people exchange and joint efforts to improve livelihoods. The role of Kyrgyzstan in hosting the Transit Centre at Manas International Airport and its contribution to international efforts to stabilise Afghanistan was fully acknowledged. It said, "The role played by the Kyrgyz Republic in this critical global security issue is illustrative of the transformation in this country in a mere twenty years."[54]

The US report card issued on the 20th anniversary only confirmed what Valentin Bogatyryov, a well-known Kyrgyz strategic expert had concluded that the US was focusing in on two fronts.[55] One is on the internal processes and the other is geopolitical processes in the Central Asian countries. The democratisation crusade by the US, according to Bogatyryov, had failed with the exception of Kyrgyzstan being only best student in this regard. The US now is focusing on the second crusade of finding entry and exit from Afghanistan.

In fact, US interests were getting sharper in 2012. The Obama administration had listed Kyrgyzstan and Tajikistan as priority assistance countries in Central Asia.[56] The administration had recommended $40.8 million for Kyrgyzstan for 2012 to address among other things Kyrgyzstan's underlying development challenges and chronic instability.[57] The assistance was also meant for boosting Kyrgyz security forces, strengthening civil society and democratic institutions, and to empower the private sector. Therefore, it did suggest that the US was providing sufficient incentive with the aim to prevent the Kyrgyz taking abrupt decision on the Manas Transit Centre.

In fact, the Deputy of State Secretary on South and Central Asia Robert Blake was appreciative of constructive dialogue with Kyrgyzstan on Manas Transit Centre.[58] He also allayed the doubt that US will use Manas for military operation against Iran. However, Blake said "I cannot answer for what the government of Iran is going to do. One reason for our concern about Iran is that it is very unpredictable. But, of course, we do not support Iran's efforts aimed at the destabilisation of situation in Kyrgyzstan or in any other friendly country."[59]

In fact, Blake held talks with President Almazbek Atambayev on April 2, 2012 about further cooperation between Kyrgyzstan and the USA. While the Kyrgyz position on Manas remained unchanged, Blake was seen offering incentive to the Kyrgyz, especially about giving Kyrgyzstan an important role in reviving the economy of Afghanistan and in other regional projects. The US was also discussing about expanding trade and economic cooperation, creating a favourable investment climate, providing assistance in fighting threats and challenges of the modern world, such as terrorism, extremism and others.[60] Blake has been articulating Washington's "new silk route" strategy,[61] and also had been selling the idea of how Kyrgyzstan can promote Sustainable Development in Afghanistan by linking its infrastructure and energy transmission grids and pipelines to Central Asia. In essence, the US wanted to play (a) the security role through the Transit Centre and (b) contribute to regional integration role by linking up with development projects in Afghanistan.[62]

Robert Blake was accompanied by the Head of US Central Command (USCENTCOM) James N. Mattis who held talks with Kyrgyz Defence Council Secretary Busurmankul. There was a media report that the Kyrgyz side had agreed to assist the US post 2014 in view of national interest.[63] The news came against the backdrop of an earlier statement coming from American officials that the US will be leaving weapons and equipments to friendly countries after the withdrawal from Afghanistan. This had even prompted the Kyrgyz officials to ask the US to leave drones to Kyrgyzstan after the withdrawal. It was not clear, whether the Kyrgyz had been instructed by the Russians for such a demand from the US.[64] Interestingly, US Marine Corps (USMC) General James Mattis, reportedly replied that Washington is ready to consider the request. Tabaldiev told the US delegation that Bishkek is ready to cooperate beyond 2014 "taking into account Kyrgyzstan's interests, its security, and public opinion."[65] This had proved that Kyrgyz were bargaining with US and their position to vacate the Transit Centre is negotiable.

Profiting from the Drawdown

As the drawdown dates of Alliance forces from Afghanistan were approaching nearer, Central Asian states were redesigning their security charts to profit from the reverse transit.[66] Since May 2012 year, they have signed fresh agreements with NATO on ground transport routes to move out non-lethal equipments along the NDN.[67] Moreover, following the visit by a series of political and military level visits to Kyrgyzstan, the US in a new game plan sent its kite flying test by suggesting that (a) it could consider Tajikistan as a possible alternative to Manas Transit Centre in Kyrgyzstan, (b) it may also leave behind military equipments to Central Asian states after the withdrawal from Afghanistan. This was announced by Robert Blake on August 15, 2012. The US Assistant Secretary said "First of all, the process of allocating Excess Defence Articles (EDA) is only just beginning. We are beginning the consultations on that. It won't be just for Uzbekistan but for all countries partnering on NDN. There will be quite detailed conversations with our military people based in embassies in each of these posts, with host nation counterparts on this thing."[68] Earlier, the Obama administration had lifted a ban on foreign military sales to Uzbekistan. It was reported that the Uzbek government had long list of items including drones to be sought from the US. As mentioned above, the Kyrgyz also sought similar weapons from the Americans. Blake however stressed that there will not be any lethal weapons of any kind that will be offered.[69] In fact the US announcement in many ways changed the overall context of politics in the region. The signing of the surface transport agreements though came against the backdrop of Russia's own approval of a trans-shipment centre for NATO in its Ulyanovsk city.

The developments since then had snowballed into weakening of the Russian-led CSTO.[70] After Uzbekistan announced its withdrawal from the CSTO, Tajikistan and Kyrgyzstan too had started bargaining for more dividends from Russia's military presence in their territories. While Tajikistan had demanded $300 million yearly rent for the presence of Russia's 201st military base in its territory, Kyrgyzstan announced plans to increase the rent and placed new conditions for the presence of three Russian military facilities including a Torpedo testing centre No 954 in Karakol, the 338th communications centre in Kara-Balta, and a radio seismic laboratory in Mailuu-Suu starting from 2014, when the existing term expires. Even the Kant airbase, which was operating under the CSTO auspices, the Kyrgyz President, during his visit to Moscow in 2012, made a huge hue and cry about a $15.5 million debt outstanding against Russia. The amount was immediately released by the Russian Defence Ministry following a direct intervention by the Russian President.[71] The other three bases have been in existence under a 1993 agreement by which Russia agreed to train Kyrgyz military personnel and provide military equipment, though media reports have said these conditions have not been met since 2008, allegedly due to the worsening political situation in Kyrgyzstan. Some of these issues have since been resolved after Putin visited Bishkek in 2012 when Russia managed to gain heavy strategic presence in Kyrgyzstan. (*Details are covered in the Kyrgyzstan-Russia chapter*)

In Tajikistan, the 201st Motorised Infantry Division was deployed in 2005 under a mutual assistance agreement. About 7,000 Russian servicemen were deployed in Dushanbe, Kurgan-Tyube, and Kulyab, serving as a key element of the common security system in Central Asia. The fate of the 201st army base had been turned into a riddle for quite some time as both Moscow and Dushanbe have exchanged conflicting signals for the continuation of the facility after 2014. But like the Kyrgyz, the Tajiks too asserted that the issue was not about money but about respect of their national interests. Tajikistan had been taking tougher stance linking the issue with host of problems such as from the ill-treatment of Tajik laborers working in Russia to seeking lower import duties on oil products coming from Russia. Besides the above, there was also a dispute over the lease of the Gabala radar station in Azerbaijan by Russia.

But, it was also clear that individual states were trying to readjust their policies to meet the post 2014 security scenario. For example, Uzbekistan's decision seems to be based on much deeper considerations of its domestic politics and the security challenges it foresees from Afghanistan. It had done such a rebalancing earlier as well.

The new contest was linked to US preparation to leave Afghanistan in 2014. Washington was trying to reorient itself to Russia and Central Asian countries and conclude agreements on surface transit with them. The US was though expecting to reach an agreement with Pakistan at the NATO summit in May 2012 in Chicago, but Islamabad insisted on a public apology for the killing of its servicemen, a revision of US policy on drone strikes in Pakistan, and an increase in the fee for transit from $250 to $5,000 for every vehicle, which was unacceptable to the US. This led President Barack Obama to delete Pakistan from the list of nations he thanked but expressed gratitude to Russia and Central Asian countries for supporting the anti-terror efforts in Afghanistan.[72] Obama even refused to have one-on-one meeting with President Asif Ali Zardari. It seemed, the US trick worked. Kyrgyzstan's Foreign Minister Ruslan Kazakbaev, who participated in the NATO Summit in Chicago, quickly emphasised on the importance of bringing stability to Afghanistan and signed an agreement on surface transit for the international coalition's freight with NATO Deputy Secretary General Alexander Vershbow.[73]

Interestingly, on the one hand, the Kyrgyz were threatening to close down the US Transit Centre, they were happy at the same time that they got additional opportunity to make money from the US by allowing surface route for NATO's exit. In this context, Ravshan Jeenbekov, the Deputy Head of the Kyrgyz parliament was quoted in Russian newspaper *Nezavisimaya Gazeta* by saying that earlier arrangement with the US was only for the use of base at Manas Airport, but the new agreement with NATO would allow Kyrgyzstan to participate in two NATO transit routes: Afghanistan-Tajikistan-Kyrgyzstan-Kazakhstan-Russia and Afghanistan-Uzbekistan-Kyrgyzstan-Kazakhstan-Russia.[74] It seemed the route through Uzbekistan was already operating.

As compared to the Pakistani route that cost the NATO approximately $17 million a year, the NDN route was costing more than $500 million a year. Bill Speaks, spokesman for the USCENTCOM, complained that the US DoD was quoted as saying that $500 million is probably not the final sum.[75] Transit would include shipment of 120,000 freight containers, 70,000 armoured vehicles and more than 100,000 servicemen and civilians.

Of course, this development was unfolding after Russia agreed to offer its Ulyanovsk airport for NATO's freight transit.But the Kyrgyz had financial compulsion to bow down to the American request. Although, both the Kyrgyz and Tajiks had cited "inflation" for increasing the rent for the Russian bases, the issue seemed more to do about posturing to the US that they were willing to bargain for any financial and military dividends in the post 2014 scenario. Interestingly, even Kyrgyz President Almazbek Atambayev, who vehemently opposed the presence of the Manas Transit Centre after 2014, made such a bold turn to facilitate transportation of NATO cargo and even started showing inclination to extend the lease of Manas beyond 2014. The Kyrgyz probably also saw how, on the one hand, Russia itself had agreed to opening a transit centre for NATO in the city of Ulyanovsk that too without consulting its CSTO allies, while pressurising others for the closure of the US bases.[76]

But, what actually put the Kyrgyz into a spin was the new US signal over considering relocation of Transit Centre from Kyrgyzstan to Tajikistan and the possible offer of weapons to Central Asian states once the US forces leave Afghanistan. The new American maneuvering of offering non-lethal weapons to Central Asian states could also impact the Russian security calculations.[77] Some Russian defence experts like Vladimir Kudelev commented that the move will though not conflict with the CSTO agreements, but it could complicate Russia's military-technical cooperation with the former Soviet partners.[78]

The underlying motives of Kyrgyzstan, therefore, seemed driven less by geopolitics but more due to economic interests. Since the 9/11, politics of military bases in Central Asia had been determined mainly by question of commercial yield, and in the face of rising economic recession and the lack of substantial sources of income (budget deficit of Kyrgyzstan in 2012 stood $532 million and there was no way the country would have got help from other sources) the Kyrgyz bargaining tactics were going to be a continuing feature and there was sufficient indication that the Transit Centre will continue to stay even after 2014.

As the efforts to strengthen the NDN as an alternative to transit through Pakistan began in early 2012, regional calculations had begun to change making it tough for Russia to sustain its military interests in Central Asia. But assessing the general situation, there was visible signs of shifting balance of power due to a three-way geopolitical struggle. Both the US interest for using Central Asia as a staging ground, and China's intention to build Central Asia as a shield and buffer for Xinjiang were impacting the Russian interests in the region.

China was following a blend of foreign aid and investment policy in Central Asia which suited the local regimes. Tajikistan and Kyrgyzstan were virtually looking at Beijing than Moscow for all possible support. Beijing already seemed to have gained upper hand in the political and economic game if not in the security structures of these two states

While on the surface, interests of major actors seemed coinciding, however in reality there was resentful enabling of each other; and the Central Asian leaders have learnt the art of playing the game. All of them have essentially tried to move closer to either US or China with the aim of invoking the interests of Russia to be more sensitive of their economic needs. Kyrgyzstan had been long frustrated with Moscow's inability to implement economic projects committed long before.

They were likely to play along these lines and be objects of competition for a long time to come. Unfortunately, such competitions were also entailing corrupting influence on these states. One of the widespread complaints heard in the informed circles in Bishkek was that the US had been complicit in propping up corrupt regime for its narrow interests. Washington supported Bakiyev in return of leasing the airbase. Bakiyev and his family had profited from the base through financial interests in Mina Corporation and Red Star Enterprises that supplied jet fuel worth millions of dollars to Manas. Even after Bakiyevs left the power, the small Kyrgyz political elite continue to earn millions from the American military installation. Despite Russian pressure, Kyrgyz continue to see it as a major source of earning.

Interestingly, they were asserting vis-à-vis Russia under Putin's new Presidency. It was hard to believe how these states can sever ties from Moscow to deal with their basic security and socio-economic stability. But it was also true that Russia had considerably lost its instrument of power especially in the softer areas of Central Asian life. Thousands of Western funded NGOs were operating in the south of Kyrgyzstan alone especially in the garb of implementing educational and humanitarian projects.

New pressures were developing against Russia in the region. However, it was not easy to write off Russia easily. The Uzbek withdrawal from CSTO and others challenging the presence of Russian military bases, Moscow could be forced to make its own moves that could be quite tough. There were visible signs of Moscow trying to arrest its declining control and thus may take steps initially to negotiate with the regimes. However, if that does not work, Russia still retains sufficient leverages to apply hard options.

NOTES

1. Jim Nichol, "Kyrgyzstan: Recent Developments and U.S. Interests", *CRS Report for Congress*, http://fpc.state.gov/documents/organization/150182.pdf Retrieved on May 20, 2013.
2. Walter Pincus, "Bethesda-based development firm gets Kyrgyzstan contract", *Washington Post*, October 24, 2010.
3. David Trilling, "Money That Belongs in Kyrgyzstan's Toilets", *Eurasianet*, October 26, 2010http://www.eurasianet.org/node/62241.
4. "U.S. Secretary of State Hillary Clinton applauded the country's efforts to establish a democratic government", *Associated Press*, December 12, 2010.
5. www.akipress.kg, 15 March 2011, Also read Erica Marat, "Otunbayeva Open to Military Cooperation with the US and Russia", The Jamestown Foundation, *Eurasia Daily Monitor*

8(56), April 23, 2011.

6. The idea of creating facility in Batken was discussed during Bakiyev's time. The US Central Command, General David Petraeus, pledged $5.5 for the center to be operated under the US International Military Education and Training (IMET) programme.
7. www.ng.kg, March 16, 2011.
8. Andrew Higgins, "In Central Asia, a new headache for U.S. policy", *Washington Post,* August 31, 2010.
9. http://mayavision2012.wordpress.com/tag/current-events/page/2/
10. "Foreign Minister Kazakbaev, Deputy Secretary of State Burns discuss U.S. assistance for continued democratic reforms in Kyrgyzstan", *AKIpress,* February 17, 2012.
11. "PM Atambaev offers resumption of Kyrgyz-American security consultations", *AKIpress,* February 20, 2012.
12. "Kyrgyzstan President Insists on 2014 Deadline To Close U.S. Military Base", *RTT News,* February 20, 2012.
13. *AKIpress,* February 20, 2012.
14. "President Atambaev meets with delegation of U.S. Congressmen", *AKIpress,* February 22, http://eng.24.kg/community/2012/02/21/23065.html
15. "Group of members of Kyrgyz Parliament on visit to U.S", *AKIpress,* January 30, 2012.
16. "Delegation of Kyrgyzstan Defence Ministry attends conference in U.S. to produce scenario of upcoming anti-terror drill", *AKIpress,* January 27, 2012.
17. "Nation-wide congress of political parties speaks against U.S. military presence in Kyrgyzstan", *Bishkek, AKIpress,* June 1, 2011.
18. "Rally in Kyrgyz capital demands US air base closure", *Kyrgyz Telegraph Agency, KyrTAg,* April 2, 2012.
19. Ibid.
20. Erica Marat, "U.S. Image in Central Asia", http://jamestownfoundation.blogspot.in/2011/03/us-image-in-central-asia.html (Accessed March 28, 2011).
21. "Kyrgyzstan, U.S. sign new Manas base fuel deal after criticism of supplier", *People's Daily,* February 9, 2011.
22. "Kyrgyzstan wants to slap tax on US base", *Associated Press,* February 3, 2011.
23. Aizada Kutueva, "Kyrgyzstan's parliament postponed consideration of bill on special tax introduction on jet fuel supply at Manas", *24.kg news agency,* March 9, 2011.
24. In an interview with national TV, broadcast on March 7, 2011.
25. Through discussion with the Commander of Transit Centre.
26. URL: http://eng.24.kg/politic/2012/04/09/23758.html.
27. "No meeting scheduled between Kyrgyz president, US secretary of defence", *AKIpress,* March 13, 2012.
28. "Defense Ministry of Kyrgyzstan: The Manas Airbase infrastructure will be used as a civil transit center after 2014", *24.kg news agency,* March 14, 2012.
29. "No military facilities should be stationed in Manas Airport after 2014, Defense Council Secretary tells U.S. Secretary of Defense", *AKIpress,* March 14, 2012.
30. "Kyrgyzstan wants USA to use air base as civilian transit centre", *Kabar,* March 13, 2012
31. www.knews.kg/ru/politics/12517, *Kabar,* March 13, 2012.
32. Elisabeth Bumiller, "Kyrgyzstan Wants Military Role to End at U.S. Base", *The New York Times,* March 13, 2012.
33. Viola Gienger, "Panetta Hears Kyrgyzstan Open to Talks on Extending Base Deal", http://www.bloomberg.com/news/2012-03-13/panetta-in-kyrgyzstan-seeking-talks-on-renewing-base-agreement.html (Accessed March 13, 2012).
34. Joshua Kucera, "Pentagon Starts Manas Renegotiation with Soft Sell" *Eurasianet.org,* March 14, 2012.

35. "Panetta seeks to boost support for Kyrgyzstan base", *Associated Press*, March 13, 2012.
36. "Special Representative for Afghanistan and Pakistan Ambassador Grossman to visit Kazakhstan, Kyrgyzstan, Uzbekistan, Tajikistan, Pakistan, and Afghanistan", Bishkek, *AKIpress*, May 18, 2011. Also read Hillary Clinton's speech at the Asiatic Society, February 2011.
37. "U.S. Ambassador: Discussion about future of Transit Center at Manas in progress", *AKIpress*, May 8, 2012.
38. "A rally for the withdrawal of the U.S. air base from Kyrgyzstan is held in Bishkek", *AKIpress*, March 14, 2012.
39. "Head of Transit Centre confirms information about landed aircraft with Secretary Clinton on board in Manas one month ago", *AKIpress*, June 8, 2012.
40. Ibid.
41. Daniel Wagner and Luca Costa, "Recalibrating Relations between the U.S. and Central Asia *"Foreign Policy Journal,* May 27, 2011.Joshua Kucera, "Should the U.S. Be Ignoring Central Asia Even More Than It Already Does?", *Eurasianet*, May 25, 2011.
42. Joshua Kucera, "Uzbekistan Achieves U.S. Military Aid Parity with Neighbors", *EurasiaNet*, February 13, 2012.
43. "High-Ranking U.S. Official in Uzbekistan for Talks", *RFE/RL*, August 16 2012.
44. Ibid.
45. Richard Weitz, "Global Security Watch Russia: A Reference Handbook", *World Politics Review*, February 10, 2009.
46. "Russian and U.S. Cooperation in Kyrgyzstan", *EurasiaNet*, March 2, 2011.
47. Ibid.
48. Ibid.
49. *RIA Novosti* news agency, February 25, 2011.
50. "U.S. considers Kyrgyzstan as "field" of cooperation with Russia", *Xinhua*, February 25, 2011.
51. "U.S. Ambassador makes statement on occasion of 20 years of diplomatic relations between Kyrgyzstan, U.S.", *AKIpress,* December 27, 2011.
52. Ibid.
53. Ibid.
54. Ibid.
55. "Kyrgyz expert likens US presence in Central Asia to crusade", *24.kg website,* July 12, 2012
56. Washington-based Silk Road Newsline on February 15, 2012. Executive Budget Summary released by the Department of State said "The FY 2012 request prioritizes assistance for the Kyrgyz Republic to support the new Government's efforts to reform core institutions, law enforcement, and increase economic opportunities".
57. "Obama administration lists Kyrgyzstan and Tajikistan as priority assistance countries in Central Asia for 2012", *AKIpress,* February 16, 2012.
58. "USA appreciate constructive dialogue with Kyrgyzstan on Manas Transit Centre – Robert Blake", *Trend,* Baku, April 19, 2012.
59. "Robert Blake: U.S. Transit Centre "Manas" will not be used for any military operations", *AKIpress,* April 4, 2012.
60. "Kyrgyz leader says civilian shipping centre must be created at air base", *AKIpress news agency*, April 2, 2012.
61. "Blake's Testimony on U.S. Engagement in Central Asia, U.S. Department of State, Testimony by Robert O. Blake, Jr. Assistant Secretary, Bureau of South and Central Asian Affairs, House Foreign Affairs Committee, Subcommittee on Europe and Eurasia, Washington, DC July 24, 2012/// US Department of State press release, July 25, 2012 see annexure 4.
62. Deputy of State Secretary on South and Central Asia Robert Blake called a meeting with Ambassadors of major countries in Bishkek and conveyed US policy goals. Author attended

the meeting hosted by the US Ambassador in Bishkek.

63. Our party is ready to assist US government after 2014 in view of Kyrgyz people interests, opinion and security – Ministry of Defence", *24.kg news agency*, April 2, 2012.
64. "Bishkek Asks U.S. For Pilotless Drone Aircraft", *RFE/RL's Kyrgyz Service*http://www.rferl.org/content/bishkek_asks_us_for_pilotless_drone_aircraft/24535241.html.
65. Ibid.
66. Alexander Cooley, "After Afghanistan, a New Great Game", *The New York Times*, August 21, 2012.
67. "Kyrgyzstan signs Afghan surface transit agreement, requests budget assistance", *Nezavisimaya Gazeta,* May 24, 2012.
68. "U.S. to leave military equipment to Central Asian states after withdrawal from Afghanistan", Bishkek, *AKIpress*, August 17, 2012.
69. Ibid.
70. "Used weapons giveaway in Central Asia concerns Russia", http://rt.com/politics/us-afghanistan-central-asia-084/ June 18, 2012.
71. This is being elaborated in Kyrgyz-Russia relations section.
72. "Obama snubs Pakistan as conflict over supply routes continues", *Associated Press*, May 21, 2012, Read more: http://www.foxnews.com/politics/2012/05/21/obama-snubs-pakistan-as-conflict-over-supply-routes-continues/#ixzz1vaWzSL00 "President Obama, NATO leaders at Chicago Summit thank Central Asian countries for their "important perspective" on Afghanistan, critical transit for ISAF supplies", Bishkek, *AKIpress,* May 22, 2012. "U.S. Defense Secretary Panetta thanks Central Asian nations for distribution network", *AKIpress*, May 22, 2012.
73. "Kyrgyz signs Afghan surface transit agreement, seeks budget assistance", *Nezavisimaya Gazeta,* May 24, 2012.
74. *Nezavisimaya Gazeta,* May 24, 2012.
75. Ibid.
76. The Russian decision on Ulyanovsk was much criticised in Kyrgyzstan as double standard by Russia.
77. "Used weapons giveaway in Central Asia concerns Russia", *Interfax*, June 18, 2012.
78. *Interfax*, June 18, 2012.

CHAPTER 11

The Chinese Forays

For China, Kyrgyzstan like other Central Asian countries is too critical a frontier for its security, trade expansion, source of natural resources, and ethnic stability. In fact, in the last one decade, the balance of economic power in Kyrgyzstan has already been shifted in favour of China. After capturing the consumer market over the years, China has recently started embarking on large-scale strategic projects in Kyrgyzstan with an eye on harnessing its rich natural resources, minerals, land and water. It was aptly mentioned by Gen. Liu Yazhou of the People's Liberation Army (PLA) "Central Asia is the thickest piece of cake given to the modern Chinese by the heavens."[1] Trade between China and the five Central Asian countries had totaled $25.9 billion in 2009, an increase from just $527 million in 1992.

At the bilateral level, Kyrgyzstan's relations with China have been warm and cordial since proclamation of its independence. In the last few years, bilateral trade has grown manifold and the overall cooperation has blossomed rapidly especially in the economic encompassing construction, energy, infrastructure projects, and technical cooperation in defence sectors.

However, China's earlier attempts to make deeper inroads into Kyrgyzstan were frustrated by the successive periodic revolutions which intermittently kept the country tied to Russia. In the post second Kyrgyz revolution, new Kyrgyz Prime Minister Atambayev in a balancing game consistently signaled to look away from the traditional support base of Russia (and the US). As a result Chinese were making renewed attempts for forays into the Kyrgyzstan in a major way. The reorientation of Kyrgyz economy towards China had already begun during the period of previous regimes. China had been the main beneficiary in Central Asia after the collapse of the Soviet political and economic structures. The Kyrgyz initial adoption of the multi-vector policy facilitated the process.

China has become Kyrgyzstan's largest trade partner. In 2008, trade with China had reached to $9 billion officially but the unofficial figure was said to be much more. The Chinese had been dumping large-scale goods into Kyrgyzstan without customs which then are re-exported to other post-Soviet republics. However, the trade figure declined in 2009 to $5.3 billion. According to Chinese statistics, the trade between Kyrgyzstan and China amounted to $4.2 billion in 2011. But other sources indicated that the trade turnover was $10 billion in 2011, the second highest bilateral trade with CIS countries after Russia. According to Kyrgyz vice Prime Minister for Economy and Investment, Joomart Otorbaev, China exports to Kyrgyzstan amounted to $10 billion.[2] The Kyrgyz Foreign Ministry (MFA) gave a figure of only $2.1 billion during 2012.[3] The steady decline of trade does not reflect the Kyrgyz-China relations, but it is an indication that other CIS countries have stopped importing Chinese goods through Kyrgyzstan. Ironically, the trade figure was far more than the $5 billion GDP of the country.

Kyrgyzstan has attracted large numbers of Chinese businessmen, who have come to dominate most of the republic's import and export of small goods. More than 80 per cent of goods in the three largest markets of Kyrgyzstan, Kara-Suu Bazar in Southern Kyrgyzstan and Dordoi and Osh Bazar in Bishkek come from China. These include consumer goods, construction material, electronics and even food items. Most of the Chinese imports are re-exported to neighbouring Central Asian countries through the porous borders. Many ascribed to this as "Chinese invasion"[4] though the statistics never reflected the true nature of Kyrgyz-Chinese trade. Almost all the Chinese goods illegally pass through Kyrgyz border to CIS markets.

Tragically, after the Soviets left, Kyrgyzstan's own industrial production had stopped. The remaining manufacturing capacity eventually got killed by the Chinese businessmen selling cheap goods, almost being dumped from across the border. The cross-border trade has been the key for the availability of consumer goods. It seemed impossible for the majority common men in the country to live without the availability of cheap Chinese goods. Most of the Chinese businesses in Kyrgyzstan were in the shadow market and the Kyrgyz authorities had no control. Even in 2010, it appeared that the Kyrgyz authorities were facing tough time regulating the Chinese businesses. The Kyrgyz Minister of Labour, Employment and Migration Aigul Ryskulova, was warning the Chinese companies to comply with regulations that stipulated 80 per cent of personnel must be Kyrgyz citizens.[5] Most Kyrgyz feared increasing Chinese migration into Kyrgyzstan. Many politicians had been raising serious concerns about China threat only to be silenced later when the most vocal among them get special invitation from Beijing and given huge hospitality.[6] With China's increasing presence, analysts fear that Kyrgyzstan may eventually be regressed into a Chinese raw material appendage. This will become a reality once the Chinese complete the planned Chinese-Kyrgyz-Uzbek railway in the next five to six years.

In 2010, more than 300 Sino-Kyrgyz joint enterprises were operating in Kyrgyzstan. According to the Kyrgyz National Statistical Committee's (NSC's) 2009 data, Chinese investment grew 89 per cent from 2008-09—reaching about

$51 billion. Kyrgyzstan's foreign debt to China's Export-Import Bank (EXIM) was $760 million in 2010.

China has been providing huge credit and assistance to Kyrgyzstan. In the last few years, more than $150 million was extended by Beijing. In 2011, China Development Bank (CDB) had assured to extend $136 million credit to Kyrgyzstan. In 2011, talks were being held for China's Sinohydro Corporation for the construction of a cascade of Hydropower plant in the Suusamyr River with overall capacity of 1,300 megawatt in five years at an estimated cost of about $2 billion. China too had shown interest to import electric power from Kyrgyzstan. In the recent years, China Jundu firm showed interest in constructing an oil refinery in Kara-Balta. Besides, many Chinese companies have acquired license for gold mining in Kyrgyzstan.

By 2012, China's presence in Kyrgyzstan was all pervasive. In order to expand its trade and investment, China has been looking for upgrading transport connectivity through Kyrgyzstan to other parts of Central Asia. Discussions on a rail link from China to Uzbekistan through Kyrgyzstan were also in progress. It has embarked on massive infrastructure construction projects that would link Kashgar in Xinjiang with Bishkek and Osh with high quality roads. China's long term strategy is to build a high-speed railway corridor through Central Asia to Europe.

China has joined hands with Kyrgyzstan to conduct close cooperation within the bilateral and SCO frameworks, and jointly combat terrorism, extremism, separatism and trans-national organised crimes like drug trafficking, so as to safeguard security and stability of the two countries and the region at large. China's interests vis-à-vis Kyrgyzstan centre around pre-empting any support from Kyrgyzstan to the Uighur separatists and in countering US and Russian influence in Kyrgyzstan.

As mentioned before, negotiations with China for major investments have been going on for decades. But the progress was slow due to internal political instability in Kyrgyzstan. In the changed political environment, induced by a plethora of Chinese commercial and economic grants, assistances, investments etc, Kyrgyz leadership had shown stronger inclinations towards China. In the post-Second Kyrgyz Revolution, the rising Chinese influence was mirrored by the frequency of high level bilateral visits; starting with First Vice Prime Minister Babanov (April 2011), there have been a plethora of visits in recent past, including by President Otunbayeva (September 1, 2011), visit of Foreign Minister Kazakbaev and the Prime Minister Almazbek Atambayev (September 15, 2011) and President Atambayev's two visits in 2012. In addition to the routine aid, the Chinese, through these visits, had stepped up their involvement in Kyrgyzstan in a major strategic way i.e., construction of railway line passing through Kyrgyz territory; import of rare earth and other strategic minerals from Kyrgyzstan; export of Chinese manpower to do manual labour and other works; establishment of Consulate in

Osh; Kyrgyzstan to open one in Guangzhou; construction of major projects, including hydro power, highways etc.

The first high-level visit from Kyrgyzstan led by First vice Prime Minister Omurbek Babanov took place on April 6-8, 2011. Babanov met Chinese Vice President Xi Jinping, Vice Premier of the State Council Wang Qishan, senior management of CDB, Minister of Commerce, Minister of Railways of China and representatives of major energy companies. Interestingly, the Chinese leadership including Xi Jinping and Wang Qishan acknowledged the Kyrgyz choice for democratic reforms. They told Babanov "The chosen political course will bring benefit for Kyrgyzstan and will contribute to stability, development and peace in the region. The Government of China supports your efforts aimed to keep the national accord. We are ready to continue providing support to development of bilateral relations. We consider Kyrgyzstan as a friendly neighbour and important partner of China."[7]

In a bit to lure Kyrgyzstan, Beijing lauded Kyrgyz coalition government's achievements and agreed to dole out millions of dollar aid and credit to stabilise Kyrgyzstan's economy. Kyrgyzstan had received the following pledges:

- To receive assistance through both bilateral means and under the SCO framework,
- To receive $5 million no-strings financial aid for the reconstruction of southern Kyrgyzstan,[8]
- To extend $136 million credit CDB,
- To strengthen friendship, deepen cooperation and coordination on regional and international issues,
- To enhance political mutual trust, mutual support on major issues in UN and SCO,
- Kyrgyzstan to abide by bilateral agreements and legal documents inked in the past by two sides,
- To promote cooperation in areas of trade, economy, transportation, electricity and infrastructure construction,
- Kyrgyzstan to adhere to one-China policy and back China's stance on Taiwan, Tibet and on the strike against the "three evil forces" of separatism, extremism and terrorism.[9]

Babanov had proposed a US $200m Kyrgyz-Chinese investment fund for financing of collaborative priority projects in Kyrgyzstan.[10] Both sides agreed to implement previously reached agreements, including construction of cross-border roads, credit line for reconstruction of power supply system in southern Kyrgyzstan, construction of agricultural technology parks in Kyrgyzstan. Priority projects included construction of railways, export of electricity, construction of the Datka substation and Datka-Kemin power line, combined heat and power plants, and speeding up the supply of tractors in line with a grant allocated earlier. Two sides also explored the prospects of reconstruction of small hydropower plants in Kyrgyzstan. The Chinese had conveyed to the Kyrgyz that implementation of several collaborative projects was suspended in the previous year over the world financial and economic crisis. Xi Jinping said "With the recovery of world economy and stabilisation of the situation in Kyrgyzstan, good opportunities of business cooperation arise."[11]

Babanov also met with heads of Godyan Corporation, SYNOHYDRO, Huawei Symantec Technologies Co. Ltd and ZTE Corporation. China promised to send specialists from Jinhua Corporation to assess investment opportunities in construction of railway, hydroelectric stations, development of coal and iron fields in Kyrgyzstan.[12] Babanov had been pushing China's plan to construct a railway line from Western China to Uzbekistan through Kyrgyzstan. China had agreed to provide assistance in construction of China-Kyrgyzstan-Uzbekistan railway.[13]

Babanov's China visit gave impetus to Chinese businessmen returning to Kyrgyzstan who suffered losses due to crisis in Osh in 2010. Lot of Chinese workers/businessmen had to leave the region following the events. Bilateral trade with Kyrgyzstan reached $9 billion once, but it had declined in 2011.

Another important visit was by the Kyrgyz President Roza Otunbayeva to Urumqi, to participate in the first China-Eurasia Expo on September 1, 2011 and met Chinese vice Prime Minister Li Keqiang and Secretary of the Xinjiang Uygur Autonomous Region, Zhang Chunsyan. At the meeting, China agreed to allocate 100 million Yuan grant to Kyrgyzstan. Roza Otunbayeva stated on the occasion that "Kyrgyzstan and China have close links almost in all spheres and our cooperation should only grow and consolidate."[14]

Finally, the visit to China by the Prime Minister Almazbek Atambayev took place on September 14-15, 2011 when he attended the World Economic Forum. He held a series of meetings with China's top leadership, including Prime Minister Wen Jiabao, Foreign Minister Yang Jiechi and Science & Technology Minister Wan Gang.[15] Earlier, Atambayev had mentioned China as one of the few countries that does not link its assistance to any political conditions.[16]

All in all, it appeared in 2011 that the space ceded by Russia was being occupied by China. On the commercial front, Beijing seemed to be taking advantage of Kyrgyzstan not being a member of Russian-led Custom Union (CU). This was helping the process. Though, Russia has been insisting on Kyrgyzstan to join the CU and the Kyrgyz too have been mulling over to joining the CU, but the Chinese were trying hard to prevent it from happening. The decision to join CU was postponed several times. For China, Kyrgyzstan's WTO status had thus far suited to use Kyrgyzstan as a transit zone to flood its goods into CIS market. In a counter move, China lately offered Free Trade Agreement (FTA) with Central Asia. During the China-Eurasia Expo in September 2011, the Chinese vice Minister of Commerce Zhong Shan suggested the Shanghai Cooperation Organization (SCO) states should consider setting up a FTA.[17] Significant resistance to joining CU continues because over hundred thousand Kyrgyz traders benefit from re-exports of Chinese goods to Russia and Kazakhstan. The Kyrgyz political elite who are essentially business tycoons have a huge interest in continuing the cross-border trade with China.

A flurry of activities was witnessed in 2011. China's EXIM Bank was financing the reconstruction of Osh-Sarytash-Irkeshtam road for $75.3 million and reconstruction of Bishkek-Naryn-Torugart road for $200 million. China was mulling to invest $2 billion for the construction of the Kokomeren hydroelectric power station's cascade—a joint venture between Sinohydro Corporation Elektricheskiye Stantsii Company. The project will have the capacity to produce 1,300 MW power.

Railway Connectivity

Most significantly, Bishkek and Beijing, during Atambayev's visit to China in September 2011 had finally decided to go ahead with the long-anticipated agreement on the construction of the China-Kyrgyzstan-Uzbekistan railway on the lines of New Silk Road that will pass through the thickly populated Fergana Valley.[18] The idea was floating since the Shanghai Five was born in 1996. Once this $2 billion project is fully laid in the next 12 years the Chinese expansion into Eurasia will be fully realised with wide geopolitical implications (economic, political, social, demographic and security). China will have full access to the natural resources and mineral reserves of Kyrgyzstan, Uzbekistan and Turkmenistan and a spin off could be that the Chinese railway will be even effectively linked to Afghanistan, Pakistan and Iran. The 268 km railroad would become China's main Gateway and it would considerably shorten the existing 900 km long connection between China and Central Asia.

Notwithstanding both internally and externally induced criticism, China's National Precision Machinery Import & Export Corporation (CPMIEC) was to finance the project in return of Kyrgyzstan offering several key mineral deposits —gold, aluminum and iron ore—to China. Kyrgyzstan had earlier proposed to use the principle of resources in exchange for investments in order for Kyrgyzstan to get rid of external debt. In January 2011, Kyrgyzstan offered its Terekkan and Perevalnoye gold deposits, Sandyk aluminum and Jetim iron ore deposits for consideration of China.[19] Later, Kyrgyzstan changed its mind and agreed to offer four deposits of natural resources instead in exchange for construction of the railway. As mentioned earlier, Chinese Ministry of Railways had agreed to provide assistance in construction of China-Kyrgyzstan-Uzbekistan railway when First vice Prime Minister Omurbek Babanov visited Beijing.

However, there had been instant public criticism regarding the sudden increase in the Chinese influence especially with regards to proposed railway project. Many Kyrgyz leaders had reservations about benefits to Kyrgyzstan on transit of goods from China to Uzbekistan; especially when the infrastructure will be used by

Uzbekistan and China. Some prominent Kyrgyz thought it as an open surrender and compared with the earlier ceding of land to China in a dubious means. A Kyrgyz MP Karganbek Samakov wrote in an appeal "Kyrgyzstan's people want to know the terms of the memorandum signed by Kyrgyz First Deputy Prime Minister Omurbek Babanov in China. We are concerned about the project's consequences. Will the fate of Uzengu-Kuush and Karkyra (plots of land allegedly given to China and Kazakhstan respectively) be repeated?"[20] The appeal was signed by several pubic associations like Lustration, Kyrgyzstan Jany Kuchtoru, Kurultay, Obshestvennyy Parliament public organisation and the Kyrk Choro Movement. Atambayev, however, has been dismissing the China threat perception and instead talked about taking advantage from China. In an interview with the Public Service Broadcasting Company OTRK on May 2, 2012, he said "Even if we do not build this railway, they (Chinese) will come here anyway. There are 1.5 billion Chinese. We will have jobs and trade.... If we want to become an economically independent and developed state, we need to develop the transport network."[21]

One of the major and critical obstacles so far has been replacing the Russian standardised track or gauge width with narrow gauge of the Chinese. China had been insisting on its own railways gauge size. Most analysts assumed that Russia perhaps would not allow that for security considerations. It seemed Uzbekistan has already begun to change its rail gauge to meet Chinese standards and Kyrgyzstan will have to follow suit despite Russia's security concerns. But off late no specific objections were visibly coming from Moscow. Beijing, it appeared, has been waiting for this moment. However, both China and Kyrgyzstan had agreed to treat the gauge issue as internal matter of the participating countries. It seemed that an expert group was to visit Kyrgyzstan soon to assess the details.

Energy Deals

China made a major breakthrough when it had finally agreed to provide soft loan to Bishkek for the construction of the Datka-Kemin power transmission line stretching from south to the north of Kyrgyzstan. This was agreed when Kyrgyz President Almazbek Atambayev paid his official visit to China on June 5-6, 2012. It was also announced that China's Tebian Electric Apparatus Stock Co., Ltd. (TBEA) was to build 500 kV Datka-Kemin power transmission line for $400 million.[22] In fact, a series of Chinese delegations had been visiting Bishkek to discuss the construction of Datka-Kemin high voltage line project which is meant to provide the southern regions of the country with independent power supply and join Kambar-Ata hydro power stations. Earlier, Kyrgyzstan and EXIM Bank of China signed $208 million loan agreement for construction of power transmission line 500 kV Datka station in Jalalabad and construction of 220 kV power transmissions line stretching for 256.5 km through Datka-Osh-Uzlovaya and Osh-Uzlovaya-Alay.[23] The official capsule laying ceremony of the Datka Project took place on in Akman village, Bazar-Korgon rayon of Jalal-Abad oblast in July 2011.

It seemed Atambayev gave major concessions to Chinese energy companies to enter into Kyrgyz energy market. Reports suggested that the Sinohydro Corporation will build a series of hydropower plants (1,300 MW) on the Naryn River and other hydropower sources. Atambayev said "It is significant for Kyrgyzstan; we are beginning to diversify supplies and will be independent in terms of energy. These are real steps towards independence of the country."[24] It only appeared that this pattern will continue and China will harness major water resources of Kyrgyzstan both for hydropower and possibly for eventual diversion of river waters from the Pamirs and Tien-Shan.

Beijing did achieve significant gains from Atambayev's visit, who also met Chinese President Hu Jintao and Foreign Minister Wen Jiabao. Commitment for China-Kyrgyzstan-Uzbekistan project was made from the highest Chinese leadership. The joint statement mentioned that 'Kyrgyz-Chinese relations is a priority direction in the foreign policy of two states, and serves the fundamental interests of the nations of Kyrgyzstan and China. Parties are committed to continue to provide mutual support on issues affecting sovereignty, territorial integrity, stability and security of each state, as well as peace and stability in Central Asia."[25]

Of course, the Chinese had huge concerns about expanding business and investments in Kyrgyzstan that is being elaborated later in the chapter. To mollify the Chinese concerns, Atambayev tried to lament at the incidents where Chinese projects were halted by protesters and in many cases Kyrgyz citizens had man-handled Chinese mining workers. He was 'ashamed' of his citizens' behaviour[26] and said, "I was ashamed of such excesses. I think all citizens of Kyrgyzstan should be ashamed...it is unpleasant when you are reminded that the country helps you for free. What our people are doing with Chinese workers at Solton-Sary, Ishtamberdy? Such things disallow development of normal relations in Kyrgyzstan, attraction of bigger investments, this should be said openly. It is time for citizens of Kyrgyzstan to get accustomed to living in a civilised manner."[27] Almazbek Atambayev appeared very concerned on the China issue. In the same context he said "They beat Chinese citizens, banish them from the enterprise. Despite that they agree to help us. Not due to our deeds, but despite them. We need stability. Kyrgyzstan should be stable. Frankly speaking, this chaos will be over soon...there were conflicts, the criminal cases were launched, and actions are taken regarding those who orchestrated the events. Very often certain people, certain business structures are behind our ordinary citizens, who put forward some demands, they command, give money, finance such actions. People of Kyrgyzstan do not need instability. Certain politicians and businessmen need it, who wants to gain some dividends or to take away the license...look at Ishtamberdy deposit. The agreement was signed many years ago, the road was almost built for this money and after all that we want to cheat China. This is not nice."[28] Of course, such incidents described by Atambayev were not confined to the Chinese investors alone. Almost all the countries including the Russians have been lodging similar complaints.

The year 2011 witnessed Kyrgyz leadership putting the Kyrgyz-China relations in full swing. The increased Chinese activities in Kyrgyzstan was coming at a time when the Russians were showing scant interest in the region due to domestic political scenario and serious mistrust with Kyrgyz leaders. The momentum was maintained even in 2012 with maximum number of high level visits between China and Kyrgyzstan taking place in April 2012. As stated earlier, Kyrgyz President visited Beijing in June 2012 (Kyrgyzstan assumed chairmanship of SCO in 2012) and the Chinese Premier Wen Jiabao was to visit Kyrgyzstan. The pace of high level visits was unusual and could have been attributed primarily to the cracks that appeared in Kyrgyz-Russia relations after Atambayev visited Moscow in March 2012.

Earlier in January 2012, when all countries celebrated the 20th anniversary of diplomatic relations with Kyrgyzstan, China did something extra diplomatically. The Chinese President sent his special envoy Chen Zhili (Vice Chairman of the Standing Committee of the NPC of China to mark the occasion. Zhili in a statement at the anniversary said "Relations between Kyrgyzstan and China must be treasured.... Kyrgyz-Chinese relations are based on principle of equality, mutual respect and benefit. We are cooperating in economic, transport, communication, security and humanitarian sphere. There is a strong legal foundation under relations of two countries; every part pays contribution in development of peace and stability in region."[29] He further added "As for further prospect, cooperation between Kyrgyzstan and China have embarked on a new historical level and stand before great opportunities of further development. There are no contradictions between our countries. There are only principles of mutual benefits and complementarities. No matter how the international situation changes China is ready to remain friendly neighbour and reliable partner of Kyrgyzstan." This was more than a normal gesture from China's side that reflected how small state like Kyrgyzstan figured so much in Beijing's scheme of things. This was also a bit surprising for everyone. President Almazbek Atambayev quickly reminded Zhili about the China-Kyrgyzstan-Uzbekistan railway project. Chen Zhili was assured that all the obstacles for Chinese investors in Kyrgyzstan will be resolved. Chen Zhili made it clear that there were no contradictions between China and Kyrgyzstan.[30]

Selling Soft Power

The Chinese were not only coming into large strategic projects but also in other spheres that involved projection of its soft power. These were perhaps part of Beijing's policy to enhance its outreach and improve its image in Central Asia. Quite often, in fact, almost on daily basis, news of Chinese assistance to various Kyrgyz institutions had become a routine thing and had become difficult to keep track of. But the most visible ones included allocation of colossal funds ($2 million grant in 2011 alone) for the development of capital Bishkek city. A grant of $1 million was aimed at creating a service station for municipal buses, another $1 million for purchasing spare parts. China, earlier provided Kyrgyzstan with 161 buses that ply all over the country with labels written on the buses 'Gift from China'. Bishkek transport agency had more than 450 Chinese made buses.[31] The Chinese were also donating tractors to Kyrgyz farmers to earn goodwill.

The cornerstone of China's cultural diplomacy in Kyrgyzstan included opening of Confucius Institutes at both Bishkek Humanities University and the Kyrgyz National University in 2007 and 2008 respectively. The Chinese were paying for the teachers and classes for Chinese language enrolled more than three thousand local students every year. In 2012, 38 Chinese teachers were teaching in schools and universities across Kyrgyzstan. It appeared that over 100 Kyrgyz graduates headed to China every year in search of jobs or for higher learning. In fact, reports appeared that the Chinese language lessons were introduced at Kyrgyz schools such as School No. 69 located in Yug-2 micro district. The parliamentary committee for education approved the ratification of the draft signed in 2007 for the construction of a special Chinese language school on January 24, 2012.[32] The Bishkek City Mayor's office had announced that it had allocated 2.44 hectares of land for construction of the school at Djal (outskirt of Bishkek) with Chinese grant.[33] Later, it was also announced by the Kyrgyz officials that China's Xinjiang University had discussed the idea of opening Kyrgyz-Chinese university, kindergartens and schools with Chinese language of instruction. In a meeting held with Chinese on August 27, 2012 in Bishkek, Kyrgyz vice Minister Gulnara Asymbekova said "We should build a chain, since education and upbringing starts in kindergartens and schools."[34] This meant that China was beginning to mould the next generation Kyrgyz people to think in Chinese way. Of course there had been much criticism about allowing Chinese schools to be opened in the country.[35] On the reverse side, over 2000 Chinese students study in Kyrgyzstan. Though, the number had reduced after 2010 June events. But an interesting aspect was that the Chinese students were learning local Kyrgyz and Russian languages. In contrast 1,000 students from India studying in Kyrgyzstan opted for medicine course.[36] In addition to this, the Chinese were giving aid to cultural, educational, financial, health and other institutions. In 2011, China announced to build a150-bed hospital in Ak-Tilk micro district of Osh.[37] Thrust was also given to coordinate works on media between the two countries. This was seen by analysts as a step by China to curb anti-Chinese and change Central Asian negative perception of China. During the China-Eurasia Expo., in September 2011, China took a major initiative to tie media relations with Central Asian counterparts, including Pakistan, Kazakhstan and Kyrgyzstan. The aim was to coordinate on news features, reporting intrinsically to promote peace and development in the region. Wang Chen, Minister of the State Council Information Office was quoted by *China Daily* as saying "The exchange and cooperation in the news and media field is the key promoter for friendly relationships between China and its neighbouring countries."[38] This was viewed in the context of growing threat to China from social media and information that was considered by China as destabilising.

In fact, China had expressed interest in strengthening cooperation in media earlier also at the SCO meeting. China suggested to Kyrgyzstan to cooperate through an agreement to train journalists, organise courses to improve the skills of Kyrgyz journalists, mutual visits by delegations of the media, exchange of experiences, participation in conferences, symposia, help to improve material-technical base of public and private internet sites, publications, television and radio broadcasting facilities. In fact, the Kyrgyz side was careful on this regard and instead had suggested that there should be high degree of openness and freedom of speech. The Kyrgyz Foreign Minister noted "Kyrgyzstan had chosen the path of democratic development, and freedom of speech is an integral part of building a stable, prosperous and safe country."[39]

Security Nexus

China was simultaneously gaining grip over Kyrgyz security system. For Beijing, Kyrgyzstan like Kazakhstan remained a critical frontier for its security. Some of China's strategic concerns are being covered in the first chapter. Here, the Chinese approach appeared quite diligent. They knew that the Kyrgyz aspirations for democracy could not be stopped. Yet, security concerns arising out of Kyrgyz democracy for China had to be addressed carefully. Beijing was sending stream of high-level delegations to tie up security measures that also included Kyrgyzstan's security apparatus. In April 2011, Chinese State Counselor Meng Jianzhu visited Bishkek to strengthen security and law enforcement ties. Meng Jianzhu, who is also China Public Security Minister, importantly said that China respects Kyrgyz's choice of political development and will support the Bishkek government's efforts to achieve domestic stability and boost the economy.[40] The emphasis was to strengthen cross-border control, and drug trafficking. By 2011-12, every sensitive Kyrgyz Government structures, including Ministry of Interior, NSA, and Ministry of Defence were receiving large scale aid and assistance. Importantly, K. Dushebayev, Chairman of Kyrgyz State Committee for National Security (Head of Kyrgyz Intelligence Agency) visited China in September 2011 and an agreement to jointly fight the "three evils" was signed.[41] Kyrgyz spy chief met with Chinese Public Security Minister Meng Jianzhu and State Security Minister Geng Huichang and received an aid of $1 million to improvise the Kyrgyz security infrastructure.[42] In April 2012, the Chinese Minister for Public Security (MPS) Meng Jianzhu visited Bishkek again and had agreed to give more than $3 million to help Kyrgyzstan strengthen security. Meng Jianzhu had extensive discussion with the Kyrgyz Defence Council Secretary Busurmankul Tabaldiyev on regional security, cooperation between security forces, and strengthening collaboration in combating challenges and threats.[43] Besides, China and Kyrgyzstan has annual consultations on security under the SCO Security Council mechanism. On April 17, 2012, the Vice Chairman of the Internal and Judicial Affairs Committee of the NPC, Zhang Xuezhong visited Bishkek to discuss the fight against organised crime with the Kyrgyz officials.[44]

Similarly, China had been consistently supporting Kyrgyzstan's efforts to develop its military and national defence. Following a meeting between Defence Minister Liang Guanglie and Kyrgyz Minister of Defence Omuraliev Taalaibek at the SCO military Chiefs meeting in Beijing on April 23, 2012, the defence ties between the two had been further boosted.[45] The talks for cooperation included among others to modernize the Kyrgyz Defence Ministry and intelligence apparatus. The Chinese military delegation headed by Deputy Chief of Staff of Foreign Affairs under the Ministry of Defense arrived in Kyrgyzstan in April 2012 to participate in the ceremony of laying a capsule for the construction of residential buildings for Kyrgyz Army. China had committed to build two nine-storey houses with 108 departments for the military personnel of the Ministry of Defence of Kyrgyzstan. Construction was to be completed by August 2013.[46] In a return gesture, Kyrgyzstan allowed Chinese military subunits to transit through its territory to Tajikistan for their participation in the SCO's joint military counter-terrorism exercises "Peace Mission-2012".[47] The PLA transited through Irkeshtam - Sary-Tash - Gulcha - Osh - the Kyzyl-Kiya - Batken - Isfana on June 4-5, 2012.

The intelligence and security analysts viewed such cooperation in the defence and security fields as heavy Chinese penetration into the Kyrgyz establishment, especially to keep track of the trends detrimental to Chinese security. With over 850 kilometres of border and home-grown problems like the Uighur/East Turkistan Islamic Movement (ETIM), and a high Kyrgyz Diaspora living in Urumqi, China naturally desired stronger cooperation in intelligence-defence with Kyrgyzstan. While combating the ETIM was considered important, China's outreach to Kyrgyzstan was more nuanced than holding its interests in Xinjiang. An increased intelligence arrangement with Kyrgyzstan was part of a key element in its tacit strategy to hedge competing influences from actors especially monitoring US, Russia, Turkey and India. Beijing has been suspicious of the US (Transit Centre) and the Russian airbase located close to its sensitive Xinjiang border. The discomfort was more particularly to the US military presence in Kyrgyzstan. Though, China has been conducting its own war game under the SCO rubric with all the Central Asian states, including Kyrgyzstan, it had tried through several means including allurement and arms twisting of Kyrgyz elite for closing down the US base. This was widely known but became public when *WikiLeaks* released a cable of the State Department which cited American officials having suspected China of offering Kyrgyzstan $3 billion to shut down the US air base in Kyrgyzstan. The cable, dated February 13, 2009, revealed that in an awkward meeting between Tatiana C. Gfoeller, the US Ambassador to Kyrgyzstan, and Zhang Yannian, the Chinese

Ambassador, in which Ms. Gfoeller confronted Zhang with her suspicions of the $3 billion bribe. The cable said "Visibly flustered, Zhang temporarily lost the ability to speak Russian and began spluttering in Chinese to the silent aide diligently taking notes right behind him."[48] The *WikiLeaks*' revelations had created quite fervor in 2010 among the diplomatic circle in Bishkek. Tatiana C. Gfoeller was later moved to Pentagon as advisor to the US military chief.

The intelligence nexus with China evoked sharp reaction within Kyrgyzstan; many suggested that it would harm the country.[49] Two Chinese telecommunications giants Huawei and ZTE operating in the region were under scrutiny by a US congressional committee. The Americans indicated that the probe could have revealing "cyber-security threat" to Central Asian states from China, whose companies had modernised their telecom sectors. The two companies were suspected to have been working for the Chinese Government.[50]

Kyrgyz Resentment

Notwithstanding all the good things happening between the two countries, Kyrgyzstan's heavy reliance on Beijing over the years had increased the country's economic vulnerability that entailed huge public resentment. The fears that Chinese migrants will follow Chinese goods into Kyrgyzstan in massive numbers have, since the early days of independence, been a source of unease in Bishkek. Over the years, Chinese relentless economic push in Kyrgyzstan had put the ordinary people in a fix. On the one hand, the flood of Chinese imports had been considered as a blessing, because (a) it was affordable, (b) Chinese imported goods are re-exported to larger and better-protected markets in Kazakhstan, Uzbekistan and even Russia.[51] In fact, the ordinary Kyrgyz had developed a love-hate relationship with the Chinese. It had come to a stage where they did not like the Chinese but couldn't do without them, whereas, the Kyrgyz liked the Russians but could do without them.

But now, with the Chinese corporate heavily investing in strategic projects including infrastructure, electricity supply, mining, metallurgy, and refinery, the discontent was further intensifying especially among the among think tanks and the general public. Whereas the political class viewed the Chinese influence differently. The overwhelming local perception was that Kyrgyzstan's economy will eventually be entirely dominated by China. People have been complaining about the country becoming a dumping ground for Chinese junk. The most pro-Russian media were fuelling fears about the negative impact of hazardous Chinese goods and Chinese immigration.

Informal statistics suggested that some 150-200 Chinese cross the Kyrgyz border every month but not all of them return. Some unofficial reports revealed more than 50,000 Chinese are presently staying in Kyrgyzstan. In an article in the Kyrgyz newspaper "*Sayat press*"Turdugul Karimova quoted more than 100,000 Chinese living in Kyrgyzstan.[52] Analysts feared illegal Chinese migration would lead to social problems in the future. Media also reported about the Chinese companies were fuelling massive corruption in the country.

Apprehensions were also being raised over the sovereignty concerns. The Kyrgyz have been historically suspicious about the Chinese. The historian cited the Manas epic depicting various wars between the two peoples. Many people still wonder why Kyrgyzstan settled their hundreds year old border dispute with China and gave away country's valuable land of Uzengy-Kuush to China after independence in a clandestine border deal. A local journalist K. Kumkova wrote in this context "among its Central Asian neighbours, China these days is more often feared than loved. This attitude is perhaps most apparent in Kyrgyzstan, where despite an overwhelming dependence on Chinese imports, Chinese-owned malls and mining pits have been the subject of attacks in recent years; nationalist editorials in the local press play on fears of the Middle Kingdom. But all the negative press is not deterring Beijing's efforts to win friends and promote Chinese culture in the region."[53] One of the reasons for the Chinese success was attributed to vested interests among Kyrgyz political elite, who seemed hesitant to enforce law to check Chinese forays. Not only the Kyrgyz authorities were deeply corrupt but were also unable to regulate the flow of Chinese immigrants. It was generally known that the Chinese come on short-term visas and then continue to stay illegally. Karimova observed that "if this phenomenon is not stopped at the state border, then several years from now, the Chinese may completely 'drown' Kyrgyzstan. Unfortunately, there are no measures to limit the flow."[54]

One of the fallouts of the influx of Chinese was growing intermarriage between Han Chinese men and Kyrgyz women. This was a threatening phenomenon for ordinary Kyrgyz. These sentiments at popular level were getting reflected on the ground. In fact, there had been organised protests against Chinese migrants, workers and companies. The incident of attacks against Chinese had been on the rise. Throughout 2011, there were reports of ugly incidents of local Kyrgyz harassing and beating Chinese workers. The protestors demanded cancellation of licenses of Chinese companies. For example, Kara-Balta town was protesting against setting up of Chinese refinery near the town due to environmental concerns. Members of the Jayil Regional Assembly's Environmental Commission had claimed that the construction of an oil refinery Chinese firm, Jundu would negatively impact air and rivers.[55]

Issyk-Kul and Naryn region of Kyrgyzstan were demanding to ban Chinese haulers from delivering cargo in Kyrgyzstan. One of the demands of the Lorry Drivers in Kyrgyzstan was the installation of scales at the Torugart post on the Kyrgyz-Chinese border to weigh goods. They wanted Lorries to reduce the weight from 55 tonnes to 44 tonnes. Their demands also included banning of Chinese Lorries entering into Kyrgyzstan and to be replaced by Kyrgyz transporters.[56] The Kyrgyz Cargo Carriers Association also complained how Chinese and Tajik cargo carriers had monopolised the transport market in Kyrgyzstan.[57]

Residents of Terek-Sai village of Chatkal rayon, Jalal-Abad oblast blocked the road in August 2011 in protest against China's Full Gold Mining demanding to suspend development of the mine. The mining came under controversy after the local workers demanded payment of leave and sickness allowances. Invariably, the government had taken the sides of the workers.[58] It was the second foreign-run gold mine in the country. The project was launched by the Kyrgyz Prime Minister in September 2011.[59] The Chinese company was to produce 300,000 tonnes of ore annually by 2012 that would yield up to two tonnes of gold concentrate annually.

Earlier in August 2011, hundreds of protestors from village of Daroot-Korgon in southern Kyrgyzstan had blocked a major highway against illegal mining by two Chinese companies Asia Gold Enterprise, and Inter-Business Kaidi.[60] On August 26, 2011, some 300 people beat up three Chinese miners at Chinese-operated Solton-Sary gold mine in Naryn region. The locals were opposed to Chinese mining and accused them of ignoring environmental standards and poor treatment of Kyrgyz workers.[61] The incident was among series of demonstrations held against Chinese companies operating in Kyrgyzstan.

Not just this, the environmentalists had been raising concerns about China's relentless economic push into Kyrgyzstan and the Kyrgyz Government's hesitation in forcing environmental statutes. Given the political instability, rampant corruption and perceived lack of security have deterred other countries from investing in Kyrgyzstan. The Chinese have taken advantage of this and in fact, their push has been quite aggressive. Head of Taza Tabigat (Clean Environment) public association, Anara Dautalieva during the press conference accused the Chinese foundries operating on the territory of Kyrgyzstan for damaging the environment and health of people. She said "Their production is too primitive and local officials ignore it due to benefits that they receive."[62] In fact, Atambayev had to admit all these atrocities against Chinese investors in Kyrgyzstan before he was to visit Beijing in 2012.

China's increasing foray into the mining sector, supposedly through manipulative means, had led to deep public anger. In fact, the media described the phenomenon as 'resource nationalism'.[63] Government was forced to react to the rising public protests. In October 2011, the State Agency for Environmental Protection and Forestry (SAEPF) banned the work of China's Kay Enterprise, which was developing placer gold deposit at Nizhnyi Chanach, until it compensated environmental violation.[64] Similarly, the Ministry of Natural Resources (MNR) annulled licenses of China's Mylin Resources for geological exploration of iron ore deposit at Jetim and had begun its work only one year ago.[65] In March 2012, the State Agency on Geology issued a statement to the Chinese Embassy that no license for deposits will be issued through intermediaries. Director of the Agency Uchkunbek Tashbaev said "We change the mechanisms fundamentally to ensure transparency and we will issue new licenses only by auction. Each Chinese investor should know about it."[66] Tashbaev identified several factors, which included among others; differences between the two cultures, intermediaries with questionable reputations, and investors obtaining permits through dubious ways. Tashbaev said "We need to establish some code of behaviour for Chinese businessmen working directly on the fields. Since even the smallest detail can lead to more unwanted problems, we have witnessed last summer...we want investors to comply with all laws of Kyrgyzstan. Those, who violated these laws, shall be punished."[67] There were reports of Kyrgyzstan's secret services having stopped the work of three Chinese companies under anti-corruption act. It was widely known that the Chinese companies were involved in illegal financial transaction, and custom evasion apart from indulging in corrupt practices.[68]

Such events indeed reflected the uneasy relationship at least in the public perception. Yet, the Chinese side was trying to play down the incidents. The Chinese Ambassador to Kyrgyzstan Wang Kaiwen blamed unnamed political groups behind the protests against foreign investors. The Chinese side had come to a conclusion that the mining sector in Kyrgyzstan was complex and needed streamlining if investment from China had to come.[69]

Increasing attack against Chinese investors, however, did not deter China pursuing more aggressive policy in Kyrgyzstan. In fact, to further enhance cooperation in trade, economy and investment, China sent the Vice-Premier Hui Liangyuto Bishkek on September 10, 2012.[70] Earlier in July 2012, Kyrgyz First Deputy Premier Karashev Aale had visited Beijing and met with Vice Premier Hui Liangyu.[71] The Kyrgyz Government had ensured the Chinese leaders that it will take efficient measures to protect Chinese investments in Kyrgyzstan. Instead, the cooperation was expanding into other areas such as machine building, cotton processing, fertilizers plants, agriculture and irrigation projects.[72] Following documents were signed during the vist of Hui Liangyu:

- Agreement on technical and economic cooperation between the governments of Kyrgyzstan and China (10 million yuan grant);
- Agreement on cooperation and exchange in agricultural sector between the Chinese Ministry of Agriculture and the Ministry of Agriculture and Land Improvement of Kyrgyzstan for 2013-14;
- Exchange letters on delivery of police materials;
- Memorandum of cooperation between the branch of State Development Bank and Kyrgyztelecom.

The media had reported Chinese had opened two well equipped garment factories with 500 sewing machines each in Kara-Balta near Bishkek. Importantly, the Ministry of Economy and JSC Central Asian Power and Energy Company signed a memorandum of cooperation in Beijing on June 6, 2012 with China for the construction of oil processing plant in Kara-Balta.[73] The China National Petroleum Corporation (CNPC) had promised to invest $250 million into the project which will produce 20 thousand tons of oil products by the ends on 2012 and 800 thousand tons by 2013. The plan was to build a pipeline from Shymkent (Kazakhstan) to Kara-Balta and then eastward to China.

By 2012, the Chinese were funding National Institute of Strategic Research of Kyrgyzstan (NISS) that had been assigned by the government to come out with national project proposals which could be implemented under the development strategy of 2012-14. This was being done under the China-Kyrgyz technical and economic cooperation agreement. A decree was passed by the Kyrgyz Prime Minister in May 2012 to this effect. China had approved five million Chinese yuans grant for preparing the feasibility projects.[74] NISS later came out with 40 national projects for the country.[75] Author was present when the projects were launched at the government office in the summer of 2012.

China-Eurasia Trade Initiative

For decades now, China had been making consistent effort to open up its Xinjiang Province for economic integration with Eurasia under the auspices of China-Eurasia Trade Expo. The Expo is held annually under the rubric of the New Silk Road revival with the aim to move westward by developing economic, commerce, investment and connectivity. China's plan has been to build an expressway across the Pamirs Plateau into Central Asia and then move towards Europe.[76] Kyrgyzstan has 850 km long border with Xinjiang.[77] With Kyrgyzstan and Kazakhstan in mind, Chinese were constructing the Special Economic Zones (SEZ) in Khorgos and Kashgar. Construction of Kashgar zone started in 2010. The zone covered 50 square km that included Irkeshtam at the China-Kyrgyz border.[78] Of course, by brining economic revival to Xinjiang, China hopes to quell the separatist ideas.

China had invited Kyrgyz President Almazbek Atambayev as the chief guest for the China-Eurasia Expo 2012 held in Urumqi. In his inaugural speech, President Atambayev said "we are witnessing a revival of the Great Silk Road that used to connect the East and the West, including Kyrgyzstan and China, with commercial, economic, cultural, humanitarian, political and diplomatic ties for centuries. Just like in history, the Great Silk Road begins from China today. In this respect, it is pleasant to point out that Chinese people's wisdom and China's effective and purposeful government policy, which is reflected on large-scale social and economic reforms, have enabled the country to take one of the leading positions in the world."[79] Besides unveiling the ceremony, Atambayev had extensive talks with Premier Wen Jiabao. The two leaders once again discussed economic and security issues, especially to fight against three evils. Importantly, China expressed readiness to provide support to Kyrgyzstan during its Chairmanship of SCO and to provide assistance in organisation of SCO summit in 2013.[80] Kyrgyzstan had asked China to consider the possibility of construction of the facility in Bishkek for the events.

It is now being learnt that China will provide $30 million to Kyrgyzstan towards the expense for organising the SCO Summit in June 2013. The Chinese helped the Kyrgyz Government construct residential suites for the Heads of States during the SCO Summit held in Bishkek in 2007.

The China-Eurasia Expo opened up fresh opportunities for trans-border economic cooperation. The areas of active cooperation included:

- To build machine and tractor factories, nitrogen fertilizers, soft goods and processing cotton.
- To build infrastructure in agriculture sector.
- China showed interest in building an oil pipeline (from Kazakhstan) across the north of Kyrgyzstan and a gas pipeline (from Turkmenistan) across the southern part of Kyrgyzstan.
- Kyrgyzstan was keen to develop the existing and new trade routes and transit corridor between China and Kyrgyzstan.
- The idea of interconnecting the power grids of Central Asia and China were of a major significance.
- To boost domestic industry in view of Kyrgyzstan's possible entry into the Customs Union.
- China to construct a three-storeyed building for secondary level Chinese school with 20 classrooms and for 750 students.
- Plans were afoot to set up Kyrgyz-Chinese University and a chain of kindergartens and schools with Chinese language instruction.

Atambayev and Wen Jiabao reviewed the implementation of ongoing strategic joint projects including construction of the Datka-Kemin power transmission line and the proposed China–Kyrgyzstan–Uzbekistan railway project. Atambayev met with Chairman of the Board of TBEA Zhang Xin in Urumqi. The President asked TBEA to complete the project within two years and three months period.[81]

Besides, China was also mulling granting a soft loan for construction of Osh–Batken–Isfana road. Interestingly, Kyrgyz Economy and Antimonopoly Minister Temir Sariyev had revealed to the media that China had shown keen interest in building an oil pipeline (from Kazakhstan) across the north of Kyrgyzstan and a gas pipeline (from Turkmenistan) across the southern part of the country. It seems the issue was also discussed between Presidents Atambayev and Hu Jintao earlier. The minister said that the pipeline route could run from Kazakhstan through the south of Lake Issyk-Kul to China.[82] The Kyrgyz agency JSC Kyrgyzgaz was quick to offer four variants for building gas pipeline through Kyrgyz territory to China: (a) Andijan-Jalal-Abad-Kazarman-Torugart-Kashgar; (b) Andijan-Osh-Gulcha-Irkeshtam-Kashgar; (c) Tashkent-Shymkent-Bishkek-Balykchy-Naryn-Torugart; (d) Modification of the existing pipeline along the route Tashkent-Shymkent-Bishkek-Almaty- Taldy Corgan (Panfilov) and later in China.

Kyrgyzstan was also developing direct relations with China's Xinjiang Uyghur Autonomous Region (XUAR). The two have a Special Coordination Group and protocol signed to boost cooperation in commerce, transport, agriculture, customs and cross-border cooperation in culture, health care, and tourism. In August 2012, they decided to expedite launch of Kyrgyzstan-Kashgar international flight and Kashgar-Osh-Bishkek flight. Bishkek-Urumqi flights already exist. Motor roads between Bishkek-Torugart-Kashgar and Osh-Irkeshtam-Kashgar carry major transit goods between China and CIS countries. It is clear that Central Asia states were actively supporting the development of all existing and new transit routes to China which lessens their dependence on Russia and also gain access to the cheap Chinese goods.

Conclusion

Clearly, China was deepening ties with Kyrgyzstan with an aim to make the Central Asian country as the gateway to Eurasia, Southern Central Asia and South Asia. The leaders of the two countries were meeting too frequently with focused agenda. When China's Vice-Premier Vice-Premier Hui Liangyu visited Bishkek in September 2012, Atambayev said relations with China is a priority.[83] On one hand, China was busy building roads, rail networks, hydro plants, etc. On the other hand, it was also actively promoting Pakistan's engagement in the region through several cooperation measures such as promoting an integrated media policy among Pakistan, China, Kazakhstan and Kyrgyzstan, as well as enhancing surface connectivity among the four countries.

As for the internal political situation, most Kyrgyz politicians having business background were developing good rapport with Beijing. Atambayev too, before the Presidential elections, had become an admirer of China. It was evidently visible that China had become a factor in Kyrgyz internal politics.

Even though China-Kyrgyzstan economic dependency is likely to continue, the latter's overall dependence on Russia tends to put limits on the Kyrgyz aspirations. It is widely known that Moscow played a key role in overthrowing the former President. The post-revolution period also witnessed attacks on Chinese business establishments in Kyrgyzstan. Major Chinese investment projects came to a halt since April 2010. But in 2012, most projects have been revived.

By beginning of 2012, Atambayev was already pushing hard for engagement with Russia though a lot of problem between the two countries had been festering for some time. Russia had been trying to promote its economic interests through expansion of CU to Kyrgyzstan. An eventual inclusion of Kyrgyzstan into CU would certainly restrict expansion of Chinese trade and investments in Kyrgyzstan. Chinese Ambassador to Kyrgyzstan Wang Kaiwen admitted when he said at a conference in Bishkek "Kyrgyzstan's accession to the CU will hurt the re-export of Chinese goods. But, nevertheless, we intend to foster our economic relations in other ways, for example, making investments. We are developing a number of projects that we intend to invest in. We have already begun implementing some of them and others are in development stage. These are quite major projects."[84] At another occasion, Ambassador Wang Kaiwen said Kyrgyzstan's entry to the CU will not affect the economic and trade relations with China because he felt the terms of Kyrgyzstan joining the CU was not clear to him. He thought with both Russia and Kazakhstan joining the WTO, the CU will have to work in accordance with WTO rules. Wang felt that all these points need to be considered carefully. In any case, he felt, China will remain an active partner in economic cooperation with Kyrgyzstan under the SCO and through other arrangements.[85] certainly, upon Kyrgyzstan joining the CU, Chinese will face problems for 2-3 years. But, they would look for an alternative solution and this would include creating manufacturing units in Kyrgyzstan rather than relying on cross-border trade.[86] Kyrgyzstan has the resources, energy, water, labour and most importantly well connected to CIS market. In fact, Chinese Ambassador was proposing to invite a group of experts to study the impact of Kyrgyzstan's accession into the Customs Union.

Even though Atambayev may try to push Kyrgyzstan joining the CU, other politicians appeared loath to break lucrative business connections with China, which was actually conducted through illegal channels. Russia had slapped duty hikes on export of fuels to Kyrgyzstan several times to leverage its economic influence. A malign campaign (presumably by pro-Russian elements) against the Kyrgyz leadership had started off to deter the Kyrgyz leaning Chinese way. But those favoring enhancing links with China argued that Russia's role in Kyrgyzstan had reduced to supply of fuel and extending security cover under CSTO only. Absence of any substantial economic assistance from Russia and tangible investments by any other foreign investors would create more favourable situation for the Chinese to induce the Kyrgyz leadership for innocuous trade and investment agreements.

There has been certainly large scale absence of any tension between Kyrgyzstan and China since many of the long pending border issues between the two had long been resolved. However, Beijing's attempt to push politically and economically in Kyrgyzstan had failed in the past due to frequent change in regime in Bishkek; as a result many Chinese economic investment projects got derailed with negotiations lasting for decades now. For example, negotiation over building China-Kyrgyzstan-Uzbekistan railroad had been lasting for decades.Kyrgyzstan's offer of valuable gold, iron and aluminium deposits to China for in exchange of the railway though still being criticised by a large section of Kyrgyz intelligentsia is likely to be realised unless Russia seriously decides to scuttle it. There have been numerous incidents about Chinese mining companies violating legal and environmental obligations that entailed strong public reaction in Kyrgyzstan. The common men in Kyrgyzstan were also not happy about quality of commodities being exported to Kyrgyzstan. Therefore, despite all the good developments taking place, developing a robust relation with China still remains uncertain.

NOTES

1. Quoted by Edward Wong, "China Quietly Extends Footprints into Central Asia", *New York Times*, January 2, 2011. Also see, http://chinaincentralasia.com/2013/04/19/afghanistan-has-what-china-wants/
2. *AKIpress*, June 7, 2012.
3. Ivan Marchenko, "Trade turnover between China and Kyrgyzstan reaches $ 2, 140 B in 2012", Bishkek,*24.kg news agency*, September 4, 2012.
4. Ulan Nazarov and Aibek Karabayev, "Chinese business footprint grows in Kyrgyzstan Trend has supporters and naysayers", *AKIpress*, March 22, 2010.
5. Ibid.
6. Through private conversation with Askar Aimatov, former Foreign Minister of Kyrgyzstan.
7. "Coalition government of Kyrgyzstan achieves success in economic development, improvement of living standards of population – Vice Premier of State Council of China", *AKIpress*, April 7, 2011.
8. "China gives Kyrgyzstan 5m dollars in aid to restore south", *Kyrgyz news agency 24.kg*, April 7, 2011.
9. "Chinese Vice President appreciates Kyrgyzstan's support on Taiwan and Tibet issues during meeting with Omurbek Babanov", Bishkek, *AKIpress,* April 8, 2011.
10. "$200m Kyrgyz-Chinese investment fund proposed by Kyrgyz", *24.kg*, April 7, 2011.
11. Ibid.
12. "Chinese companies ready to make investments into energy sector, telecommunications and railways in Kyrgyzstan", Bishkek, *AKIpress*, April 8, 2011.
13. Erica Marat, "Kyrgyzstan and China Move Closer to Joint Railroad Construction", *The Jamestown Foundation*, September 8, 2011.
14. "Kyrgyzstan and China have close links almost in all spheres and our cooperation should only grow and consolidate – Roza Otunbayeva", Bishkek – *24.kg news agency*, September 2, 2011.
15. "PM Atambaev meets with Chinese Premier Wen Jiabao", Bishkek *AKIpress*, September 15, 2011. "Prime Ministers of China, Kyrgyzstan decide to begin construction of China-Kyrgyzstan-Uzbekistan railway", Bishkek, *AKIpress*, September 15, 2011.
16. "PM Atambaev: China—one of few countries that does not link its assistance to any political conditions", Bishkek, *AKIpress*, May 12, 2011.
17. "China mulls free trade zone among SCO member states", *Xinhua,* English.news.cn September 3, 2011.
18. "China to provide sustainable growth of Kyrgyzstan's economy", Bishkek, *24.kg*, September 15, 2011.
19. The Kyrgyz Minister of Transport and Communications Erkin Isakov had proposed to use the principle of resources in exchange for investments in view of Kyrgyzstan's big public external debt during discussion of construction of China-Kyrgyzstan-Uzbekistan railway at the meeting of *Ata Meken* faction on January 11, 2011. Aizada Kutueva, "Erkin Isakov: Kyrgyzstan suggests China to develop several deposits", Bishkek – *24.kg news agency*, January 11, 2011.
20. "Protest held in Kyrgyz capital over China-bound railway project", *24.kg*, Bishkek, May 24, 2011.
21. "President Atambaev says Kyrgyzstan should take advantage of its neighbourhood with China", Bishkek, *AKIpress*, 3 May 2012.

22. "Sinohydro Corporation (China) plans to build a hydropower facility in Kyrgyzstan", Bishkek, 24.kg *news agency*, September 14, 2011. "China's TBEA ready to build Datka-Kemin power transmission line for $400 mln", *AKIpress14* September 2011. "Kyrgyz PM urges China to build HPP in Kyrgyzstan", *The Times of Central Asia*, September 15, 2011.
23. "Export-Import Bank of China approves disbursement of $208 million for construction of Datka-South overhead power transmission line in Kyrgyzstan", Bishkek, *AKIpress* May 12, 2011.
24. "Kyrgyz president upbeat on major projects with China", *Russian news agency Interfax*, June 6, 2012.
25. "President Atambaev and Chairman Hu Jintao adopt joint declaration", Bishkek, *AKIpress,* June 6, 2012.
26. "Prime Minister Almazbek Atambaev admitted he was ashamed of excesses that happened with Chinese companies working at deposits Ishtamberdy and Solton-Sary in Kyrgyzstan", *AKIpress,* September 15, 2011.
27. Ibid.
28. Ibid.
29. Anastasia Bengard, "Relations between Kyrgyzstan and China must be treasured – Chen Zhili", http://eng.24.kg/politic/2012/01/11/22344.htmBishkek,*24.kg news agency*, January 11, 2012.
30. President Atambaev offers broader participation of Chinese capital in economic projects in Kyrgyzstan, *AKIpress,* January 10, 2012.
31. URL: http://eng.24.kg/bishkek24/2011/04/27/17831.html.
32. "Parliamentary committee approves construction of Chinese language school in Bishkek", Bishkek, *AKIpress*, January 24, 2012.
33. "New school to be constructed from China's grant in Bishkek", Bishkek, *AKIpress*, March 1, 2012.
34. "Construction of Kyrgyz-Chinese university, kindergartens and schools with Chinese language of instruction discussed in Bishkek", Bishkek, *AKIpress*, August 27, 2012.
35. Aizada Kutueva, "Kyrgyz MP asks the Ministry of Education to know why the Chinese language lessons introduced at school", *24.kg news agency*, April 6, 2012.
36. A large number of students from India were doing their medicine course in Bishkek, Osh and Kant cities.
37. "China to build a hospital in the southern capital of Kyrgyzstan", Bishkek, *24.kg*, September 12, 2011.
38. "China sets eyes on new media, Internet technology to end Western media dominance", http://www.andhranews.net/Intl/2011/China-sets-eyes-new-media-Internet-14799.htm#ixzz1XQn8Q0dc September 2, 2011.
39. "China expresses interest in strengthening cooperation with Kyrgyzstan in the sphere of media and press", Bishkek, *AKIpress,* May 11, 2012.
40. "Kyrgyzstan, China vow to strengthen law enforcement and security ties", *AKIpress* April 27, 2011.
41. Xiong Zhengyan, "Chinese, Kyrgyz ministers pledge cooperation on security", *Xinhua,* September 6, 2011.
42. "China to provide equipment worth around 49 million som to Kyrgyz State National Security Committee", Bishkek, *AKIpress*, September 12, 2011.
43. "Chinese officials discuss cooperation, regional security", *AKIpress,* April 17, 2012.
44. "Kyrgyzstan Interior Minister, representative of National People's Congress of China discuss cooperation in fight against organized crime" Bishkek, *AKIpress,* April 17, 2012.
45. "China, Kyrgyzstan pledge to strengthen military ties", *Xinhua*, April 23, 2012.
46. "China to build two 9-storey houses for officers of Kyrgyz Defence Ministry", *AKIpress,*

April 4, 2012.

47. "Kyrgyzstan to ensure cargo transit of Shanghai bloc for drills in Tajikistan", *Interfax,* 4 June 4, 2012.
48. "Viewing cable 09BISHKEK135, CHINESE AMBASSADOR FLUSTERED BY KYRGYZ ALLEGATIONS", http://wikileaks.org/cable/2009/02/09BISHKEK135.html (Accessed May 23, 2013).
49. Marat Sartpaev, "Kyrgyz-Chinese spy cooperation will harm, not help", http://www.neweurasia.net/homebase/kyrgyz-chinese-spy-cooperation-will-harm-not-help/ September 14, 2011.
50. Deirdre Tynan, "Are Chinese Telecoms Acting as Ears for C.A. Authoritarians?", *Eurasianet.org,* February 16, 2012.
51. "Kyrgyzstan: China's Economic Influence Fostering Resentment", *EurasiaNet,* April 28, 2011.
52. Paul Goble, "Kyrgyzstan: Influx of Ethnic Chinese Causing Concern – Analysis", http://www.eurasiareview.com/27032011-kyrgyzstan-influx-of-ethnic-chinese-causing-concern-analysis/ (Accessed March 27, 2011) Also see (www.gezitter.org/society/1901/).
53. K. Kumkova, "Kyrgyzstan: China Expanding Influence, One Student at a Time", *EurasiaNet,* January 4, 2012.
54. Paul Goble, "Kyrgyzstan: Influx of Ethnic Chinese Causing Concern – Analysis", http://www.eurasiareview.com/27032011-kyrgyzstan-influx-of-ethnic-chinese-causing-concern-analysis/ (Accessed March 27, 2011).
55. Chris Rickleton. "Kyrgyzstan: Chinese Refinery Riles Environmentalists, Raises Transparency Concerns", *EurasiaNet,* March 31, 2011.
56. "Protest held in Kyrgyz east demanding ban on Chinese haulers", *24.kg,* Bishkek, August 18, 2011.
57. Temirbek Shabdanaliev, "Chinese, Tajik cargo carriers occupied transport market of Kyrgyzstan - head of Association of Cargo Carriers", Bishkek, *AKIpress,* August 12, 2011.
58. "Acting PM Babanov: China's Full Gold Mining should pay compensations to workers", *AKIpress,* October 3, 2011.
59. "Chinese miner launches gold plant in Kyrgyzstan", *Reuters*, September 21, 2011.
60. "Kyrgyz Villagers End Protest against Chinese Gold Mining", *RFE/RL* August 16, 2011 (The local council of Chon-Alay sought international experts to review the Chinese gold mining companies).
61. "Kyrgyz Officials Probe Attack At Chinese-Operated Gold Mine", *RFE/RL* August 30, 2011.
62. "Kyrgyz "TazaTabigat" urges to shut down Chinese foundries", *AKIpress,* May 30, 2012.
63. A widely used term to describe the Kyrgyz protests over foreign investors, especially in mining sector.
64. "Operation of China's Kay Enterprise suspended in Kyrgyzstan until removal of environmental violations", Bishkek, *AKIpress,* October 26, 2011.
65. *AKIpress,* October 26, 2012.
66. "Director of State Agency on Geology proposes to establish code of behavior for Chinese businessmen on fields in Kyrgyzstan", *AKIpress,* March 20, 2012.
67. Irina Dudka, "Chinese investors in Kyrgyzstan not to obtain licenses for mining through intermediaries with dubious reputation", *24.kg,* March 22, 2012.
68. Makhinur Niyazova, "Kyrgyz secret services stop the work of three Chinese companies", *24.kg,* August 13, 2012.
69. "Chinese Envoy: Situation in mining sector in Kyrgyzstan is complex, needs streamlining, *AKIpress,* May 18, 2012.
70. "Chinese investment", *24.kg,* September 10, 2012.
71. "China, Kyrgyzstan vow to boost relations", *Xinhua,* July 31, 2012.
72. "Kyrgyzstan, China agree to build 3 plants", Bishkek, *AKIpress,* September 11, 2012.

73. "Agreement on construction of oil processing plant in Kara-Balta", *AKIpress*, June 6, 2012.
74. "Kyrgyzstan-China working group to attract investments for 40 national projects", *AKIpress*, May 18, 2012.
75. Ibid.
76. Interestingly, The Region Initiative (TRI), a body comprised of a network of responsible tourism organisations from south and central Asia and Eastern Europe, including Pakistan, Nepal, Armenia, Turkey, Kazakhstan and Kyrgyzstan had appealed to China not to use name 'New Silk Road' for its new cross border road project. The TRI argued that 213 kilometre expressway between Kashgar and Erkeshtam, should not be call 'New Silk Road' because such a name may undermine the historic original Silk Road.
77. Hu Yue, "Building a New Silk Road The first China-Eurasia Expo attempts to boost economic ties between west China, Asia and Europe", *Beijing Review*, September 15, 2011.
78. *AKIpress,* September 27, 2011.
79. "Visiting Kyrgyz president upbeat on cooperation with China", *Kyrgyz Television-1,* September 3, 2012, Also read, "President Atambaev: We witness revival of Great Silk Road", *AKIpress*, September 3, 2012.
80. "Kyrgyzstan, China reach agreement on cooperation in security sphere", Bishkek, *AKIpress*, September 3, 2012.
81. "President Atambaev asks TBEA to complete construction of Datka-Kemin, *AKIpress,* September 3, 2012.
82. "Kyrgyz premier pledges "active" measures to protect China is interested in building gas pipeline through territory of Kyrgyzstan –Temir Sariev", *AKIpress*, September 9, 2012.
83. "Kyrgyz president says relations with China priority*", Kyrgyz Television 1, Bishkek,* September 11, 2012.
84. "Chinese envoy concerned over Kyrgyz plans to join Russia-led Customs Union", Kyrgyz Telegraph Agency, *KyrTAg,* January 12, 2012.
85. "Kyrgyzstan's entry to the Customs Union will not affect on economic and trade relations with China - Ambassador Wang Kaiwen", *Kabar*, January 3, 2012.
86. "Kyrgyzstan and China need to open joint enterprises at the territory of Kyrgyzstan – Ambassador Kaiwan on Customs Union accession", *AKIpress*, June 12, 2012.

CHAPTER 12

The Indo-Kyrgyz Relations

Historical Relations

Historically, India has had close contacts with regions of Central Asia. Interactions between India and Kyrgyz people had begun since the time of the Sakas or the Scythians. The Sakas had originally inhabited around Issyk-Kul Lake in Kyrgyzstan and later expanded southward to establish the Indo-Scythian kingdom in the second century BC. Intense contact took place through Indian traders who visited Fergana Valley to trade along the Silk Route.

Kyrgyzstan in return received a stream of philosophical ideas especially the influence of Buddhism from India to Central Asia and beyond. The Silk Route that passed through Kyrgyzstan had notably served as cultural and commercial contact points between India and China. The archaeological finds of Buddhist complexes in the Chu Valley and the Semirech'e region are indication of the historical links that existed between India and Kyrgyzstan. The ancient towns of Suyab and Navaket that had formed important trading points on the Silk Route has strong historical linkages with ancients institutions of learning in India. The Buddhist sites located around Tokmak (Ak-Beshim and Krasnaya Rechka), and in the vicinity of Bishkek (Novopakrovka and Novopavlovka) were linked to Buddhist centres in Kashmir.

History is full of friendly interactions among Indians, Chinese and Central Asians through movement of people, goods and ideas, including spiritual interface that were not without advantage to our common heritage. Mahmud-al-Kashgari, a widely traveled native of the Lake Issyk region, appended to his work an original circular map of the world datable to the 10-11 centuries, incorporating Bilad-i-Hind (Hindustan) and Bilad-i-Sind (present day Pakistan).

It was from Fergana Valley that Babur came to India and founded the Mughul Empire which shaped the destiny of the Indian sub-continent for centuries. The Mughuls introduced in India multifaceted Central Asian culture and artifacts including, art, architecture, music, songs, theatrical traditions, epics, poetry and even cuisines. Babur died in India (1530) but in his autobiographical works the

Baburnama, he nostalgically wrote about his former life and home in Osh. Babur's retreat house *Chilla* is still standing on the Suleyman Mountain in the centre of Osh.

Another Indian link to Osh was Khwaja Syed Muhammad Qutbuddin Bakhtiar Kaki (1173-1235) who was born in Osh in 1173 and became a highly respected Sufi saint of the Chishti order founded by Moinuddin Chishti. Qutbuddin Bakhtiar Kaki was instrumental in establishing Chishti order in Delhi. Qutbuddin Bakhtiar Kaki was highly regarded by many rulers of Delhi like Qutbuddin Aibak, Iltutmish who named the Qutub Minar and the stepped well (baoli) after the saint. Sher Shah Suri built a grand gateway; Bahadur Shah built the Moti Masjid nearby and Farrukhsiyar added a marble screen and a mosque. Mahatma Gandhi visited Kaki's Dargah during the Annual Urs, 1948. Kaki's variant of Sufism is known for universal brotherhood and charity that continue to attract large number of followers from South Asia. His dargah in Mehrauli is the venue of his annual Urs.

The great Kyrgyz epic *Manas* has inspired and thrilled many Indians, which also has a reference to India and historians have drawn parallels between *Manas* and Mahabarata. In a mark of respect, India has named a road after *Manas*. As a mark of respect and recognition of Kyrgyz identity, India had awarded the great Kyrgyz writer Chingiz Aitmatov with Jawaharlal Nehru Award.

Much before Kyrgyzstan gained independence, during the Soviet period, India had a limited but warm relationship with Kyrgyz people. With the visit of Rajiv Gandhi along with Sonia Gandhi to Bishkek and Issyk Kul Lake in 1985 and the Festival of India in USSR (1987-88) these contacts became closer and cultural and people-to-people interaction increased. They had planted a tree in Bishkek's main square.

Contemporary Relations

After the independence of Kyrgyz Republic on August 31, 1991, India was among the first to establish diplomatic relations in 1992. The Kyrgyz Republic opened its resident mission in New Delhi in 1993 and India opened its Embassy in Bishkek in 1994. Two countries have maintained close bilateral ties during the last two decades. Political ties with the Kyrgyz Republic have been traditionally warm and friendly. The former Prime Minister of India Narasimha Rao visited Kyrgyzstan in September 1995. He had addressed Joint Session of both the Houses of Kyrgyz Parliament. During his meeting with President Akayev the latter conveyed verbal support to India's case for permanent membership of UNSC. An important street in Bishkek was renamed after Mahatma Gandhi during the visit. Late K.R. Narayanan and the late Krishna Kant, former Vice-Presidents, visited Kyrgyzstan in September 1996 and August 1999 respectively. In 2003, two Indian Cabinet Ministers, External Affairs Minister, Yashwant Sinha and Raksha Mantri George Fernandes, visited Bishkek in January and November respectively. Murli S. Deora,

Minister of Petroleum and Natural Gas led a delegation to Kyrgyzstan during SCO Summit on August 15-16, 2007. Raksha Mantri A.K. Antony visited Kyrgyzstan on July 4-6, 2011 to inaugurate Kyrgyz-India Mountain Bio-Medical Research Centre. E Ahamad, Minister of State for External Affairs visited Bishkek to inaugurate the First India-Central Asia Dialogue in July 2012.

From Kyrgyzstan's side President Askar Akayev visited India four times (March 1992), (April 1999), (August 2002), and (November 2003). Akayev during his first visit reiterated Kyrgyzstan's commitment to secularism and opposition to Islamic fundamentalism and desire to collaborate closely with India in the foreign policy sphere. The Joint Declaration issued at the time of the visit, inter alia, included a mutual commitment to grant each other the Most Favoured Nation (MFN) treatment. He also expressed keenness to learn from Indian experience in drawing up Constitution, economic liberalisation, experience of India's green revolution, development of small scale industry and private entrepreneurship. During his second visit to India, Akayev conveyed Kyrgyz opposition to cross-border terrorism and welcomed the Lahore Declaration as well as initiatives taken by India for promoting peace and stability and cooperation in the region. In August 2002, President Akayev paid a brief stop over visit to India. A joint statement issued at the end of the visit, inter alia, included Kyrgyz support for India's candidature for a permanent seat in the expanded UNSC. This is significant as this was the first occasion when Kyrgyzstan publicly announced its support to India's candidature in UNSC. During his visit to India in November 2003, he had participated in the UNESCO Conference "Education for All". He met with President as well as with Prime Minister Vajpayee. India proposed to set up an IT Centre in Bishkek and also announced $2 million grant to set up two hydro projects in Kyrgyzstan.

Other important visits from Kyrgyzstan included a visit by Lt. General I. Isakov, Kyrgyz Defence Minister, (November 2005), Turatobek Djunushaliev, Minister of Emergency Situation (November 2007), Kyrgyz Foreign Minister Ednan Karabaev Oskonovich (2008), Kapar Kurmanaliev, Minister of Natural Resources (March 2010), Kyrgyz Defence Minister Kudaiberdiev Abibilla Alymovich (September 2011), Nurlan Aitmurzaev, the Kyrgyz Deputy Minister of Foreign Affairs (August 2011).

A Parliamentary delegation led by Usup Mukambaev, the then Chairman of the Legislative Assembly of the Kyrgyz Parliament visited India in August 1997. A four-member group of the Kyrgyz Parliamentarians visited India in February 1999 to study the Indian experiences in infrastructure and agricultural sectors. Two Kyrgyz MPs visited India in April 2002 as part of invitation to young MPs from Central Asian countries.

Both countries share common concerns on threats posed by terrorism, extremism and drug–trafficking. The Kyrgyz leaderships have been largely supportive of India's stand on Kashmir and have welcomed the ongoing peace process. Kyrgyzstan has been against the internationalisation of the Kashmir issue. In the past, when the resolution on Kashmir was being discussed in the OIC, Kyrgyzstan had, on many occasions, expressed its reservations on the resolutions. Of late, there appeared to have been an increasing pressure on Kyrgyzstan to coordinate position on international issues, including Kashmir.

President Akayev had been supportive of India's bid for a permanent seat in an expanded UNSC. However, while claiming that there has been no dilution of support for India's bid for a permanent UNSC seat, the government, headed by Bakiyev, Roza Otunbayeva and now by Atambayev appeared to shy away from an endorsement of the G-4 position, citing the need for ensuring that the Kyrgyz stance is in line with the position of the countries in the region, as well as the importance of consensus (which, it is claimed, is particularly significant for safeguarding interests of small developing countries like Kyrgyzstan.) The Kyrgyz non-committal on G-4 position is now guided by the Chinese and Russian policy. Kyrgyzstan had contested (with Pakistan in the Asian category) for non-permanent seat in the UNSC 2012-13 for which India had internally pledged support. However, it lost in the final voting by two votes.

Kyrgyzstan is supportive of India's role in the SCO, and had earlier indicated that it would support any Indian bid in this connection. (Kyrgyzstan has also been supportive of Pakistan's bid to join SCO). Due to growing Chinese influence, one could see a nuanced change in Kyrgyz policy towards India.

While the Kyrgyz authorities have taken note of India's sensitivities with regard to the implementation of the Quadrilateral Traffic in Transit Agreement (QTTA) which is a key transit corridor to pass through Pakistan Occupied Kashmir (PoK). However, it had gone ahead and signed it in March, 1995 citing only as economic consideration and for keenness to having access to a sea port. Although, the transit corridor has been ineffective, Pakistan has been trying hard to revive the QTTA project since 2011. To remove obstacles, the Kyrgyz side agreed to revive the pact and Pakistan will host a meeting of experts from the four member countries.

Institutional Relations

Since the establishment of diplomatic relations in 1992, the two countries have signed several framework agreements, including on Culture, Trade and Economic Cooperation, Civil Aviation, Investment Promotion and Protection, Avoidance of Double Taxation, Consular Convention etc. At institutional level, Foreign Office Consultations (the Fourth Session was held in Delhi in August 2006) have provided a useful forum for exchange of views on bilateral and international issues, thereby facilitating greater understanding. Nurlan Aitmurzaev, the Kyrgyz Deputy Minister of Foreign Affairs led a delegation to attend the sixth Foreign Office Consultation meeting held at New Delhi on August 4, 2011. The Indian side was headed by Secretary (East). An Indo-Kyrgyz Joint Commission on Trade,

Economic, Scientific and Technological Cooperation set up in 1992, is the inter-governmental framework for promoting trade and economic cooperation; five sessions of The Joint Commission have been held so far (the last being in Delhi in March, 2010), facilitating cooperation in areas as diverse as tourism, civil aviation, technical assistance, etc. The progresses in these entire sectors have been rather very tardy.

Trade

India's trade with Kyrgyzstan is very low and remained stagnant over the years. However, trade had increased 19 per cent to 37 million in 2012-13. India's exports to Kyrgyzstan totaled around $35 million (up by 15 per cent) whereas Kyrgyz exports to India amounted to only $2.13 million in 2012-13. Apparel and clothing (both knitted and crocheted as well as not-knitted and crocheted), leather goods, drugs & pharmaceuticals, fine chemicals, and tea are some of the important items in India's export basket to Kyrgyzstan. Kyrgyz exports to India consist of raw hides, metalifers ores & metal scrap etc. Trade with India faces stiff competition from China, Turkey and CIS countries. Lack of connectivity and lengthy and unreliable surface trade routes become major hurdles for the export of goods from India. In 2004, Kyrgyzstan became a party to the Trilateral Transit Agreement between India, Iran and Turkmenistan (signed in February, 1997).

Investments

Indian investments to Kyrgyzstan have not been forthcoming for various reasons. Firstly, the country lacks the investment climate. Secondly, the banking system and financial institutions are not developed for attracting FDI and repatriation of profits. Thirdly, the present visa regime of Kyrgyzstan also puts up numerous obstacles for travelling Indian businessmen. Fourthly, frequent changes in the government formation are yet another problem for the investors. Fifthly, Kyrgyzstan has opened up too much to China; as a result others are not able to compete.

Notwithstanding, at least one Indian corporate, the Rateria Group of Companies of Kolkata, had invested in mining and manufacture in Kyrgyzstan but without any success. A few Indian companies have just entered the manufacturing sectors, but their success is yet to be seen.

Line of Credit

In 1995, India had extended a $5 million line of credit to Kyrgyzstan for purchase of equipment and machinery from India for projects to be set up in this country. A plant for manufacture of toothbrushes, a plant for manufacture of polythene bags, a toothpaste production plant and a pharmaceutical plant were set up in Kyrgyzstan. The Kyrgyz side had repaid $1.66 million and the remaining amount was written off in 2007.

Assistance Programmes

The Government of India had provided Grant Assistance to Kyrgyzstan for the following projects:

1997-2000: Mini Dairy Plant	Rs. 20,000,000
2002: Potato Processing Plant	Rs. 10,80,44,00
2007: Indo-Kyrgyz Centre for Information Technology (IKCIT)	Rs. 44.70 million
2010: Assistance for Parliamentary Elections	Rs. 794,218
2011: Supply of Medical Equipment	Rs.9.61 crore
2012: Setting up a multi-media language laboratory	$31703.00
2012: Printing of school text books	$62424.00

Disaster Relief and Humanitarian Aid

(i) Medical Assistance: Rs. 22.13 lakhs (2005)
(ii) Earthquake Relief: $100,000 (2008)
(iii) Humanitarian Relief: $1 million (2010)

Potato Processing Plant

In 200, during the visit of President Akayev to New Delgi, Indian Prime Minister announced the gifting of a food processing plant to the Kyrgyz Republic. The Kyrgyz authorities requested for setting up of a potato processing plant in Talas oblast (province).[1] The Governor of Talas offered to provide a suitable building to house the proposed plant. Feasibility study was undertaken by M/s Suman Foods Consultants and M/s Chemprojects Consulting Private Limited in 2003. The project is planned to produce 100 kg of conventional potato chips per hour and another 95.2 kg of dehydrated potato flakes. An agreement to this effect was signed by both the countries in May 2009. M/s. PEC Limited has been appointed as nodal agency for implementing the project from the Indian side while M/s. Agro-food Corporation is the implementing agency from the Kyrgyz side.[2] Project was undertaken under India's Aid to Central Asia at a total cost of Rs. 10, 80, 44,000. Finally, the potato processing plant was inaugurated on June 11, 2012 by the Minister of State for External Affairs, E Ahamad. The plant took a long time to complete. But it is still not functional due to technical problems.

There have been many problems in implementing Indian assistance programmes in Central Asia. They include operational deficiencies, supply of outdated machinery, inordinate delays, rampant corruption in the local governance among others make the implementation of schemes less efficient. The recent experience in Kyrgyzstan is no better. Save the dairy plant and a computer centre, all other projects assisted by India have long been shut down. The potato plant (inaugurated in July 20120) ran into rough weather, with lack of desired quality of potato and the local agency demanding technical modifications and training support, which cannot be met without additional grants. It has also been noticed that the grants offered by India have not yielded commercial opportunities for Indian companies. Such a picture, however, does not deter the traditional partners. As such, Kyrgyzstan has been receiving huge funds, grants, aid in the fields of infrastructure mineral exploration etc from aid-wings. In view of the past experience, India should focus on more specialised sectors like hydro-power, infrastructure, hospitals, IT sector and agro-food for which a huge potential exists in Kyrgyzstan. An effective proposal should include creation of a region specific investment fund, for example India-CA Investment Fund for financing projects on PPP on commercial terms; a revenue model is to be envisaged, with proper accountability, cost-benefit analysis, and risk management provided by technical and financial experts.

Technical Cooperation

Technical assistance under the Indian Technical and Economic Cooperation (ITEC) Programme, particularly in terms of Human Resources Development (HRD), is the cornerstone of India's economic involvement in Kyrgyzstan. Since 1994, about one thousand professionals from Kyrgyzstan have been trained in India under the ITEC programme. The training programmes have contributed to capacity building and HRD in Kyrgyzstan. The training programme is demand-driven and subjects selected are a wide and diverse range of skills and disciplines in IT and Telecommunication, Management, SME/Rural Development, Specialised Courses, Technical Courses, Environment and Renewable Energy Courses. In accordance with the growing demand for ITEC programme, the number of ITEC slot for Kyrgyzstan has been increased from 60 to 95 in 2012-13. An additional 16 slots have allotted to Kyrgyzstan for military education in India.

Civil Aviation

As per the MoU signed between India and Kyrgyzstan in April 1999 (within the framework of Air Services Agreement signed in September 1993) the designated airlines of the two countries were entitled to operate two flights per week on Bishkek-Delhi-Bishkek sector using aircrafts of seating capacity not exceeding 160 seats. In 2003, permission was to Kyrgyzstan Airlines, to operate bigger aircrafts with greater seating capacity. However, the Kyrgyz Airlines has not been operating any flight on Delhi-Bishkek sector. The Turkish Airlines and Air Company Kyrgyzstan has made a joint proposal to start aviation service between Istanbul-Bishkek-Delhi in February 2012.

Education and Culture

In October 1992, an agreement for Cultural Exchange Programme, (CEP) valid for 1992-94 was signed by the two countries. This included cooperation in the areas of Culture, Arts, Education, Science, Mass-media and Sports. The CEP was subsequently extended up to the year 2000. However, CEP is yet to be renewed for future cooperation in the field of culture, though India has been conducting cultural programmes on a non-reciprocal basis under the auspices of ICCR.

India offers six scholarships under General Cultural Scholarship Scheme of ICCR to Kyrgyzstan annually. The Centre for Indian Studies was set up in Osh State University in 1997. This has been useful in providing an exposure to Indian culture and civilisation to academicians and intelligentsia in Kyrgyzstan. In the past, the setting up of a Centre for Gandhian Studies at the Bishkek Humanities University in 1996 and an India Centre at the Kyrgyz State National University at Bishkek in 2004 have also facilitated greater exposure to India in institutes of higher education in Kyrgyzstan. MOUs have been signed between the Kyrgyz State National University and Bangalore University and between the International University of Kyrgyzstan and Punjab University for facilitating student exchange programme etc. In September, 2004, an agreement was signed between the Indira Gandhi National Open University (IGNOU) and the International University of Kyrgyzstan in the field of distance education. However, these centres and exchange programmes are not in operation at present.

Defence Cooperation

Defence Cooperation forms an important component of bilateral relations. India has been extending assistance to the Kyrgyz armed forces through a MoU on Military-Technical Cooperation signed in 1997. There has been significant progress in defence cooperation between India and Kyrgyzstan over the years. Among landmarks in defence cooperation were the visits of Raksha Mantri to Kyrgyzstan in November, 2003 and 2011 as well the visit of the Kyrgyz Defence Ministers to India in November 2005 and September 2011.

The visit by Defence Minister A.K. Antony to Kyrgyzstan in July 2011 was of a great significance. Apart from inaugurating the Kyrgyz-India Mountain Bio-Medical Research Centre (KIMBMRC), he held extensive talks with his Kyrgyz counterpart Abibilla Kudayberdiev on regional security issues, particularly terrorism emanating from the South Asian region. The two discussed the potentials of further cooperation in defence, especially relating to training of Kyrgyz armed forces in India. He also met President Roza Otunbayeva and Health Minister Sabyrbek Jumabekov.[3] Antony's was accompanied by a high level defence delegation that included DRDO chief V.K. Saraswat, Special Secretary R.K. Mathur, Defence Finance Secretary Vijay Lakshmi Gupta and DRDO chief controller of R&D Dr. William Selvamurthy. The Defence Minister also decided to present to Kyrgyzstan's Health Ministry equipment such as critical-care ventilators, coronary stents, dental implants, special ambulances, bio-digestors and mobile catheter laboratory, all valued at Rs.9.7 crore.[4]

The training of Kyrgyz officers in India has been the main component of defence cooperation. Kyrgyz defence personnel at present undergo training in Indian defence establishments such as DSSI and IMA.[5] In 2009, seven officers from Kyrgyzstan were trained in India under the ITEC program. The training courses included English language training, training in IT, Mountain Warfare and Counter Insurgency Operations. The Kyrgyz Ministry of Defence could not avail the courses in the year 2010 due to unstable political and security situation in the country after ethnic riots. By 2012, eight officers from Kyrgyzstan have been trained on UN Peace Keeping Operation Courses conducted by the Centre for UN Peace Keeping at New Delhi. The Kyrgyz side has been keen on having an agreement to provide training on a structured basis.

A 20 member special task force of the Defense Ministry of Kyrgyzstan took part in a joint commando exercise codenamed Kanjar-2011 [Dagger] at Nahan, HP during the period December 1-20, 2011.[6] From the Indian side, servicemen of the ninth battalion's commando parachute regiment participated in the exercise. The military exercise Kanjar-2011 was majorly highlighted by the Kyrgyz media.

A four member Indian Army Training Team (IATT) provided nine months' training to Kyrgyz military personnel at Osh and Batken in UN Peace Keeping Operations and English language during August, 2011 and April, 2012.[7] The training was given to servicemen of Kyrgyzstan's south-west regional command and military unit No 30630. Military unit No 30630 was designated as a peacekeeping subdivision for participation in international operations to maintain peace. However, in the absence of a national law to send Kyrgyz troops on foreign missions, such trainings by Indian team remained futile. For any future cooperation, Kyrgyzstan has to enact a law to this effect.

The visit by Defence Minister in 2011 to Kyrgyzstan had paved the way for a higher interaction between the two countries in the defence sphere.[8] Kyrgyz Defence Minister Major Gen. Abidilla Kudaberdiev paid a return visit to India in September 2011. Defence Minister A.K. Antony once again assured his counterpart, Major Gen. Abidilla Kudaberdiev that India will extend full support to Kyrgyz defence apparatus.[9] The two sides discussed the enhancement of military engagement, including training, exchanges between the armed forces of both countries, enhancing military technical cooperation and R&D in non-defence sectors such as physiology, medicine, animal husbandry and nutrition. The Kyrgyz Defence Minister, during his visit to India, also visited the Khadakvasla-based National Defence Academy and other defence institutions in Pune.

The Kyrgyz-India Mountain Bio-Medical Research Centre (KIMBMRC)

The defence cooperation has been a major booster in India's relationship with Kyrgyzstan; as such it also meets India's strategic requirements. On the request of Kyrgyz Government, India had approved a joint collaboration project to be undertaken by Defence Institute of Physiology and Allied Sciences (DIPAS) under the DRDO and Kyrgyz National Centre for Cardiology and Therapy (NCCT). The KIMBMRC was opened in Bishkek in June 2011. The Centre was inaugurated on July 5, 2011 by Rakhsa Mantri A. K. Antony along with President Roza Otunbayeva.[10] The DRDO had contributed Rs.six crore for the project. The Research Centre is in Bishkek but it also has a field station at Tuya Ashu, located at a height of 3,200 metres. India has deputed a team of physiologists, biochemists and molecular biologists, headed by India's Defence Institute of Physiology and Allied Sciences (DIPAS director Shashi Bala Singh. They were assisted by 20 Indian Army soldiers. The KIMBMRC aims to study the short-and long-term high altitude acclimatisation procedures; find strategies for rapid and efficient acclimatisation with special reference to molecular mechanism of human performance promotion and amelioration of maladies in mountain operations. It will identify markers for screening of people for high altitude resistance and susceptibility to high altitude sickness and development of mountain maladies. It aims to conduct experiments in improving the physical endurance; do research on the effects of using the nitric-oxide delivery system, aloe vera cream, bio-digestors, and heating gloves and socks for protection against cold injuries; and to improve the treatment of bronchial asthma, vascular diseases, anemia and hypertension caused by exposure to moderate altitudes. The project has high significance for India and especially for Kyrgyzstan whose territory is largely mountainous and over 10 per cent of the country's GDP is generated in high-altitude regions.

The benefits of these studies would help in improving the life and health of people living in high altitude areas across the globe. The Chief Controller (Life Sciences and International Cooperation) in the DRDO Dr W. Selvamurthy was quoted in the media saying "We have deployed soldiers at an altitude of 22,000 feet in the Siachen glacier. We have populations living in altitude areas in Himachal Pradesh. Our pilgrims undertake '*padayatra*' to Amarnath. Kyrgyzstan has several high altitude areas. So research related to high altitude is important to both India and Kyrgyzstan."[11] He further said "in high altitude, hypoxia and cold are the major threats. We face solar radiation there. Soldiers posted there face psychological stress in the form of isolation, separation from family, fear of the unknown, sensory deprivation and so on. So the DRDO's mandate is how to keep soldiers fighting-fit in the high altitude areas."[12] The Centre is also meant for mobilising and synchronising the expertise of the two countries in the area of high altitude research.

Ties with Kyrgyz Defence Industry

India has strong business ties with Kyrgyzstan's only functional defence production unit the Joint Stock Company JSC Dastan located in Bishkek. The Indian Navy has been procuring spares for its Russian made electric torpedoes as well as procures torpedoes from Dastan. On a functional basis, apart from Indian Navy, the DRDO's scientists from Naval Scientific and Technological Laboratory (NSTL) have maintained regular touch with Dastan and ULAN companies in Kyrgyzstan since 1997.

The Dastan is a 40-years old Soviet time enterprise that produces naval weapons, rocket systems, aerial and armoured systems, radio engineering monitoring and reconnaissance. The Dastan produces well-known weapon systems such as USET-80, modernised oxygen torpedo 53-65KE as well as recently developed mobile ground mine "MURENA" and multifunctional homing electric torpedo SET-92HK. It also produces most innovative ongoing maritime weapon systems, the super-cavitating 220 mph Skhval-type rocket torpedo, which has a six-mile range and can be made both in nuclear (up to 150 kiloton yield) and conventional (210 kg of chemical explosives) variants. The Shkval anti-ship complex with the M-5 missile was created by Research Institute No. 24. The length of the missile is 8,200 mm; caliber - 533.4 mm. The missile can be launched from ordinary torpedo tubes. The jet torpedo weighs 2,700 kilograms. The maximum cruising range is 11 kilometres. The maximum underwater speed is 90 to 100 metres per second.

All Shkval torpedoes were dismantled from Soviet submarines in accordance with the agreement between the USSR and the US in 1989. It is said that the Western navies currently have no countermeasure against the weapon. Only in 2005 Germany managed to create a Skhval-like torpedo. A new modification was created on the basis of the Shkval torpedo in the late 1990s. Its export version was called Shkval-E. The weapons system was first offered for sale at the IDEX-99 arms exhibition in the United Arab Emirates.[13] In early 2011, there were reports that components of Skhval were sold to Iran in 2010.[14]

The Dastan Company has a full range of test and repair facilities, which has been used by the Indian Navy as well since mid-1990s. But, for a long time, Russia's Rosoboronexport has been seeking to control the Dastan manufacturing plant. Since 2009, talks have been underway for transferring 48 per cent stake of Dastan to Russia in exchange of writing-off $180 million Kyrgyz debt. The initial agreement was signed during the reign of President Kurmanbek Bakiyev under which 48 per cent was to go to Russia and the remaining shares was owned by President's son Maxim Bakiyev. The deal got mired into controversy over kickbacks and even after Kyrgyzstan received the first tranche on time and in full ($300 million in mid-2009), shares were not transferred then. Following the ouster of Bakiyev, the company was nationalised and 98 per cent shares were taken over by the new Kyrgyz authorities. However, faced with critical economic crisis, the new government in October 2010 renewed its intentions to transfer the shares to Russia after Parliament ratification.

The transfer of Dastan to Russia was expected after the April 2010 change in power, but the Kyrgyz leadership abruptly announced in February 2011, during the visit to Bishkek by Turkish Prime Minister Recep Tayyip Erdogan, that it would sell Dastan torpedo plant to Turkey instead. The Kyrgyz leadership however later ruled out selling it to Turkey—a NATO member. However, for over a year, the issue of Dastan remained mired into major controversy directly linked to Kyrgyz inability to settle debt with Russia. Moscow has been critical of Kyrgyz bargaining on the Dastan. The issue was considerably played up by Russian and Kyrgyz media. In fact, it became a major sore-point leading to worsening of bilateral relations from 2009-12. (The issues involved have been illustrated in detail in the Chapter Kyrgyzstan-Russian relations)

As the negotiations restarted in early 2012, Russia demanded revision of the earlier arrangement and sought 75 per cent stake instead of 48 per cent in the Dastan.[15] This was to be done in exchange for $180 million debt to be written-off by Russia. Russia demanded 75 per cent on the pretext that since 2009, the assets of Dastan depreciated due to wear and tear of the equipment. The Kyrgyz were against such plan.[16] The Kyrgyz insisted that they will abide by the previously reached agreements and if Russia wanted 75 percent it will be on a different terms.[17]

Under a new agreement signed in September 2012, the handing over of 48 percent shares of Torpedo Plant to Russia stands resolved. Kyrgyzstan has reserved the right to offer Dastan shares for sale through the auction to interested investors. Key experts were to study this issue. In fact, there was a clear doubt whether Russia really wanted the Dastan Plant. The Chief of Russian President's Administration Sergei Ivanov, in an interview with the television company MIR on April 8, 2012, expressed doubts about staking 48 per cent shares in the Dastan torpedo plant. He said, "I am not sure if we need this plant at all. It was not upgraded during the last 25-30 years. We need to think if there is sense to invest big resources into the plant. The second issue is the price. As far as I remember, a part of shares of this plant is missing somewhere, let's put it this delicate way. Ownership of 48 per cent of shares won't give anything for Russia. We won't be able to govern it. This is why either the controlling package of shares should be acquired or some other agreement should be achieved. The two sides are holding the dialogue on this issue now."[18]

The plant itself has witnessed numerous scandals on account of mismanagement, financial irregularities, and illegal deliveries of special-purpose devices.[19] The Company lacks funds to maintain the plant at a normal functional capacity.[20] Marketing is another problem as only few CIS countries buy the torpedoes. India remained the sole consumer of the Dastan's product apart from services it provides to Russian naval fleet. According to the Chairman of the Dastan Albek Ibraimov, Russian order was 26 per cent and 70 per cent was from India.[21] The Chairman of the Board of Directors said that the plant could serve for 20-30 years.

According to media reports, Rosoboronexport's interest in the Dastan plant for production was linked with prospective deliveries of the Shkval-E torpedoes to India. Russia also intended to arm the Shuka-B (project 971) submarines with such torpedoes. Of late, there were reports about Dastan selling its assets, including land and building premises, to private entrepreneurs.

Under the old contract, the value of shares to be passed on to the Russians totalled $19.4 million. In 2012, 98 per cent of Dastan was nationalised and was administered by the Ministry of State Property, while the remaining two percent of the securities were in the hands of private individuals and company employees.

ULAN Open Joint-Stock Company

ULAN OJSC or ULAN Torpedo Range (UTR) is located in the world's second largest mountain Lake IssykKul (180km long and 60km wide). It is a unique Soviet built facility set up in 1943 as a Test Range of S. M. Kiro Machine-Building Plant. In the past, it was a leading manufacturer and a test range for naval armament and for specific submarines.[22]

The UTR facility carries out trial of thermal torpedoes of various calibers from 324 mm to 650 mm. It manufactures and supply spare parts for CET-65E, TEST-71ME, and 53-65 KE torpedoes. The plant has the capacity to service CET-65E, TEST-71ME, 53-65KE torpedoes.

It has access to a wide test bed with necessary capability to test and qualify maritime warfare equipments. The bed has an average depth of 410 metres and a maximum depth 702 metres that makes it easy to retrieve, recover torpedoes. The range ensures conditions are similar to sea in a calm environment and offers testing facility for almost all the time of the year. Karakul's remoteness makes it an ideal weapons testing site, though located close to China border but away from Western intelligence eyes.

The UTR is currently maintained and operated by individuals and company employees. A prominent Kyrgyz leader and the former speaker of the Parliament Ahmatbek Keldibekov and the Director, External Relations of M/S ULAN Alexander holds majority 67 per cent of the securities. The other main share holder is the Kazakh Company *Kirov Mash Zavod* factory with 22 per cent and the remaining 11 per cent are in the hands of private investors including two per cent by M/S Dastan.

The UTR's infrastructure include a vessel, assembly and repair shop, oxygen and air compressor stations and accumulator preparation section. But they are in a depleted state and require massive up-gradation. The vintage ship available at the range has no deck launch facility. But there is another torpedo-testing range Ozero, which is presently owned by Russia Navy. There has been rumour about Russians abandoning the Ozero range. But in a new defence agreement Russian has created a unified defence facility that included the Ozero range at Issyk-Kul.

India has been using UTR range since 1997 and on an average 20 trials is being conducted in a year. Besides, the torpedoes procured from Dastan by Indian

Navy, the prototype torpedoes developed by Naval Scientific and Technological Laboratory (NSTL) are also tested at the UTR.[23]

During the visit by Defence Minister to Karakul on July 6, 2011, he was acquainted with the ULAN Torpedo Range (UTR) as well as with the work of the 40-years old Dastan Joint Stock Company that produces torpedoes.[24] After the Russians have dropped the idea of staking claims in Dastan, both ULAN and Dastan Companies would be keen to have an arrangement with India for a possible future collaboration, including their willingness of leasing the facility for a specific period of time. Though, of late delegations from Turkey have been surveying these facilities in Kyrgyzstan. China too has been eyeing these facilities. The OJSC ULAN was quoting a rent of $568,000 per year for test range for a lease to be signed for five years and extendable for another 20 years.

The Dastan has tremendous prospects for joint production. As mentioned before, the Dastan also produces components of super-cavitating 220 mph VA-111 Shkval-type rocket torpedo. In 2012, Russia has finally decided not to take up the Dastan project and Kyrgyzstan has reserved the right to offer Dastan shares for sale through an auction to interested investors. However, the plant is likely to remain mired in internal political controversy and legal complications, and many of the critical issues are unlikely to be resolved any time soon. As mentioned earlier, numerous scandals have also blazed up around Plant's leadership on account of financial irregularities and illegal deliveries of devices.

It should be noteworthy that the International media gave a strategic dimension to A.K Antony's Issy-Kul visit where he inspected the UTR in July 2011. Washington based Joseph Farah's G2 wrote "India is developing nuclear torpedoes at a deep-water lake in land-locked Kyrgyzstan and intends to equip its navy with them because of the threat posed by Chinese warships in the Indian Ocean and South China Sea"[25] While quoting, William Selvamurthy, Chief Controller of DRDO, the Bulletin wrote "India is willing to develop the centre to test all kinds of torpedoes such as heavy weight torpedoes and those having thermal navigation system."[26] Similarly, Russia media also expressed envy about India's interest in the UTR. A news headline said "India to Use Torpedo Plant in Kyrgyzstan, But Where Are the Russians?" The article illustrated the sensitiveness of the Kyrgyz facility that tests torpedoes of highly sensitive prototype designs including the VA-111 Shkval, a super-cavitating torpedo capable of speeds of more than 200 knots, or 230 miles per hour.[27] The VA-111 Shkval is rocket-propelled and is capable of carrying a nuclear warhead. The Bulletin said that the US Navy is not known to have any defence to repel this type of torpedo. China too has no such equivalent torpedoes. It said "in working with Kyrgyzstan, New Delhi is attempting to increase its influence throughout Central Asia through various training programmes and military production efforts which analysts say are indicative of an alarming trend of the militarisation of Central Asia."[28] The Russian media was surprised by the flurry of Indian military activities in Kyrgyzstan and questioned what Russia's role in all these was. "Will India be sharing it with Russia? It's curious that neither Russian nor Kyrgyzstani sources have appeared to say anything publicly about this deal", the media commented.[29]

Another media write up said "India may have been thwarted in its attempt to set up an air base in Tajikistan, but now it's building military ties with Kyrgyzstan, agreeing to train UN peacekeeping troops and establishing a joint high-altitude military research centre in Bishkek."[30] Apart from linking India's interests in Kyrgyzstan with the situation in Afghanistan, the media also assumed that this was an effort by Kyrgyzstan's president, Roza Otunbayeva to lessen Kyrgyz dependency on Russia. Kyrgyzstan was a better fit for India than Tajikistan, which was more susceptible to Russian pressure to not allow India's use of the air base in Dushanbe. The story further cautioned that 'if India is still interested in a base in Central Asia, and decides to focus on Kyrgyzstan rather than Tajikistan, that would certainly get interesting quickly."[31]

In the backdrop of mystery created by Russian media over Indian Defence Minister's visit to Karakol, the ULAN OJSC's Director General Vladimir Stepanov finally did give a clarification to the media after two months. Stepanov, on September 20, 2011, said that the Indian Minister indeed visited the facility and confirmed that India and the Kyrgyz Government were planning to develop a torpedo testing centre in Karakol. He added that the company was expecting a delegation from India's military and industrial complex in October 2011. At the same time Stepanov also told media that the "ULAN had repeatedly come up to Russia with an offer of possible cooperation for many years, but Russians have not shown interest."[32] The ULAN was also not keen to sell its facility to the Russian company Ozero located closed by in Issyk-Kul near Koy-Sara village. The Director General announced that ULAN had maintained a mutually-beneficial cooperation with the Indian MoD since the mid-1990s. Without the Indian support, the company would not have survived, he added. Vladimir Stepanov said. "Carrying out tests on the Indian Navy's orders will give us an opportunity to buy new equipment and modernise our company's logistics base. We are counting on this very much."[33]

The DRDO Chief Controller William Selvamurthy did tell the media that India was planning to develop a facility in Kyrgyzstan to produce state of the art torpedoes in order to strengthen its under water attack capabilities.[34] The DRDO announced that it would develop existing infrastructure at the centre and has proposed to engage local companies with available know how in torpedo technology to co-develop the facility. DRDO said, India is also planning to use the facility to test the Autonomous Underwater Vehicle (AUV) Developed by NSTL. For India, both Dastan and UTR have strategic significance as both can be used as test bed and production facilities.

To step up diplomatic footprints and to project its soft power, the Minister of State for External Affairs E. Ahamed visited Kyrgyzstan on June 12-13, 2012.

Apart from inaugurating the Potato Processing Plant, which has been set up with the assistance by the Government of India as a gift to the people of Kyrgyz Republic, E. Ahamad also inaugurated the First India-Central Asia Dialogue jointly with the former President Roza Otunbayeva in Bishkek. The Dialogue was held under the joint aegis of the Indian Council for World Affairs (ICWA) and the World Diplomatic Academy, Bishkek. The visit by E. Ahamad was also to coincide to mark the 20th anniversary of establishment of the diplomatic relations between the two countries. The Minister had wide-ranging meetings with Kyrgyz Foreign Minister Ruslan Kazakbaev and Prime Minister Omurbek Babanov.[35] During the meetings both sides noted the significant progress in bilateral relations and expressed satisfaction with the regular dialogue between India and Kyrgyzstan in the spirit of equal and mutually beneficial cooperation.[36] They underlined the intentions of Kyrgyzstan and India to strengthen the partnership relations at all levels of interaction for the benefit of the people of both countries. The sides reviewed the existing level of bilateral relations and discussed future prospects of cooperation and also exchanged views on wider range of international and regional issues. Both the Ministers reiterated their readiness to continue regular political consultations between the two Foreign Ministries for the purpose of strengthening and development of bilateral cooperation.[37]

The two-day Dialogue, attended by participants from across the Central Asian region, was followed by a business interaction 'Discover Asia' organised jointly by the International Public Foundation 'Roza Otunbayeva's Initiatives' and Embassy of India in Kyrgyzstan.[38] The meeting was attended by a delegation from India and hundreds of representatives from business, science and civil society, government officials and journalists from Kyrgyzstan. The event served India in reaching out to wider business community wishing to seek partnership with Indian entrepreneurs.[39] In fact, during 2010-12, the Kyrgyz leadership has shown great interest in learning from India's experiences covering social and cultural areas. The visit of former President Roza Otunbayeva to India in February 2012 paved the way for wider interaction between the entrepreneurs and NGOs of the two countries. Roza Otunbayeva has, in fact, become a major catalyst for learning from Indian experiences of nation building process especially in the socio-economic spheres.[40] Roza is fond of India and Indian culture and philosophy. She practices *Vipasana* meditation and visited India earlier. Her interactions with officials of E-Choupal, Self Employed Women's Association (SEWA), Micro-credit institutions, SEWA, handicraft and textile industry, interest for learning from India's silk industry etc in 2012 were reflection of this growing interest. The ex-President also met with Vice President of India Mohammad Hamid Ansari and Indian Minister of State for External Affairs Preneet Kaur and exchanged views on the prospects for furthering cooperation and learning from Indian experiences.[41] Otunbayeva also addressed a special session of the Asian Security Conference at the Institute for Defense Studies and Analysis in New Delhi.

The focus on India was more related to promoting sustainable development in countries like Kyrgyzstan, which does not have many natural resources to export. Learning from Indian traditional craft, silk fabric, wool industry etc were viewed as reliable sources of economic stability and environmental friendly. Indian experience was attractive for three things: create jobs in rural areas, remove poverty, and a means to preserve national traditions. It was found that such an interaction serves to promote India's positive image of handling social, cultural, and governance issues. This is a low cost option with assurance of a high visibility, positive publicity, and provides dividends in terms of goodwill.

At the invitation of *Mekendeshter* (Forum of Fellow Citizens of Kyrgyzstan), Secretary, Ministry of Overseas Indian Affairs, (MOIA) Parvez Dewan was able to pay a visit to Kyrgyzstan in August 2012. This was a great occasion to share and highlight India's diaspora experiences, i.e., the annual and regional *Parvasi Bhartiya Divas* and other diaspora issues with the Kyrgyz. The Kyrgyz diaspora event was attended by the highest political leadership and business elite. The Secretary MOIA's interaction with the attendees was a tremendous success. There was a great enthusiasm amongst the participants to understand the way India has been dealing with the problems and prospects of its diaspora staying abroad. Interests were also shown for learning from Indian experiences of tourism industry, health system and national integration programmes launched by the Government of India. Several Kyrgyz Ministers queued up to interact with Secretary MOIA including the Foreign Minister, Deputy Foreign Minister, Tourism Minister and others.

Future Prospects

Kyrgyzstan perceives India as a large and successful model of democracy and secularism with expanding political and economic influence not only on Asian affairs, but also on the global stage. Kyrgyzstan has also opted for parliamentary form of democracy since last year. From this perspective, it seeks to further deepen the vibrant relationship with democratic India.

India's Central Asia policy is quite remunerative and the recent high level visits have added impetus to relations of India with these countries. Such interaction is essential and is beneficial from the multi-dimensional angles, viz. energy, security, metals, social, multilateral issues etc. During this author's interaction with the wide spectrum of Kyrgyz political and official establishment, and also based on personal assessment, the need to engage in a more meaningful way was widely felt. The author recalled the meeting with President Atambayev in 2012 who had a natural affection and love for India. He praised the role of India as a champion of democracy, for upholding cultural values in a diverse society and expressed great satisfaction at our bilateral relations. Atambayev mentioned about the difficulties of being a poor and landlocked state; compared India with China in economic prosperity and sought larger engagement indicating high value investment.

India's engagement with Kyrgyzstan is presently at a nominal yet at steady rate. It may have, in the short term, several limitations for enhancing economic relations with Kyrgyzstan. However, Kyrgyzstan is gaining enormous strategic significance for regional security and great power interests and in this regard our interests and engagement with Kyrgyzstan should gain merit on the following grounds:

- Strategic Importance: Kyrgyzstan has become a hub for power-play among great powers. The great power interests in Kyrgyzstan are unlikely to diminish soon. The Russians and Americans have their agendas well drawn. In fact, the difficulty in managing great powers interests, especially playing one off against other by the earlier Kyrgyz regime underpinned the turmoil in the country. Both US and Russia are likely to retain their existing military bases, if not acquire more, for a longer-term basis, and hence India needs to watch and understand the politics of air-base in the region. Kyrgyzstan will emerge as an important transit point for NATO's withdrawal from Afghanistan. Deeper security relations to meet any contingency are needed.
- SCO Member: Kyrgyzstan, as a border state to China, should receive India's close attention. The Chinese are mutely expanding their spheres of influence in Kyrgyzstan, especially on the economic and strategic front, and in the longer term, it would be fair to assume that Kyrgyzstan would largely fall under the Chinese economic influence. At the same time Kyrgyzstan is also a trouble-spot for China and therefore Beijing is following a very cautious and vigilant approach.
- As US-Pakistan relations strain, Islamabad is realigning with Russia. This will allow Pakistan gain credibility in Central Asia. Russia benefits by gaining surface access up to Afghanistan. India cannot be left behind in the rebalancing scenario;
- Regional Stability: The southern Kyrgyzstan, especially the Osh region in the Fergana Valley has long been an incubator of political and religious radicalism. It is now a breeding ground for clandestine outfits like the Islamic Movement of Uzbekistan (IMU) and Hizb ut-Tahrir (Party of Liberation). Most of them have nexus and operational linkages with the Taliban, Al-Qaida and other extremist groups in Pakistan. The Osh region is the other face of Kyrgyzstan where India has little presence. India should enlarge its cultural engagement especially in Osh region.
- Southern Kyrgyzstan which is increasingly becoming a hub for Islamic extremism, drug trafficking and terrorism; cooperation in security and intelligence is important to counter negative threats from the region;

- Nascent democracy: shifted to multi-party parliamentary mode in 2010; striving to gain international recognition. The Kyrgyz experiment with parliamentary democracy is likely to survive and may even influence changes in the neighbourhood;
- Erstwhile Soviet State with profound likeness for India: Bollywood, Yoga, IT etc were extremely popular in the past. Now the Western world, China, Korea are occupying that space. India needs to revive the diluted link;
- India's ties with Kyrgyzstan in the defence sector have been sound and beneficial. India should explore the possibility of seeking joint venture projects for weapons manufacturing and testing in Kyrgyz facilities. The need for enhancing defence cooperation with Kyrgyzstan should be imperative for India to deploy a full time presence of a Defence Attache;
- Connectivity: Kyrgyzstan's territory offers north-south and east-west transit routes;
- India should exploit Kyrgyzstan's enormous hydro-electric potential and vast mineral resources;
- With stability returning to Kyrgyzstan, prospects of businesses have grown. India needs to seek opportunities in mining, agriculture, health and education sectors on commercial terms viz. Apollo Hospitals in Tanzania etc. Kyrgyzstan joining the CU will also benefit India;
- Engagement at highest leadership level needs to be revived; the last high level visits were by PM Narasimha Rao in 1995 and President Akayev to India in 2002. A high level visit will cement ties and dispel notions of lesser import. In the absence of it, India may go off their radar! As it is, Kyrgyzstan is increasingly getting guided by Chinese thinking on multilateral issues. In right earnest, India should include Kyrgyzstan in the VVIP schedule (incoming or outgoing) in the coming years. India should be generous in extending assistance in the hours of Kyrgyzstan's economic crisis and international debt exceeding US$ 2.6 billion.

NOTES

1. "Grant as a grant 100 kgs of chips per hour", *Vecherniy Bishkek,* August 16, 2011.
2. "The Agrifood Corporation plans to launch the potato plant in Talas before November 1, 2012", *AKIpress*, September 21, 2012.
3. Erica Marat, "India Boosts Its Presence in Kyrgyzstan", *Jamestown Foundation Eurasia Daily Monitor*, August 7, 2011.
4. T.S. Subramanian, "Kyrgyzstan Minister's visit to boost defence-related biomedical research", *Hindu*, September 9, 2011.
5. "India to train Kyrgyz Armed Forces", *Express news service*, July 6, 2011.
6. "Special task force of Kyrgyz Defense Ministry to receive counter-terrorism training in India", *AKIpress*, November 29, 2011.
7. "Indian military instructors train Kyrgyz servicemen", *Telegraph Agency, KyrTAg*, Bishkek,

August 8, 2011 quoted the Press Secretary of Kyrgyzstan's Defence Ministry, Ayzada Igibayeva informing the press.

8. "The Kyrghyz defence minister expressed happiness that the two sides have worked out a cooperation plan for the year 2011", *IANS*, July 5, 2011.
9. "India offers to strengthen Kyrgyz armed forces", *IANS*, New Delhi, September 9, 2011.
10. "India opens high-altitude medical research center in Kyrgyzstan", *IANS*, July 6, 2011.
11. T. S. Subramanian, "Kyrgyzstan Minister's visit to boost defence-related biomedical research", *Hindu,* September 9, 2011.
12. Ibid.
13. *Rossiiskayagazeta,* March 24, 1999.
14. "Russia's secret torpedoes sold to Iran from Kirghizia?' World-weapons.ru (Accessed January 26, 2011) noted that the editorial staff of Russian news agency *REGNUM* obtained unverified information that components of secret torpedoes *Shkval* which are currently in service at Russian Navy were sold to Iran in 2010. The news was confirmed by Kyrgyz scientist to the author. The person responsible was from Kazakhstan and is supposed to be in prison.
15. "Russia wants Kyrgyz torpedo plant", *AKIpress*, March 23, 2012 http://www.upi.com/Business_News/Security-Industry/2012/03/23/Russia-wants-Kyrgyz-torpedo-plant/UPI-30151332524423/#ixzz1qTcFjz83
16. "Kyrgyzstan insists on its positions and waits for reply from Russia regarding handover of Dastan torpedo plant shares—Deputy Finance Minister", Bishkek, *AKIpress*, May 2, 2012.
17. "Kyrgyzstan will abide by previously reached agreements concerning handover of stake in Dastan Corporation to Russia—President Atambaev", Bishkek, *AKIpress*, February 27, 2012.
18. "Russian President's Administration Chief expresses doubt if Russia needs Kyrgyz torpedo plant", *AKIpress,* April 10, 2012.
19. The Chief Engineer of Dastan, Boris Udot, was detained for illegal supply of equipment of Dastan factory. Earlier the Chairman of the board of Dastan, Sergey Danilenko was detained at Manas international airport on his way to Istanbul. Read "In Kyrgyzstan a chief engineer of TNK Dastan OJSC detained", http://eng.24.kg/community/2010/11/24/14961.html Also read "Kyrgyz Frontier Service: Turkish Airlines initiated detention the head of TNK Dastan OJSC", Bishkek, *24.kg news agency*, November 23, 2010.
20. Julia Mazykina, "Kyrgyzstan may lose Dastan factory as the leader of the industry in Central Asia forever - Oskar Daminov", *24.kg news agency,* November 6, 2010.
21. "TNC "Dastan" delivers 70% of torpedoes to India", Bishkek, *AKIpress*, February 12, 2012
22. "Navy Trial Complex: ULAN Open Joint-Stock Company", Manual, Bishkek, 2012.
23. T.S. Subramanian, "Kyrgyzstan Minister's visit to boost defence-related biomedical research", *Hindu*, September 9, 2011.
24. http://www.defencenow.com/news/307/india-proposes-to-initiate-production-of-torpedoes-in-kyrgyzstan.html
25. "India's new weaponry: Nuclear torpedo Using Kyrgyzstan testing site to refine arsenal", Joseph Farah's G2 Bulletin http://www.wnd.com/2011/10/357753/ (Accessed October 21, 2011).
26. Ibid.
27. "India To Use Torpedo Plant In Kyrgyzstan, But Where Are The Russians?" http://www.eurasianet.org/node/64200 (Accessed September 21, 2011).
28. Joseph Farah's G2 Bulletin http://www.wnd.com/2011/10/357753/ (Accessed October 21, 2011).
29. "India To Use Torpedo Plant In Kyrgyzstan, But Where Are The Russians?" http://www.eurasianet.org/node/64200 (September 21, 2011).
30. Ibid.
31. Ibid.

32. "Kyrgyz official upbeat on India's plans to develop torpedo testing centre", *AKIpress news agency,* September 21, 2011.
33. "India does not put claims for Russian torpedo testing base at Issyk-Kul – Ulan JSC Director General", *AKIpress,* September 20, 2011.
34. India to develop torpedo testing centre in Kyrgyzstan", http://www.thehindu.com/news/national/india-to-develop-torpedo-testing-centre-in-kyrgyzstan/article2464999.ece (Accessed September 18, 2011).
35. "Kyrgyzstan and India enhance cooperation", *AKIpress,* June 12, 2012.
36. "Kyrgyz Prime Minister and State Minister of Foreign Affairs of India discussed prospects for bilateral cooperation", *Kabar,* June 12, 2012.
37. Kyrgyz Foreign ministry Press Release, June 12, 2012.
38. Victor Winner, "Opportunities for cooperation between India and Kyrgyzstan", *Times of Central Asia,* July 10, 2012.
39. Tolgonai Osmongazieva, "Kyrgyzstan's ex-president of transitional period advises citizens to greet Indian students when they met them in the streets", Bishkek, *24.kg news agency,* July 11, 2012.
40. Victor Winner, "Opportunities for cooperation between India and Kyrgyzstan", *Times of Central Asia,* July 10, 2012.
41. "Ex-President Otunbaeva tells about parliamentarism experience of Kyrgyzstan during her visit to India", *AKIpress,* February 23, 2012.

CHAPTER 13

India's "Connect Central Asia" Policy

Central Asia had been historically a zone of India's civilisational influence. Many specialists on the region have argued that India's historical interface and cooperation, alliances and exchange of trade, frequent scholarly exchanges and spiritual advancements were not without advantage to the humanity. According to them, India still enjoys a range of cultural attributes and justification and it could be one of the stakeholders in Central Asia. A proactive policy therefore could entail India with huge advantage and potentially facilitate its speedy access into Central Asian economic resources.

Since the emergence of new Central Asian states, India has forged a strong political relationship with them. However, lack of easy connectivity with the region has been an impediment for India's inroads into the region. Several initiatives made in the past decades have failed to realize their operation.

The entire Eurasian region is now rapidly changing in the face of increased international attention. Fresh initiatives are being made by the Western governments and institutions focussing on various transformational schemes for regional integration that also aim to embed Afghanistan into regional cooperation dynamics. This has resulted in increased capital flows and expansion of regional trade. The spate of Chinese investments and trade has triggered large-scale infrastructure, shipment of goods and flow of people across the region.

Geopolitics is particularly driving major external powers jockeying for influence both for maximising economic and security stakes in Central Asia. International interests for redefining the contours of the region have become more palpable since the 9/11. Major Powers have leapt into fray using various traditional and non-traditional instruments of powers to increase their presence. Both the US and Russia have their military bases and military ties with Central Asian states. China has raised its profile in Central Asia through economic, energy and military cooperation under the SCO's auspices.

The developments in Central Asia should potentially engage India's security concerns. The struggle against terrorism and attempts to stabilise Afghanistan will always remain a challenge. The events that may unfold in Central Asia in the aftermath of the US withdrawal from Afghanistan will assume critical importance with wide ranging security ramifications for India. Sharing of perceptions and informed discussion with the regional experts therefore becomes imperative. As India prepares to join the SCO, it will have to define the role it wishes to play in the organisation.

Central Asia traditionally played a role of bringing Europe and Asia together. It continues to provide large scale potentials for commerce and trade. India's commercial interest is not likely to expand without creating investment or financing small and medium size enterprises in Central Asia. India, therefore, needs to create an integrated platform for investors, entrepreneurs, bankers, marketers, traders and other types of business groups and stakeholders.

In recent years, Central Asia itself has witnessed numerous political and social conflicts. The societies in the region faced serious stresses, social and economic dislocation and other forms of threats and challenges. The ancient cities of Andijan and Osh, in the Fergana Valley have been volatile since the Soviet collapse. India had uninterrupted links with the Fergana Valley through ancient, mediaeval and contemporary times. It was a transit town and a cross-point on the Great Silk Road—connecting India, China and Europe. Buddhism once flourished here during the Sogdian period. Zahir-ud-Din Babur was born in Andijan (1483) but lived in Osh until he came to India and established the Mughal Dynasty (1526-27).

While the Fergana Valley remains prone to instability, it is incumbent on India to provide, through close cultural interaction, a poignant perspective of peace and harmony besides conjuring them up of their common cultural, historical and ethnic roots. India is viewed in the region as the principal proponent of peace. The voice of peace will still be relevant should India considers as its destiny to take lead as well as share its experiences with the people of Central Asia, so that they could safeguard their multi-ethnic understanding and inter-religious communication. India's historical affinity with the region would serve as a compelling alternative to offset conflicting forces, domestic nationalists and potentially be acceptable to regional and international audiences.

Interestingly, the major powers, in their pursuit of a realist strategy, have not discounted altogether the application of their ideologies and ideals. The major countries have already established specific institutions in Central Asia in order to further their interests. Russia has Slavic Universities, while Turkey has set up Turkic Universities in all the countries. The US too has opened American Universities and besides China has established Confucius Centres in Central Asian capitals. In fact, China, with its long term interests in mind, has started setting up Secondary level Chinese language schools in the region. India has set up three Cultural Centres in the region. Considering a greater demand for an Indian University, the idea of establishing an Indian University in Central Asia has been mooted by the author through India's new "Connect Central Asia" Policy (CCAP).

This will help to revive and re-harness the Indo-Central Asia linkages through regular intellectual and institutional resources available in both regions. The idea is also to be able to draw on the understanding of the past while emphasising its relevance to the future, especially in the context of an Asian renaissance for reinvigorating cultural, socio-economic and intellectual aspects of Asia. It will also help to showcase India's soft-power and the idea of promoting the Asian knowledge cooperation. Besides, the Indian University should play the catalyst role for broadening India's operational scope and presence in the region.

The above points should suggest that Central Asia is a critical strategic lynchpin to India's external interest. In order to clarify India's interests and find a new platform that could lay the groundwork for evolving an enduring policy, the Government of India had envisaged its new CCAP in 2012. The CCAP is meant to be a smart policy that outlines India's multifaceted pro-active political, economic and people-to-people engagement with Central Asian countries, individually and collectively.[1] The policy is anchored in broadening India's firm and long term strategic interest and that will also serve to be commensurate with India's rising profile on the global stage.[2] The greater emphasis is given on some of the niche areas that India enjoys in the region. These include extending India's soft power, for example by setting up of a Central Asian University in Bishkek that could evolve as a Centre of excellence to impart world class education in areas like IT, management, philosophy and languages.[3] The new policy also envisaged replicating India's success of the Pan Africa e-network by creating a similar project of tele-education and tele-medicine connectivity, linking all the five Central Asian states.[4] The CCAP was launched at India's first Track 1.5 diplomacy in the framework of India-Central Asia Dialogue held in Bishkek on June 12-13, 2012. The dialogue was inaugurated jointly by the Minister of State for External Affairs E. Ahamed and the former Kyrgyz President Roza Otunbayeva. The Dialogue was held under the joint aegis of the Indian Council for World Affairs (ICWA) and the World Diplomatic Academy, Bishkek. Broadly, the "Connect Central Asia" Policy envisaged the following:[5]

1. To build on the strong political relations through the exchange of high level visits at both bilateral and multilateral fora.
2. To strengthen strategic and security cooperation with focus on military training, joint research, counter-terrorism coordination and close consultations on Afghanistan.
3. To step up multilateral engagement with Central Asian partners using the synergy of joint efforts through existing fora like the SCO, Eurasian Economic Community (EEC) and the Custom Union; proposed a Comprehensive Economic Cooperation Agreement (CECA) to integrate with Eurasian market.
4. To develop a long term partnership in the field of energy, natural resources and agricultural land use with value addition.

5. To cooperate in the medical field by setting up civil hospitals and clinics in Central Asia.
6. To set up a Central Asian University in Bishkek as a Centre of excellence to impart world class education in the fields of IT sector, philosophy, language etc.
7. To set up a Central Asian e-network with its hub in India, to deliver, tele-education and tele-medicine connectivity, linking all the five Central Asian States.
8. To encourage Indian companies to showcase their capabilities in building world class structures at competitive rates.
9. To improve land connectivity, by reactivating the International North-South Transport Corridor (INSTC) and bridging the missing links in the Corridor.
10. To promote a viable Indian banking infrastructure in the region,
11. To improve air connectivity with Central Asia with a view to promote tourism between our countries.
12. To promote people-to-people contacts through exchanges of youth, future leaders, scholars, academics, and civil society in order to gain deeper insights into each others' cultures.

NOTES

1. "India unveils ambitious 'Connect' with Central Asia", *IANS*, June 18, 2012.
2. "India embarks on "Connect Central Asia" policy, *TNN,* June 13, 2012.
3. "India to open Indian-Central Asian University in Kyrgyzstan", *AKIpress*, June 13, 2012.
4. "India to gift e-network to Central Asia, *IANS*, June 12, 2012.
5. See the MOS speech in Annexure 5.

Conclusion: Emerging Trends in Central Asia

Central Asian states have been undergoing an arduous and complex nation-building process, which is far from complete. The shortcomings include their inability to move out of the past Soviet era of political and economic structures. The leaders of Kazakhstan, Tajikistan, Turkmenistan and Uzbekistan had strongly resisted political change and have successfully adopted internal political mechanisms with varying style to stay in power. Among them the former President of Kyrgyzstan, Askar Akayev was the only leader who initially embraced political and economic reforms, but later on he too began to develop authoritarian tendencies and stopped sharing power with his opponents. During the last two decades Kyrgyzstan went through a very difficult political transition. The major test has been the transition from a Soviet Republic to a parliamentary democracy, though since 2005 it had witnessed two major uprisings, something not known in the former Soviet republics.

On the other extreme was the Turkmen President Saparmurat Atayevich Niyazov who served as President for life until his death in 2006 being the most repressive dictators. President Karimov of Uzbekistan too retained his power for over two decades now. He does not want to demolish the old house until he is able to build a new one. Similarly, Kazakh President Nursultan Nazarbayev also managed to survive by shrewdly manipulating the internal politics and devising internal means to gain political legitimacy.

Political Trends: With the exception of Kyrgyzstan, the politics in other states remain unpredictable. None of the aging Presidents of Kazakhstan, Tajikistan, and Uzbekistan appear to have clear succession plans despite some surreptitious intrigues among members of the ruling elite. To some extent, the Kyrgyz uprising and the Arab-Spring syndrome had compelled Nazarbayev to drop the referendum extending his rule until 2020. Instead he preferred to hold an early presidential election. However, post December 2011 Zhanaozen events, Nazarbayev removed his influential son-in-law, Timur Kulibayev from power; and scheduled parliamentary elections in January 2012. This was critical to strengthen at least the Parliament body. Uzbekistan is unlikely to see any change until Islam Karimov leaves office. But, the post-Karimov Uzbekistan is likely to be marked by significant instability because of the presence of a strong political Islam. Turkmenistan's Gurbanguly Berdymukhamedov has though shown some liberal attitude and called exiled opposition leaders to participate in the 2012 elections. But, in essence he too is likely to follow the course of his late predecessor.Tajikistan continues to remain locked in a difficult combination of poverty, authoritarianism, and Islamic extremism that keeps the country prone to instability. Kyrgyzstan has switched to a parliamentary democracy and the institution of democracy and the rule of law remain underdeveloped. A shaky experiment in coalition government is in place; there are also many unresolved issues including the ethnic rifts in the south. However, for the time being none of the ruling Presidents are likely to face any real opposition, though the basic politico-economic characteristics of these countries are no different from those in West Asia. Moreover, unlike in the West Asian case, both Russia and China will firmly insulate the Central Asian regimes from failing, viz., Uzbekistan after 2005 Andijan crisis; Kazakhstan after 2011 Zhanaozen events. Even the Kyrgyz crises were contained affectively and not allowed to cross a threshold.

Radical Islam: Behind the secular settings a major shift to a far more religious pattern of society is underway in the region. Islamic forces are getting stronger in Tajikistan and southern Kyrgyzstan (Osh & Batken). To some extent, the semblance of democracy seemed to have succeeded in channeling popular anger, but pro-Islamic tone and language of debate in the Kyrgyz Parliament is beginning to impact the government policies. Kazakhstan and Turkmenistan have been the least affected by extremist forces. However, the unequal distribution of wealth generated from oil export has begun to instill public discontent and protests on streets. A series of serious explosions and terrorist acts by Islamists took place in Kazakhstan in which at least 30 people have been killed during 2011 alone. The fight against extremism so far carried out covertly by the state has now come out open in the surface. The official Kazakh (OIC Chairs OIC 2012) was seen as moving towards warmer ties with the Muslim world. Turkmenistan too has forged closer relations with Iran and with the Gulf region. Uzbekistan has firmly resisted extremist drive but the society is already Islamised and soon religion is likely to be a dominant factor for polity in the country.

Regional Conflicts: The interstate and interethnic conflicts are likely to intensify further. The Uzbek-Tajik conflicts over water, energy and surface transport have worsened the relations. Border incidents have become a regular feature as Uzbekistan builds up armoured tanks along the Sughd enclave. Tensions have heightened following the halting of gas supplies, closer of Amuzang-Khatlon railway section and sudden increase by 32 per cent tariffs on transit of freight by Uzbekistan for Tajikistan. Tajikistan's plan to build the Roghun hydroelectric dam on the Vakhsh River is strongly opposed by Uzbekistan. The Uzbek-Kyrgyz relations have also deteriorated over the years, especially since the June 2010 ethic riots in Osh. The two have differences over land, enclaves, border and water. Uzbekistan is strongly opposed to Kyrgyzstan going ahead with the building of Kambar-Ata mega hydroelectric projects with the Russian support. Uzbek President has warned about an imminent war if hydropower dams are built on the upstream of *Amu Darya* and *Syr Darya*. Energy crises are causing frictions; Uzbekistan and Kazakhstan have threatened to pull out from the Soviet-era built Central Asian electricity grid due to serious shortage of power. The Kyrgyz-Tajik tensions over resources are also building up in the Batken region. These issues are unlikely to be resolved in the short and mid-term period.

The Afghan Reconstruction and Central Asia: The Afghan stabilisng process may have unintended consequences for the regional states. For example, any effort to boost Afghan agricultural production will cut into Central Asian water resources; hydro-power projects are likely to cause strain on downstream water supplies, which is already fueling anxieties in Uzbekistan and Kazakhstan. Some sort of skepticism remains about the US-authored New Silk Road (NSR) idea for creating regional infrastructure networks (roads, rail, and electricity). The NSR aims to knit the region together and embed Afghanistan into a regional integration process. Several connectivity projects have been envisaged to realise the idea. In 2010, Afghanistan, Kyrgyzstan and Tajikistan have signed the Cross-Border Transport Agreement (CBTA) under the aegis of the CAREC. The CBTA forms a significant part of the NDN logistics corridors. Both TAPI gas pipeline and CASA-1000 hydroelectric power lines are encouraged by the US to make Afghanistan a linchpin of South-Central Asia integration process. But, there are rivalries erupting over who will anchor these projects. The US goal seemed only to secure its short term security interests. Russia has also actively sought participation in both TAPI and CASA-1000 projects.Iran too is keenly pursuing hydropower projects in Tajikistan. Uzbekistan has its ambitious projects to control power supplies to Afghanistan and also Pakistan. China on the other hand is trying to implement its own project to revive the historic Silk Route and connect its Xinjiang province with Central Asia and beyond. The planned China-Kyrgyzstan-Uzbekistan railway line that will be completed in the next five year will change the geo-economic and political landscape of South and Central Asia. The Xinjiang Trade Expo-2011 envisaged new ideas to broaden China's cooperation with South and Central Asia including a FTA among SCO member states.

Growing Uzbek Role: Tashkent is intrinsically acquiring a high pedestal in the US policy goals in Afghanistan projecting itself as a frontline state and as a hub for the NDN in the post-2014 scenario. Importantly, Uzbekistan has opened a major strategic railway line (75 kilometres) in December 2011 from the Uzbek border to Mazar-i-Sharif. Besides, leveraging the transport route, Uzbekistan also plans to control power supply to Afghanistan and beyond. Tashkent is likely to exploit the evolving situation fully in its favour. This may upset the regional equations.

US in Central Asia: The continuation of the US military facilities in Central Asia is also likely to become a critical issue, and in fact, it may fuel regional and domestic discord. In the past, despite the SCO's firm opposition, Kyrgyzstan and Tajikistan had supported transit rights for the coalition efforts in Afghanistan. In fact, the US had several blueprints until recently for constructing several airbases in the region i.e., in Osh (Kyrgyzstan), Karatog (Tajikistan) and Almaty (Kazakhstan). The situation has changed since then. However, the US is trying to retain its Transit Centre at Manas beyond 2014, although Kyrgyzstan has repeatedly threatened to close it down when the lease expires in 2014. The Kyrgyz new administration perceives Russia to be strategic partner and has decided not to renew the lease citing a possible threat of Iranian missiles hitting the US Transit Centre in Bishkek. But, at the same time, opposition to closing the US Transit Centre is not uniformly strong as many politicians see the leasing of Manas a very important source of finance to Kyrgyzstan's state budget.

Post-2014 Scenario: The US withdrawal from Afghanistan will result in increased security threat for Central Asia and to Russia also. Islamic extremists, emboldened by their victory over the Western coalition, will try to expand their influence into Central Asia. Uzbekistan, particularly, could be seriously exposed to terrorist attacks. The poverty and ethnic conflicts in the Fergana Valley will provide the extremists the right conditions. In the scenario of the Taliban's revival, the Central Asian states would neither have the means nor are they likely to take responsibility on their own, and if the Russians and Chinese have their say, they would not let the US and NATO to cross certain threshold. But the past trends have shown that regional states will seek cooperation with the West against the wishes of Moscow and Beijing and in the process extract maximum advantage for themselves in the post 2014 drawdown. The process in this direction has already begun after the US has announced to leave behind weapons to friendly countries of Central Asia. The opposition to closing the US Transit Centre in Kyrgyzstan was not uniformly strong as many politicians see the leasing of Manas a very important source of finance to Kyrgyzstan's state budget. Similarly, Tajikistan too may not be opposed to having a deal with US for a base to be stationed in its territory.

In the past, Moscow has handled internal turmoil in the CIS states with pragmatism. By not intervening in the ethnic conflict, Russia gained more trust among Kyrgyz and started to depend more on Moscow than before. To fend off the looming threat, Russia in December 2011 had consolidated its leading position within the CSTO and CIS structures by blocking deployment of foreign military bases in the CSTO member countries without the consent of all its members; and legitimising its military intervention in case of internal conflicts. Differences though persist whether the collective rapid deployment forces should be used not only in the case of foreign aggression, but also in the case of interference by those states within the CSTO. Only Karimov stubbornly resisted any interventionist role and opted out of the CSTO. Russia has also signed fresh security agreements with Tajikistan and Kyrgyzstan in 2012 for longer term stationing of Russian military bases in both the countries.

China's Influence: Notwithstanding the Customs Union (CU), China seeks an increasingly powerful and ambitious presence in Central Asia, projecting itself as a factor of stability. China's plans for large-scale energy and transport links would mean gradual integration of Central Asia into Chinese economic space. Beijing wants to enter the region's agriculture, mineral ore, gold, coal mines, hydropower, and manufacturing sectors. This is already happening in Kyrgyzstan. Chinese farmers are buying Tajik land. Rumors of Chinese leasing land in Kazakhstan evoked strong public protests in 2011. Among other things, the wage gap between local and Chinese are already fuelling discontent in Kyrgyzstan and Tajikistan. If the current comfort level and overlapping of security interests between Beijing and Moscow continues, it would affect a range of regional security issues. Undoubtedly, Central Asia presently remains a unifying factor in their shared security interests. The SCO has essentially become an interesting condominium, but the content of relationship remains low. And no two countries trust each other completely. The regional experts feel that SCO is just a show.

Common Economic Space: The CU is now expanded into Common Economic Space (CES) from January 2012 between Russia, Belarus and Kazakhstan – and possibly Kyrgyzstan and Tajikistan will join soon. The CU must be viewed in the context of countering challenges of economic expansion posed by China into Eurasia. The CU also means Russia's search for a stronger regional integration model like EU and as a necessary process to evolve as an economic bloc on line of the EU, APEC, NAFTA and ASEAN.The long-term success of CU would remain a subject of intense debate, but Beijing is likely to seek new strategy to turn economic relations with Central Asian states in its favour. China may suffer commercially in the short term, but it will seek greater economic space including manufacturing capacities through investments and concessionary loans within Eurasia. Moscow is unlikely to withstand the economic push by China in Central Asia in the longer run.

Role of Iran: Iran is increasing its stake in Central Asia. Tehran is engaged in developing the Sangtuda-2 plant in Tajikistan. To demonstrate its strength, Tehran forced Uzbekistan to revoke its decision to block Iranian freight meant for Sangtuda-2. Lately, Kyrgyzstan has cited the threat of Iranian missile hitting the Manas military base as an excuse to evict the US military base from its territory.These are indications of Iranian growing influence in the region. Besides, Iranian role would remain vital for any Central Asia's connectivity projects in future.

Role of India: For an affective Indian response, it would be prudent to take a wait-and-see approach. However, India must seek to engage with the CU, especially identifying commercial and investments opportunities to benefit from such an integrated market of the CES. India's decision to work out a FTA plus or CECA with the CU will give a major fillip to economic engagement with the entire Eurasian region. But, in the short term, Uzbekistan and Tajikistan are likely to become a lynchpin for regional security development and our engagement—economic and political—with Tashkent and Dushanbe should be improved. As India prepares to join the SCO, meaningful gains can be achieved if India identifies schemes for economic cooperation with China in Eurasia and Western China that will facilitate trade and create a sound environment for regional economic cooperation. India's newly launched 'Connect Central Asia' policy aims to achieve these goals.

ANNEXURES

ANNEXURE 1

Kyrgyzstan Inquiry Commission (KIC)

Report of The Independent International Commission of Inquiry into the Events in Southern Kyrgyzstan in June 2010

(The report is 140 pages)

Executive Summary

1. The Independent International Commission of Inquiry into the Events in southern Kyrgyzstan was established after the President of the Kyrgyz Republic; H.E. Ms. Roza Otunbayeva asked Dr. Kimmo Kiljunen, Special Representative for Central Asia, Organisation for Security and Co-operation in Europe (OSCE) Parliamentary Assembly to coordinate the preparation process to establish it. After broad consultation with numerous international bodies, including the United Nations (UN), the OSCE, the European Union (EU), the Commonwealth of Independent States (CIS) and the Office of the High Commissioner for Human Rights (OHCHR), the terms of reference were established and endorsed. The Kyrgyz Inquiry Commission (KIC) was mandated to investigate the facts and circumstances relevant to incidents that took place in southern Kyrgyzstan in June 2010, qualify the violations and crimes under international law, determine responsibilities and make recommendations, particularly on accountability measures, so as to ensure the non-repetition of the violations and to contribute towards peace, stability and reconciliation.
2. The present report is based upon extensive interviews and analysis conducted by the KIC in Kyrgyzstan and elsewhere. In excess of 750 witnesses, 700 documents and many thousands of photographs and video extracts were considered by the KIC. The KIC has been able to establish a detailed and accurate narrative of the June events in Osh and Jalalabad. The events must be viewed in context of the historical and political background of the region, particularly the relationship between the communities of ethnic Kyrgyz and ethnic Uzbeks. In this regard the KIC notes the under-representation of ethnic Uzbeks in public life and the rising force of ethno-nationalism in the politics

of Kyrgyzstan. The KIC notes further the power vacuum and consequent political rivalries, fragile state institutions and the weak rule of law in southern Kyrgyzstan in the wake of the April 07 overthrow of the Bakiyev government.

3. The events resulted in significant loss of life and injury, of which the majority of victims were ethnic Uzbeks. In total about 470 people died. It is expected that this figure will grow but not substantially. About 1,900 people received medical assistance at hospitals. Many thousands of people were displaced. About 111,000 people were displaced to Uzbekistan and a further 300,000 were internally displaced. There was also significant property damage, again to a disproportionately high number of ethnic Uzbek owned properties. In total about 2,800 properties were damaged. The KIC notes that ethnic Kyrgyz also suffered significant losses, in terms of life, health and property. The KIC has found that both communities suffered loss.

II

4. The seizure, distribution and use of weapons during the events are a particularly disturbing feature of the events. In many instances crowds of attackers seized firearms and ammunition from the military and police in circumstances largely unopposed by troops or officers. Armoured Personnel Carriers (APCs) were also surrendered. The KIC notes, with some concern, that some 80 weapons and about 19,000 rounds of ammunition have not been recovered. The authorities of Kyrgyzstan have failed to carry out appropriate criminal and disciplinary investigations into the loss of weapons.

5. Further to the narrative of facts and circumstances, the KIC has qualified the violations under international law. It is the view of the KIC that the violence of June does not qualify as either war crimes or genocide. However, if the evidence of some acts committed during certain attacks against the mahallas in Osh on June 11, 12 and 13 was proven beyond reasonable doubt in a court of law, those acts would amount to crimes against humanity. These are murder, rape, and other forms of sexual violence, physical violence (as another inhumane act) and persecution against an identifiable group on ethnic grounds. The KIC is of the view that no acts of violence committed in Jalalabad would qualify as crimes against humanity. There were many other criminal acts committed in both Osh and Jalalabad during the events that fall under the Criminal Code of Kyrgyzstan.

6. Sexual and gender based violence committed during the events remains underreported and largely unacknowledged by the authorities. While the KIC has corroborated around 20 rapes and other incidents of sexual violence, the true figure is certain to be considerably higher. Women have continued to suffer sexual and gender based violence in the aftermath of the events. In the rare cases where victims have chosen to file claims for rape the response of the authorities has been inadequate if not obstructive.

7. The KIC was not mandated to conduct a criminal investigation, which remains the responsibility of the authorities of Kyrgyzstan. Neither is it a prosecuting authority or tribunal. The KIC is not in a position to identify named individuals as being responsible for the crimes that have been documented. These results in part from the limitation of its mandate, but other factors are also relevant, including: the short timeframe for its work; the limited investigative capacities available to it; and its inability to require individuals to testify. It is essential, both in fulfilment of domestic and international legal obligations and in order that justice be done and community wounds healed, that every effort be made by the authorities of Kyrgyzstan to establish individual criminal responsibility.
8. In addition to the documented international and domestic criminal acts, the KIC has found that there have been and still are serious violations of International Human Rights Law (IHRL) committed by the state in the aftermath of the events. There is a consistent and reliable body of material which tends to show that acts of torture were committed in detention centres by the authorities of Kyrgyzstan in the aftermath of the June events. Of particular concern to the KIC is that such acts of torture are ongoing and that the response of the authorities to allegations of torture has been grossly inadequate.
9. Criminal investigations and trials which have resulted from the June events have been marked by breaches of the International Covenant on Civil and Political Rights (ICCPR) fair trial rights. Large scale sweep operations conducted in Uzbek mahallas from June 21 to 23 and the smaller scale search operations which then followed have involved ill-treatment and arbitrary arrest and detention. There has been selective prosecution targeting the ethnic Uzbek minority. Defence lawyers representing ethnic Uzbek defendants have been subject to improper interference and intimidation.
10. The KIC has examined the institutional and political responsibility of various actors and institutions. The Provisional Government (PG), which had assumed power two months before the events, either failed to recognise or underestimated the deterioration in inter-ethnic relations in southern Kyrgyzstan. Arguments advanced by President Otunbayeva that the eruption of violence was of such magnitude that it made it difficult for the Provisional Government to contain do not absolve the government of its basic responsibility to protect the population. The KIC finds that the violence of June was reasonably foreseeable and that the Provisional Government should have developed a contingency plan that would, in the event that it occurred, have contained it. Particularly, the Provisional Government had the responsibility to ensure that the security forces were adequately trained and appropriately equipped to deal with situations of civil unrest.

11. The KIC considers the actions of other actors to have been inadequate. General Ismail Isakov, the Special Representative of the Provisional Government for Southern Kyrgyzstan took effective command over the operational headquarters and security forces in Osh city and province. His failure to deploy the security forces with clear orders and rules of engagement providing for the use of non-lethal force on June 11 or subsequent days constitutes a serious omission. The Commandant of Osh city and province, Bakyt Alymbekov, unlawfully abdicated control over law enforcement in favour of General Isakov and failed in his duty to ensure that human rights were respected during the restoration of order. The Commandant of Jalalabad, Kubatbek Baybolov, failed to take all measures within his power to end the violence in Jalalabad. He is now the Prosecutor General and has failed to ensure that the investigation and prosecution of crimes committed during the events and aftermath have been conducted in accordance with the domestic and international legal obligations of Kyrgyzstan. The nationalist rhetoric of the Mayor of Osh, MelisMyrzakmatov, was not conducive to the calming of inter-ethnic tensions.
12. The role of the security forces in the events was significant. The military personnel under the command of the Provisional Government numbered 2,000. The KIC is of the opinion that had those troops been properly instructed and deployed; it would have been possible to prevent or stop the violence and to block the access to Osh city by the attackers who moved from rural areas. The failure of members of the security forces to protect their equipment raises questions of complicity in the events, either directly or indirectly. Further, some members of the military were involved in some of the attacks on the mahallas.
13. In accordance with its mandate the KIC has made recommendations as to conflict prevention and reconciliation, accountability and impunity.
14. As to conflict prevention and reconciliation, the KIC recommends measures on inclusive state building; language, culture and education; good governance; women's rights and gender equality; the media; public safety and security; and the prevalence of weapons among civilians. Kyrgyzstan should take a strong public stand against extreme nationalism and ethnic exclusivity. The restoration of the name "Republic of Kyrgyzstan" would be a concrete example of how this may be achieved. The Uzbek language should be given special status at municipal and regional levels in southern Kyrgyzstan. Schools, theatres and other cultural facilities destroyed or damaged should be rebuilt and the educational curriculum should be inclusive of various cultural, language and historical traditions and perspectives. The government should establish an independent national body for the promotion of women's rights and gender equality and adopt a zero tolerance policy on violence against women. The security forces should execute their function according to law and without

reference to extraneous loyalties. The government should organise an effective disarmament campaign for the surrender of illegal weapons in Kyrgyzstan.

15. As to accountability, the KIC recommends measures on criminal and disciplinary accountability, gender based violence, violations of human rights and fair trial principles and on international follow up. The government should ensure the conduct of thorough, independent and impartial investigations into crimes or other human rights violations without reference to ethnicity and should consider seeking international assistance to do so. The government should undertake an immediate investigation into the actions of the security forces and, specifically, into the loss of military and police equipment and weapons. The government should incorporate crimes against humanity in the Criminal Code of Kyrgyzstan and ratify the Rome Statute. The government should ensure the prosecution of perpetrators of sexual and gender based violence. The government should immediately stop all arbitrary arrests, torture in detention and other human rights violations. The KIC recommends that the government should request the assistance of the UN OHCHR, the OSCE High Commissioner for National Minorities and other relevant international bodies to monitor and report on the implementation of the recommended measures.

16. As to impunity, the KIC makes recommendations on truth seeking and reconciliation and reparation. The government should establish a truth and reconciliation commission to examine the June events, their causes and consequences with the support and active participation of the international community. A comprehensive reparation programme to provide victims with adequate material compensation for loss and rehabilitation should be established as a matter of priority.

Concise Chronology of Main Events

April 7, 2010	The President Kurmanbek Bakiyev is overthrown after popular demonstrations. A Provisional Government headed by Roza Otunbayeva assumes power.
May 13, 2010	Bakiyev's supporters seize administrative buildings in Batken, Osh and Jalalabad.
May 14, 2010	Supporters of the Provisional Government re-capture the administration building in Jalalabad. A crowd of Kyrgyz and Uzbek marches to Bakiyevs? home village of Teyit. Houses belonging to Bakiyevs are set on fire.
June 10, 2010	At 10 pm, a clash near the casino sparks rioting around the dormitory, *Philarmonia* and various parts of the city. The authorities are unable to contain the crowds. Unfounded rumour of rape at the dormitory mobilises rural Kyrgyz at extraordinary speed.

June 11, 2010 At 2am, the Provisional Government establishes a state of emergency and introduces a curfew.

At 4am, the burning and looting commence near the Frunze market in central Osh.

A delegation from the Provisional Government arrives in Osh.

Uzbek villagers in Nariman block the central road, which connects Osh to both the airport and Bishkek.

Mass Kyrgyz mobilisation from villages to the west and east of Osh begins.

At noon, automatic weapons are distributed amongst civilian and military Kyrgyz in Furkhat. The Uzbek barricade is brought down and extensive burning and killing ensue.

At 1.30pm, an APC, followed by armed men, penetrates the Cheremushki *mahalla.* Many Uzbeks are beaten or shot, women raped and houses burnt.

Near midday, an APC followed by a Kyrgyz crowd enters the *mahalla* [near the Al-Hakim hospital] near the clothing market. Houses are burned and many are killed.

Tension rises in Jalalabad. Uzbeks begin to barricade their *mahallas*

June 12, 2010 The rumour spreads that the Uzbekistan military will intervene. Kyrgyz start to withdraw from the *mahallas*in Osh.

At 7am, 2 APCs break through the Uzbek barricade into Majrimtal *mahalla*. Houses are looted and burned.

The looting and house burning continue in Cheremushki and Furkhat. Violence spreads to Onadyr, a neighboring part of Furkhat.

A Kyrgyz crowd attacks Navoi Street. Wholesale looting, murder and arson take place.

An APC breaks into the Teshik-Tash*mahalla.* The attack continues to the *mahalla* near the Shait Tebe mosque.

Violence erupts in Jalalabad. Uzbeks establish a barricade in Suzak and shot at Kyrgyz cars. The Kyrgyz-Uzbek University of People's Friendship is looted and set on fire.

June 13, 2010 Scale and intensity of violence decreases in Osh, although attacks against *Mahallas* continue. Hostage taking is particularly active.

During the morning, Kyrgyz crowds seize weapons and ammunition from several police and military locations in Jalalabad Province.

Uzbeks establish a roadblock at the Sanpa crossing. They burn cars and shoot Kyrgyz.

	At 1.30pm, Kyrgyz crowd moves from the Hippodrome to Jalalabad city. The TashBulak*mahalla*, then Suzak, are attacked. Buildings and houses are burnt. At 4pm, the police chief of Karasuu district and his driver, both Kyrgyz, are murdered in Nariman. During the afternoon, the provisional government declares state of emergency across the Jalalabad Province and establishes a curfew.
June 14, 2010	Situation stabilises in Osh. Sporadic incidents of violence, including looting, sexual violence and hostage taking, will continue in the next days. Clashes continue in Jalalabad during the day and looting throughout the night. The situation stabilises early the next morning.

Map of Osh

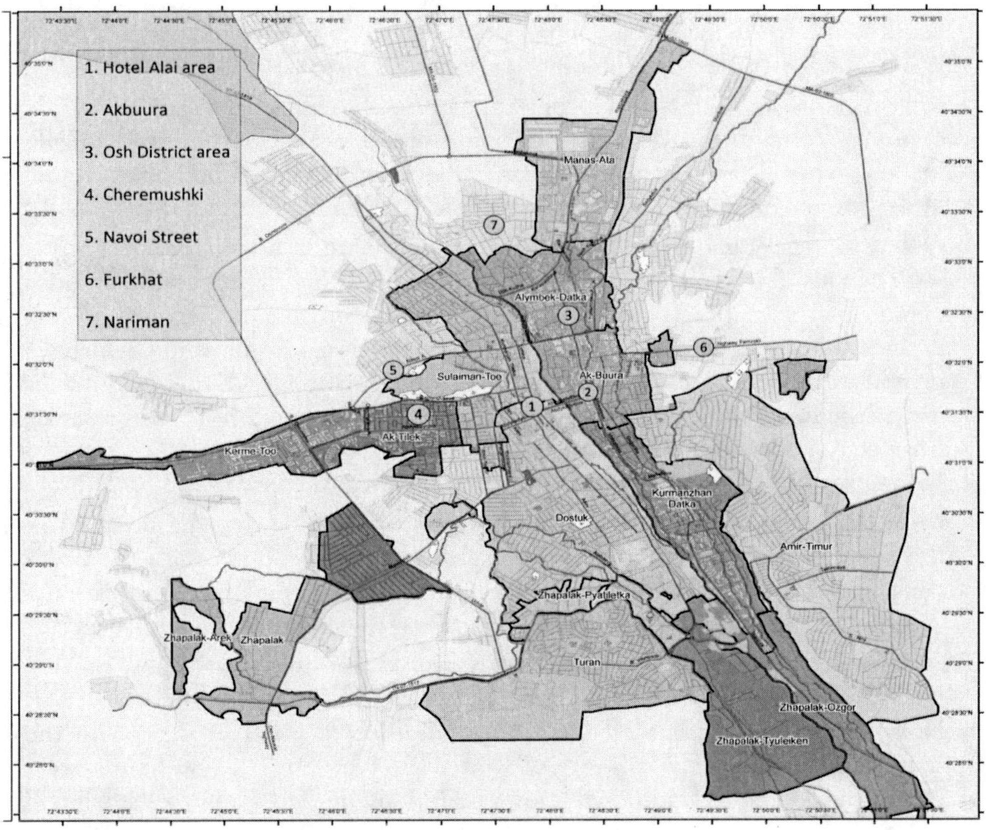

ANNEXURE 2

Kyrgyz Response to Story by the Economist

Weak Fences, Bad Neighbours
(August 13, 2011)

SIR – You had published a report in August about the situation of Uzbeks in southern Kyrgyzstan following the events of June 2010 ("Weak fences, bad neighbours", August 13). The article raised a number of themes and problematic issues connected to the process of post-conflict recovery. We would like to remind you about the context surrounding last year's events.

Inter-regional and inter-ethnic contradictions were used to instigate the tragic events in the south of Kyrgyzstan during a situation of sharp political struggle in 2010, when the people of Kyrgyzstan had overthrown the authoritarian regime of the former president Kurmanbek Bakiev.

Owing to the mutual efforts of government and the whole nation the conflict was settled in just four days and a further escalation prevented. The working findings of more than 10 national and international commissions and reports on the events in the south, including of the Independent International Commission, which we invited to demonstrate to the whole world the openness of Kyrgyzstan that is unprecedented in the post-Soviet region, show that the June 2010 events resulted from complex socio-political causes.

That is the reason why overcoming its consequences and restoring confidence between communities is not an easy task. Acknowledging that the situation in this region remains complicated, nevertheless, we consider it necessary to inform you about the measures and reforms we have undertaken in Kyrgyzstan with the aim of achieving the real results in overcoming the conflict's consequences.

The first action, undertaken by the Kyrgyz Government in the post-conflict period, was the reconstruction of houses and destroyed infrastructure. Notwithstanding the hardest conditions, all affected were provided with the transition shelters before advance of winter last year. Some 1,780 houses were reconstructed and 41 additional houses built. No one "faced a homeless winter" as you stated in your article. Also your assertion that, a "sole apartment block built for the families of last summer victims", does not correspond to reality.

The reconstruction work was conducted by a specially created directory under the strict control of the supervisory board consisting of civil-society representatives. Taking into account that the transitional shelters were small in size, work on the construction of the completed living houses, including 34 multi-storey houses, continued in 2011. This process caused internal debate. Part of the population supports the idea of joint, mixed settling for these houses. However, the residents of some areas do not support this idea. The process of discussion is taking place, and different opinions are expressed, but no one will be settled into these houses without his personal wish.

Reacting to the issue of human-rights violations rose in the article, it is necessary to note the wide scale of judicial reform being carried out in the country, such as changing the selection principle of all 445 judges from local courts to the Supreme Court and starting the inter-regional rotation programme for appointed judges. The role of the prosecutor's office in torture prevention has been strengthened. UN special rapporteur on torture to Kyrgyzstan was invited to study the reforms; this serves more evidence about the country's openness and readiness for the reforms.

There is also no justification for your observations about efforts to renounce the Russian language. The Russian language has an official status according to the constitution and is one of our international languages that has a strong position and carries an important role in the country's development.

Notwithstanding the pre-election presidential campaign under way work is continuing on fulfilling the recommendations of reports and investigations on the summer 2010 events in the south of Kyrgyzstan, primarily those of the Independent International Commission.

Conducting a thorough analysis of all the recommendations, a working commission has been set up in Kyrgyzstan to look at implementing the recommendations. Its activity will be followed by the monitoring committee consisting of human-rights groups, including civil-society activists from the Uzbek minority.

Embassy of the Kyrgyz Republic.

ANNEXURE 3

Non Paper

The Candidature of the Kyrgyz Republic for a Non-permanent Seat of the United Nations Security Council (Issued by Ministry of Foreign Affairs)

The Kyrgyz Republic has declared its intention to become the United Nations Security Council (UNSC) Non-Permanent Member for the term 2012-13 in 1997, five years after joining the United Nations (UN);

The Kyrgyz Republic is a landlocked country located in Central Asia on the crossroads of Asia and Europe;

The Kyrgyz Republic is a small, friendly, peaceful and multiethnic country;

The Kyrgyz Republic has never been a member of the UNSC before, although it has taken an active part in the peacekeeping efforts of the UN through its participation in UN peacekeeping operations in Europe, Asia and Africa;

The Kyrgyz Republic has been most actively participating in the world actions to combat illicit drugs trafficking, trafficking in human beings, transnational organised crime and volunteered its assistance to the Anti-Terrorism Coalition (ATC) in accordance with the UNSC Resolutions;

Every UN member state should have a chance to be a non-permanent member of the UNSC regardless of their size, economic or political development. Kyrgyzstan's election will be proof of the recognition of the right of small countries to be present in the UNSC;

Election of small states to UNSC will bring confidence into the principle of equality of member states and thus will strengthen authority of UN;

Election to the council of countries which have never served in this UNs organ before can bring to its work a variety of views, regional and sub-regional experiences, as well widen interests of different categories of states;

The Kyrgyz Republic is one of the initiators and depositary of the Nuclear Weapon Free Zone (NWFZ) Treaty in Central Asia and signatory to Non-Proliferation Treaty (NPT) and member of other non-proliferation regimes;

The Kyrgyz Republic has experience of mediation in resolving conflicts and is ready to provide its expertise in creation favorable conditions for incessant global peace and stability, as well as promotion of human rights and equitable sustainable development in the world;

The Kyrgyz Republic is ready to become a responsible, reliable and effective member of the Council.

If elected into the UNSC, the Kyrgyz Republic will:

- Be ready to share responsibility for maintaining peace and security with a purpose of ensuring stability in all corners of the world while securing the principles of transparency and sovereign equality of all states;
- Call for abiding by the norms of international law including by the principles of territorial integrity, sovereignty, independence, non-interference into internal affairs of states and peaceful settlement of conflicts;
- Support the reforming of the UNSC and call for more democratic and wider representation in the Security Council that will reflect fair regional presence including developing and small countries;
- As a member of group of landlocked countries, group of small countries and countries with transition economies be ready to call for wider representation of small countries in all organs of the UN;
- Contribute to the establishment of permanent mechanism of political consultations with all countries aimed at creating a balanced decision-making process that will take into account opinions of small countries. Also will strengthen cooperation with multilateral regional organisations;
- Call for keeping paying attention to the issue of non-proliferation and for destruction of nuclear weapons, small arms and their excesses;
- Actively cooperate with the international community in the fight against all forms of international terrorism;
- Call for enlargement of UNs peacekeeping operations and increase of their effectiveness;
- Promote preventive diplomacy; provide mediation in accordance with the United Nations Charter in post-conflict settlements;
- Oppose hatred and violence, including against peaceful and non-armed civil population, women and children. Call for maximum restraint and abiding by norms of humanitarian law;
- Pay special attention to energy, food and climate security that are essential elements of sustainable development of all states;
- Organise weekly briefings for small countries on the work of Security Council for promoting transparency of this UN body and interests of small countries.

ANNEXURE 4

Blake's Testimony on U.S. Engagement in Central Asia

U.S. Department of State, Testimony by Robert O. Blake, Jr. Assistant Secretary, Bureau of South and Central Asian Affairs, House Foreign Affairs Committee, Subcommittee on Europe and Eurasia, Washington, DC
July 24, 2012

U.S. Engagement in Central Asia

Chairman Burton, members of the committee, thank you for giving me the opportunity to speak today on the status of U.S. engagement in Central Asia. I would particularly like to thank you, Mr. Chairman, for all you have done to support our efforts, including your leadership of one of the largest Congressional delegations ever to Central Asia earlier this month. The high level reception you received testifies to the desire of our Central Asian partners to strengthen relations with the US and your visit was a major step in that direction. So, thanks to you and other members of your delegation for making this grueling but very productive trip.

In my testimony today, I would like to review our regional priorities with Central Asia, and then discuss briefly each country.

Central Asia is an increasingly important region to the US, and we work with each country on a broad range of policy priorities. The Obama Administration's review of Central Asia policy identified a number of key strategic priorities, ranging from enhanced support for Afghanistan to economic development, including the economic empowerment of women, energy cooperation, promotion of democracy and human rights, and working together to combat transnational threats such as narcotics trafficking and violent extremism. The countries of Central Asia are an important part of our vision of a secure and stable Afghanistan integrated into a stable, secure, and prosperous region. The drawdown of forces from Afghanistan between now and 2014 makes our engagement with Central Asia even more critical.

Through our annual bilateral consultation mechanism, or in the case of Kazakhstan, a strategic partnership dialogue, we seek to achieve increased cooperation on regional security and support for Afghanistan; greater economic and commercial ties; progress on democracy and human rights issues such as preventing trafficking in persons, freedom of religion, greater space for political expression, and support for civil society; and enhanced scientific, cultural and educational cooperation.

Regional Security

Mr. Chairman, the Central Asian Governments share our priority to maintain security in the region after the 2014 transition in Afghanistan. We continue to view our security assistance funding as an important mechanism for ensuring the future stability of Afghanistan and its neighbors. In fiscal year 2011, we provided about $170 million in security assistance in the areas of border security, counternarcotics, counterterrorism, law enforcement and military. In the latter area, we will have provided more than $6 million in Foreign Military Financing and $3 million in International Military Education and Training. Looking forward to 2013, the administration has requested a slight increase in military assistance levels to continue support for these same efforts.

Uzbekistan, Tajikistan, Kyrgyzstan and Kazakhstan have played a significant role in our efforts in Afghanistan by participating in the Northern Distribution Network (NDN). Over the last year we have expanded the capacity of the programme to include multiple, alternate routes for our personnel and cargo transiting into Afghanistan and concluded agreements and arrangements for reverse transit. As such, the NDN will remain of critical importance as transition reaches culmination in 2014 and Afghan National Security Forces take over security lead and international forces conduct a responsible draw down.

Additionally, I want to note that Kyrgyzstan has hosted the Transit Centre at Manas International Airport for over a decade. As you know well, Mr. Chairman, the Transit Centre fulfills crucial roles in support of Operation Enduring Freedom, both as a key stop for all our troops entering and exiting Afghanistan, and as a hub for aerial refueling, among other missions. As a result of the recently concluded Strategic Partnership Agreement with the Government of Afghanistan, we are evaluating what support will be needed as we fulfill our partnership commitments to Afghanistan. We continue to have preliminary discussions on the post-2014 future of the Transit Centre with the Kyrgyz Government. However, let me be clear that the US does not seek to establish any permanent bases in Central Asia.

New Silk Road

Beyond security cooperation, regional economic integration and opportunity will also be essential for a secure, stable and prosperous Afghanistan. Secretary Clinton has highlighted many times over the past year her vision of economic cooperation, trade liberalisation, and increased trade flows throughout the region, referring to it as a 'New Silk Road.' This New Silk Road envisions a network of economic and transit connections running throughout Central and South Asia, with Afghanistan at its heart. Success, of course, will depend on the continued engagement of its neighbours and we are collaborating closely with the Central Asian Governments to make this vision a reality.

The Central Asian countries have also consistently supported Afghanistan through the Istanbul Process, in which Afghanistan's neighbours have committed to a series of ambitious confidence building measures and a process of regular consultations. Three of the seven Istanbul Process Confidence Building Measures (CBMs) focus on economic cooperation and there are several initiatives underway to increase trade and promote a shared prosperity. Other regional groupings to advance Central Asian and Afghan economic cooperation include the Regional Economic Conference (RECCA) on Cooperation on Afghanistan, which endorsed in March an Afghan blueprint for regional integration that we support.

In the context of the New Silk Road, I would like to highlight our work to empower Central Asian and Afghan women economically through the Women's Economic Symposium. The inaugural event was held in Bishkek, Kyrgyzstan in July 2011 with the complete support of the Government of Kyrgyzstan. Women from Central Asian and Afghanistan attended to learn develop women run enterprises and to foster relationships amongst themselves. As we promised the House Foreign Affairs Committee staff in a conference call during the Congressional Notification process, when discussing our intent for the Symposium, we have worked hard to ensure it was not just a one-off conference, but an event that launched an initiative. Since last year, we have committed over $1.7 million to supporting the action recommendations from the Symposium. Although, efforts are still ongoing, Women's Economic Symposium follow-on activities have been directly responsible for increasing the number of businesses owned by women, increasing their access to credit, capacity training and increased political participation. I look forward to discussing additional impacts after we formally evaluate the initiative.

Human Rights

Mr. Chairman, I would also like to emphasise that our enhanced engagement with the Central Asian Governments does not focus only on security and economic issues, but consistently includes frank and open discussions about the need for political liberalisation, more operating space for civil society, and respect for universally recognised human rights. These are not always easy conversations, but our bilateral relationships cannot reach their full potential without support for these human rights and fundamental freedoms. Our engagement with the Central Asian Governments at every level includes an open discussion of the importance of an active civil society, independent media, democratic reforms and the rule of law. We also meet with civil society and non-governmental organisations at every opportunity. But we believe that the path to progress on these issues is more engagement with these governments, not less. As Secretary Clinton has said, "Once you state your concerns, if you do not engage, you have no influence."

Mr. Chairman, I will now briefly highlight key issues in our relations with each country.

Kazakhstan

As I noted in my introductory remarks, in recognition of an expansion in the depth and breadth of our cooperation with Kazakhstan, this year, Secretary Clinton elevated our engagement to the level of a strategic partnership dialogue. Kazakhstan is considered to have the best investment climate in the Central Asian region as evidenced by the numerous international firms that utilise Kazakhstan as a regional headquarters. Over the past 20 years, U.S. companies have invested just over $16.5 billion in Kazakhstan. Currently, a GE-Kazakh joint venture manufactures locomotives in Kazakhstan, while FedEx operates a successful shipping centre in Almaty. North Dakota is exporting Angus and Hereford cattle to Kazakhstan, as part of a deal which promises to revitalise the country's cattle industry. Boeing has also been very successful in Central Asia, announcing deals worth nearly $2 billion in just the first quarter of 2012. Kazakhstan has supported expanded trade in the region and has invested in the Central Asia Regional Economic Cooperation (CAREC) infrastructure network. We strongly support Kazakhstan's bid to join the World Trade Organisation (WTO) and look forward to its anticipated WTO accession.

The US appreciates the commitment Kazakhstan made in June during the Istanbul Process conference to help fund the Afghan National Security forces after 2014 and its generous programme to educate 1,000 Afghan students in Kazakhstani universities and vocational schools. These are excellent examples of Afghanistan's close neighbours stepping in to provide support for stability. Kazakhstan has also been a strong and consistent partner on non-proliferation issues. For example, in November 2010, we completed a long and complicated project to safely shut down the BN-350 reactor in Aktau, secure the spent fuel it produced, and then package and transport the spent fuel more than 2,100 miles for secure storage in Eastern Kazakhstan. At the 2012 Nuclear Security Summit in Seoul, Kazakhstan affirmed its commitment to establish a regional nuclear security training center.

While Kazakhstan has made progress in fulfilling the promise of their chairmanship of the Organisation for Security and Cooperation in Europe (OSCE) and the OSCE Summit they hosted in 2010, we will continue to work with the Government of Kazakhstan toward our mutual goal of a fully democratic system and strong civil society that work together to protect internationally recognised human rights. In this context, I would note that the US was disturbed by the use of deadly force against protesters in Zhanaozen last December, and while we appreciate the legal process that has resulted in convictions of both protestors who used violence and police who reacted with excessive force, we have raised our concerns about allegations of torture, mistreatment and selective punishment of some who were detained during and shortly after the events in Zhanaozen. We have called on the government to ensure these allegations are fully investigated and that individuals are held accountable for their actions. More broadly speaking, we continue to urge progress on a range of human rights issues, including freedoms of expression and religion, in our dialogue with Kazakhstan on support for civil society and human rights. As part of our strategic partnership dialogue, our governments routinely host forums with democracy and human rights NGOs in Astana and Washington.

Kyrgyzstan

The US has made support for Kyrgyzstan's democracy a cornerstone of our Central Asia strategy. We remain committed to the people of Kyrgyzstan as they work to further develop democratic institutions and practices. The U.S. has allocated nearly ten million dollars in support of civil society, rule of law, human rights and democratic reform in fiscal year 2012 and in our 2013 request. As part of the 2010 parliamentary and 2011 presidential election cycles in Kyrgyzstan, our assistance funded training for over 50,000 election officials across the country.

That support and the hard work of the government and voters in Kyrgyzstan have enabled great progress towards democracy, with competitive elections in 2010 and 2011. As a result of the 2011 elections, the people of Kyrgyzstan accomplished a peaceful and democratic transfer of presidential power, something that has never happened before in Central Asia. This is profound change that affirms the rights and expectations of ordinary citizens, and shapes our long-term view of the close partnership between our countries.

In order to fully realise and sustain its democratic goals, we continue to urge Kyrgyzstan to work actively on national reconciliation. Meaningful democracy requires that the rights of all of Kyrgyzstan's citizens be respected and upheld fully throughout the justice and law enforcement systems, as required by Kyrgyzstan's constitution and its international obligations. The US continues to engage interlocutors regularly in Kyrgyzstan so that we make clear the critical importance of ending abuses of detainees and holding the perpetrators of such abuses accountable under the rule of law. This is especially important for all cases arising out of the June 2010 violence.

Next month, I will lead the U.S. delegation to the Annual Bilateral Consultation with Kyrgyzstan in Bishkek. Kyrgyzstan continues to be a strong partner in international coalition efforts in Afghanistan, especially in hosting the Transit Centre at Manas International Airport in support of coalition operations. The US looks forward to continuing our longstanding cooperation with the Kyrgyz Republic to address regional challenges of terrorism and narcotics trafficking.

Turkmenistan

Turkmenistan has supported Afghanistan through humanitarian aid and by the construction of rail and energy infrastructure that will more fully integrate Afghanistan into the region. The recent signing of gas sales and purchase agreements between Turkmenistan, Pakistan and India enables the Turkmenistan-Afghanistan-Pakistan-India pipeline to move to the commercial phase. This project is one example of the potential Turkmenistan has to be a leader in the economic prosperity of the region. We encourage Turkmenistan to build clear and transparent mechanisms for investment in its country.

In order to realise its potential, Turkmenistan must make significant steps to fulfill its international obligations on human rights. The US consistently raises concerns about respect for human rights at every appropriate opportunity and we have offered assistance to help advance space for civil society and building democratic systems.

Tajikistan

Tajikistan remains a strong supporter of efforts to help Afghanistan. It also has made accession to the WTO a key priority in our bilateral relationship: the US supports Tajikistan in its efforts to increase trade. Through Embassy Dushanbe, we are providing technical assistance to help Tajikistan make the necessary changes to meet the requirements for membership. Tajikistan also needs to develop the agriculture sector, and improve the regulatory environment for foreign investment.

We recognise that energy issues and water management are challenging issues for Central Asia and have been sources of tension between Tajikistan and Uzbekistan. Regarding the Roghun dam project, the US has had a long-standing policy to support the World Bank process. The World Bank is funding two feasibility studies to assess the technical, economic, environmental, and social impact of the proposed Roghun Dam. We continue to encourage the Government of Tajikistan to fully cooperate with the World Bank and not to move forward with construction or river diversion for the Dam until the completion of the feasibility studies.

The US is concerned about Tajikistan's continuing efforts to limit human rights, including religious freedom and media freedoms. While we recognise the government's desire to promote security and prevent violent extremism, long-term peace and stability are only possible when accompanied by respect for human rights, the rule of law, the fostering of transparent and democratic governmental and civic institutions, and an open and unrestricted media environment. We continue to encourage Tajikistan to protect religious freedom, and to respect media freedom and refrain from interference in the media sector.

Uzbekistan

Next month, I will also lead the U.S. delegation to Tashkent to participate in this year's Annual Bilateral Consultation with Uzbekistan. Uzbekistan has been a critical part of regional support for Afghanistan, building a rail line connecting Afghanistan to Central Asia and providing electricity that benefits the Afghan people. In addition, Uzbekistan has a central role in the NDN, with the majority of supplies transiting through the Uzbek-Afghan border. As you know, the secretary certified in January that it is in the national security interest to waive the restrictions on security assistance for Uzbekistan, and as a result, we have been able to provide equipment and training necessary to counter threats from terrorist groups and narco traffickers in the region.

During our upcoming annual bilateral consultations, we will work to make progress on creating the business environment necessary to increase economic investment by U.S. firms, boost education and cultural exchanges, address ongoing human rights concerns, and strengthen our security and defence cooperation.

We look forward to increasing cooperation with Uzbekistan in several areas. We are encouraged by General Motors' (GMs) significant investment in the country, including its construction of a new automotive power train factory, and we hope Uzbekistan will take steps to attract more U.S. companies by addressing restrictive currency conversion laws and pervasive corruption issues. We are slowly increasing our science and technology cooperation. The U.S. Department of Agriculture is working with Uzbekistan's Institute of Genetics on cotton genomes, and the American Association for the Advancement of Science plans to hold a conference in Tashkent this September. Still, registration requirements have slowed our cooperation, and we hope Uzbekistan will permit greater peer-to-peer interaction. Finally, we are pleased to welcome Uzbek students and educators to the U.S. as part of several educational exchange programs, but we have asked Uzbekistan to strengthen its commitment to allow our Fulbright scholars to study and teach there.

While we work hard to strengthen relations with Uzbekistan in our mutual interests, the US continues to urge the Government of Uzbekistan to improve its record on human rights and we continually advocate for those who seek peaceful democratic reforms. In particular, we ask the government to take steps to eliminate the forced labour of children and adults during the cotton harvest and to prosecute those labour traffickers. We are also working with the Government of Uzbekistan to increase religious freedom by addressing its overly restrictive religious registration policies and allegations of arbitrary arrests and detentions of peaceful religious leaders. We also regularly engage with members of civil society from Uzbekistan and the diaspora community on these issues.

Conclusion

In conclusion, Mr. Chairman, we are working toward a future in which the US and the countries of Central Asia are partners for peace, security, economic development, democracy, and prosperity. We envision a region where goods and services flow easily and efficiently between the Central Asian countries, Afghanistan and South Asia. Changes occur slowly in Central Asia. However, our consistent engagement with these countries can be mutually beneficial, as demonstrated by progress over the last few years in security cooperation and regional projects in support of the New Silk Road vision. We will continue to strengthen our ties with these important countries and their people and thereby advance U.S. interests in this strategically important region.

Thank you. I look forward to your questions.

US Department of State press release, July 25, 2012.

ANNEXURE 5

Keynote address by MOS Shri E. Ahamad at the First India-Central Asia Dialogue

June 12, 2012, Bishkek

India's 'Connect Central Asia' Policy

Excellency Madame Roza Otunbaeva,

Excellency Madame Dinara Kamelova, Deputy Foreign Minister of Kyrgyz Republic,

Distinguished scholars and academics from Central Asia and India,

Excellencies, Ladies and Gentlemen

It is an honour and privilege for me to speak to such a distinguished audience of scholars, experts and business leaders, in the beautiful city of Bishkek. I congratulate the Indian Council of World Affairs (ICWA) on putting together this pioneering dialogue forum and thank the Kyrgyz Republic for being gracious enough to host this event with so much aplomb and enthusiasm. We have had many events in India where we have welcomed scholars from Central Asia, but this is the first instance, where we have reached out to Central Asia's intellectuals and opinion leaders in their own home, bringing to the table the rich knowledge and experience of India's scholars and business persons.

Today's event is also a fitting celebration of the two decades of India's diplomatic relations with the Kyrgyz Republic, which has been our valued friend in Central Asia, and with which we now have a special empathy after the recent bold experiment in parliamentary democracy.

In my remarks, I will dwell upon India's vision of its role in Central Asia today. India is looking intently and seriously at this neighbourhood, with which we are bound by the silken bonds of centuries of common history.

Central Asia, over the last two decades in general and recently in particular, is witnessing an unprecedented integration into the global economic and political mainstream. We, in India, rejoice in this trend of the expanding influence of Central Asia, particularly on the world energy scene. We recognise Central Asian countries as close political partners in our 'extended neighbourhood', a precept which has become a key element of our foreign policy.

Our civilisational bonds with Central Asian countries have been translated into warm and friendly relations, with India being among the first countries to open diplomatic missions in all the five capitals. We have had a robust exchange of visits of our leaders and have signed numerous cooperation agreements. Our policy has been marked by deepening relationships based on political, economic and technical cooperation as a partner, rather than a mere contender for the region's vast oil and gas resources. We have shared our experiences and expertise, built capacity and focused on training through our Indian Technical & Economic Cooperation Programme (ITEC), and other assistance programmes.

India's cultural heritage is deeply rooted in the Eurasian past. Indian traders and travelers had actively traded along the Silk Route and Buddhism had flourished across the vast Eurasian steppe. History is full of friendly interactions between India and Central Asia, through movement of people, goods and ideas, including spiritual interfaces that enriched us both. The fondness for Indian culture is expressed in Central Asia's deep interest in Indian cinema, music, and art. This interest intensified further in Soviet times.

However, in the last few decades, we have been struggling to build economic links that match our political and cultural interaction. Our trade with the whole region is at a relatively low level of around 500 million US dollars. We face some natural obstacles like limited land connectivity and the limited size of the Central Asian markets. India has thus not seen the sort of commercial interaction in Central Asia, which we saw in Southeast Asia, East Asia and West Asia. This has led to a joint quest for innovative answers, some of which we look upon this dialogue to throw up.

India is now looking intently at the region through the framework of its 'Connect Central Asia' policy, which is based on pro-active political, economic and people-to-people engagement with Central Asian countries, both individually and collectively.

I believe that India's active presence in the region will contribute to stability and development in the entire Central and South Asia region. In this analysis, we must factor in the regional situation and especially the challenge of rebuilding the Afghan nation. A cooperative approach for embedding Afghanistan into a more meaningful regional economic and security framework would have benefits for the entire region. One way is to work towards converting Afghanistan into a hub for trade and energy, connecting Central and South Asia. The landmark agreement for the construction of the Turkmenistan-Afghanistan-Pakistan-India (TAPI) pipeline has put the spotlight on the importance of Central Asia for India's future energy plans. It would also greatly benefit Afghanistan.

Central Asian countries could also gain from the techno-economic- potential of India, which could be accessed in cooperative, mutually beneficial partnerships. Your desire for diversifying hydro-power and energy export routes would correspond with India's quest for diversifying imports. India will be keen to invest in setting up downstream production facilities, instead of exporting raw materials out of the region through expensive pipelines. The approach could differ from those seeking exclusively to pump out Central Asia's riches.

It is also important to remember that India has never been prescriptive in its political approach. We represent our liberal democratic values, particularly in the Asian context. We believe in a nation building model based on participatory democracy, economic growth, building civil societies, pluralistic structures, ethno-religious harmony and the rule of law.

Against this backdrop, let me outline some of the elements of India's 'Connect Central Asia' policy, which is a broad-based approach, including political, security, economic and cultural connections:

1. We will continue to build on our strong political relations through the exchange of high level visits. Our leaders will continue to interact both in bilateral and multilateral fora.
2. We will strengthen our strategic and security cooperation. We already have strategic partnerships in place with some Central Asian countries. In focus will be military training, joint research, counter-terrorism coordination and close consultations on Afghanistan.
3. We will step up multilateral engagement with Central Asian partners using the synergy of joint efforts through existing fora like the Shanghai Cooperation Organisation (SCO), Eurasian Economic Community (EEC) and the Custom Union. India has already proposed a Comprehensive Economic Cooperation Agreement (CECA) to integrate its markets with the unifying Eurasian space.
4. India looks to Central Asia as a long term partner in energy, and natural resources. Central Asia possesses large cultivable tracts of land and we see potential for India to cooperate in production of profitable crops with value addition.
5. The medical field is another area that offers huge potential for cooperation. We could extend cooperation by setting up civil hospitals/clinics in Central Asia.
6. India has excellent higher education system imparted at a fraction of the fees charged by Western universities. Keeping this in mind India would like to assist in the setting up of a Central Asian University in Bishkek that could come up as a centre of excellence to impart world class education in the fields of IT sector, philosophy, language, etc.
7. We are working on setting up a Central Asian e-network with its hub in India, to deliver, tele-education and tele-medicine connectivity, linking all the five Central Asian States.
8. Our companies can showcase India's capability and build world class structures at competitive rates. Central Asian countries especially

Kazakhstan, have almost limitless reserves of iron ore and coal, as well as abundant cheap electricity. India can help set up several medium size steel rolling mills, producing all its requirement of specific products.

9. As for land connectivity, we have reactivated the International North-South Transport Corridor (INSTC). We need to join our efforts to discuss ways to bridge the missing links in the Corridor at the earliest and also work on other connecting spurs along the route.
10. Absence of a viable banking infrastructure in the region is a major barrier to trade and investment. Indian banks can expand their presence if they see a favourable policy environment.
11. We will jointly work to improve air connectivity between our countries. India is one of the biggest markets for outbound travelers estimated at US$ 21 billion in 2011. Many countries have opened tourist offices in India to woo Indian tourists. Central Asian countries could emerge as attractive holiday destinations and to the Indian film industry which likes to depict foreign locales in its films.
12. Connections between our peoples are the most vital linkages to sustain our deep engagement. I would particularly like to emphasise exchanges between youth and the future leaders of India and Central Asia. We already have a robust exchange of students. We will encourage regular exchanges of scholars, academics, civil society and youth delegations to gain deeper insights into each others' cultures.

India thus stands ready for a deep, meaningful and sustained engagement with Central Asia. We need our Central Asian friends to create favourable visa conditions to accept India's benign presence. Perhaps the governments of all the five states will agree to simplify these procedures.

India's "Connect Central Asia Policy" will be consonant with our overall policy of deepening engagement in Eurasia, our policy of strengthening relations with China, with Pakistan, and building on our traditional relationship with Russia. We hope that our membership in numerous regional forums including at the SCO, would help India's renewed linkages with the region.

Collectively, we must also think about creating a cooperative security structure for maintaining peace in Asia. Our policy of peaceful coexistence and of playing a constructive and meaningful role in the United Nations (UN) (now also as a non-permanent member of the UN Security Council (UNSC) will drive us to work with a deep sense of responsibility on all global issues. India's engagement in Central Asia, therefore, must be seen in the context of a quest for a world order which is multi-polar.

With these remarks, I invite the galaxy of experts and thinkers present here to take the stage and deliberate more on some of these ideas. I wish the seminar all success.

Index